INFLIGHT CATERING MANAGEMENT

INFLIGHT CATERING
MANAGEMENT

Audrey C. McCool

William F. Harrah College of Hotel Administration
University of Nevada, Las Vegas

John Wiley & Sons, Inc.

New York • Chichester • Brisbane • Toronto • Singapore

Library of Congress Cataloging-in-Publication Data:
McCool, Audrey Carol.
    Inflight catering management / Audrey C. McCool.
        p.   cm.
    Includes bibliographical references.
    ISBN 0-471-04253-6 (cloth : acid-free paper)
    1. Food service management.   2. Airlines—Food service-
  -Management.   I. Title.
  TX911.3.M27M35   1995
  647.95'068—dc20   94-42490

Printed in the United States of America

10 9 8 7 6 5 4 3 2 1

Preface

This book is a unique publication within the hospitality industry. It marks the first time, to our knowledge, that a textbook has been published that focuses exclusively on the inflight foodservice industry. While it is our understanding that there is a similar project underway in Europe, the focus of that book will be primarily on European and international inflight catering operations. In contrast, this publication focuses on the United States domestic catering, with some attention given to the international perspective in recognition of the trend toward globalization of the airline industry and of all of its supportive services. It is anticipated that the European text will be an excellent source of ancillary information for someone using this book in an academic course in the United States—and vice versa for someone teaching in any of the European Hospitality programs.

Note that I say *our* here, and not *my*. This book is also unique in that it is the product of a true collaboration between the world of academia and the industry that is the topic of the text. This project was initiated through the efforts of Robert Arnold, chairman of the Inflight Food Service Association's Education Committee, and the members of his committee. The Association and its president, James J. O'Neill, sensed that there was a need to create an interest in the inflight foodservice industry among students studying for degrees in the hospitality field. The Inflight catering industry has had varying degrees of success in recruiting professionally trained young persons into the management of its catering operations, and many who did enter the field at some point in their careers did so by accident. The committee felt that by creating a complete course structure, including a textbook and related course materials, it would be possible to have both two- and four-year colleges and universities initiate a complete course or a significant component of a course in noncommercial foodservices that would focus specifically on inflight foodservice management. Having such courses available would offer hospitality students an avenue through which they might learn about the inflight foodservice industry, gain skills that would better qualify them for entry into this field, and lead them to seek employment with inflight catering firms. To ensure that the course was scholastically oriented and suitable for use in Hospitality academic programs, the committee sought the assistance of the academicians for the development of the course. Throughout the development of this book and the initial course that has been taught, there has been close interaction between industry and academia. It is hoped that this interaction has resulted in a text that is reflective of the inflight foodservice industry.

The material in this book has been structured to readily fit into one academic semester. However, it is realized that not all programs may be able to accommodate an elective such as this one, which is focused on one specific segment of the noncommercial foodservice industry. In that case, it is suggested that course instructors review the entire text and focus their attention on those chapters they feel best present the unique perspectives of this industry segment. However, it should be noted that the inflight foodservice industry is rapidly diversifying into new markets. The inflight catering kitchen is singularly well situated to handle the production and distribution of meals and other types of food and beverage products to service many types of foodservice operations, such as those in health care, schools, recreational facilities, special events or off-premise catering. Because of this very broad perspective that a once closely focused industry is now taking, hospitality programs are encouraged to consider a complete course in inflight foodservice operations that would utilize the resources presented here.

This book should also be helpful for someone considering entering or who has recently entered the inflight foodservice industry. It can provide valuable insights into many aspects of the industry, which would be helpful in learning about and adjusting to an entry-level management position in this field.

We hope that readers of this book will find answers to many of their questions about the inflight industry and become excited and want to join us in working to meet the food and beverage needs of airline passengers,—as well as in the many new areas into which this industry is diversifying.

Join us, and find new adventures in the world of inflight catering!

Acknowledgments

This text was completed under the direction of the Education Committee of the Inflight Food Service Association. It could not have been completed without the support of the members of the committee, as well as the other assistance received from many people. The author would especially like to thank the members of the Education Committee who worked very hard on this text. Robert Arnold, Chair, whose vision developed this project, and Michael Kasnia, Vicky Stennes, Robert Novak, and Ernest Tosi.

In addition, the management of the Caterair and Ogden Aviation Services flight kitchens at McCarren International Airport were instrumental in providing information for the text, as well as in getting the actual classroom instruction off the ground. The author would particularly like to mention the contributions of Joe Morgan, Vincent LaRuffa, David Diamond, John Lacy, Nancy Halama, Richard Kalesz, and Chef Heinz Schoeffel. All of these people spent a great deal of their time reading draft versions of the text, making corrections, offering suggestions, and locating materials. Not only did they read materials, but they also took the time to come to the class to talk about the industry with the students and accommodated the students on-site at their kitchens to help them get a real-world perspective of the inflight catering industry.

The author would also like to thank the many people in the airline and inflight foodservice industry who contributed materials, photographs, and other needed input that made this text possible, particularly Robert Sobczewski, Arthur Taylor, Irma Todd, Lynda Zane, and Alexander Morton.

Of course, none of this would have been possible at all, if the Inflight Food Service Association had never been founded. Two people instrumental in the development of the Association were also helpful with this project. Many thanks to Philip Parrott and Gerald Lattin for taking the time to review the industry history as discussed in the text, and especially to Mr. Parrott for authorizing the use of many historical pictures used as text illustrations.

Finally, a note of thanks to my husband and other family members who put up with stacks of paper, short tempers, typing for hours and hours at all times of the day or night (even on weekends and holidays), and the many other inconveniences associated with the completion of a major project such as this text. Your support is very much appreciated!

Contents

INFLIGHT CATERING MANAGEMENT

1

Introduction to the Inflight Foodservice Industry

LEARNING OBJECTIVES

After studying this chapter, the student should be able to:

1. Describe the inflight foodservice industry.
2. Identify at least two features of inflight foodservices that make this industry a unique sector of the total foodservice industry.
3. Explain the need for flawless logistics in inflight foodservice.
4. Describe one way in which domestic providers of inflight foodservices differ from international providers.
5. Discuss the increasing diversity of inflight catering operations.
6. List six major inflight caterers in the United States.
7. Discuss the background of at least four of the major domestic inflight caterers.

INTRODUCTION

Every year, over 755 million people, worldwide, fly on commercial aircraft. Airlines from many countries operate over 9,000 aircraft which service more than 1,000 worldwide airports every day. Flight schedules are such that one of these more than 9,000 aircraft are landing somewhere in the world almost every minute of the day. There is little doubt that air travel has changed our way of life throughout the world. Indeed, commercial flight has become so common that having to travel without flying as an option would be inconceivable to many people.

However, flying involves much more than just a fleet of well-maintained aircraft and smiling flight crews to welcome passengers on board. People working in the airline industry realize that a vital part of any airline's success lies with the catering firm that is providing one of the most important inflight amenities, inflight foodservices for the airline's passengers.

INFLIGHT FOODSERVICES

Anyone who has flown on a commercial aircraft today has come into contact with inflight foodservices, yet few have an understanding of what is involved. Most airline passengers now expect to receive some type of food or beverage service as a routine part of their flight, no matter where their seat is on the plane. They see meals regularly served with efficiency and ease. However, few passengers ever realize that the provisioning of inflight foodservices is a highly complex task that is performed by a unique segment of the total foodservice industry. Whenever a plane lands anywhere in the world, the race is on. In the airline industry, time is money, and inflight foodservices are part of the race to meet the close time schedule characterizing the airline industry's concern with passenger service.

Inflight foodservices may be defined as that part of the foodservice industry that is concerned with the provision of meals and beverages served to passengers on board aircraft. These foodservices are usually provided by firms specializing in the inflight catering business (inflight foodservice caterers). Figure 1.1 shows samples of meal trays and snack plates that might be served to passengers during airline flights.

Many persons often confuse inflight foodservices with the foodservices found in airports, or terminal foodservices. The foodservices found inside the airports represent a different part of the foodservice industry than the food and beverage services provided enroute during actual flight times. While both are considered to be segments of the noncommercial foodservice industry (as opposed to the commercial foodservice industry composed of restaurants and quick-service foodservices), the operation of foodservices inside the airport is similar to that of foodservices found in any other type of host organization, such as a football stadium, a university campus, a manufacturing plant, or a hospital. While some inflight caterers may also have the contract to provide some or all of the foodservices inside the airport (particularly if the airport is very small), in most instances the two types of foodservices are provided by two different firms with different areas of foodservice management expertise.

UNIQUE FEATURES OF INFLIGHT FOODSERVICES

While inflight foodservices have many features in common with other components of the overall foodservice industry, these foodservices are

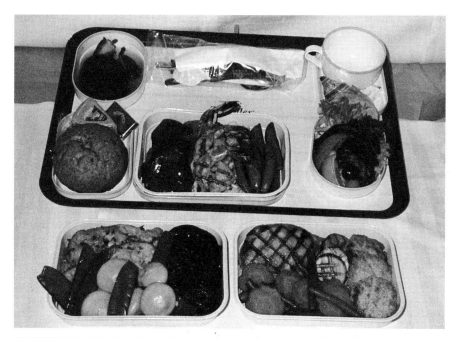

FIGURE 1.1 Meal and snack trays that might be used for inflight foodservice. (Courtesy of De Ster Corporation, Atlanta, GA, USA.)

unique in many ways. One of the most unique aspects of inflight foodservices is that the people who prepare, package, and deliver the foods and beverages consumed by the airline passengers have little opportunity for direct contact with the consumers of their products. They have only indirect contact with the passengers through the flight attendants who are responsible for accepting the prepared products from the inflight foodservice caterer and for serving the meals and beverages to the passengers. Thus, there is typically no opportunity for the caterer's personnel to interact with the actual consumers to learn about their likes and dislikes and no opportunity for these consumers to either compliment or complain directly to the people involved in the preparation and packaging of their foods and beverages. As a result, the inflight catering industry must rely on feedback through the airline and its flight attendants or market research and other such indicators, such as published reports of trends in consumer eating patterns, to gain an understanding of the consumers they are serving.

Inflight foodservices are characterized by other unique features. One such feature is the very high volume of foods and beverages that must be handled by any one foodservice operation. Indeed, inflight foodservices can be thought of as a food factory where many similar products which meet very precise specifications are produced in very large quantities in a highly efficient assembly line. As an example of the high volume of foods handled, passengers on Delta Air Lines' flights originating from Atlanta, Georgia consume, among other foods, 18,532 dinner rolls, 2,495 pounds of chicken, 1,390 gallons of wine, 550 pounds of broccoli, 2,698 pounds of lettuce, and 5,257 gallons of coffee daily. Of course, there are many other airlines with flights that originate from Atlanta, and many other Delta flights originating in other cities which serve foods not included in the figures listed here.

Another factorylike characteristic of inflight foodservices that is different from many other foodservices is that the preparation site, or inflight kitchen, may or may not be at the airport, the point where the food products produced by the kitchen are boarded for inflight service to the aircraft's passengers. While the food products are not immediately served when they are loaded on the aircraft, the aircraft may be considered to be the point of service for the products prepared by the caterer. A second characteristic is that most flight kitchens operate 24 hours per day, 365 days per year. These kitchens never close, and they never have an opportunity to stop and catch their breath.

No matter where the kitchen is located, the prepared products are precisely packaged in appropriate shipping or transport containers (such as aisle carts, trolleys, or transport modules) transported to the airport departure ramp area, and then loaded on board the aircraft. The meals and beverages may not actually be consumed by the passengers for an hour or two—or even for many hours on an intercontinental or transoceanic flight. Although the time lines and the transportation distances are shorter between the meal production stage and the actual consumption of the food, the process is not dissimilar from that which would be found in the production and ultimate consumption of products, such as many frozen or chilled convenience foods, found in grocery stores today. It is also similar to many of the cook–chill systems now used in many noncommercial foodservices, such as hospitals or prison systems.

More than most other foodservices, except perhaps foodservices provided on board cruise ships, inflight foodservices are dependent upon flawless logistics. Technically, *logistics* is a term referring to that aspect of military science dealing with the procurement, storage, maintenance, and transportation of supplies, facilities, and personnel. Applied to inflight foodservices, it refers to the management of the details of procurement, storage, maintenance, transportation, and distribution of the large amounts of foods, beverages, supplies, and equipment needed to service the world's fleets of passenger aircraft. There is little room for error in inflight foodservices. The right amounts of the right products have to be in the right places at the right time, or the flights don't fly—or at least will not fly on schedule. It is very important that inflight caterers *not* be the reason for a delayed flight or for passenger disservice!

Indeed, it is essential that inflight caterers are *never* late boarding the food and beverages products on the aircraft. Late delivery can mean a late departure for a flight, and the caterer can be assessed heavy financial penalties for causing that delay. Generally, a passenger aircraft will not depart without the required food and beverages loaded on board. Although the aircraft captain or certain airline management staff can make a decision to have the flight leave without the necessary foodservice supplies in unusual situations, some airlines will not fly without certain galley components which are generally delivered to the aircraft as a part of the catering delivery process. Thus, the importance of precise logistics in the operation of inflight catering services is underscored.

Other logistical considerations of concern to the inflight caterer are that the food products used must be able to withstand holding conditions at the caterer's production kitchen, the transport conditions, and the extended hot or cold holding period that occurs between the time the products are loaded for transport to the aircraft and the time they are actually served to the passengers. Generally, if a food item is to be served hot, it is transported in the chilled state. Therefore, it must be a product that freezes or refrigerates well, yet will rethermalize well in bulk or on the plate once on board the aircraft. Even more significant considerations are (1) that the products used must fit into the space available on the aircraft for food and beverage service storage, and (2) that the total weight of the products and the transport equipment used must not exceed the weight allocation for food and beverage services that is factored into the total weight of the aircraft. Table 1.1 summarizes some of the factors that make inflight foodservices unique.

WHO PROVIDES INFLIGHT FOODSERVICES TO THE AIRLINES

Today, almost all of the foodservices for U.S.-based airlines are provided by inflight caterers. At one time, as will be discussed in Chapter 2, some of the airlines, such as American, Continental, Northwest, Pan-American, TWA, and United, provided their own foodservices and operated inflight kitchens at many airports where their flights landed. However, most airlines today have found it more economically feasible to contract with specialized management firms for necessary support services, such as their food and beverage services, at most of their landing sites. United Airlines was one of the first to develop their own kitchens and one of the most recent to almost completely withdraw from the flight kitchen business. United sold fifteen of their seventeen inflight kitchens to Dobbs International Services in November 1993. TWA has recently contracted with Ogden Aviation Services to operate its kitchens at John F. Kennedy International Airport in New York and at Los Angeles International Airport.

There are still some U.S. airlines who own and operate some flight kitchens. Delta, for example, owns its kitchens in Atlanta, one of the airline's primary hub airports (managed by Dobbs International), and United

TABLE 1.1
Unique Features of the Inflight Foodservice Field

1. There is limited opportunity for contact between food production personnel and passengers who eat the food products.
2. The caterer's customer is not the one who consumes the products.
3. There is heavy reliance on market research, consumer eating trend reports, and other such data as the determinant of menus served.
4. A very high volume of foods and beverages must be handled by any one foodservice operation.
5. Products served by an airline are prepared by multiple caterers in diverse locations.
6. Caterers must prepare products in accord with very rigid specifications to achieve product consistency for the customer.
7. There are unusually long holding times between the time the finished products leave the production kitchen and when they are actually consumed by the airline passengers.
8. The meals produced by the caterer are often served in a location that may be far from the caterer's kitchen.
9. The caterer generally does not see the garbage (or what was actually eaten) from the meals prepared and provided by the caterer's kitchen.
10. There is a zero tolerance level for errors in the products prepared and the amounts boarded onto the aircraft.
11. The scheduled service time for products is often changed on very short notice to the caterer, yet the caterer must meet the new scheduled time.
12. Food products used must be able to withstand severe handling, transport, and storage conditions without a significant loss in quality.
13. All foods, beverages, serviceware, and equipment must fit into the designated storage spaces in the aircraft galleys.
14. The foods, beverages, serviceware, and equipment cannot exceed the weight allocated for these items.
15. Most inflight catering kitchens must operate 24 hours per day, 365 days per year.
16. Inflight caterers must meet their obligations for product quality and service times despite the uncertainty of conditions such as the weather or airline mechanical problems.

retained one of its kitchens in the 1993 sale. (The remaining United kitchen was sold to Caterair.) Also, Continental owns six Chelsea Catering kitchens. Figure 1.2 illustrates a typical midsize inflight catering kitchen.

The international situation is different. Several major airlines are also the leading inflight caterers in their countries. British Airways, for example, owns and operates the European Catering Center near Heathrow Airport (London), which is one of the largest, most highly automated inflight catering facilities in the world. Another example is Lufthansa (from Germany), an airline that is very active in the inflight catering industry through their catering subsidiary, LSG, Lufthansa Service. LSG has now formed a

FIGURE 1.2 Employees prepare cold food products in a typical inflight catering kitchen.

consortium with Delta Daily Foods (headquartered in the Netherlands). In addition, Lufthansa (as LSG Lufthansa Service) and Delta Daily Foods have recently entered into a cooperative partnership with Sky Chefs (headquartered in the United States in Dallas, Texas).

Another difference between European and U.S. caterers is that in Europe, caterers are generally full service firms that provide an array of services to the airlines. In addition to foodservices, they also provide inflight services such as fueling, baggage handling, or aircraft cleaning for the airlines that have service contracts with them. With the exception of Ogden Aviation Services, most U.S. inflight catering firms are primarily in the foodservice business.

Generally, most U.S. airports have two or more caterers who compete for inflight foodservice contracts with the airlines serving an airport. This competition is very intense, and the successful bid for a contract is contingent on many factors, as will be discussed later. However, there are a few (often smaller) airports where one caterer has been able to obtain exclusive rights to locate a kitchen on airport property. The airports at Allentown, Pennsylvania and Fresno, California are examples of such small airports. Being located on airport property offers a caterer a competitive advantage because of lower aircraft service times and lower transportation costs. While airports can limit the number of contractors to whom they grant the right to locate one or more kitchens on airport property, anyone has the right to open a kitchen off of airport property and compete for business from the airlines. However, in order to service passenger aircraft, the owners of such kitchens must be able to obtain the right to make deliveries to the aircraft located on airport property, and they must have the capability to meet the service requirements of the airlines, which includes an investment in needed transport equipment.

When an aircraft lands at an airport (usually a small one) where one caterer has exclusive service rights, the aircraft must use the services of that caterer at that site or the airline must double-provision the aircraft landing at that site from a kitchen at another location. Double provisioning the aircraft means that enough food and beverage supplies are boarded at a previous landing location so that no additional supplies are needed when the aircraft lands at the site where one caterer has the exclusive service rights, or there is no catering facility available.

THE DIVERSITY OF INFLIGHT CATERING OPERATIONS

Recent changes in the airlines' perspective regarding passenger foodservices and the highly competitive inflight foodservice market have made many inflight caterers, who were once primarily in business to service the needs of the scheduled airlines, diversify into new catering markets. Many flight kitchens, capitalizing on their ability to produce and distribute food products efficiently, now also cater to AMTRAK trains, hospitals, and other health care facilities, corporate jets, charter flights, and even the growing market of home-delivered or congregate meals for the elderly.

Charter flights are very diverse, and they can provide significant business opportunities for many kitchens. Some vacation locations, for example, may do a sizable business with charter operations. Charter aircraft can range from six-seat Lear Jets to the Supersonic Concorde as well as from various military aircraft to Boeing 747-400s seating nearly 400 passengers. Charter flights may carry passengers, such as sports teams, with very special dietary requirements, or they may be religious pilgrimage flights that call for special meals made to religious specifications. Military charters and military flights have increasingly been using flight kitchen contracts to provide needed meals, largely as a result of federal government emphasis on downsizing and contracting with the civilian market where possible.

As health care operations have diversified, a number of inflight kitchens have begun to cater meals to local hospitals and nursing homes. Such locations rely heavily on in-house registered dietitians to work with the hospital accounts and their diverse meal needs. The needs of some congregate and home-delivered meal programs, most of which are now funded under the provisions of Title IIIc of the Older Americans Act, have grown beyond the capabilities of small church kitchens or other such local food production facilities. As contracts for these programs have become more formalized and as food safety needs have been recognized, flight kitchens have successfully entered this market.

Some flight kitchens cater meals and supplies to AMTRAK trains and even to riverboats. Some are also doing a good business preparing everything from box lunches to full meal services for local conventions, meetings, and sports events.

Given all the various day-to-day catering opportunities that inflight caterers are now actively involved in, many flight kitchens are able to participate in the recycling of off-loaded aluminum, plastics, and cardboard waste. Additionally, many kitchens work with groups such as Second Harvest so that others in their communities can benefit from production and flight delay leftovers.

The inflight foodservice industry has long had, and will continue to have, close ties with all aspects of aerospace development. One inflight caterer has been working with NASA on the development of food systems for the first commercially viable space station. Indeed, the diversity of the inflight foodservice industry is limited only by the imagination of its managers and employees.

A very important approach to diversification that many inflight caterers are taking is to expand the range of services that they offer to the airlines. Caterers such as Ogden Aviation Services, Dobbs International Services, and many European catering firms that offer a range of services to the airlines are referred to as full-service caterers. Some of the services that caterers are beginning to offer, in addition to food production and distribution, include aircraft cleaning, refueling, baggage handling, menu development, culinary design, equipment repairs, and laundry service.

THE MAJOR INFLIGHT CATERING FIRMS

There are several large inflight catering firms that provide food and beverage services to a majority of the airlines today. In addition to these large caterers, there are a number of small firms in the inflight catering business that provide services at smaller airports or have small, specialized inflight contracts—usually with charter airlines or general aviation operators for private corporate aircraft needs. Inflight catering firms in the United States include: Caterair International, Dobbs International Services, Inc., LSG Lufthansa Service/Sky Chefs, Ogden Aviation Services, Chelsea Catering, CA One Services, Inc. (formerly Concession Air), and other independents. A conglomerate in Europe that is expected to play an increasingly large role in worldwide catering is Gate Gourmet International.

Caterair International

Caterair International is a very large inflight caterer that provides inflight foodservices both in the United States and in approximately twenty-six other countries on six continents around the world. Internationally, Caterair kitchens can be found in such diverse locations as Australia, Belize, Germany, Russia, Mexico, and Japan. As of early 1994, Caterair operated 118 different flight kitchens around the world. Until the 1993 sale of most of United Airlines' flight kitchens to Dobbs International Services and the 1993 partial stock merger between Sky Chefs and LSG Lufthansa, Caterair was the largest inflight catering firm in the world. Now Caterair is second only to Dobbs in the domestic market, but is still larger than Dobbs, overall, when both their domestic and international components are combined. Internationally, Caterair is second in size to the LSG Lufthansa/Sky Chefs group, now the world's largest international combination providing inflight catering services.

Although it is officially one of the newest companies providing inflight catering services today, it may also be thought of as the oldest company in this industry. Caterair was formed through a leveraged buyout from Marriott Corporation in 1990. However, as will be seen in Chapter 2, Marriott Corporation was the first firm to provide any type of airline foodservices. So, although the name "Caterair" may be new, the firm actually has many years of experience providing inflight foodservices to a wide variety of airlines.

Dobbs International Services, Inc.

With the purchase of fifteen flight kitchens from United Airlines in 1993, Dobbs International Services, Inc. became the largest inflight catering firm in the U.S. market. Under the terms of this sale, Dobbs is United's exclusive caterer at the twelve airports where these kitchens are located. While Dobbs operates flight kitchens in many airports in the United States, to date it operates only six kitchens outside the United States, all in England and Scotland. However, because of the growth in international traffic, Dobbs is pursuing possible joint ventures with firms in Europe, Asia, and the Pacific rim.

Dobbs, headquartered in Memphis, Tennessee, first entered the inflight catering business in 1941. It is a subsidiary of The Dial Corp., a consumer products and services company headquartered in Phoenix, Arizona, having been purchased by Dial in 1987. As of early 1994, Dobbs operated 68 domestic kitchens in 51 different U.S. airports.

LSG Lufthansa Service/Sky Chefs

Sky Chefs, now associated with LSG Lufthansa in an international consortium, is the second oldest inflight caterer. Originally a subsidiary of American Airlines, Sky Chefs was created in 1941 when American decided to compete with airport terminal restaurants, which American felt were charging exorbitant prices for inflight foodservices. American Airlines, one of the earliest airlines to provide commercial passenger services in the United States, operated its own flight kitchens for many years under the auspices of its wholly owned subsidiary, Flagship International, Inc., which operated as Sky Chefs.

However, in 1986, American sold Sky Chefs through a leveraged buyout with Onex Capital Corporation and the firm's management, and American Airlines is no longer in the inflight foodservice business. In 1987, Sky Chefs' airport restaurants and concessions division was sold to Delaware North Companies, Inc., where they are now operated by a Delaware North Subsidiary, CA One Services, Inc. This sale allowed Sky Chefs to better focus its efforts on the development of its inflight catering operations.

In 1993, Sky Chefs partially merged with LSG Lufthansa Service in a move enabling LSG Lufthansa to enter the U.S. inflight market while also enabling Sky Chefs to expand its activities in the international marketplace. The Sky Chefs portion of this very large organization is now headquartered in Dallas, Texas.

Ogden Aviation Services

Ogden Aviation Services has a long history in the inflight catering arena, dating back nearly fifty years. Today its inflight operations are based primarily in major hub airports throughout the United States, including John F. Kennedy International in New York, Los Angeles International, Miami International, Dulles International in Washington, D.C., Honolulu International, and McCarran International in Las Vegas.

Ogden's inflight client base of over 85 airlines is composed primarily of leading international carriers (carriers based outside of the United States) that service the U.S. Market, but this base also includes several of the dominant U.S. carriers. One of the company's strengths is its longstanding reputation for highly customized service programs among foreign airlines, and it has held contracts with many of its major customers for fifteen years or more. A key part of Ogden's approach is to work closely with airline customers to customize menus and cuisines which reflect the unique tastes and preparation techniques of the international airlines' home countries. Ogden has, in some cases, recruited chefs from Asia, Europe, and other regions to run U.S.-based operations, and the company has sent its own employees overseas to study with renowned chefs and food experts in other nations.

Unlike many of its competitors, Ogden Aviation is a full-service aviation service company for which inflight catering constitutes approximately one-third of its business mix. In total, the company has operations at 90 airports throughout North America, Europe, Latin America, the Pacific, and other regions. In addition to its inflight operations, Ogden Aviation Services provides a full range of ground handling, aviation fueling, and related services. It is a $500 million division of Ogden Services Corporation, a Fortune Service 100 company listed on the New York Stock Exchange.

Chelsea Catering

Continental Airlines was one of the last of the major airlines to enter the inflight catering business. It was not until the late 1950s that Continental developed kitchens in Chicago (O'Hare Airport), Denver, Houston (Intercontinental Airport), and Los Angeles. Some time later, the Chicago kitchen was sold.

In 1983, the International Association of Machinists (IAM) struck Continental. Generally, within the airline industry, when an airline has owned and operated flight kitchens, the workers in those kitchens have been unionized by the same union that has organized other airline employees such as their mechanics and other ground crew personnel—the IAM—and *not* by local culinary unions. Thus, the IAM strike not only impacted Continental's ability to keep its planes flying, but also inpacted its ability to keep its kitchens operating. As a result, Continental furloughed all of its kitchen employees and contracted with Marriott In-Flite to operate and manage the flight kitchens.

On January 1, 1986, Continental created Chelsea Catering as an independent caterer to handle catering at its hub airports. Chelsea started with two catering locations, 200 daily inflights, and 600 employees. From 1989 to 1991, Chelsea opened nine flight kitchens and was the fastest growing airline catering company in the country. In 1988, Chelsea Catering became a wholly owned subsidiary of Continental Holdings, Inc. However, in 1993, after Chapter 11 reorganization, Chelsea returned to being a division of Continental, and that is the status of the firm as of this writing. The company now caters more than 240,000 flights a year at six airports, employs more than 2,300 people, and produces nearly 40 million meals annually.

CA One Services, Inc.

The genesis of CA One Services, Inc. (formerly known as Concession Air) started with a simple idea—feed hungry travelers as they wait to depart on their flights. Thus, today CA One's primary business is the design and operation of food, beverages, and retail concessions at nearly forty airports in the United States.

In the beginning, airport foodservice consisted of simple luncheon counters adjacent to single runway airfields. Such operations were basically diners in huge airplane hangers. The operators were local, and the emphasis was on simplicity and quick service. No one could have predicted the success of commercial air travel. As the airlines expanded, passengers demanded more amenities at airfields. Higher-quality foodservice was of particular concern.

During the 1930s, various air terminal operators had a vision of creating opulent havens for the comfort and convenience of airline passengers. One of them was an early airline pioneer, C. R. Smith, the founder of American Airlines. In 1940, he created Sky Chefs as a division of American Airlines to develop air terminal foodservice facilities. Sky Chefs lunch counters and coffee shops sprang up at American Airlines terminals across the country.

Also in 1940, three brothers in Buffalo, New York created their own airport foodservice firm as a subsidiary of their successful sports and theater concessions company. These three brothers, Charles, Marvin, and Louis Jacobs, started their business with the foodservice contract for the Washington National Airport in Washington, D.C. This new company was called Air Terminal Services (ATS). At the time, ATS and Sky Chefs were competitors, but their destinies connected almost two generations later.

The ensuing forty years were good to the two firms and to the airline and terminal foodservice business in general. Commercial air travel boomed, and the ancillary industries experienced a tremendous growth spurt. Sky Chefs became a dominant player in both the air terminal concessions market and the inflight catering industry. At the same time, ATS nurtured its standing as the concession contractor of choice for small and midsized airports. In this environment, it did not take long for airports to surpass railway stations in amenities, passenger traffic, and scope of operations.

In 1986, the Sky Chefs' Catering and Concessions Division was spun off from American Airlines and subsequently sold twice, as indicated previously in the Sky Chefs discussion. In 1988, this division found a permanent home at Delaware North, the corporate ancestor to the tiny concessions firm founded by the Jacob Brothers in Buffalo. The new holding was merged with ATS to form Concession Air. With the combined portfolio, the new company became the second largest airport foodservice firm in the United States. It remained known as Concession Air until 1994 when its name was changed to CA One Services, Inc. The new name was chosen to reflect management's commitment to make this firm number one in customer services in the airport and inflight environment.

Because of the number and type of airports that CA One Services, Inc. serves, it has also been quite active in inflight catering. At the present time, the company services airlines through the convenience and capacity available in its in-terminal concessions kitchens at nearly one-third of its locations. The company's inflight catering niche is at small to medium-sized airports where the terminal concession's production facilities are built to accommodate the airlines' service needs on either a scheduled or on-call basis.

Gate Gourmet International

Although it is not a domestic caterer, Gate Gourmet, SwissAir's catering company, has long been one of the major international inflight caterers. It is a growing company that is looking toward the United States as a possible area for future expansion. Indeed, Gate Gourmet is now a partner with Dobbs International Services, Inc. in a joint venture known as International Service Partners. This partnership is now operating flight kitchens at Chicago's O'Hare Airport.

Gate Gourmet is somewhat unique among the larger catering firms in that it is one of the few still wholly owned by an airline, although airline ownership has been more characteristic of European catering companies (such as the LSG/Lufthansa relationship and British Airway's ownership of its own catering firm). In mid-1994, Gate Gourmet purchased SAS Service Partner (SASSP), the inflight catering arm of Scandinavian Airline System (SAS). Gate Gourmet had previously purchased controlling interest of a firm called Aero Chef, which also services many of the same airports at which SAS Service Partner has kitchens. Thus, there was some concern on the part of Scandinavian officials about the new Gate Gourmet purchases leading to its having a monopoly on the catering services at a number of European (and especially Scandinavian) airports. However, Gate Gourmet plans to operate these two companies as two totally separate subsidiary operations to avoid the concern about a monopoly interest.

With the purchase of SAS Service Partner, Gate Gourmet has become one of the three largest international catering firms (along with LSG Lufthansa/Sky Chefs and Caterair). One of Gate Gourmet's objectives in purchasing SASSP was to take advantage of the technological sophistication in their kitchens, where they have incorporated high production volume equipment and industrial production procedures to give them very high volume and highly efficient production and distribution capability. The new Gate Gourmet/SASSP conglomerate has kitchens throughout Europe, and looks to expand its operations into new markets throughout the world.

SUMMARY

The inflight foodservice industry provides foods and beverages to the airlines for consumption by passengers during flights. The food and beverage products are prepared and packaged at an inflight caterer's kitchen facilities, then transported to the airport for boarding on the proper aircraft. It is essential that all food and equipment required for a particular flight be on board that flight and ready for departure at the scheduled time. Having a flight delayed because of problems with the foodservice is a serious problem for the inflight caterer.

The inflight catering industry is highly competitive today as airlines are changing their foodservice requirements and shortening their flight times. In response to this environment, many inflight caterers are diversifying their operations to make improved use of their production facilities and generate new revenue sources. Indications are that this diversification movement is a trend of the future for inflight caterers.

Several caterers handle a large proportion of the inflight foodservices at the larger domestic airports. Among them are some of the oldest and largest inflight catering firms in the world. There is increasing globalization of inflight catering operations, and expansion of domestic inflight catering firms seems most likely through the development of kitchens in the international market and through acquisitions, mergers, and partnerships among catering companies.

KEY TERMS

Boarding	Galley
Charter Flight	Inflight Caterer
Commercial Foodservices	Inflight Foodservice
Cook–chill Foodservice System	International (Foreign)
Delay	Logistics
Diversification	Noncommercial Foodservices
Domestic	Registered Dietitian
Double Provisioning	Rethermalize
Flight Kitchen	Scheduled Charter
Food Factory	Terminal Foodservices
Full Service Firm	

DISCUSSION QUESTIONS

1. Describe the inflight foodservice industry. Is the provision of foodservices inside airport terminals part of the same industry as the provision of food and beverage services on aircraft? Why or why not?

2. Identify and discuss at least three features which make inflight foodservices a unique sector of the total foodservice industry. What impact do you think these features would have on the management of the inflight foodservice industry?

3. Discuss why it might be said that the successful provisioning of inflight foodservices is dependent upon flawless logistics.

4. Discuss why U.S. domestic airlines are generally no longer in the flight kitchen business while many non-U.S. airlines, such as British Airways or Lufthansa, remain in the flight kitchen business.

5. Identify factors making the domestic inflight foodservice industry so highly competitive. Why has that competitive level led to increased diversification within the industry? How are inflight caterers diversifying their operations?

6. Identify six major inflight caterers in the United States today. Briefly discuss the background of each of these firms and their current position in the industry. How did each of these firms get into the inflight catering business?

2

Development of the Inflight Foodservice Industry

LEARNING OBJECTIVES

After studying this chapter, the student should be able to:
1. Discuss the historical development of food and beverage services on board aircraft prior to World War II.
2. Discuss the development of the inflight catering industry as opposed to in-house provision of food and beverage services by the airlines.
3. Describe the development of inflight foodservices aboard DC-3 aircraft.
4. Discuss the developments in inflight foodservices since World War II.
5. Discuss the development of the Inflight Foodservices Association and the reasons for the creation of a professional association to service this industry.

The first airlines were created after World War I by former military pilots. Their purpose was mail delivery, not passenger transport. Passengers were gradually included on flights, sometimes sharing an open cockpit with the mail. Since passengers were considered a necessary evil by the pilots who ran (and controlled) the airlines, no thought was given to any foodservice for them, although the pilots and other members of the crew might sometimes share a box lunch sandwich or a thermos of coffee with them.

EARLY FOODSERVICE DEVELOPMENTS

It was not until 1936, with the development of the DC-3, that the first airplane galley was introduced by American Airlines. That galley was quite primitive by modern standards as there was no electrical power available for heating foods or beverages, and all hot foods and liquids were boarded at ready-to-serve temperatures and held hot in thermoses. Three years later, the Boeing 307 Stratoliner, the first aircraft with a pressurized cabin that permitted commercial flights above the weather, was developed with a galley no more advanced than that of the DC-3. Primitive though it was, the DC-3 (illustrated in Figure 2.1) revolutionized air travel in the United States, and it was in this plane that routine, planned passenger foodservice became the standard for the industry. Figure 2.2 shows lunch service on Western Airlines in 1935, while Figure 2.3 illustrates American Airlines cold luncheon service in 1937. Prior to this time, stewards, rather than stewardesses, were used as passenger service attendants, as shown in Figure 2.4.

Also in the 1930s, Pan American Airways developed extensive galleys on their flying boats, the clippers that were used for overseas flights. Although there was no electric power available for these galleys for either heating or cooling food products, the last of these famous aircraft, the Boeing 314, had food-heating capability from a glycol circulating

FIGURE 2.1 DC-3 aircraft flown by Nevada Airlines. (Photo courtesy of Scale Model Research, Costa Mesa, CA)

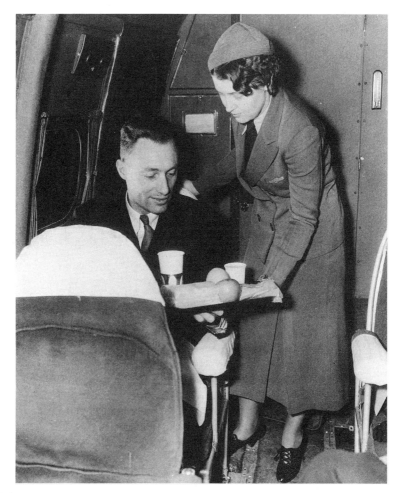

FIGURE 2.2 Western's first flight attendant, Ursala Brown, serving a sandwich lunch in 1935. (Photo courtesy of Delta Air Lines)

system which piped glycol from the galley to one of the plane's four engines. The engine heated the glycol, which, in turn, heated water in the galley. Unfortunately, if that engine had to be shut down for any reason this heating system became nonfunctional for the flight. However, from the very first, these flying clippers had the capability of making fresh coffee on board through the use of the circulating glycol heating system.

There was no refrigeration system on board the flying clippers, and weight limitations precluded boarding more than the minimum amount of ice that was needed for bar service requirements. However, because of the poor reliability of the glycol heating system, cold meals

FIGURE 2.3 American Airlines cold luncheon service in 1937. (Photo courtesy of Philip J. Parrott)

or cold buffets were served on these flights whenever climatic conditions allowed.

Except in places such as Wake Island, where there were no amenities available and Pan American had to establish and staff kitchens, food for the clipper flights was procured from high-quality local hotels or restaurants. The finest foods were procured as Pan American was competing with the elegant steamships of the day for their passengers. However, canned foods, such as ham, potatoes, peas, and so on were always carried on board for emergency purposes and for second meals that were required on long flights. Figure 2.5 illustrates the dining service on Pan American flying clippers. Figure 2.6 shows Delta Airlines passengers enjoying first-class lounge service similar to the meal services provided by Pan American during this early flight era.

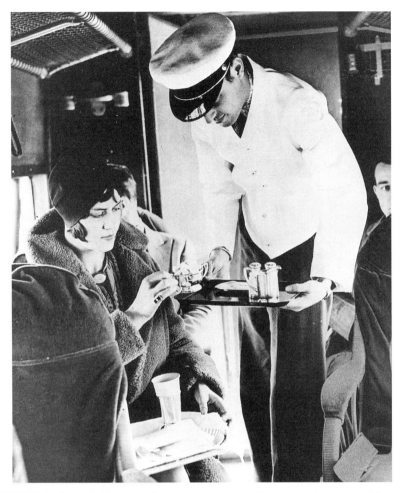

FIGURE 2.4 Initially the attendants on passenger flights were stewards. Note the silver and crystal condiment service used along with paper trays and cups for after dinner coffee service aboard Western Air Express in 1928. (Photo courtesy of Delta Air Lines)

By the mid-1930s, airlines were beginning to realize the importance of inflight foodservices and were becoming concerned about both the quality of the food products available and the high prices charged by the airport terminal restaurants where they usually bought their food supplies. United Airlines, under the guidance of their chairman, W. A. "Pat" Patterson, was the first airline to recognize the marketing potential of inflight foodservice as competition among the airlines increased. The development of the DC-4, which could carry fifty passengers, further emphasized the need for improvement in inflight foodservice procedures and products. Figure 2.7 illustrates Delta Air Lines' meal service on a DC-4.

FIGURE 2.5 Passengers enjoying fine dining service on board Pan American's Flying Clippers. (Photo courtesy of Philip J. Parrott)

THE DEVELOPMENT OF AIRLINE-OWNED INFLIGHT KITCHENS

Pat Patterson engaged a consultant, Don Magarrell, to advise them how to proceed. Magarrell developed United's answer to the problem—build its own flight kitchens at airports where its flights landed. Its first experimental kitchen was completed in Oakland, California in December 1934. Operating its own kitchen was so successful for United that Magarrell was given the go-ahead to rapidly expanded this concept. United eventually built a chain of twenty kitchens throughout the United States. Figure 2.8 is a photo taken in the United Airlines kitchen at Salt Lake City, Utah in 1946. United quickly became the largest inflight caterer in the United States, and eventually catered to other airlines as well as to its own flights.

American Airlines and Transcontinental Air Transport (TAT)—the forerunner of Trans World Airlines (TWA)—took an alternative approach to their local suppliers at each airport they serviced. In the early years of the airline industry, airline activities were regulated by the federal government, and governmental decisions made in the mid-30s were an important influence on these airlines' decisions.

FIGURE 2.6 Delta Air Lines passengers enjoying first-class lounge service on early long distance flights. (Photo courtesy of Delta Air Lines)

In 1934, President Franklin Roosevelt, in an unprecedented action, canceled all federal airmail contracts. This action made the airlines realize the need to market themselves to emphasize passenger service. Now, with the loss of the mail delivery services, their primary revenue source would be passenger accommodations. Following the airmail contract cancellation, there were three major transcontinental airline routes remaining which were allocated between United, American, and TAT by the federal regulatory agency, the Federal Aviation Administration (FAA). United was given the northern route via Chicago. TAT was given the shortest route via Pittsburgh, Kansas City, and Albuquerque. American received the long, sparsely populated southern route via Washington, D.C., Nashville, Memphis, Fort Worth, El Paso, Tucson, and Phoenix. Because TAT's flights were concentrated at only a few airports and its food purchase volume at each airport was large, it was able to demand and receive good-quality products for its flights. American, though, had difficulty with its foodservices. Its route allocation covered a large geographic area, including the sparsely populated Southwest. As a result, American needed services from a substantially larger number of airports, and it required a lower volume of meals per airport, compared with the service requirements of United and TAT.

FIGURE 2.7 Delta Air Lines meal service on board a DC-4. (Photo courtesy of Philip J. Parrot)

Thus, there was little question that American's food quality was well below that of its competitors, especially United, by the end of the 1930s. Still, American surpassed United as the leading passenger carrier in 1939 because of its many other service innovations, such as the Air Travel Plan (the forerunner of the credit card), the ground air conditioning units to climatize the plane cabins prior to boarding, and new ticketing and reservation systems, which expedited boarding and provided flight attendants with passenger information. However, American realized that it could not retain its dominant position in the passenger industry without an improvement in its foodservices.

In 1940, American Airlines decided that it, too, had to go into the flight kitchen business to stay competitive with United. In contrast to United's

FIGURE 2.8 United Airlines flight kitchen in Salt Lake City, 1946. Note the lidded trays used at that time. The lid was placed under the tray for service, bringing the tray to a comfortable level for dining when placed on the passenger's lap. (Photo courtesy of Philip J. Parrott)

concept of building and operating kitchens exclusively to service passenger aircraft, American's original concept, formulated and implemented by Newt Wilson, was to develop terminal restaurants that could also cater to aircraft. They opted to develop special inflight catering kitchens only at those airports where the development of dual-purpose terminal restaurants was impractical. Sky Chefs, Inc. was approved by American's stockholders in 1941 as the name of its subsidiary organization tasked with the development of its terminal restaurants and inflight foodservices. Newt Wilson became the first president of Sky Chefs and remained in that position until 1971.

While United, American, TWA, Northwest, and Continental were concerned with the development of their domestic foodservices, Pan American Airways (Pan Am) was concerned with the provision of foodservices on its international routes. It established commissaries headed by port stewards at each of its provisioning points, but the frequency of its flights was insufficient to justify in-house food preparation where good hotel and restaurant facilities were available to service its inflight needs. Thus, in locations such as Lisbon, Honolulu, or Hong Kong, the duty of the port steward was to see to the resupply of all equipment and to assist the chief steward on each flight in securing the needed foods from a quality local hotel or restaurant. However, in more remote areas, such as Wake Island, Guam, or Horta (in the Azores), the commissaries were expanded to include food preparation capabilities also managed by the port steward as there were no local facilities able to service Pan Am's flights.

As previously noted, Pan Am's competitors at the time were the cruise ships, not the other domestic airlines. Therefore, many of the terms adopted for its aircraft, personnel, and procedures were nautical in nature and modeled from cruise ship tradition and practice. Indeed, as has been mentioned, a major focus of Pan Am's foodservice activities was to provide the fine dining ambiance and gourmet cuisine which characterized the cruise ships of the period. This perception of an aircraft as a ship spread throughout the industry; thus terms such as *galley*, *steward*, *port*, and *starboard* are still used in the industry.

Continental Airlines and Trans World Airlines (TWA) were the last airlines to enter the inflight kitchen business. It was not until the 1950s that these airlines developed their own kitchen facilities at a limited number of airports that were key to their flight activity. In the early 1960s, one of the pioneers of inflight foodservice, Phil Parrott, became the director of foodservices for Continental, and he was instrumental in the development of its kitchen operations. Later on, in 1986, Chelsea Catering was set up as a subsidiary of Continental Airlines to operate the Continental-owned flight kitchens. TWA has since sold most of its kitchen operations, but Continental still incorporates Chelsea as one of that airline's divisions. At present Chelsea operates flight kitchens in nearly all of Continental's hub locations—Denver, Houston, Newark, Los Angeles, Cleveland, and Honolulu.

THE DEVELOPMENT OF INFLIGHT CATERERS

Marriott was one of the earliest inflight caterers as a result of innovative actions by William Kahrl, the manager of a new Marriott Hot Shoppe across the road from Washington's Hoover Airport (now Washington National Airport) in the late 1930s. In late 1937, at the request of one of his customers who was the manager of American Airlines' operations there at that time, Kahrl started putting coffee and sweet rolls on American flights coming from the west coast. These flights stopped in Washington enroute to their final destination (New York City) after flying all night across the country. The airline furnished the thermoses; the Hot Shoppe furnished the food and the paper supplies; everything was loaded on a flat pushcart and pushed across Route 1 from the Hot Shoppe to the airport in the very early morning hours and loaded onto the airplane. These activities were the beginning of Marriott's inflight catering activities.

Unlike Marriott's beginnings, Dobbs' entry into the inflight foodservice field was in response to James K. Dobbs' concern with the poor-quality food that he received on flights as he traveled around the country checking on his Toddle House operations. He enjoyed quality food, and felt that airline passengers were entitled to the best food possible, given the serving constraints associated with airline foodservices. His work was instrumental in the airlines' transition from serving only cold box lunches to serving hot, restaurant-style meals. His entry into the airline business was through the purchase of the Memphis Airport Restaurant, which also serviced American Airline's DC-3 flights through that airport.

Mr. Dobbs' concept was to service the airlines through the terminal restaurants. He also had a theory that there should be a recipe for everything, and he demanded that all the products in all these restaurants be prepared by approved recipes. Thus, Dobbs was able to provide consistent food products from one airport to the next as they were able to expand their operations. Because planes had to stop about every two hours for fuel, Dobbs' expansion strategy was to acquire terminal contracts for many small cities such as Shreveport, New Orleans, or Amarillo before trying to expand to airports that were major terminals during the 1940s and 50s. Dallas Love Field was Dobbs' first major airport, but its first independent airline kitchen was built in Atlanta in 1946 in order to cater to Delta Air Lines when Dobbs was unable to secure the terminal feeding contract there.

FOODSERVICES ON THE DC-3

Figures 2.9 and 2.10 illustrate meal service using trays set on pillows on passengers' laps. Even though the lap pillow was soon replaced by alternatives for most passengers, the pillow was still used to support the meal trays of passengers seated in bulkhead rows as late as the 1960s and early 1970s, as illustrated in Figure 2.11.

The service items for one meal were packaged in paper bags by the caterer. The bags were stored on the plane in bins above the racks holding the thermoses with the hot foods (2-gallon jumbo thermoses with wide mouths) and hot beverages (2-quart thermoses). The service items for each passenger consisted of a paper mat for the aluminum tray, a linen napkin, a china plate, three pieces of silverware, two paper cups, one aluminum cap holder, and salt and pepper containers. Cold foods, such as milk, rolls, butter, and desserts, were placed in a cold buffet unit which fit under the racks holding the hot food thermoses. To prepare a tray, stewards and stewardesses (referred to as *flight attendants* since the early 1970s) placed an empty tray on the buffet top; removed the service items from the bag and arranged them on the tray; placed chilled foods from the buffet drawers on the tray; spooned hot foods from the jumbo thermoses onto the plates; and drew liquids from the thermoses into the cups. Because of all the handling required, the meal service process was very slow. Figure 2.12 shows meal provisions using this equipment being loaded onto a DC-3 aircraft flying inland routes in Australia.

Two or three years later, United introduced lidded trays made of paper maché, which replaced the aluminum trays. (Note lidded trays in Figure 2.8.) These new trays were relatively inexpensive and had surfaces impreg-

FIGURE 2.9 A 1940's passenger samples the fried chicken box lunch served during his flight. In order to be at a more comfortable height for eating, the meal tray was placed on a pillow on the passenger's lap. (Photo courtesy of Delta Air Lines)

nated with a paint or varnish, which made them easy to clean. The lids for these trays were approximately five inches deep, making it possible for the trays to be preset with the service items and the chilled foods in the flight kitchens. Presetting the trays encouraged the use of more variety in salads and desserts, helped speed meal service and allowed foods to be presented with improved finesse. The trays and mats were color-coordinated to complement the foods served.

The new lid, when inverted, served as a bottom for the tray, supporting it on passengers' laps for dining and eliminating the need for the pillow as the tray support. Because it was firmer and steadier than a pillow, it helped passengers eat more comfortably from the trays. After the passengers finished their meals, the lid again became the tray cover, enabling the stewardesses to store the tray back into the service buffet without removing the dirty dishes and other debris as they had to do originally. (See Figure 2.8 for an example of these trays being packed in a United Airlines kitchen.)

Controlling the distribution of catering equipment became a steadily increasing logistical problem for both the airlines and the caterers as the number of airlines operating DC-3s increased. There was a continuous

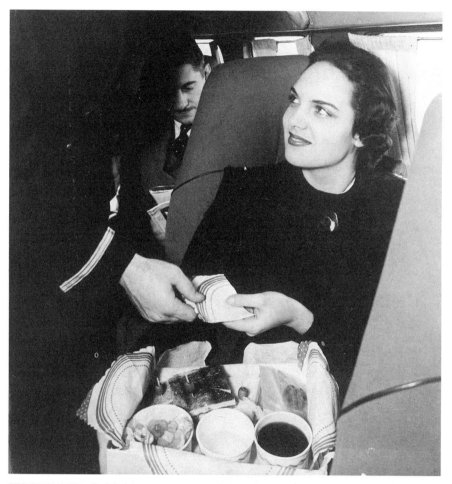

FIGURE 2.10 Celebrities were some of the early airlines passengers. Here Linda Darnell, flying on a Lockhead Electra in the 1930s is served her meal in a tray set on a pillow on her lap by Mr. Jack Slaton. (Photo courtesy of Delta Air Lines)

shortage of equipment as a result of passenger pilferage of items that were not replaced and because of some airlines' failure to repair damaged equipment. When caterers were short of equipment, they would substitute that of another airline to the amusement of passengers and the embarrassment of the airline serving the meals. Such substitutions were possible because the food equipment of all airlines was either identical or sufficiently similar in design (as all airlines were flying DC-3s) that it could be used interchangeably. To protect themselves from shortages, caterers began hoarding equipment, especially the thermoses and silverware necessary for any service. Hoarding was accomplished by shorting dummies, or the sets of equipment that were supposed to be boarded over and above the actual number of meals boarded on a flight. This hoarding of equipment

FIGURE 2.11 United Airlines stewardesses practice serving trays to persons seated in bulk head rows. Note that the trays are still served on pillows placed in the passengers' laps as late as the early 1970s. (Photo courtesy of Dr. Kathleen S. Bell)

ultimately gave rise to a more systematic approach to equipment control, as will be discussed later in this text.

Airlines that did purchase replacements and make equipment repairs were soon providing equipment for other airlines that did not. By 1939 or 1940, American estimated that it was providing enough foodservice equipment for about one-half the airline industry, and issued an edict that such competitor support had to stop. As a means of stopping it, a Passenger Service Committee was sponsored under the auspices of the newly established Air Transport Association. It was hoped that this committee could solve the problem by obtaining the cooperation of all airlines concerned with the issue.

FIGURE 2.12 Loading catering supplies on board a Quantas DC-3 airliner which was providing airline service in Queensland, Australia. (Photo courtesy of Philip J. Parrott)

DEVELOPMENTS AFTER WORLD WAR II

World War II brought a halt to much of airline development and expansion as all resources, including new aircraft, were diverted to the war effort. After World War II, though, inflight foodservice developments were rapid. One of the most important developments from the war was the capability of some aircraft to generate electric power during flight. On these aircraft, it was possible to divert power to the galleys so that coffee could be brewed on board and food could be kept hot.

Other postwar developments, most of which are either still in use or very similar in design to equipment in use today, included: (1) Howard Baumgardner's (American Airlines) development of the holding oven, which was manufactured by Mapco; (2) Baumgardner's development of the automatic coffee brewer; (3) Pan American's development of the convection oven (1945) as a means of rethermalizing the frozen meals it, and TWA, had pioneered before and during the war; (4) William Littlewood's (American Airlines) development of the plug-in tray table, which eliminated the need for a pillow or tray lid under the tray to raise it to a comfortable level for eating; and (5) Baumgardner's development of a tray carrier which reduced the space requirement for on-board tray storage. This new tray carrier also had provision for slabs of dry ice as well as for air circulation throughout the box; thus, it provided effective refrigeration on board the aircraft for the first time. Problem-solving work at Sky Chefs (American Airlines) also resulted in the development of the flight-type dishwasher for ware washing and drying without touching a dish with a towel, drying agents for wash water to prevent dishes and glassware from streaking while air drying, and the gas-fired grill.

THE ARRIVAL OF JET AIRCRAFT IN THE 1950s

The development of jet aircraft in the 1950s began a new era in inflight foodservice. Not only were the galleys in the aircraft newly designed, but changes were required in the inflight kitchens as well to accommodate the larger boarding modules and the much heavier weights involved. Some of the boarding packages were as large as ten by fourteen feet and weighed almost a ton for planes such as the jumbo jet. The arrival of the 747 and two-deck service in the 1970s meant new adaptations to be able to load very heavy equipment (which had to be rolled as it was too heavy to lift) into the lower deck area using the airlines' loading systems. The end result was a near doubling in size of inflight kitchens to provide the space to handle the much larger boarding equipment requirements.

In the early 1950s, hot food packaging was changed from the thermoses of the 1930s and 1940s to heated ovens which could weight 150 pounds or more. Although it had been possible to board the required food and equipment onto a DC-3 by backing a truck under the wing, standing on the bed of the truck, and handing the supplies and equipment up to personnel on the plane, it was quickly apparent that improved methods were needed to get the food and equipment to the proper height for boarding the newer aircraft. This need drove the development of the high-lift truck in the 1950s. The whole bed of this type of truck was raised to the level of the aircraft doorway. Figure 2.13 shows food being boarded by Dobbs personnel in the early 1950s before the development of the high-lift truck. Figure 2.14 shows one of the early high-lift trucks used by Dobbs House (now Dobbs International Services, Inc.).

Getting supplies for the inflight kitchens to use in meal preparation was no simple task, either. The extensive product distribution systems which support the foodservice industry today had not yet been well developed in the 1940s and 1950s. Many airlines purchased the products that they wanted used for their meals and transported them as COMAT (Company Owned Materials) in their own aircraft to the different catering kitchens that serviced their flights. When the plane arrived at an airport with food or supplies, it was the responsibility of the caterer to pick up those products from the airline and bring them back to the inflight kitchen for use there.

FIGURE 2.13 Hand-operated carts like the one shown in this photo were used by Dobbs to load food into planes in the early 1950s. The aircraft was accessible only by climbing up a steep set of narrow stairs. (Photo courtesy of Dobbs International Services, Inc.)

Figure 2.15 illustrates catering employees off-loading cases of produce shipped in by an airline from an aircraft.

FROZEN MEAL DEVELOPMENT FOR TRANSOCEANIC FLIGHTS

Throughout this period, Pan American Airways continued its development of elegant service for its transoceanic flights. An innovation developed by Bert Snowden was the precooked frozen entree, the forerunner of today's

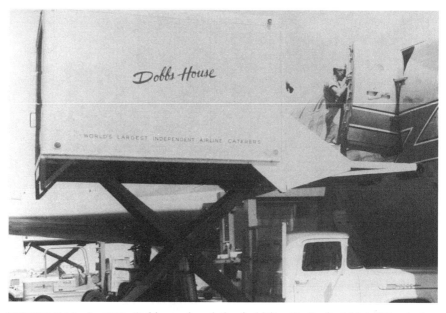

FIGURE 2.14 In 1958, Dobbs replaced the forklift with its first high-lift catering truck like the one shown here boarding meals on an aircraft in Memphis. (Photo courtesy of Dobbs International Services, Inc.)

pop-out meals. Its development of the convection oven in 1945 (termed the Maxson Oven since the Maxson Company agreed to manufacture it) led to Pan American's increased usage of these frozen meals to solve its transoceanic meal service problems.

The new precooked frozen entree was a flexible item that could be used in any system. In addition to being heated on board planes equipped with the new convection oven, it could also be thawed, heated on the ground, and boarded as a hot casserole meal. However, the precooked frozen entree was very controversial. Many chefs felt that it posed a threat to their security. Also, in spite of the careful research work of Mr. Snowden, many of the early products that appeared on the market were of inferior quality and gave the system a bad reputation. However, it should be remembered that the development of any type of frozen food for the retail market was barely in its infancy at this time. These concerns with meal quality caused Pan American to seriously consider eliminating this frozen meal concept in 1948. However, to revert to locally prepared meals at that time would have meant the development of flight kitchens in areas such as Damascus, Syria; New Delhi and Calcutta, India; Bangkok, Thailand; and Johannesburg, South Africa. At the same time, they were in need of new aircraft to expand their fleet; so the funding and development of inflight kitchens in these rather remote areas was not economically feasible.

FIGURE 2.15 Dobbs employees manually off-load cases of fresh produce from an aircraft for use in their Memphis inflight kitchen. (Photo courtesy of Dobbs International Service, Inc.)

Kenneth Parratt came to Pan American from United Airlines to try to solve the problem. He recognized that the problem was not the system, but the quality of the food products being prepared for the system. Therefore, he pioneered the establishment of a frozen meal production facility operated by Pan American in the United States. He installed equipment such as high-velocity blast freezers and low-temperature storage freezers and employed an Italian chef with hotel fine dining experience as the food production manager.

Products produced in this facility were shipped around the world to the Pan American commissaries for boarding on flights originating from those airports. While his system essentially solved Pan Am's foodservice problems at that time and significantly increased meal quality, the system was not without its problems. For example, it was reported that the first shipment to Karachi, Pakistan was lost because transfer from the ship at the port dock to the airport freezer storage facility was done by camel-drawn cart with the food unprotected and exposed to the broiling noonday sun.

Pan American was not the only airline developing frozen entrees for its flights at this time. TWA was also producing frozen entrees at its flight kitchens at Orly Field in Paris and at Laguardia Airport in New York City.

The entrees produced in Paris were shipped to airports around the world for use on TWA's international flights.

THE DEVELOPMENT OF STANDARDIZED FOOD AND BEVERAGE PRODUCTS

The 1950s was also the era for the development of many standardized products suitable for use in inflight foodservices. Chicken had been a mainstay for inflight foodservice since foods were first offered to passengers in the 1930s. Fried chicken was one of the few foods that could be held hot over long time periods and still be of an acceptable quality. Prepared other ways, chicken still held up much better than many other protein products such as beef or pork. It could be cooked, held, chilled, frozen, rethermalized and still be tender and moist if properly cooked and plated. Idle Wild Farms' development of the oven-ready stuffed rock cornish game hen brought product consistency and a gourmet quality to the use of poultry products for inflight meals.

Other developments in this era included the initial marketing of portion cut meats based on the Meat Buyers' Guide for Standard Specification, first published in laymen's terms in the 1950s; the development of filling machines by the Dixie Cup Company, which enabled caterers to fill and seal individual cups of items such as salad dressings, cream, and other condiments; the development of portion packs for items such as sugar, salt, and pepper; and the replacement of refillable glass bottles for carbonated beverages with cans.

The boarding of glass carbonated beverage bottles had been a major problem for the airlines as the bottles were not disposable, the deposit costs forfeited by the airlines were substantial, the bottles were very heavy and added significantly to the weight of the food and beverage service items, and there was always potential for injury from bottle breakage and explosions. The highly carbonated beverages (particularly club soda) became quite explosive at high altitudes as the atmospheric pressure dropped and the volume of the dissolved gas in the beverages expanded within the bottle. The shaking caused by aircraft vibration and air turbulence added to the problem. It was not uncommon to have a bottle neck break and a sharp projectile fly through the cabin, sometimes seriously injuring cabin attendants. The new cans were not only lighter and disposable, but their flexibility helped alleviate the explosion problem.

FINE DINING ABOARD THE AIRCRAFT

The advent of the 707 jet aircraft brought fine restaurant dining to first-class passengers in the late 1960s. Efforts were made to adapt menus from well-known fine dining establishments to airline service. Figure 2.16 illustrates a menu used by Pan American for their first-class service from Paris to New York during this era. Their restaurant partner was Maxim's of Paris. Initially, the problems encountered with this type of service were enormous, as each service had its own linen, glassware, and china—all of which had to be kept in stock at each terminal boarding that particular style of service. Figure 2.17 illustrates a place setting typical of this era. As the fine dining concept developed, it was simplified away from being modeled after existing restaurants. Instead, it was developed as a particular service for the airline which used a consistent linen, glassware, and china service.

However, new transport and service equipment was required as fine china and glassware could not withstand the handling required for inflight service in the existing unpadded carts. Sky Chefs pioneered the development of rubber-coated racks for handling the fragile serviceware to help reduce the breakage problem. Wheeled carts were also developed to facilitate the handling of the new food products and service equipment as well as to provide a means of displaying and serving menu items to the passengers in the first-class cabin.

Throughout the 1970s and the 1980s, developments in food products, packaging alternatives, and equipment continued as inflight foodservice needs expanded. The Boeing 747 and other wide-body aircraft were introduced in the 1970s. The 747 was revolutionary in terms of changes in galley equipment and inflight service procedures as (1) airlines tried buffet service on board the aircraft where passengers selected their food at display areas and (2) lounges were installed complete with pianos and bars. Snack flights were added to the foodservice repertoire as some flights were too short to allow for full meal service to all passengers in the time available. A business class was developed, which called for an intermediate service style blending many aspects of first-class service with some coach-class customs. Throughout this time, though, there were only limited changes in the actual equipment and production and service methods used on narrow-body aircraft with many inflight foodservice operations continuing much as they had previously.

THE FORMATION OF THE INFLIGHT FOODSERVICE ASSOCIATION

Although there had been annual informal gatherings of airline industry people at foodservice industry events such as the National Restaurant Show, there was no organized effort to provide a forum for interaction among airline foodservice personnel or to provide a means of sharing problems and possible solutions to those problems prior to 1966. On January 19, 1966 the first commercial airline foodservice seminar was convened at Cornell University under the guidance of Gerald Lattin, then Assistant

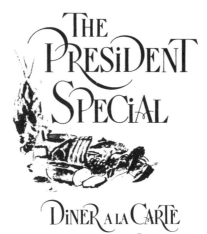

THE PRESIDENT SPECIAL

DINER A LA CARTE

HORS D'OEUVRE

Le Caviar frais d'Iran Le Foie–gras de Strasbourg aux Truffes Les Délices culinaires de la Voiture
FRESH IRANIAN CAVIAR   STRASBOURG GOOSELIVER WITH TRUFFLES   SELECTED DELICACIES FROM THE CART

POTAGES

Le Billi – By au Chablis   Le Potage Saint Germain aux Croûtons
MUSSEL SOUP WITH CHABLIS   GREEN PEA SOUP

ENTREES

Le Homard Thermidor   La Sole "Albert"   Le Ris de Veau Financière
LOBSTER THERMIDOR   FILLETS OF CHANNEL SOLE   SWEETBREAD "FINANCIERE"

Le Médaillon de Veau "Orloff"   Le Faisan du Marquis à l'Armagnac — Riz sauvage
VEAL STEAK "ORLOFF"   PHEASANT IN CREAM AND BRANDY SAUCE   WILD RICE

ROTI

Notre Spécialité : Le Contrefilet de Boeuf à la Broche
OUR SPECIALTY ROAST SIRLOIN OF BEEF

GRILLADE

La double Noisette de Pré – Salé
DOUBLE LAMB CHOPS

LEGUMES

Les Haricots verts au Beurre   Les Pommes Dauphine
BUTTERED STRINGBEANS   "DAUPHINE" POTATOES

SALADE

Les Coeurs de Laitues à l'Estragon
HEARTS OF LETTUCE WITH TARRAGON

FROMAGES

Les Spécialités régionales
REGIONAL SPECIALTIES

ENTREMETS

La Tarte "Maxim's"   Le Gâteau St. Honoré
TART "MAXIM'S"   CAKE "ST HONORE"

FRUITS

Un Choix de Fruits des Iles et des Continents
FRUIT BASKET

Café Américain   Café Sanka   Thé Orange Pekoe
AMERICAN COFFEE   SANKA COFFEE   ORANGE PEKOE TEA

NOTRE SELECTION DES GRANDS VINS DE FRANCE

BOURGOGNE BLANC Tête de Cuvée   BORDEAUX ROUGE Grand Crû classé

CHAMPAGNE Brut Millésimé — Cuvée spéciale pour Pan American

COGNAC Réserve et LIQUEURS de Marque

PAN AMERICAN CUISINE BY MAXIM'S DE PARIS

"La bonne Cuisine est la base du véritable bonheur." A. Escoffier

FIGURE 2.16 Menu served on Pan American flights during period of airline association with fine dining restaurants. (Photo courtesy of Philip J. Parrott)

FIGURE 2.17 Passenger place setting used on Eastern Airlines restaurant flights. China and crystal is by Rosenthal; silver by Reed and Barton. (Photo courtesy of Philip J. Parrott)

Dean of the School of Hotel Administration, and Philip Parrott, then Director of Food Service for Continental Airlines. These two gentlemen recognized the uniqueness of the inflight foodservice industry and realized a need to develop a separate forum to help members of the industry better address industry issues. From day one, these airline seminars were designed to promote communication and an interchange of ideas among *three* groups—the airlines, their caterers, and the suppliers to the industry. Indeed, the 1966 seminar was the first time that representatives from these three groups had met under one roof.

Forty-three people attended the first conference, only one of whom—Inez Jobe of United Airlines—was a woman. Jobe was joined by other female pioneers at the next conference—Helen Bowen (Eastern Airlines), Helene Hickey (Marriott), and Susan Walters (Seagrams). These conferences continued annually at Cornell until 1972. Eric Paalsgard of SAS was the first international speaker to address these conferences when he spoke at the third conference in 1968. Marion Sadler, then president of American Airlines, came to address the graduation banquet in 1971, indicating that the group had achieved stature and recognition in the airline industry.

By 1972, the size of the group had outgrown the capacity of Statler Hall at Cornell, and the meeting was moved to the Inn of Six Flags, at that time owned and operated by American Airlines, in Arlington, Texas. This was the first seminar to have hospitality suites and was the site of the first conference golf tournament.

More importantly, the 1972 seminar was the site of the actual formation of the Inflight Food Service Association (IFSA). The idea for a formal association was the product of a discussion panel chaired by Al D'Agostino. The association concept presented would be a formal association composed of airline and inflight catering organizations. The idea was accepted, and IFSA was born on May 9, 1972.

One of the first concerns of IFSA was to develop a program to satisfy the U.S. Food and Drug Administration. Until a change by President Richard Nixon put the inflight kitchens under the jurisdiction of the Food and Drug Administration, they had always been under the regulatory auspices of the U.S. Public Health Service for approval of kitchen and galley equipment and their sanitary operation. Now, however, the Food and Drug inspectors tried to impose the same standards applied to commercial food factories and the drug industry to working food production kitchens. This application did not work, and the result was the arbitrary closing of flight kitchens at a number of locations. What resulted was embarrassment and loss of revenue for the caterer as well as an interruption of airline schedules and inconvenience for passengers. IFSA reacted quickly and, with special input from Marriott and Sky Chefs, developed a formal program for self-inspection. This IFSA program, along with the *Airline Catering Sanitation Guide*, was initiated throughout the industry and satisfied the Food and Drug Administration. The FDA's Interstate Travel Sanitation Inspectors were subsequently given training in the application of the 1962 Public Health Service's *Food Service Sanitation Manual* for inspecting flight kitchens. Although this manual was meant for restaurants, it was not an enforceable regulation. However, it was cooperatively agreed upon as an acceptable interim measure.

Since 1972, IFSA has held annual educational conferences at various locations throughout the United States. By 1975, the format of having speakers and panel presentations in the morning and having the afternoons available for a series of workshops was developed. However, it was not until 1978 that the tradeshow portion of the conference became a permanent part of the format.

IFSA has now grown to an international organization with a 1995 membership of more than 337 members, including 78 airlines, 70 caterers, 189 allied members, and one individual member. It is recognized by the airline industry for its leadership role and proactive efforts to represent members' interests before regulatory agencies, the development of viable educational programs for its memberships, and its service as a forum for discussion among all facets of the inflight foodservice industry. IFSA's current efforts are focused through various committees which handle mutual industry concerns of food safety, government affairs, education, waste management, recycling, and compatible computer systems (electronic data interchange).

SUMMARY

The inflight foodservice industry is a relatively young industry first developed in the mid- to late 1930s. While there was limited industry development during World War II, significant technological developments occurred as a result of the war which facilitated rapid development of the airline industry and corresponding development of inflight foodservices after the war. The unique demands of this foodservice field have always been a driving force stimulating the development of new products, equipment, and service concepts to better meet the needs of the industry.

Recognizing a need for communication within the industry, in the mid 1960s, pioneers such as Gerald Lattin and Philip Parrott spearheaded the development of inflight industry seminars which brought together representatives from all three facets of the industry—the airlines, the caterers, and the product suppliers. In 1972, the group in attendance at the annual seminar voted to establish a formal association to represent the needs and interests of the industry. Thus the Inflight Food Service Association (IFSA) was born.

The inflight foodservice industry is an exciting and challenging industry. Since its inception, it has been in the forefront of developments that have often been adopted by other facets of the foodservice industry. Inflight foodservice is still on the cutting edge of the foodservice industry. Educational sessions at the annual IFSA conference continue to offer challenges to all in attendance regarding the future of inflight foodservices—challenges which serve to stimulate thought for everyone working with the foodservice industry in any way.

REFERENCES

Haynes, Karla (ed.). (1992). *Sky Chefs: From the Beginning.* Arlington, TX: Sky Chefs, 36 pps.

Lattin, Gerald W. (1990). *Our First 25 Years.* Published for the Inflight Food Service Association by Alexander C. Morton, *Onboard Services,* Miami Springs, FL, 22 pps.

McCool, Audrey C., Fred A. Smith, and David L. Tucker. (1994). *Dimensions of Noncommercial Foodservice Management*. New York: Van Nostrand Reinhold, chapters 2 and 13.

Parrott, Philip J. (1986). *The History of Inflight Food Service*. Miami Springs, FL: International Publishing Company of America, 86 pps.

KEY TERMS

Blast Freezer	Plug-In Tray Table
Boarding Module	Port
Cart Service	Portion Packs
Commissaries	Pressurized Cabin
Convection Oven	Snack Flight
Dummies	Standardized Product
Flight-Type Dishwasher	Starboard
High-lift Truck (Scissors Truck)	Steward
Holding Oven	Tray Carrier

DISCUSSION QUESTIONS

1. Discuss the early developments of the inflight foodservice industry. Who were W.A. "Pat" Patterson, Don Magarrell, Newt Wilson, WIlliam Kahrl, Howard Baumgardner, and James K. Dobbs?

2. What prompted some early airlines to develop their own inflight kitchens while others began the development of relationships with inflight caterers?

3. Describe how food and beverage services were provided on early aircraft such as the DC-3.

4. Identify at least four post–World War II developments in inflight foodservices and discuss the long-range impact of each development on both the inflight foodservice industry and the foodservice industry as a whole.

5. What was the impact of the development of jet aircraft on the inflight foodservice industry?

6. Describe some of the unique contributions to the development of the inflight foodservice industry made by Pan American Airways through its work to provide quality food and beverage services on their transoceanic flights.

7. What are some of the more recent developments in products and packaging that have helped alleviate problems in inflight foodservices? Describe these problems and explain why the new products were helpful in resolving them.

8. Discuss the development of the Inflight Food Service Association. Who are the members of this association? What is the purpose of this organization; what functions does it perform for its members?

3

Meeting Passengers' Foodservice Needs in a Competitive Marketplace

LEARNING OBJECTIVES

After studying this chapter, the student should be able to:

1. Identify the multiple roles of food in inflight services.
2. Discuss the physiological impact of food and beverage services on aircraft passengers.
3. Discuss the role and impact of liquor services in inflight services.
4. Discuss the psychological impact of inflight food and beverage services on passenger behavior.
5. Describe the impact of the passengers' need for food on airlines' decision regarding meal services.
6. Discuss the airlines' use of food and beverage services as a marketing tool, particularly in regard to first-class passengers.
7. Describe the use of food and beverage services as a marketing tool from a historical perspective.
8. Discuss current airline marketing practices in regard to food and beverage services for passengers in first-class, business-class, and coach-class cabins.
9. Describe how airlines with *classless* service are using food and beverage services to market their flights.
10. Identify at least three trends in the foodservice industry which are being reflected in the meals served on board aircraft.

INTRODUCTION

The inflight catering industry is currently a four-billion-dollar industry (at wholesale rates; a retail sales equivalent would be approximately ten billion in sales volume). Inflight catering is an integral part of the airline industry. As the airline industry undergoes changes—streamlining operations, economizing, and becoming increasingly global—so, too, is the catering industry changing. The structure of inflight foodservices must be fluid and able to respond quickly to airline industry changes as they occur. The markets served by airlines are expanding, even to small urban areas, and especially to Third World countries as people become more accustomed to airline transportation being available. The industry is becoming increasingly competitive as deregulation and the constant effort to create and implement new ideas for airline service always brings new competitors into the market.

Food and beverage services have become an expected part of airline services today. All airlines have some type of food and beverage service which they offer to their passengers, and foods and beverages are often components of the competitive strategy of the commercial airlines. Food is not offered to airline passengers just because they are hungry (although hunger may be one reason for service). Indeed, satisfaction of passenger hunger may be the least important reason motivating airlines to offer their passengers food and beverage services. However, each airline has a different management strategy; thus, each has a different perspective about its foodservices and the role that food and beverage services should play in its operations.

ROLE OF FOOD IN FLIGHT MANAGEMENT

Although it was not recognized by the airlines for some time, inflight foodservice has always played a very important psychological and physiological role in the management of passengers on board the aircraft. It is a fact that fear and its accompanying tension is an integral part of flying for some people. Indeed, in the early years of flight, when it was not uncommon for many passengers on the aircraft to be on their first flight, evidence of prayers by passengers was not uncommon, particularly during takeoff and landing or during turbulence. Although the airlines did not recognize it at the time, their foodservices were an important distraction helping the passengers control their fears as well as helping the flight crews manage the behavior of their passengers.

Even though today's passengers are far more sophisticated in regard to the concept of flying, the airlines have a long, enviable safety record, and modern aircraft are often able to fly above weather problems (drastically reducing encounters with turbulence during flights), fear is still a factor that must be taken into account. One needs only to watch passengers on a flight when turbulence is encountered to see that fear. Better yet, ask someone to tell what it was like to be on an aircraft that suddenly climbed or dropped 500 or 1,000 feet when it got caught in a thunderstorm up- or downdraft! Surprising as it may be, there are still many people in the United States who have never flown, and it is quite likely that there will be someone on almost any flight who is a first-time flyer. Passenger logic knows that it is just not natural for the human body and several tons of aircraft equipment, baggage, and passenger weight to be suspended in mid-air, held up only by jet engines and what appears to be a very frail wing surface—no matter what aeronautical engineering theories have proven to be true.

The Physiological Impact

The calm demeanor of the flight attendants and the casual stroll of the pilot through the cabin have long been methods that the airlines have used to help control passenger fears. However, as early as 1946, Pan American Airways cabin attendants were being taught a basic physiological theory that "blood cannot be in two places at once." By that time, it was known that when a meal is eaten and digestion begins, blood is drawn away from other areas of the body to the stomach to facilitate the digestive process and nutrient distribution.

·On flights, feeding the passengers and increasing the blood circulation in the stomach slows blood circulation in other parts of the body resulting in less oxygen for muscles in other areas and a reduction in the passengers' tensions. If muscles are to work hard (be tense as when the passenger's hands are gripping the arm of the seat), a high blood flow is necessary as the hand muscles are working very hard. Drawing the blood flow away from the tensed muscles leads to their relaxation. Indeed, one of the best ways to calm irate passengers (or guests in any situation) is to first feed them, and after they have finished dessert and are enjoying their coffee, come to talk to them about their problems—a common tactic among flight attendants who have to deal with difficult passengers in very confined work areas.

Liquor Service Impact

Liquor, of course, plays a role similar to that of food. However, alcohol is not only a depressant on the nervous system, it is also a dehydrating agent. Since the air in aircraft cabins is quite dry, the consumption of high levels of alcohol during an extended flight could contribute to passenger dehydration. There is also a concern with passengers' possible excessive alcohol intake which could lead to passenger behavior problems during the flight. Thus, inflight alcohol intake by individual passengers and signs of inebriation are monitored by the flight attendants.

It is of interest to note that as common as liquor service is today on board aircraft, most airlines were slow to start liquor service on their flights, primarily because of prohibition and the impact of prohibition on passengers' drinking habits even after it was lifted. With prohibition quickly followed by World War II, it was not until after the war that liquor service became commonplace.

The service of liquor during flights came under a number of legal challenges as aircraft flew over dry counties. There were attempts by some local authorities to ban the service of liquor while aircraft were over their counties. Local officials were known to book passage and, once aboard the flight, to try to get the captain to stop liquor service while over their county. These attempts failed because no one other than the captain was ever able to verify the exact location of the flight. These challenges ultimately contributed to the Open Skies policies and the control of all airspace at a federal level.

United and Delta were among the last holdouts among the major airlines in regard to serving alcohol. The management of United Airlines felt that the cocktail waitress image was demeaning to the girl-next-door flight attendant (stewardesses at that time) profile that they wanted to project on their flights. However, they finally started liquor service on flights to Honolulu in order to be competitive with Pan American's flights where alcoholic beverages were regularly served. Liquor service in coach class on domestic flights was not started until about 1961–62. It was originally complimentary as W.A. Patterson did not want United's flight attendants to become purveyors on board the aircraft.

Delta, based in the heart of the nondrinking Bible belt, delayed liquor service even longer. It was 1957 before it first started serving any liquor at all. Then, at first, it was only on its New York to Houston nonstop flights. Later, it expanded this service to its deluxe Royal Crown DC-7 flights.

The liquor industry was quick to support liquor service on passenger flights as it recognized the marketing value of having its products served to this population group—a group with discretionary funds for liquor purchases in other environments. Marketing staffs in the liquor industry developed what are today such commonplace drinks as the Bloody Mary, the Screwdriver, or Irish Coffee which, along with Champagne, gave the airlines opportunities to extend liquor service to other times of day, such as on morning breakfast flights, in addition to dinner flights.

Now, liquor service is regularly available on most flights for all classes of passengers. On domestic flights in the United States, alcoholic beverage service is complimentary in first and business class, but coach-class passengers are usually charged a fee for alcoholic beverages of all types. However, on international flights, alcoholic beverage service is usually complimentary for all classes of service.

What was once a simple liquor service has now evolved into a sophisticated service offering a variety of beers and wines to passengers as well as more traditional cocktails. The liquor industry is constantly working to improve both the product lines to reflect changing customer tastes and the packaging of their products to better meet the transport, storage, and service handling needs of inflight foodservices.

The importance of wine service today is noteworthy as a reflection of the changing alcohol consumption patterns found in the United States. The trend toward increased consumption of wine and beer, not only as aperitifs or after-dinner drinks but as an accompaniment to meals, has caused many airlines to offer an array of fine wines and a selection of beers as part of their first-class and business service as well as a selection of modest wines to their coach-class passengers. Indeed the wine demand is so high on many flights that some airlines have indicated difficulty stocking sufficient wine on board the aircraft to meet demand.

In spite of the industry's efforts to meet passengers' wants, inflight consumption of alcoholic beverages of all types in coach class has dropped an average of 10 to 15 percent over the past several years. Consumption patterns in first class, though, have remained steady. While coach-class passengers are still drinking during flights, they are just not drinking alcoholic beverages. Instead, they are consuming fruit drinks, sparkling waters, and gourmet coffees. There is also some demand for nonalcoholic beers, reflective of the growth of overall consumer demand for these products since they were introduced in the late 1980s. Some of the reasons for this change in beverage consumption seem to be (1) the high cost of cocktails, beer, and wine in coach class; (2) passengers' increasing concern with their health; (3) increased family travel; and (4) increasingly restricted time schedules and expense accounts for business travelers. While the airlines are very interested in modifying their beverage services to meet the changing passenger demands, to do so is a challenge because of the very limited on-board space for stocking a wide variety of beverages.

Psychological Impact

In addition to the physiological value of food and beverage services in helping to relieve the tensions and fears of passengers (as well as their hunger), these service are also of psychological value. Food and beverage services are a diversion for the passengers, helping to keep them from becoming bored, particularly for extended flight times. Not only do eating and drinking give the passengers something to do to pass the time during the flight, but these activities help take the passengers' minds off the fact that they are in an airplane, again helping them relax and feel more comfortable. Activities and resources such as movies, magazines, playing cards, or the new computer game systems are on board for the same purpose, but only foods and beverages have universal appeal to all passen-

FIGURE 3.1 Passengers on an early Boeing 747 relax in the first-class lounge during the flight. (Photo courtesy of Philip J. Parrott)

gers. Figure 3.1 shows first-class passengers relaxing in the lounge on one of the early wide-body aircraft developed in the 1970s.

PASSENGERS' NEED FOR FOOD

Passenger hunger may be a motivating factor prompting airlines to provide food and beverage services on their flights. Sometimes, there is a real need for passenger food and beverage services because of the length of the flight time and distance. Generally, most airlines now consider the flight segment length to be a critical factor—along with the time of day the flight is scheduled—when making decisions about the type of food and beverage service to be offered on the flight. Other factors, such as the time it takes passengers to reach the airport from their home or office or to find transportation from the airport on arrival at their destination are also considered in the airlines' service schedule decisions. Changing life styles, job time demands, home-to-work commuter patterns, and traffic congestion are drastically changing the way many people travel, their outlook on airline travel, and their potential need for on-board food and beverage services.

If the flight segment length is quite long, encompassing one or more meal periods for the passengers, then it becomes quite important for an airline to offer foods and beverages to their passengers since the passengers have no other means of satisfying their thirst and hunger needs for these extended periods. Each flight segment is considered separately. Thus, someone flying from Los Angeles to Boston on a flight that stops in Chicago flies *two* segments for this trip (even though they may not change planes in Chicago), and airlines consider *each* segment separately when evaluating the need for food and beverage services. Although the total flight time may be six to seven hours (or more depending on the layover time in Chicago), each segment is only two to four hours in length and may or may not overlap a meal period. Passengers may sometimes find that it is a long time between meals, if food service is not provided on either of the segments or only very early on the first segment or very late on the second.

Generally, the longer the flight segment length, the greater the need for food and beverage services and the more extensive such services become, even in economy (coach) class. The very long flight segment length is the reason that transoceanic flights have much more extensive food and beverage services than do flight segments within the continental United States. Not only are many people more fearful of extended flights over the ocean, the need for entertainment to alleviate boredom increases significantly as the length of the flight increases.

ALTERNATIVE MEANS OF MEETING PASSENGERS' FOOD AND BEVERAGE NEEDS

One means of meeting the hunger needs of passengers would be for passengers to bring their own food onto the aircraft when they come aboard, just as many bus and train passengers do in many parts of the world. While bringing their own food and snacks has not been customary for airline passengers in the United States and many other parts of the world, in some less developed countries, such as China, it is an accepted practice for passengers to bring the food that they want to eat along with them onto the plane.

The primary reasons for discouraging brown-bagging on board aircraft are (1) food safety, (2) flight safety, and (3) liability. Most passengers are not aware of food safety issues, such as the time and temperature parameters for potentially hazardous foods. Some passengers may not be aware of the actual length of flights when a number of time zones are involved. Time and/or temperature abuse of most foods can cause illness. Food safety is why inflight meals are specially prepared, heated, and/or refrigerated on board the aircraft during the flight.

Flights have had to be diverted for emergency landings when a passenger became critically ill from a brown-bag lunch or an improperly prepared meal eaten before boarding. Passengers who become ill during a flight or shortly after one may not want to admit that their home-prepared food may have been the cause. Rather, they may prefer to complain to the airline in an effort to receive some compensation from a firm perceived to have deep pockets and an interest in the market value of a customer. Airlines and inflight caterers go through many extra steps to ensure the safety of food served during the flight to avoid incidents of food-borne illness.

There have been instances where local restaurants, also not aware of the additional safety measures needed for inflight meals, have attempted to sell box lunches to boarding passengers only to be stopped by FDA inspectors. If these restaurants were to pursue selling meals to airline passengers, they would have to meet the same stringent construction and food safety requirements imposed on flight kitchens and airline operations in order to gain the needed FDA regulatory approval to cater flights.

Aircraft safety, as well as the safety of food products is also a concern when passengers bring their own foods on board. There have been airline disasters in third-world countries when passengers have attempted to prepare their own food while on board an aircraft. For example, passengers have attempted to light portable butane and gasoline ovens in the lavatories on board aircraft. In several cases the passengers were attempting to cook meals of religious significance. Such instances have caused inflight emergencies and even caused aircraft to crash as the ovens flared from reduced air pressure at flight altitudes, burning the passenger attempting to light the stove and catching the lavatory area on fire. In these environments, flight attendants have to be particularly alert to prevent an inflight emergency.

Currently, there is experimentation in the United States with foodservices where the passengers pick out the cold food items that they want during the flight from a complimentary food cart set up in the boarding area or purchase the foods that they want for the flight from a concession service set up in the boarding area. This practice is quite common in Europe, though in the United States it seems to be most applicable to breakfast flights and short flights which do not overlap meal periods (snack-only flights). Some airlines, such as those flying many short commuter flights, are finding this approach to be quite practical for them and very acceptable to their passengers. Such a service enables any passenger who wants food on the flight (perhaps even in addition to food that might be served on the flight) to have that food available.

If this type of service were to replace foodservice on flights for all types of meal periods and flight segments, it would mean that the flight attendants would have fewer tasks to do and may have time to give more personalized attention to the passengers. It would also mean a lighter equipment load for food and beverage service equipment and supplies. However, it would also mean that passengers who did not pick up food, but later on the flight decided that they wanted something to eat, would not have anything available to them until they reached their destination.

Northwest Airlines has successfully instituted a modification of this approach, an Á-La-Carte program which offers its passengers an opportunity to choose what they want and how much they want to eat on the flight from bulk-packed baskets circulated by the flight attendants. Although the flight attendants have to work a bit harder serving the meals since passengers pick and choose the items they want (as opposed to just serving a generic tray to everyone on board), passenger feedback has indicated a high degree of satisfaction with this program and with the foods they are served.

A variation to this concept that has been discussed, especially by some charter airlines offering very low fares to passengers, would have passengers order, and pay for, box lunches ahead of time when they make their flight arrangements or would have such lunches available for sale during the flight, much like alcoholic beverages. This was the practice of Peoples Express Airlines in the early and mid 1980s. Early in the 1950s Continental Airlines sold meals inflight and Eastern Airlines had snacks available for purchase on its "moonlight" flights. In the example where meal arrangements were made during the reservations process, the airline would board and distribute the meals only to those passengers who had pre-ordered their meals—a concept borrowed from military aircraft flights and reminiscent of early foodservice practices in commercial passenger service. This approach to passenger foodservices was fraught with logistical problems and has not met with any long-term success by an airline. Some of the problems encountered by airlines trying these approaches have been (1) determining how many snacks to provision for potential sale; (2) passengers complaining that they were not told they would not receive a complimentary meal; and (3) control of snack sale revenue.

FOOD AS A MARKETING AND COMPETITIVE INSTRUMENT

Food and beverage services are used as important marketing tools by many airlines. It was competitive pressure to recruit passengers that prompted airlines to offer food and beverages to their passengers initially. Although economic factors are much more important considerations today than they were initially in the 1930s and in the years after World War II when airline routes and fares were regulated by the government, competition is still a strong motivating factor impacting the configuration of services offered to the different classes of airline passengers. Figure 3.2 presents an example of TWA's use of foodservice as a marketing tool in the 1950s, underscoring that the airlines' usage of food and beverage services as a marketing tool

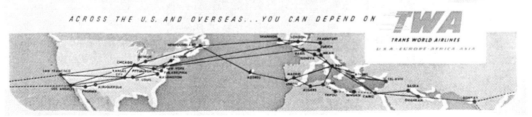

FIGURE 3.2 Example of an advertisement used in the 1950s which uses inflight dining to promote the airline's flight service. (Photo courtesy of Philip J. Parrott)

has been a long-term practice. The use of foodservice as a marketing tool was further enhanced through the services provided on board the aircraft in the 1960s. Even though the 1950s era of fine dining had passed, the airlines implemented the concept of cart service, as shown in Figure 3.3, to enhance the level of on-board service provided.

Public Perception of Inflight Foodservices

Public perception of the quality of inflight foodservice has often been less than desirable. Even books of advice for travelers sometimes refer to airline food as being high in fat, full of sugar and salt, chemically processed, bland, and lacking in wholesomeness. Unfortunately, the press often publicizes comments of this type about airline food rather than actually investigating the true food quality and reporting the constant research and development that both airlines and inflight caterers conduct to make the foods served to passengers the best possible, considering the logistical restrictions involved.

FIGURE 3.3 Cart service added to the use of meal service as a means of marketing the airline in the 1960s. (Photo courtesy of Delta Air Lines)

The Role of IFSA in Managing Public Perceptions

The Inflight Food Service Association plays an important role in regard to the public's image of inflight foodservices. One of IFSA's functions, as a professional association representing the interests of the inflight foodservice industry, is to monitor the news that is published or broadcasted regarding inflight foodservices (especially that which is detrimental to the industry). At one time IFSA employed a clipping service to try to keep up with all articles and comments written about airline foodservice. However, after three years, they found they could not deter either the comments made on talk shows or the deluge of articles and comments written by people with little or no knowledge of the industry. Now IFSA's emphasis is on public education. By carefully tracking the significant news—and public perceptions—about inflight foodservices, IFSA is able to respond to detrimental statements either by submitting a rebuttal statement to a printed article or by requesting an opportunity for someone in the industry to make an appearance to discuss the issues raised, if the news story or statements were on television or radio news broadcasts.

IFSA also has a role in public relations which may help the airlines improve the perception of their foodservices. Since IFSA represents all facets of the inflight foodservice industry, the organization is in a position to prepare press releases or articles that, if published or broadcasted, will make the public more aware of the work that the airlines and their caterers are doing to improve foodservice quality and make their foodservices as reflective of current nutritional and dietary interests as possible. Because IFSA represents the industry as a whole, and not just one airline or one caterer or even just airlines or just caterers, it is able to attract the attention of national media representatives better than a single entity might be able to do—thus helping the message of the industry to reach the public.

Current Emphasis in Airline Marketing

The current emphasis in inflight foodservice is on making first-class and business-class services the very best possible that meets the strategic objectives of the individual airline, as well as making the public aware of the high quality of these services. Airlines that offer different classes of passenger service are most interested in filling their first-class and business-class seats because these seats provide significantly more revenue per mile than economy- (or coach) class seats. It is an even more important consideration that many of the first-class and business-class passengers are frequent travelers who may make many flights on an airline in the future if they are satisfied with the service they receive. Thus, most of the marketing efforts of the airlines that involve foodservice are directed toward passengers who would potentially purchase first-class or business-class tickets or who would at least be frequent travelers in coach class.

That emphasis has changed little over time, as the focus of the advertisement portrayed in Figure 3.2 on TWA's male passengers would indicate. Then, as now, the majority of the passengers flying on business, the ones most likely to be frequent flyers, were men, although there are increasing numbers of women who are becoming frequent business flyers.

Family groups are also currently receiving increased airline marketing attention. Businesspeople are increasingly accompanied by family members or are joined by them at their business destination for a vacation or a weekend holiday. Drawing on the experiences of McDonald's, the airlines are recognizing the importance of children as an influence on their parents' decisions regarding the selection of an airline. For example, United Airlines now offers McDonald's Happy Meals as an option for children's meals on many of its flights from the Midwest into Orlando, Florida, a major vacation destination for families and a hub airport for United. But this was not the airline's first attempt to recognize the importance of serving the children to capture adult passengers. In the 1950s and 1960s, United offered a special children's menu, pictured in Figure 3.4. Delta air lines also currently offers its young flyers a "Fantastic Flyer FunFeast," a meal in a take-away tote box which includes toy novelties and promotional items.

There is little disagreement among airline personnel that food is one factor that an airline can use to distinguish its services from those of other airlines. Although schedules are the most important criteria for selecting an airline, research shows that foodservice is the fifth or sixth most important airline selection factor that passengers consider. All other things being equal, it is the quality of the food and beverage services that can make a passenger chose an airline or its competitor—a very important factor in the competitive airline environment.

Airlines do not make arbitrary decisions regarding the menu items they are going to serve passengers on their flights. They invest considerable resources to try to determine the types of products that their passengers are going to most prefer. They conduct sophisticated market research into the eating patterns and other flight preferences of their potential frequent and infrequent customers by class of service. Their research also considers the flight patterns of these passengers—are they generally flying short segments, or going cross-country? Any other characteristics about these people or their flying patterns that can be identified are taken into consideration in the airlines' planning for their food and beverage services and the products to be served. The airlines are well aware that they must know the customer if they are to merchandise their foodservice as an attraction for that potential passenger.

USING FOODSERVICE AS A COMPETITIVE TOOL IN THE PAST

Although the style of foodservice provided, particularly to first-class passengers, has been cyclical as the airline industry has developed—going

FIGURE 3.4 Example of children's menu served on board flights by one airline in the 1950s and 1960s. (Photo courtesy of Philip J. Parrot)

from no-frills to superdeluxe and back again from time to time—foodservice has always been an airline marketing tool. However, the era of the 1950s and 1960s was probably the epitome of gourmet service for inflight passengers. As was noted in Chapter 2, during this time several of the airlines formed working relationships with well-known gourmet restaurants which enabled them to pattern some of their meals and service after that found in their partner restaurant. One of the reasons for developing such partnerships and emphasizing on-board gourmet dining was the emergence of nonstop transcontinental flight. In the 1950s, the speed of those flights was slower than that of the transcontinental jets developed in the 1970s and 1980s. As a result, there was a need for passenger entertainment on the long flights and ample time to provide elegant service of multicourse meals—to only the first-class passengers, of course.

Examples of some of the relationships established at this time include American Airlines' association with New York's 21 Club and Chicago's Black Hawk Restaurant, TWA's association with Trader Vic's and later on with New York City's Stage Deli and Pan American's association with Maxim's of Paris (illustrated in Figure 2.16). Pan American's association with Maxim's was a true working relationship as Maxim's operated a frozen food kitchen in Paris which manufactured food products exclusively for Pan American Airways and distributed them to Pan Am's commissaries throughout Europe and the Middle East.

United differed from the other airlines in that it did not initially form any alliances with well-known restaurants. Because it had its own kitchens staffed with European-trained chefs, it developed its own fine dining events. Not only did United develop gourmet menus for use on its flights, but it periodically scheduled banquets in important cities and invited prominent businessmen (who controlled many airline ticket purchases) to these banquets as its guests. These banquets gave it good promotional exposure in the marketplace and did much to enhance the public's perception of United as an airline with high-quality foodservice. Figure 3.5 illustrates a menu from one of these dinners, and Figure 3.6 pictures the staff responsible for the dinner's food preparation and service. In addition to all these activities, United later developed a major program with Trader Vic's that involved menu items, beverages and support equipment several year's after TWA's involvement with this restaurant.

QUALITY FOOD AND BEVERAGE SERVICE AS A MARKETING TOOL TODAY

First-class Service

Some airlines invest considerable monies to develop very elegant food and beverage services for their first-class and business-class passengers. Highly

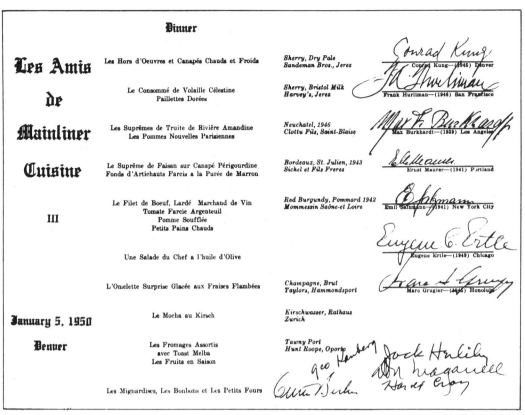

An example of the menu is the following from the dinner of January 5, 1950, in Denver, Colorado. Of special interest are the signatures of the chefs, and, at the bottom, of Don Magarrell and Jack Kansberg, both deceased. The chefs' names on the menu are opposite that part of the dinner for which each was responsible.

FIGURE 3.5 An example of United Airline's Amis de Mainliner Cuisine dinner menus. These dinners were served by United in the 1950s to help promote businessmen's use of the airline. (Photo courtesy of Philip J. Parrot)

qualified chefs are employed to develop menus and recipes to be used for these services. Indeed, many of the chefs involved with airline foodservices today compete quite successfully in food preparation competitions, and many of the menus or other service innovations of the airlines have won awards for excellence.

Items such as fresh grilled fish, stuffed quesadillas, salmon pastry with scallops or lobster fajitas can be found on first-class inflight menus today. Foods such as these reflect the public's interest in modern treatment of nutritious foods such as fresh grilled fish, which is low in fat and cholesterol. This is a common concern of many businesspeople, who are some of the most common first-class passengers. The inclusion of quesadillas and fajitas also reflect another predominant trend in foodservice today, that of the service of ethnic foods, particularly foods found in the Southwest. Even though food items such as these reflect current foodservice trends, the

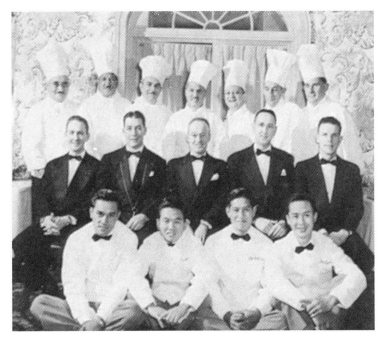

FIGURE 3.6 The foodservice staff responsible for one of United Airline's Amis de Mainliner Cuisine Dinners. (Photo courtesy of Philip J. Parrott)

airlines still research their acceptability by collecting input from passengers, carefully reviewing crew reports about the passengers' acceptance of the meal service, and studying any specific comments made by passengers that were noted in the crew reports.

Figure 3.7 illustrates a first-class menu that might be served for a lunch or dinner meal on a domestic flight. One of the objectives of first-class meal service is to make it truly first class, or comparable to both the food and the service that would be characteristic of fine dining in any restaurant environment—whether on the ground or 30,000 feet in the air.

Airlines are quite interested in using their food and beverage services to attract domestic first-class passengers to their flights, and there is a high demand for this level of service, especially from business travelers. Indeed, airlines that have traditionally attracted many business travelers, such as Delta, American, or United, are expanding the number of first-class seats available on their flights in response to this demand increase. As they expand the availability of this service on their flights, these airlines are also carefully evaluating their first-class menus and meal service procedures in an effort to offer very-high-quality meal service to these passengers.

The emphasis on fine dining for first-class passengers has been particularly characteristic of international flights. When first class is offered on international flights, the menu is generally of a high quality, and the service procedures used are based on those found in a fine dining establishment.

SALAD

Mixed Vegetable Salad
(Contains torn Boston leaf lettuce, torn red oak lettuce, blanched
cauliflower florets, blanched broccoli florets, black olives,
julienne red peppers, and shredded mozzarella cheese)
with
Honey Peppercorn Dressing

ENTREE

Seared Tenderloin with Ruby Lentil Sauce
Egg Linquini
California Stir-Fry Medley

or

Fajita Chicken
Tortilla
Black Bean and Corn Salsa
Southwestern tomato Salsa

BREAD

Choice of Dark, Soft, or Crisp Roll
Butter

DESSERT

Hazelnut Raspberry Cake

FIGURE 3.7 Example of first-class service menu that could be served for lunch or dinner (domestic flight). (Courtesy of United Airlines)

These flights are long, and there is ample time for leisurely meal service. Figure 3.8 illustrates a first-class menu that might be served on an international flight.

However, there is now a trend toward the demise of first-class service on international flights in response to a declining passenger demand for this class of service. Many companies are no longer willing to pay the high fares associated with first-class service. Further, international tourism increases mean more tourists are passengers on international flights, and most first-class fares exceed most tourist budgets. As a result, both domestic and international airlines flying international routes are changing their service patterns.

A number of both domestic and international airlines are developing two-class service for their international routes. These classes are business and economy (coach). The new business class retains the space and seat comfort of first-class service, but replaces the elegant first-class meal service with a business-class level of food and beverage services. Passengers are willing to pay the higher fares of business-class service in order to have the seating comfort for the extended flight times. However, they are indicating that the high cost of fine dining on board an aircraft is not warranted, and the casual service of more common foods, characteristic of business-class service, is what they prefer—perhaps a reflection of the overall trend toward casual dining currently found in the United States and many other parts of the world. Two recent examples of the new business-class service are Continental's BusinessFirst and Upper Class created by Virgin Atlantic Airlines.

Business-class Service

Business class is becoming quite popular with many frequent business travelers today. While some airlines still refer to business class as just that, other airlines have created new names for this class of service as a part of their marketing effort. For example, United Airlines refers to its business class as *Connoisseur Class* and Northwest Airlines uses the term *Executive Class*. Continental Airlines stresses that its Lite Fare Program offers no first-class section, but does offer BusinessFirst service, similar to that class of service on international flights.

Passengers flying this class of service receive food and beverage service that is quite similar to that offered in first class. While high-quality, sometimes gourmet, products are served which are designed to especially meet the business-class passengers' dining interests, there are fewer menu options here, and the service is generally tray service as opposed to the multiple options and cart service which may be offered in first class. In many instances, business-class meals incorporate the same foods as are served for first-class meals, but the foods are generally served in coach-

SELECTION OF CANAPES

APPETIZERS
Scottish smoked salmon
Terrine of potted game
Hot mushroom croustade

SOUP
Hot leek and potato

MAIN COURSES
Roast fillet of beef garnished with stuffed tomatoes
and bearnaise sauce
or
Steamed seabass oriental
or
Guinea fowl with orange, grapefruit and lime
or
Vegetarian pasta roulade

VEGETABLES
Steamed broccoli florets, glazed root vegetables, grilled vegetables,
basmati rice and potatoes with cream and cheese

SALAD
Mixed seasonal salad with
avocado and lime or Caesar dressings

DESSERTS
Golden steamed pudding with English custard
or
Honey, ginger, and mango ice cream
or
CHEESE
A selection of British and Continental cheeses
with celery, nuts and grapes
OR
FRUIT
Basket of seasonal fruit

BEVERAGES
Coffee, decaffeinated coffee or tea
Served with chocolates

Adapted from British Airways flight from London to the Far East.

FIGURE 3.8 Example of first-class dinner service menu for an international flight. (Courtesy of British Airways)

class format. There may also be some substitutions for very expensive first-class items, as well. For example, appetizers containing lobster or caviar might be replaced with less expensive items, such as shrimp or paté for business-class service.

As is the case with first-class meal service, there is much more emphasis placed on the food and beverage services for business-class passengers on international flights than is the case for domestic flights. Also, there is only a limited amount of business-class seating available on domestic flights, compared to a much wider usage of business-class seating on international flights—another reason for the emphasis on business-class service on an international perspective rather than a domestic one.

Figure 3.9 illustrates a menu that might be used for a business-class dinner on an international flight. Note that here there are choices offered for the entree as well as very upscale food items offered throughout the menu. Indeed, a comparison of this menu with the first-class domestic flight menu illustrated in Figure 3.7 provides a good example of the differences in the foodservice between international and domestic flights. Although Figure 3.9 illustrates a business-class menu, the foods offered on this menu might be considered to be of a more gourmet quality than those illustrated in Figure 3.7.

A comparison of Figures 3.8 and 3.9 shows that there is little differences between the food products offered on the first-class and the business-class menus on international flights. Indeed, the real difference between these two classes is the service provided during the meal period and the way that the food items are served, or presented, to the passengers.

By offering menus such as the ones in Figures 3.7 through 3.9 accompanied by quality beverages, the airlines expect to differentiate their flights from those of their competitors. Of course, the way in which the flight attendants serve the foods and beverages offered on the menu is just as important as the foods and beverages themselves. A high-quality product, poorly served, will not entice a passenger to return. Figure 3.10 illustrates some of the platters, cold plates, and chocolates that are used today by airlines providing first- and business-class service to ensure high-quality foodservice for both domestic and international passengers.

All Classes (or Airlines with Classless Seating)

Some airlines use food and beverage services to merchandise their flights in ways other than through offering fine dining enjoyment to first-class and business-class passengers. Alaska Airlines, for example, promotes the quality of its food for *all* classes as a part of its promotional efforts. Until 1993, Alaska offered full meal service of high-quality food products on all flights, whether or not the flight was scheduled for a traditional meal period. Reacting to economic pressures and the changing eating patterns

APPETIZER

A tasteful sampling of Sevruga Malossol Caviar,
chilled Pate de Foie Gras and Gravlax
Accompanied by your preferred Cocktail or Beverage

SALAD

A contemporary composition of assorted seasonal Greens,
colored with sliced fresh Vegetables
Select from Light Peppercorn Ranch Dressing or Balsamic Vinaigrette

ROLLS

An assortment of Rolls will be served with Sweet Butter

ENTREE

Choice of:

GEGRILLTES HAHNCHEN
Our German feature of grilled marinated Chicken Breast
enhanced by a Sauce flavored with Coriander and Cumin
and garnished with Shiitake Mushrooms.
Accompaniments include Black Pepper Noodles and Ratatouille
flavored with fresh Parsley

OR

FILET MIGNON
Features a grilled Tenderloin of choice Beef enhanced by
a Sauce flavored with Green Peppercorns and Pears.
Served with Sugar Snap Peas, herbed Carrots and Yellow Corn Pancakes

CHEESE SAMPLER

Features French Brie and New York Cheddar Cheese
presented with a fresh Fruit garnish
and a glass of Cockburn's Porto

DESSERT

Treat yourself to today's Dessert selection
Plus
GOURMET CHOCOLATES

THE FINISHING TOUCH

100% Columbian Coffee is recommended

FIGURE 3.9 Sample of a business-class menu for an international flight. (Courtesy of United Airlines)

FIGURE 3.10 Examples of different foods and food displays that might be used today to provide high-quality food service to passengers flying first- and business-class. (Photo courtesy of Delta Air Lines)

of their passengers, in 1993 Alaska Airlines tightened its meal service time windows and no longer serves full meals on nonmealtime flights. However, it still promotes high-quality foodservice and a range of meal options for all passengers as part of its marketing efforts.

In a markedly different approach, Southwest Airlines promotes the fact that it has no foodservices—only beverages and peanuts on its flights—as a means of promoting sales. Southwest offers *classless* service, and most Southwest flights are fairly short segments where the service of food may not be either feasible or necessary. Because its key promotional strategy is its low fare structure, Southwest promotes the absence of foodservice as an important factor in the airline's being able to keep its ticket prices low.

Although each Southwest flight segment is generally short, passengers' total flight time could be long (and thus passengers could be in need of food) if their flights consisted of several short segments put together to make a long flight (such as from Burbank, California to Chicago via two or three intermediate stops where the passenger may or may not change planes and may or may not have an opportunity to purchase food or beverages at a stopover during the flight).

Most airlines provide a basic meal service, often with a choice of entrees, to their coach-class passengers. If they are hot meals, they generally consist of either a frozen or freshly prepared and chilled entree which has been tempered and rethermalized, accompanied by a salad, roll and butter, and a dessert. Figure 3.11 illustrates a typical coach-class menu that might be served for lunch or dinner on a domestic flight.

This menu would be served to coach passengers on the same day that the menu in Figure 3.7 would be served to first-class passengers. While there is a choice of entrees indicated on the first-class menu, there is no entree choice for the coach-class passengers indicated on the menu shown

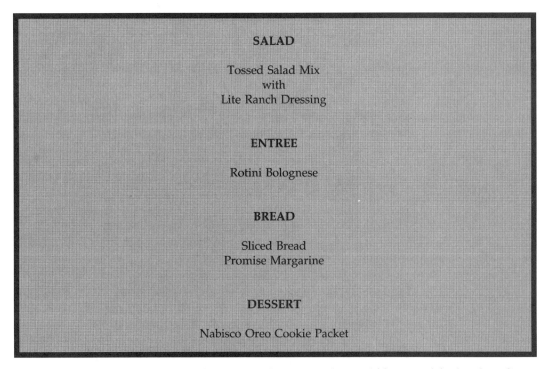

SALAD

Tossed Salad Mix
with
Lite Ranch Dressing

ENTREE

Rotini Bolognese

BREAD

Sliced Bread
Promise Margarine

DESSERT

Nabisco Oreo Cookie Packet

FIGURE 3.11 Example of a coach-class (main cabin) menu that could be served for lunch or dinner on a domestic flight. (Courtesy of United Airlines)

in Figure 3.11 even though some airlines may sometimes offer a choice of entrees in the main cabin, particularly for dinner service. Differences in the types of products used in the salad (though both are vegetable salads) and the hand preparation versus the sinpler production and preparation method of the salad components can also be noted. Another interesting difference here is the service of a low-cholesterol-brand margarine (also lower in cost than butter), on the coach-class tray and the service of butter, a high-cholesterol spread (and a high-cost quality image item), on the first-class tray, considering the concern of many first-class travelers with their blood cholesterol levels.

TAILORING INFLIGHT FOODSERVICES IN RESPONSE TO PASSENGER PREFERENCES

Most airlines that provide foodservices on their flights are responding to changing eating patterns among the public in the development of their menus for all classes of service. Some of the trends that airline foodservice personnel have noted and are responding to include:

1. An increased popularity of breakfast meals. However, the popularity increase is for cold breakfast menus, which are now offered in lieu of or as alternatives to hot, egg-based breakfasts.
2. The use of cold meals and the substitution of snacks for full hot meals, particularly on shorter flights and flights during nonmeal periods.
3. Increased popularity of pasta and other nonmeat dishes leading to the replacement of many beef-based hot meals with pasta-based meals such as meatless lasagna.
4. Increased preferences for lighter foods, such as entree salads, pasta salads, vegetable-based sauces, and grain-based dishes. One small airline has been very successful offering healthy snacks as an alternative for their passengers; another offers pretzels (usually quite low in fat or even fat free) as an alternative to peanuts for snacks with beverages.
5. Increased preference for regional and seasonal foods. Airlines are developing menus with more regional dishes and making more use of seasonal foods, reflective of currently popular restaurant menus.
6. Decline in hard liquor and caffeinated coffee consumption and increased consumption of beverages such as sparkling and still bottled waters, juices, and decaffeinated coffee.

The point here is that each airline uses its food and beverage services as a marketing tool to help it compete in the highly competitive airline transportation market. To use their foodservices effectively, the airlines incorporate their foodservices strategies into their total marketing plan.

The food and beverage services offered must be carefully planned and developed if they are to be effectively merchandised to today's discriminating airline passenger.

Passengers have certain food and beverage expectations for different airlines, different types of flights, and different classes of services. These expectations are the result of a combination of the passengers' previous flight experiences and the promotional efforts of the airline. Satisfied passengers are those whose expectations (including their food and beverage service expectations) are met or exceeded. By matching the services offered with the service expectations of the people an airline wants to attract as passengers, airlines have excellent potential to use their food and beverage services as a most effective merchandising tool.

Just how the food and beverage services are used varies from one airline to another, and the airlines' perspective regarding food and beverages can be quite diverse. The inflight caterer servicing airlines' food and beverage needs must be aware of each different airline's point of view regarding the expected role of its food and beverage services if they are to design and ultimately provide the type of foods and services for an airline that will enable it to meet its marketing and sales objective.

SUMMARY

Food and beverage services have become an expected part of airline services today. Although inflight foodservice was originally initiated as a means of airlines increasing their competitive position for passengers, the service of food and beverages on flights serves physiological and psychological purposes for the passengers as well. Liquor service, not originally a part of inflight food and beverage services, is now a significant service component which both serves the airlines' marketing objectives and helps meet passenger needs.

Inflight foodservices are still an important part of an airline's marketing plan. By incorporating foodservice planning into their overall strategic plans, airlines are able to distinguish between the several classes of service offered on their flights and to distinguish their flight services from those of their competitors. The use of inflight foodservice for this purpose is particularly notable on international flights covering long, overwater distances.

Alternative means of providing food and beverages for passengers are being considered in an effort to make inflight food and beverage service more efficient while still satisfying passengers. The most feasible alternative seems to be passenger self-service of cold foods for breakfasts on short flights as the passengers are waiting to board the flight. It is important for the airlines to remain aware of eating patterns and trends in the areas they serve if they are to be innovative in their inflight foodservices and structure their services in a way that best markets them to their potential passengers.

REFERENCES

Coomes, Steve. (Winter, 1994). "One Less for the Road." *IFSA Quarterly*, 3(1): 1, 4–5.

Parrott, Philip J. (1986). *The History of Inflight Food Service*. Miami Springs, FL: International Publishing Company of America, 86 pps.

KEY TERMS

Business Class	Open Skies Policy
Deregulation	Stewardess
Coach (Economy) Class	Tempered
First Class	Transoceanic Flights
Flight Attendant	Tray Service
Flight Segment	Turbulence
Main Cabin	Wide Body

DISCUSSION QUESTIONS

1. Discuss the physiological impact of food and inflight foodservices on airline passengers. Why are airlines interested in the calming effect of food on their passengers?

2. Discuss the impact of liquor service on airline passengers. Why was liquor service not originally a part of inflight foodservices—but added only after World War II?

3. Discuss the psychological impact of food and beverage service on airline passengers.

4. Do passengers have a need for foodservice to satisfy their hunger? How does that need impact on airlines' decisions regarding the type of services to offer on a particular flight? Or does it impact at all?

5. Do all airlines offer food and beverage services on all flights? Are there other options besides the foodservices provided by the airlines for passengers who become hungry while traveling?

6. Describe the public perception of inflight foodservices. Can (or does) IFSA play a role in molding public opinion regarding inflight foodservices?

7. Discuss the current emphasis of most airlines in regard to their use of inflight food and beverage services as a marketing tool.

8. Describe how airlines have used food and beverage services to market their flights in the past.

9. What kinds of foods are served to first-class passengers on domestic flights? On international flights?

10. What kinds of foods are served to business-class passengers on domestic flights? On international flights? How do these foods and their service differ from that found in first class?

11. Discuss other approaches that some airlines are taking to use their food and beverage services (or lack thereof) as a means of marketing their flights.

12. What kinds of foods are served to coach-class passengers? What is their range of menu selection? How does coach-class service compare with first class? With business class?

13. Identify changes in public eating patterns which are being reflected in changes in the on-board food and beverage services offered by the airlines. Discuss how those changes are reflected in the airlines' menus or services.

14. Discuss why it is important for an airline to match its passengers' food and beverage service expectations with what is actually served and the quality of the service provided.

4

Flight Kitchen Functions

LEARNING OBJECTIVES

1. Discuss the activities and responsibilities of the inflight caterer in regard to at least six functional areas.
2. Explain the relationship between the inflight caterer's personnel and U.S. customs agents on the arrival of international flights.
3. Discuss the requirements governing the handling of trash and garbage that arrives on international flights and the reasons for these requirements.
4. Explain why managing the flow of equipment in the caterer's kitchen is a complex, critical responsibility.
5. Describe the different approaches to meal preparation characteristic of first class/business class and coach class in the United States.
6. Explain why the inflight caterer may be involved with bonded storage facilities.
7. Identify possible resources required to appropriately store products belonging to the airlines on the caterer's premises.
8. Discuss the airlines' and the inflight caterers' responsibility and liability for food wholesomeness and safety.
9. Explain why staff who are assigned driver and transport responsibilities are some of the most qualified and experienced personnel employed by the caterer.
10. Discuss at least three differences between domestic and international flights in terms of the functional responsibilities of the caterer.

In order to support the needs of the airlines' inflight food and beverage service, the inflight caterer is responsible for accomplishing a number of functions, including (1) off-loading inbound flights; (2) managing the flow of equipment used to board meals and beverages; (3) purchasing pre-prepared food products; (4) preparing food products; (5) setting passenger trays; (6) preparing, assembling, and bulk packing supplies and utensils to be boarded on aircraft; (7) storing airline-owned products; (8) transporting products and equipment to the aircraft; and (9) boarding the products and equipment. Should the inflight caterer fail to properly manage and accomplish any one of these functions, difficulties will be encountered, and it is quite likely that aircraft may be delayed or the quality of the products and service will fall below a level acceptable to the airlines.

OFF-LOADING INBOUND FLIGHTS

The catering function begins with inbound flights. The caterer must meet the flight and off-load the carts, carriers, and containers that hold the service equipment, trash, garbage, and any excess food and beverage products. Generally, the caterer's staff are the first people on board an aircraft after it lands. Therefore, it is necessary for the caterer to carefully track the arrival of inbound flights and have the appropriate truck for the type of aircraft that is landing and a crew in place at the gate area when the plane arrives.

As soon as the aircraft's engines are shut down, the truck is able to move into place, usually at the plane's rear service door, so that the catering crew can enter the plane and begin the off-loading, often even before all of the passengers have exited the aircraft. If the flight is a terminating flight, most airlines prefer that the caterer clears all of the equipment off the aircraft as soon as possible so that the cleaning crews can come on board to clean the aircraft at their scheduled time. While airlines' policies differ in this regard, some would like the aircraft cleaned within 30 minutes of its arrival, if possible.

When the caterer is servicing international flights, customs inspections become a consideration, and it is important for the caterer to maintain a good working relationship with the customs agents at the airport. As will be noted later in this chapter, the caterer's personnel must work closely with U.S. customs officials as well as officials from the U.S. Department of Agriculture (USDA) when off-loading any international flight.

One caution is quite important here. The off-loading crew must *always* knock on the aircraft service door before opening it from the outside to be sure that the flight attendants have detached or disarmed the emergency evacuation slide that is attached to the door sill. If the slide is not disarmed, it will deploy, causing serious injury and even death to the off-loading crew opening the door. Beyond the danger and harm such a deployment could cause, the slide must be repacked by airline maintenance personnel before the aircraft can leave on a flight. Repacking the slide is a major job which would likely cause a lengthy delay for the flight with resulting penalty fees assessed to the caterer.

Once the equipment, trash, and other materials are off-loaded from the plane, they are returned to the caterer's facilities. There, the trash and garbage is disposed of, and the dishes, utensils, and so on are separated for washing. The dishes and utensils that are washed for reuse are termed *rotable* equipment, in contrast to *disposable* or single-service items that are sometimes used for serving snack meals. The use of rotable versus disposable equipment for a particular type of meal or type of service is a decision made by each individual airline.

If the caterer is handling an international flight, however, the trash may not be returned to the caterer's kitchen unless the caterer has special equipment for handling international trash, as discussed later in this chapter. Unless the caterer has the required equipment for international trash disposal, trash from international flights must be taken directly from the plane to a site on the airport designed to handle this type of trash. This procedure is required to assure the protection of the U.S. agricultural industry from pests or diseases that might be carried into the country through foods and beverages from another country. Usually trash from an international flight is put into specially colored or marked bags when it is taken off the plane to help insure proper handling and disposal of this trash.

Proper handling and washing of dishes and utensils coming into the caterer's kitchen from the inbound flights is an important step for maintaining a high level of food sanitation. Because of the high volume of dishes handled by most caterers, dishwashing operations are automated as much as possible, and continue throughout much of the day.

MANAGING THE FLOW OF EQUIPMENT

Rapid washing of all the dishes, equipment, and serviceware used is important as the caterer must have clean stocks of these items to get the next day's meals (or maybe meals to be served in the next several hours) ready for boarding on the airline's flights. There is only a limited inventory of dishes, serviceware, utensils, and equipment available for any one airline. Typical inventory levels are adequate for only 6 to 36 hours of catering operations; what is available must remain in circulation as much as possible. Indeed, this cleaning, sorting, and staging process is the *lifeblood* of a flight kitchen.

Once washed and sanitized, clean dishes, serviceware, carts, and other equipment that have come in from the inbound flights are properly positioned in the kitchen for reloading. The eating utensils (flatware) are usually individually packaged, often with a napkin and salt and pepper packets, according to each airline's specifications, and stored for use on the passenger tray setup. As will be discussed in Chapter 11, this packaging can be done manually, but it is generally automated in the larger inflight kitchens where thousands of flatware packets must be prepared daily.

Each airline has its own equipment, dishes, and so forth, and it is the caterer's responsibility to insure that one airline's equipment, dishes, and utensils are kept separated from that of other airlines. It is not acceptable (and prohibited in the service contract) for a caterer to interchange airlines' equipment and use what belongs to one airline on a flight of another airline. Because inbound flights provide the equipment that is required for the meals to be prepared for outbound flights, the start of the catering process is considered to be the arrival of inbound flights.

The flow of inbound equipment (including dishes, trays, utensils, etc.) rarely exactly matches the outbound flow. Either the food and beverage services on the inbound flight are different from those needed for the outbound flight or a full complement of equipment was not boarded by the caterer originally servicing the inbound flight. Caterers are supposed to send a full load of equipment out on a flight even if the passenger count is low. This practice is termed *deadheading* equipment. However, when caterers are short of certain equipment, they will conserve it by boarding less than a full complement.

It is important that backup stocks be provided by the airline and maintained by the caterer. Caterers may still need to periodically prepare a request to the airline for additional stocks of certain items from another caterer's kitchen or directly from a manufacturer. Also, caterers that have accumulated excess stock of some items may need to pack and ship excess equipment to other kitchens serving the particular airline. Although all of the equipment used for the service of inflight meals is the property of the airlines, managing the flow of that equipment by boarding it in proper quantities and maintaining an appropriate stock level is one of the caterer's functions.

Managing the flow of equipment, dishes, glassware, and so on through an inflight caterer's kitchen is not a simple task. Even a moderate-size kitchen serving several different airlines will need a large floor space just for equipment storage. Daily or weekly inventories must be maintained for each separate item for each airline. Thus staff working with clean equipment must be able to count inventory levels and know precisely where to find information to tell them what quantity of each item is required for a particular aircraft in an airline's equipment inventory. To make the most efficient use of the available storage space, the trolleys and other types of carriers should be washed first so they are clean and ready to be immediately repacked with the correct amount of the proper dishes, glassware, serviceware, and utensils.

FOOD PREPARATION (OR UNPACKING MEAL COMPONENTS)

Another responsibility of the caterer is the preparation of food for the meals. Most of the foods served in first class and in business class are produced in the caterer's kitchen, usually under the direction of a qualified chef. These products are generally prepared just as they would be in any type of production kitchen for any type of foodservice. Figure 4.1 shows salad plates prepared for use in first-class meal service.

However, an important difference in the handling of the prepared products and in the production schedule used is that the inflight catering production system is a cook–chill system similar to the type of system now being used in many health care facilities and other large institutional settings. In a cook–chill system, the food items are prepared ahead of the day they are needed for service. In the flight kitchen, foods are generally prepared at least one day ahead of the day they are to be served on the plane. Depending on the handling required, though, a food item (a beef roast, for example) could be cooked one day, portioned onto trays the next day (after being sliced cold that day), and boarded on the plane for service later that day. Figure 4.2 illustrates entree casseroles being plated in the flight kitchen prior to chilling.

As soon as the food items are cooked, they are rapidly chilled to a temperature of 40°F or less. In the flight kitchen, the items are often por-

FIGURE 4.1 Cold salad plates prepared for use in first-class service. (Courtesy of Ogden Aviation Services)

FIGURE 4.2 Inflight caterers prepare many food products, including meal entrees, in their kitchens in very large quantities. Generally, cook–chill systems are used for meal production and distribution.

tioned into individual portions prior to being chilled to expedite both the chilling process and the handling required for preparing the passenger's trays later on. Except while they are being served onto the passengers' plates on the tray line, once chilled, food items are held at refrigerator temperatures at all times until they are heated for service on the plane. In some kitchens, with more sophisticated equipment available, it is possible to hold all items under refrigeration throughout most of the serving period, thus reducing the potential for food contamination during the production process. No matter what equipment or system is used, federal Food and Drug Administration (FDA) regulations require all cold food products to be chilled to 38°F at least four hours before they are to be boarded onto an aircraft.

Coach-class meal production, though, is quite different from that of first or business class in the United States. Many of the meal entrees served in coach class on domestic flights are prepared to airline specifications by commercial manufacturers, and are purchased by the caterer as prepre-pared, frozen, individual entrees. These entrees are often referred to as pop-out meals or pop-outs because they are packaged in plastic formed to the shape of the entree. When the entree is to be plated for use, it is pushed out—or popped out—of the plastic into the casserole or onto the plate from which it is to be served. Thus, preparation of these meals by the caterer entails unpacking, plating in individual casseroles (after popping them out of their plastic packaging), and tempering at refrigerator temperatures prior to being packed into the boarding equipment for transport to the aircraft.

In Europe and other parts of the world, coach-class production is still primarily done in the caterers' kitchens. This would also be true for economy meals on many U.S. carriers' international flights. However, change is underway there, too, as these kitchens look to gain labor economies to reduce operating expenses as well as to maintain better control over food safety. Airlines and flight kitchens outside of the United States are looking more and more at the pop-out meals—their quality, acceptability to the passengers, increased control over food safety, and the labor cost savings possible. The trends everywhere are toward economy in production labor costs and increased concern with food safety.

SPECIAL MEALS

Passengers often want to have special meals when they are flying. They may want these meals for health, medical, or religious reasons. There is an ever-increasing number of requests for such meals. This trend seems to be the result of passengers' increased concern with healthful meals, the changing age demographics of airline passengers, and the ever-present public image of airline food as "unhealthy."

At one time there were many differences among the special meals served by airlines and much passenger confusion regarding the terminology to use to get the type of meal desired. To resolve these issues, airlines from the United States, Europe, and Asia jointly developed special meal guidelines that combined the common traits of each meal. Medical guidelines for these meals were based on the latest information from The Americal Dietetic Association. Meal codes were then agreed upon so that a passenger ordering a particular type of meal on any airline anywhere in the world could be assured of getting the type of meal desired, if the airline offered it.

While it was nearly impossible to standardize all the special meals and meal codes to the agreement and satisfaction of all airlines worldwide, the objective of this joint effort was to identify the most commonly requested meals and at least standardize the terms and descriptions that characterize each meal. The guidelines developed were intended to give airlines general information about foods allowed or not allowed on particular types of special meals. Each airline still has the latitude to individualize the special meals served to fit ethnic, regional, or cultural needs by creating its own special meal menus and recipes while staying within the parameters of the special meal guidelines.

Figure 4.3 lists the special meals that are typically available by prior customer request on most airlines' flights today and the codes that are used to identify those meals. Figure 4.4 is an example of the meal descriptions that were developed to serve as guidelines for each meal. As can be noted, the descriptions indicate other names that the diet might be called, give medical indications for usage (if any), describe the characteristics of the diet, and then list the guidelines for the foods that can be used on the diet and any restrictions in preparation methods that can be used.

When passengers request special meals, with the exception of kosher meals, caterers must prepare these meals individually in their flight kitchens. Because of the highly specialized procedures and production conditions that are involved in the preparation of kosher meals, most of the airlines (other than El Al) use frozen kosher meals that are prepared and marketed to the industry by kosher production kitchens. El Al is the airline of Israel, and it does all of its own food preparation as only kosher food is served on all flights. However, because of the high demand for kosher meals at some international airports, there are some U.S. kitchens at these airports that now have their own kosher section. Since all special meals

	Special Meal Codes
BLML	Bland Meal
DBML	Diabetic Meal
GFML	Gluten Free Meal
HFML	High Fiber Meal
LCML	Low Calorie Meal
LFML	Low Cholesterol, Low Fat Meal
LPML	Low Protein Meal
LSML	Low Sodium, No Salt Added Meal
NLML	Non Lactose Meal
PRML	Low Purine Meal
VLML	Western Vegetarian Meal (lacto-ovo)
VGML	Vegan (Western) Vegetarian Meal (no dairy, no eggs)
AVML	Asiatic (Indian) Vegetarian Meal
RVML	Raw Fruit Vegetable Meal
SFML	Seafood Meal
SPML	Special Meal
KSML	Kosher Meal
ORML	Oriental Meal
HNML	Hindu Meal
MOML	Moslem Meal
CHML	Children's Meal
BBML	Baby Meal

FIGURE 4.3 Special meal codes used throughout the inflight food service industry (Courtesy of the Inflight Food Service Association)

DBML Diabetic Meal

Alternate Names   Sugar Free
Hyperglycemic
Hypoglycemic
No Added Sugar
Carbohydrate Restricted/Low Carbohydrate

Medical Indications   Diabetes Mellitus
Glucose Intolerance

Characteristics
Increased complex carbohydrates
High fiber

Guidelines
Use lean meats; do not fry foods.
Use low fat dairy products.
Use high fiber foods whenever possible—fresh fruits and vegetables and whole grain breads and cereals.
Canned fruits must be water packed or in their own juices. Use unsweetened fruit juices.
Use polyunsaturated fats.
Omit any items with high fructose, sorbitol, mannitol, zylitol, and sugar.
Specialized, commercially produced diabetic products and sugar substitute are acceptable.
Omit cakes, pastries, sweet biscuits, sweetened breakfast cereals, ice cream, and sweet sauces.
Low fat: (30% or less of energy intake).
Protein: approximately 12–20% energy intake.
Calories: approximatley 2,000–2,400 in 24-hour period.

FIGURE 4.4 Description of the special meal code DBML, the code for a diabetic meal. This description is typical of those that have been developed by the inflight foodservice industry for all of the agreed-upon special meal codes. (Courtesy of the Inflight Food Service Association.)

require individualized food product preparation and handling, they are labor-intensive, costly meals for the caterer to prepare. Thus, the increasing demand for these products adds to the caterer's operating costs.

TRAY SET-UP

Another function of the caterer is setting the trays for coach class and business class and, where required, for first class. Tray setting is usually done as an assembly-line process using some type of trayline equipment similar to that used in most health care facilities for assembling their patients' meal trays. Trayline equipment comes in a wide variety of sizes and configurations and is often customized for the particular kitchen's needs. However, the principle is the same for all traylines. The products to be placed on the trays are assembled at different stations on the line. Each station on the trayline is staffed by a person who places the needed items stored at the station on each tray as it passes by. When the tray reaches the end of the line, it should contain all the items required for the meal service. To help prevent errors, a checker is at the end of the line who checks the setting on each tray and corrects any observed errors.

Airline meal service trays are set with all eating utensils, condiments, and cold food items that are necessary for the particular meal for which the trays are being set. Unless high-tech carts are being used, no items are placed on the tray that are to be served hot even though they would stay chilled stored on the trays in the tray carts. The hot entrees are kept separate as they must be heated in ovens, either on board the aircraft or in the caterer's kitchen prior to service. The hot items are added to the passengers' trays during the service process on board the aircraft.

Foods not set on the tray (such as the hot entrees) must also be placed into the proper boarding equipment and stored under refrigeration until they are transported to the aircraft. These items are placed into special carriers as they are plated. When these carriers are filled, they are placed into the refrigerator for storage prior to departure.

PREPARATION OF SUPPLIES

Not only food, but beverages, serving utensils, and any other needed equipment and supplies must also be loaded into the carts, trolleys, or carriers for transport to the aircraft. Generally most of these items are packed into drawers or bins which fit into galley carts for transport. The caterer is responsible for preparing these drawers, which hold the soft drinks, beer, liquors, napkins, stir sticks, and any other products and supplies necessary for beverage service on the aircraft. Wines, champagnes, and liqueurs are usually required for first and business class and may be requried for coach class. Drawers are also prepared for needed serving utensils and other small equipment and supplies. Because the drawer contents are standardized for a particular type of aircraft (for each airline), they are prepared well ahead of time and staged, ready to use when needed.

STORING OTHER AIRLINE-OWNED PRODUCTS

Another function performed by the caterer is the storage and handling of products and supplies purchased directly by the airline, but used for the preparation and service of the meals. Any type of product could fall into this category from disposable packaging supplies for food products to precut steaks to canned soft drinks. Products purchased directly by the airlines could just arrive on the caterer's loading dock at times and in amounts the airline's purchasing department determines is appropriate to meet their catering needs. The amount may or may not accurately reflect the actual product flow at that caterer's kitchen, and the amount delivered may tax the caterer's available storage space. Unfortunately, the airlines are usually unaware of an individual kitchen's size or space constraints. They forget that other airlines may be duplicating their need for storage space in the same kitchen. Thus, unintentionally, the airlines could really put considerable pressure on a kitchen facility with limited storage space.

Preferably, products purchased directly by the airlines are purchased on an open purchase order, and each local caterer serving the airline calls the supplier to order the amount needed when their stocks of the item(s) are running low. When the order is called in, the product is delivered to the individual caterer, but the billing goes to the airline via the open purchase order once receipt of the goods by the requesting kitchen is documented.

Regardless of how the purchasing process is handled, the caterer is responsible for providing secure storage for the airline's property and for keeping one airline's property separate from that of another airline. Usually some type of caging is required to provide separate areas for the several airlines served by the caterer. As was noted for the management of the airlines' equipment, considerable space is required for airline product storage as well. Indeed, a large portion of an inflight catering kitchen more closely resembles a warehouse with provisions for freezer, refrigeration, and dry storage areas than a production kitchen because of these extensive storage requirements.

In addition to just storing product, the caterer may also be responsible for managing and maintaining the airlines' inventory of soft drinks, beers, wines, and/or spirits. The different airlines have different policies toward the inventory and accountability for these items. Some airlines may want each can and each single service liquor bottle counted, both as it is issued to a flight and as it comes into the kitchen from a flight. They want an accurate, perpetual inventory that shows the flow of product to and from each flight. Other airlines consider product consumed once it leaves the caterer's facility and are concerned only with the outbound counts used to pack the drawers. It is important for the caterer to know exactly what each airline wants, in terms of the handling of these beverage products, and to make sure that their in-house procedures reflect the desires of each individual airline.

TRANSPORTING PRODUCTS AND EQUIPMENT TO THE AIRCRAFT

Once all the products have been prepared and staged for transport, another function of the caterer is to transport all of the required foods, beverages, equipment, and supplies to the aircraft. The transport function requires careful coordination with the airlines—not only with the published flight schedule but with changes in scheduled departure times as well as gate and aircraft number changes that occur from time to time, just as was the case with off-loading the aircraft.

The transport function is a critical one for the caterer. It is critical because the caterer's transport staff (1) interface directly with the customer (the airlines' flight attendants); (2) must see that the prepared products are delivered in excellent condition; and (3) is the section of the caterer's staff that coordinates operations with the airline locally. If the transport process is not done properly, there is a potential for high penalty fees to be paid to the airline because of (1) damage done to aircraft by the truck or the crew doing the transport, off-loading, or boarding; (2) flight delays that resulted from the caterer not having the proper items on board the aircraft at the proper time; or (3) fines incurred for speeding or other improper driving. Because of the critical nature of this task, generally the most reliable and knowledgeable employees are responsible for the transport function. All products and equipment required for the flight must be on board prior to the flight's departure.

Generally, shortly before it is time for equipment and products to be transported to a flight, all of the carts, carriers, and other such items required for that flight are gathered together, or staged, in the kitchen near the loading dock. Usually a space within the kitchen, termed the *staging area*, is designated for this activity. To be sure that all of the items are there and everything is correctly done, all of the components for the flight are generally inspected one last time prior to their being loaded for transport. Dry ice is placed in carts with items that must be kept chilled. The dry ice serves as the refrigerant not only for the transport period, but also for the time the food is on board the aircraft prior to the meal actually being served if the aircraft does not have a chilling system. Required wet ice, which has been cured (discussed in Chapter 10), is added to the proper carts at the last minute to minimize exposure to melting.

The truck used to transport necessary items to the aircraft must be appropriate for the aircraft. Large, wide-body aircraft require larger high-lift trucks that can reach to the height of the aircraft doorsills. Smaller aircraft that are lower to the ground, of course, do not require as large a truck—not only because of height differential but because of the more limited amount of equipment and supplies to be boarded. On some aircraft, the space between the back edge of the wing and the rear engine is quite limited, another factor controlling the size of the truck that can be used. A caterer must know the specific types of aircraft being used by an airline and the compatibility of their trucks with those aircraft.

Two people are required to drive the truck to the aircraft and accomplish the boarding activities. The senior staffperson is the truck driver. The driver's position is one with a great deal of responsibility because of the potential impact on product quality that might result from poor product handling and the potential for caterer liability associated with transport activities. The second staffperson, referred to as the loader, assists the driver with truck movement and placement on the ramp area by acting as a guide. The two work together to handle the boarding (or the off-loading) activities.

BOARDING THE PRODUCTS AND EQUIPMENT

A final function of the caterer is to transport all of the required foods, beverages, equipment, and supplies to the aircraft and board everything in its proper place on the plane in a timely manner prior to the flight's departure. If the flight is a through flight or a turn flight, depending on the aircraft's turnaround time, it may be that the caterer's transport personnel can take off inbound equipment at the same time they load outbound equipment, thus both starting and finishing the catering cycle in one trip. Because most airlines have limited ground times scheduled for their through or turn flights, it is essential for the caterer to be at the gate area ready to accomplish the boarding process quickly and efficiently. Generally, there is insufficient time to return to the kitchen for any forgotten or incorrect items when servicing these flights; thus, it is particularly critical that *everything* be correct when the truck leaves the kitchen for the gate area.

Other flights may be originating or terminating flights. If the flight is a terminating flight (usually a late-arriving evening flight), then only off-loading is done that day. The aircraft would not have new equipment and product boarded until it was used for an originating flight, usually the next day. On originating flights, the caterer is usually expected to have the necessary equipment and products at the gate ready for boarding approximately one hour prior to the flight's scheduled departure. Although this amount of lead time does allow time for the truck to return to the caterer's kitchen to correct errors, to do so is a waste of costly labor for the caterer and should be avoided through careful preparation of the equipment prior to the truck's departure.

It is important that the caterer exercise considerable care to be sure that the products for a particular flight are loaded onto the correct aircraft. Information from the airline lists the flight number, the departure time, the gate from which the flight is to depart, and the tail number of the particular aircraft to be used for the flight. The critical item is the aircraft's tail number. The gate may be changed for a number of reasons, but the aircraft is rarely changed other than for major concerns such as significant mechanical problems. The tail number is also important as it tells the caterer the specific type of aircraft and the amount of boarding equipment that can be used on it. Even though two aircraft are the same model plane (i.e., both are Boeing 757s), their galley structures may be quite different and may require different boarding equipment. This probability of galley equipment differences is particularly true if an airline is using equipment acquired from several different airlines, rather than equipment purchased directly from the aircraft manufacturer. Staff boarding items on the plane must *always* check the aircraft tail number to be sure they are putting the correct flight's items on the correct aircraft.

To provide flexibility to accommodate changing passenger counts, which occur up until the last minute prior to departure, and to have a way to correct any errors which may occur on the spot, caterers may have supplementary (or spare) meals and other provisions stocked at the gate areas in some way. These meals may be on one or more of the trucks servicing the gates or they may be staged from a permanent location near the gate. These extra meals are sometimes referred to as banked meals.

INTERNATIONAL CONSIDERATIONS

Catering meals for international flights adds additional responsibilities for the inflight caterer. Some of the considerations for international flights may include the preparation of more elaborate food (in terms of both preparation) and special menus which include more diverse ethnic foods, the need to board additional food and beverages on each flight since multiple meals are usually served per flight, and more concern with trash and garbage handling, as will be discussed later in this section and in Chapter 14.

Bonded Storage

One consideration with international flights is the possible need to have bonded storage areas. Bonded storage areas are specially constructed areas which must meet strict U.S. Customs specifications to ensure that there can be no unauthorized entry into the area. For example, U.S. Customs specifies the gauge span of wire caging used in the bonded storage area construction: it must meet the floor in such a way that a person could not move or bend the wiring in some way to gain access to the storage area. The height of the fencing and even ceiling protection must also preclude someone from entering the area over the top of the fencing. Bonded storage areas are used to store highly valued items which are exempt from U.S. taxes—items for which theft could be a serious problem. These storage areas are called *bonded areas* because the caterer would normally carry a fidelity bond (or insurance against theft by employees) on the items stored in these special areas.

International flights may serve bonded liquor, which must be handled differently from domestic liquors because federal taxes have been paid on domestic liquors. These same taxes need not be paid on liquor kept separate (bonded) from domestic supplies and destined for use on flights departing the country (international flights), nor on liquor from outside the United States supplied to a caterer by a foreign airline for exclusive use on their outbound international flights.

Inflight caterers may sometimes be responsible for storing and boarding duty-free products sold on international flights. While duty-free products have no relationship to foodservices or the provision of food and beverage services on international flights, these products have to be stored somewhere and have to be loaded on board the aircraft by someone. Since the inflight caterer is accustomed to storing and managing airline-owned products and must load equipment and supplies onto the aircraft anyway, some caterers have also been asked to assume the responsibility of the storage and boarding of the duty-free products owned by the airlines. These duty-free items must also be stored in a bonded storage area. Just as is the case with the bonded liquor, these items are products produced in other countries on which United States federal taxes have not been levied.

Food Elegance

Carriers on international routes tend to provide more elegant food selections on their flights. They tend to have more elaborate specifications for the food products served than is the case for domestic flights, and they are less production-line oriented, even for their main cabin meals. International flights tend to rely more on in-house prepared foods than is the case for U.S. domestic flights.

However, there now seems to be some blending of the two perspectives. Economic pressures on all airlines, both U.S. domestic airlines and international airlines, are causing the international carriers to consider ways to lower food costs. One of the ways being considered is the use of more pre-prepared frozen pop-out meals in coach-class service. At the same time, U.S. domestic airlines with international flights must compete in-kind with international carriers in terms of their foodservice concepts. They are starting to use more elaborate in-house-prepared foods on their flights. The reason for this change is also economics—the use of quality foodservice to compete for international passengers to fill the aircraft scheduled for an international flight.

In all cases, though, no matter what the airline or what approach to foodservice is used, there is much more emphasis on meal and snack service on international flights. Not only is there greater concern for the overall quality and variety of all food and beverage service, but there are more meals and snacks served to passengers during the extended transoceanic flight period than is the case on domestic flights.

U.S. Customs

Another consideration unique to servicing international flights (whether for a domestic or an international airline) is the need to interface with United States Customs. Customs officials will come on board the aircraft to clear all international flight arrivals. When working with the food and beverage services, they will be checking for items such as the seals of liquor kits and the handling of bonded goods. As noted previously in this chapter, the inflight caterer's personnel are the first people allowed on the aircraft after the passengers have deplaned. Sometimes caterer's staff must remove all of the equipment, trash, and leftover food and beverage products from the aircraft before the ground service personnel are allowed to board the plane.

U.S. Department of Agriculture, Animal and Plant Health Inspection Service, and Plant Protection and Quarantine (USDA, APHS, PPQ)

The inflight caterer handling international flights works under the surveillance of the United States Department of Agriculture (USDA) in regard to handling the trash that comes off an international flight. International trash must be either steam autoclaved and landfilled or incinerated. Many international kitchens have their own steam autoclaves to treat the inbound trash while others will use local incinerators. Every step of these processes is under the jurisdiction of the USDA. The USDA also checks outbound international flights and clears those aircraft before passengers are allowed to board.

The responsibility for protecting U.S. agricultural systems is delegated to the caterers and airlines through the use of a legal compliance agreement. The system works to keep plant and animal pests that could ruin U.S. agriculture from entering the country. Such pests as the Med fly, Foot-and-Mouth disease, and African Swine Fever could cause irreparable damage to crops and livestock if they were allowed to enter the country.

If a caterer were to allow any international trash or unused fresh fruits or vegetables to escape untreated, they could lose their right to cater international flights. Fines have been levied for a single worker eating a piece of fruit from an international flight. IFSA works with the USDA to assure that proper training materials on the proper handling of international trash are available to caterers and airlines.

LIABILITY FOR FOOD WHOLESOMENESS AND QUALITY

There is great concern for food wholesomeness and quality throughout the foodservice industry today. This concern particularly impacts the inflight foodservice industry for two important reasons. The first is that food served on airline flights undergoes more handling and transport steps than is typical of most foodservices. Therefore, there are more opportunities for spoilage or contamination to occur. Also, because of the many steps involved, the time from the first point of preparation to actual food consumption is unusually long, a factor which can contribute to a higher bacterial growth level in the food products.

The second is related to the importance of food as a marketing tool for the airline. An incidence of food-borne illness related to a specific airline could have a very adverse effect on the airline's ticket sales. Any inflight incidents, whether related to mechanical problems, weather, or food, are very likely to become high-profile national or even world news. In fact, there have been several such incidents in the past which have had very negative effects on the airlines involved. Indeed, at one time it was questionable whether a major international carrier would continue in business as a result of the high-profile publicity associated with an incidence of food-borne illness related to food eaten on one of their flights. While an inflight caterer's name may not make the headlines about such an incident, the effects could be equally adverse for the caterer and may be the cause of canceled contracts.

Problems with food wholesomeness can be the basis for airlines' and caterers' legal liability as well. The general public perceives the airlines as having deep pockets, in spite of their well-publicized financial constraints. Therefore, passenger lawsuits for damages are quite likely should there be an outbreak of food-borne illness or food contamination related to food served on an airline flight. It is important to note that one safety precaution that the airlines take is to provide the flight deck crew with individual meals containing different foods. This practice helps avoid a possible situation where both pilots might become ill from a contaminated food product and both be potentially unable to fly the plane.

Depending on the situation, it is quite likely that the caterer responsible for the preparation and transport of the food would also be named as a defendant in any such lawsuits filed. The financial costs of such lawsuits and any liability for which they are found responsible can be quite high for both the airline and the caterer, and particularly so should a death occur as a result of the contaminated food. Since such situations are generally avoidable if foods and beverages are properly produced, handled, stored, transported, and prepared for service, it is in the interest of both the airline and the inflight caterer to make sure that their employees are properly trained, that proper food preparation and handling procedures are in place, and that proper sanitation and cleaning procedures are followed at all times.

The U.S. Food and Drug Administration has the responsibility for monitoring and regulating the minimum standards of food safety for all conveyances in interstate travel. FDA investigators will generally inspect flight kitchens and airline facilities during construction and twice per year thereafter. Aircraft are inspected during construction and periodically while in operation. In addition to the FDA inspections, flight kitchens are inspected by state and local health officials, the USDA, the Army Veterinarian Corps (for military charters), health officials from foreign countries (if their nationally subsidized carriers are to be catered by the kitchen), corporate food safety audit teams, and airline quality audit teams. It is probably safe to say that inflight food operations are the most inspected portion of the foodservice industry.

In an effort to fully address critical food quality and safety issues, IFSA has traditionally given these areas its highest priority. The *Airline Catering Sanitation Guide* was produced to be used as a sound sanitation program for flight kitchen operations. *Safe Food Preparation: You're the Key!* was designed as an eight-module video sanitation training program tool for hourly employees. *The Inflight Food Safety Quality Assurance Manual* was designed to update sanitation management systems to the new Hazard Analysis and Critical Control Point (IIACCP) approach. HACCP and other food safety issues will be discussed in more detail in Chapter 13.

While there have been some notable cases of food-poisoning reported that have been traced to airline food, generally illness from food on commercial airlines is thought to be rare. One such incident that was widely publicized involved about 24 members of the Minnesota Vikings football team who became ill after eating the food on their flight home from a game with the Miami Dolphins in 1988. However, there is little public information regarding food-borne illness related to the inflight industry, just as there is little such information relative to the foodservice industry as a whole.

The Centers for Disease Control (CDC) in Atlanta has indicated that there is no really good system of surveillance for food-borne illness in the United States. Thus, there is no way to know if such outbreaks are increasing or decreasing and in what sectors of the foodservice industry such outbreaks may be occurring. It is thought that the outbreak of food-borne illnesses among airline passengers is generally underreported, as there have been only 23 such outbreaks reported, worldwide, between 1947 and 1984 (the last time period that CDC extensively reviewed the literature regarding this topic). However, such underreporting is not peculiar to the inflight foodservice industry; it is characteristic of all commercial and noncommercial foodservices.

Incidents of food-borne illness that might be related to airline food are particularly hard to identify. Passengers on a flight generally go their separate ways after the flight lands. If a passenger later gets sick, there is no easy way to know if anyone else on the flight encountered a similar illness. Also, since many flights cross time zones or otherwise are physiologically stressful to the passengers (red-eye flights interrupting sleep schedules, etc.), people who do become ill after a flight may blame the passing illness on many causes other than the food they ate, or just attribute it to what they perceive as poor-quality airline food, which did not agree with them. Nonetheless, the airline industry and the inflight caterers are not relieved of any responsibility just because food-borne illness from airline food may be difficult to identify.

SUMMARY

The inflight caterer performs many functions in the provision of foodservices for the airlines. These functions begin when an inbound inflight arrives, and the caterer's personnel must off-load all the equipment, waste, and remaining supplies from the airplane. They end when the plane is reloaded with new equipment and supplies and is ready for departure.

An important concern for anyone involved with inflight foodservices is that of food safety and the prevention of food-borne illness. Although there have been few instances of reported food-borne illness that have been traced to airline food, that does not eliminate the need for everyone concerned with airline foodservice to be alert to all food contamination possibilities. The unusual amount of handling that is required for food products served on airlines make these foods particularly vulnerable to contamination.

In the United States, the FDA is responsible for airlines' and caterers' adherence to an acceptable level of food safety. Inflight facilities are generally inspected by the FDA at least twice per year. The inflight industry cooperatively shares the responsibility for monitoring and maintaining the levels of quality and food safety expected by the FDA, the airlines, and, most importantly, by the flying public. IFSA represents the airlines and the caterers in discussion with the FDA and the USDA. Relations have been good with all concerned striving for uniform programs that protect the public's health and safety during flights.

REFERENCES

Special Meal Guidelines. (1992). Technical Pamphlet, Louisville, KY: Inflight Food Service Association, 18 pps.

Food Safety Quality Assurance Manual. (1994). Technical Manual, Louisville, KY: Inflight Food Service Association, 100 pps.

Airline Catering Sanitation Guide. (August 1976). Technical Manual, Louisville, KY: Inflight Food Service Association (FDA Sanitation Committee).

Safe Food Preparation-You're the Key. (May 1985). Eight-Module Video Sanitation Training Program, Louisville, KY: Inflight Food Service Association.

KEY TERMS

Aircraft Number	Boarding Equipment
Banked Meals (or Bank)	Bonded Storage
Belt	Cured Ice

Deadhead
Disposable (Single-Service) Items
Drawers
Driver
Dry Ice
Duty Free
Galley Structure
High-Tech Carts
Inbound Equipment
Loader
Off-Loading
Originating Flight
Outbound Equipment
Pop-Out Meals (Pop-Outs)

Rotable Equipment
Ship Number
Special Meals
Staging (Staged)
Standby Meals
Steam Autoclave
Stripping the Aircraft
Tail Number
Terminating Flight
Through Flight
Top-Off Meals
Turn Flight
Tray Line
Wet Ice

DISCUSSION QUESTIONS

1. Identify activities of the inflight caterer associated with the off-loading of inbound flights.
2. Why is the inflight caterer frequently concerned about the stock of each airlines' equipment available in the inflight kitchen?
3. Where are the foods for most first-class meals prepared? For coach-class meals? Why is there a difference? Do U.S. preparation procedures for the different passenger classes differ from European procedures?
4. What other functions (besides off-loading inbound flights and preparing foods) are performed by the inflight caterer to meet the airlines' food and beverage service needs?
5. Discuss features of inflight foodservices which are likely to be of much greater concern to an inflight kitchen servicing international flights than to a kitchen servicing only domestic flights.
6. What is bonded storage? What types of products are likely to be stored in bonded storage? Why would an inflight caterer have to maintain a bonded storage area?
7. Who is responsible and liable for food wholesomeness and food safety?
8. Why is it of great concern to an airline that no outbreak of food-borne illness result from any of their inflight foodservices? Have there ever been any such outbreaks? Are they common?
9. Why must the inflight caterer's personnel work closely with U.S. customs officials on arriving international flights?
10. What types of equipment must be used to dispose of trash and garbage arriving on international flights? Why is this so? Who oversees these disposal procedures to insure the caterer's compliance?

11. Why does the inflight caterer have to carefully monitor the flow of each airline's equipment through the inflight kitchen?

12. What items are generally preset on the passenger's service trays? What items are not preset? Why not?

13. What types of items are packed into drawers? Why can drawers be prepacked and staged for use as needed?

14. How does a caterer acquire products that are purchased directly by the airlines? What is the caterer's responsibility, if any, for these products?

15. Why is the transport function a critical one for the caterer? How does the transport crew know which plane to put the products on for a particular flight?

16. Why is food wholesomeness and proper handling of food products at all times a critical area of concern for the inflight foodservice industry?

17. What agency is responsible for monitoring and regulating the minimum standards for food safety in the United States?

18. What actions has IFSA taken over the years to help the inflight foodservice industry to understand and meet the food safety standards required of all flight kitchens?

19. Explain why an inflight caterer must spend much time and effort to keep each airline's equipment separated from that of other airlines and in well-organized storage areas in the caterer's flight kitchen.

5

The Airlines' Foodservice Division
Structure and Responsibilities

LEARNING OBJECTIVES

After studying this chapter, the student should be able to:

1. Identify at least six responsibilities of an airline's foodservice division/department.
2. Discuss an airline's menu development process.
3. Explain why airlines carefully develop the recipes used in their menu cycles.
4. Explain why airlines develop detailed specifications for all products used for their inflight food and beverage services.
5. Identify who has supply responsibilities and how products are purchased for use in an airline's inflight food and beverage services.
6. Explain the purpose of packaging and presentation specifications.
7. Discuss the type(s) of meals served to airline crews, differences between those meals and meals served to passengers, and reasons for the differences.
8. Identify factors that airlines consider in determining their inflight meal and snack service policies.
9. Explain why the inflight caterer needs to be aware of the service procedures to be used to serve a particular meal on board an aircraft.

Successful inflight foodservices occur when there is good understanding between the airline and the inflight caterer. To achieve such understanding, inflight catering management must understand the organizational structure of the airlines with which they are working. Conversely, the airline must understand the caterer's organizational structure so that expectations of both parties can be clearly defined and understood.

AIRLINE ORGANIZATIONAL STRUCTURE AND RESPONSIBILITIES

Each airline has a staff component that is responsible for the food and beverage services provided for the passengers by the airline. The title of this component, its size, and its location within the airline's organizational structure may vary. Some of the titles used include *catering division, dining services department,* or *food and beverage division.* The airline's overall organizational structure determines its foodservice arm's level, be it department, division, or group. The term *department* will be used in this text to simplify the discussion.

Regardless of the title used, this component of the airline's management staff has the overall responsibility for all food and beverage services on that airline's flights, including: (1) developing menus; (2) developing recipes; (3) developing specifications for all products used, including foods, beverages, and supplies; (4) determining packaging and presentation specifications; (5) determining crew meal menus and specifications; (6) negotiating purchasing contracts with suppliers for items to be purchased directly by the airline or by the caterer for the airline; (7) determining meal and snack service policies for flights; (8) managing inflight equipment logistics; (9) determining meal service procedures; (10) negotiating service contracts with inflight caterers; (11) interfacing with inflight caterers; (12) developing budgets; and (13) conducting food and beverage service cost analyses.

AIRLINE MENU DEVELOPMENT PROCESS

Traditionally the airlines develop all of the menus that are served on their flights. The developed menus are served on all the airline's flights, regardless of where the flight originates in the world. The inflight caterer serving a particular flight at a particular airport has no responsibility (or authority) for planning the menus served on a particular airline's flight unless it is specifically directed to do so by an airline. Indeed, it is *mandatory* that the menus and the specifications for the products to be served be *precisely* followed by the inflight caterer.

However, given the close working relationship that must exist between the airline, its inflight caterers, and the product suppliers, inflight menu development has become much more of a shared process than was often the case in the past. Caterers now have opportunities to make suggestions regarding specific menu items or menu combinations to the airline. Indeed such input is now frequently solicited and some airlines like creativity on the part of the caterers' chefs. Their input is often concerned with product availability, product acceptability (waste generated from flights), and labor or food costs associated with an item or total menu. Since airlines are always cognizant of their decisions' economic effects, products that are too labor intensive to produce and serve as originally desired by the airline may be modified to improve labor productivity, a factor that could impact on the cost of a particular meal to the airline.

The suppliers of products used in inflight meals are now also part of the team concept regarding menu development. These suppliers have test kitchens and product development expertise which is used to help develop products to better meet the needs of an airline. The suppliers may conduct product research at the specific request of an airline, or they may conduct product development research on their own in an effort to develop a new product which they feel would meet an identified need of the airlines. The pop-out meals are an example of a widely used product for which the suppliers played a major role in product development.

Menu Development for Production and Service

Menu development by the airline includes the identification of the food and beverage items to be served for each meal or snack served in each class of service. Every detail of the menu and how it should appear when served to the passenger is identified in writing. The menus and all supporting documentation are delivered to all of the inflight caterers with whom the airline has contracts.

The airline determines the frequency with which its menus will change and the dates for which the menus will be effective. Some airlines will change their menus monthly, others will change them seasonally, and still others will change them weekly. The menus for all classes of service are identified by menu cycle or period, and airlines generally rotate through four to seven cycles. All menus of an airline, regardless of class of service, will be on the same cycle. While all classes of service usually change their menus on the same date, there are times when an airline might make complete changes to the menu components in one class (perhaps an upgrade to first-class menus), while continuing to rotate the same menu in other classes (such as in coach).

A situation that may occur for inflight caterers is that several of the airlines that they service schedule the implementation of new menu cycles on the same day or within the same week. Changing the menu cycle for an airline is a complex process for a caterer—indeed, it is almost as though the caterer were opening a completely new restaurant. Opening day (or the first day of the new cycle) is the first day that the employees have to produce a completely new set of food products (with zero tolerance for error) working just as efficiently as they did the day before when preparing the old menu with which they were familiar. When the caterer has to simultaneously change more than one menu cycle, the process is a significant challenge.

Part of the complexity of this process for the caterer is the need to have a new set of food products on hand in inventory at the time the new cycle begins while planning the purchase of the products used on the old cycle so that there is little or no excess stock left on hand, but there is enough to service all the airline's flights without product substitution. A midsize inflight kitchen might be required to invest anywhere from $3,000 to $4,000 just to purchase the new stock that will be needed to implement a new cycle menu. If four or five airlines were changing their cycles simultaneously, that investment could easily grow to $15,000 or $20,000.

If caterers have a substantial amount of old stock on hand at the time of the change, they may need to contact the airline and ask for an exception to the menu for certain items so that they can use up, or burn off, this excess stock before starting to use the new stock purchased for the new menus. It is undesirable for a caterer to regularly have to ask an airline for such an exception as it indicates to the airline that the caterer's staff is unable to adequately manage their inventory in a cost-effective manner.

Figures 5.1 and 5.2 illustrate one airline's cycles (5 cycles) which will be rotated on the first and fifteenth of each month, starting June 15 and ending October 14. There are eight semimonthly periods between those dates meaning that three of the five cycles would be used twice. Figure 5.1 illustrates a lunch menu for first-class passengers while Figure 5.2 illustrates the corresponding lunch menu for coach class for the same menu period. There is a marked difference in the amount of foods served for the lunch meal as well as in the type of products served. Note, too, that these menus indicate the brand name and purveyor stock number of the specific items that are to be used or the recipe number to be used to prepare the planned menu item.

In addition to these menus, this airline also distributes provisioning sheets (catering manual pages, illustrated in Chapter 12) which indicate the condiments and garnishes to be served with each of the menu items as well as catering manual pages indicating the packing requirements and the standard tray setup to be used for these menus. Figures 5.3 and 5.4 illustrate these pages for the first-class menus indicated in Figure 5.1, while Figures 5.5 and 5.6 illustrate the same supportive pages for the menus indicated in Figure 5.2. Such provisioning information also indicates the specific brand name and item stock number of the items to be used, just as the menu sheets do. Where "local" is indicated, the caterer is to purchase the item from local sources. Only about 20 percent of the products used on inflight menus are locally purchased by the caterer. The remaining 80 percent are either specified by or directly purchased by the airline.

These menus are in the format that would be distributed to the inflight caterers for use in the production and service of the meals. In some in-

USAIR - DINING & CABIN SERVICES
L11 - FIRST CLASS - LUNCH
ALL CITIES EXCEPT: BDA, MEX, NAS, SJU, STT & SXM
STANDARD EQUIPMENT

ITEMS	CYCLE 1	CYCLE 2	CYCLE 3	CYCLE 4	CYCLE 5
			(JUNE 15 THRU OCTOBER 14)		
NUTS A	Mixed Nuts in China Ramekin (43-5/8226/10-51) 1-01 MBC-FL111A	Mixed Nuts in China Ramekin (43-5/8226/10-51) 1-01 MBC-FL112A	Mixed Nuts in China Ramekin (43-5/8226/10-51) 1-01 MBC-FL113A	Mixed Nuts in China Ramekin (43-5/8226/10-51) 1-01 MBC-FL114A	Mixed Nuts in China Ramekin (43-5/8226/10-51) 1-01 MBC-FL115A
TRAY SET-UP B	Shrimp Cocktail (45-22-5) 1-01; Vienna Salad (45-21-18) 1-01; U.S. Food Service Lite Rye (43-3/USV6062) 1.5-01; Mini Loaf (43-3/USV6064) 1-01; Land O' Lakes Continental Butter (43-5/BU800) 1-01; Crystal Salt and Pepper Shakers (43-5/SH900) 1-01; MBC-FL111B	Norwegian Smoked Salmon (45-22-6) 1-01; Piccadilly Salad (45-21-14) 1-01; U.S. Food Service 3 Grain (43-3/USV6064) Whole Wheat Loaf 1.5-01; Land O' Lakes Continental Butter (43-5/BU800) 1-01; Crystal Salt and Pepper Shakers (43-5/SH900) 1-01; MBC-FL112B	Shrimp Cocktail Louis (45-21-9) 1-01; Summer Salad (45-21-31) 1-01; U.S. Food Service White (43-3/USV6063) Mini Loaf (43-3/USV6064) 1.5-01; Land O' Lakes Continental Butter (43-5/BU800) 1-01; Crystal Salt and Pepper Shakers (43-5/SH900) 1-01; MBC-FL113B	Spicy Shrimp (45-22-11) 1-01; Endive Strawberry Salad (45-21-31) 1-01; U.S. Food Service 3 Grain (43-3/USV6064) Whole Wheat Loaf 1.5-01; Land O' Lakes Continental Butter (43-5/BU800) 1-01; Crystal Salt and Pepper Shakers (43-5/SH900) 1-01; MBC-FL114B	Shrimp with Salsa (45-22-7) 1-01; Julienne Pepper Salad (45-21-27) 1-01; U.S. Food Service White (43-3/USV6063) Mini Loaf (43-3/USV6064) 1.5-01; Land O' Lakes Continental Butter (43-5/BU800) 1-01; Crystal Salt and Pepper Shakers (43-5/SH900) 1-01; MBC-FL115B
DRESSING C	Naturally Fresh Balsamic Vinaigrette Dressing (43-18/337/10-55) 1-01 MBC-FL111C	Naturally Fresh Light Lemon Vinaigrette Dressing (43-18/328/10-55) 1-01 MBC-FL112C	Naturally Fresh Herb Vinaigrette Dressing (43-18/336/10-55) 1-01 MBC-FL113C	Naturally Fresh Raspberry Vinaigrette Dressing (43-18/318/10-55) 1-01 MBC-FL114C	Naturally Fresh Herb Vinaigrette Dressing (43-18/336/10-55) 1-01 MBC-FL115C
DRESSING D	Naturally Fresh Blue Cheese Dressing (43-18/330/10-55) 1-01 MBC-FL111D	Naturally Fresh Peppercream Dressing (43-18/324/10-55) 1-01 MBC-FL112D	Naturally Fresh Ranch Lite Dressing (43-18/342/10-55) 1-01 MBC-FL113D	Naturally Fresh Honey French Dressing (43-18/310/10-55) 1-01 MBC-FL114D	Naturally Fresh Creamy Cilantro Dressing (43-18/349/10-55) 1-01 MBC-FL115D
ENTREE A E	Breast of Chicken with Harvest Vegetables (43-9/52446) 40% Per Chart 14-2-1 MBC-FL111E	Roasted Chicken with Wild Mushroom Sauce (43-14/C138) 40% Per Chart 14-2-1 MBC-FL112E	Bayou Chicken (43-9/52447) 40% Per Chart 14-2-1 MBC-FL113E	Scampi with Garlic Butter (43-9/52445) 40% Per Chart 14-2-1 MBC-FL114E	Shrimp Oriental with Ginger Sauce (43-9/52663) 40% Per Chart 14-2-1 MBC-FL115E
ENTREE B F	Filet Mignon with Southwestern Fettucini (45-26-13) Peppers, Carrots & Onion Medley Diablo Sauce 40% Per Chart 14-2-1 MBC-FL111F	Filet Mignon with Rice Palermo (45-26-13) Celery, Carrots & Mushrooms Three Pepper Sauce 40% Per Chart 14-2-1 MBC-FL112F	Filet Mignon with Spinach Tomato (45-26-14) Anna Potatoes Cognac Mushroom Sauce 40% Per Chart 14-2-1 MBC-FL113F	Filet Mignon with Pinot Noir Sauce (45-26-17) Barley Pilaf California Vegetables 40% Per Chart 14-2-1 MBC-FL114F	Filet Mignon with Green Beans & Mushrooms (45-26-17) Baked Stuffed Potatoes Morel Sauce 40% Per Chart 14-2-1 MBC-FL115F
ENTREE C G	Grilled Salmon Cold Plate (45-24-35) 30% Per Chart 14-2-1 MBC-FL111G	Shrimp Cold Plate with Putza Salad (45-24-9) 30% Per Chart 14-2-1 MBC-FL112G	Marinated Swordfish Cold Plate 30% Per Chart 14-2-1 MBC-FL113G	Grilled Chicken Cold Plate (45-24-36) 30% Per Chart 14-2-1 MBC-FL114G	Mesquite Chicken Cold Plate (45-24-34) 30% Per Chart 14-2-1 MBC-FL115G
DESSERT H	Fruit and Cheese Plate (45-23-1/10-71) Apple Cranberry Cobbler (43-5/CAO319) 1-01 MBC-FL111H	Fruit and Cheese Plate (45-23-1/10-71) White Chocolate Oreo Torte (43-3/GTC6276) 1-01 MBC-FL112H	Fruit and Cheese Plate (45-23-1/10-71) **Chocolate Walnut Torte (43-5/8852)** 1-01 MBC-FL113H	Fruit and Cheese Plate (45-23-1/10-71) Tuxedo Mousse Torte (43-5/UC1685) 1-01 MBC-FL114H	Fruit and Cheese Plate (45-23-1/10-71) Walnut Cheesecake Brownie (43-3/GTC2038) 1-01 MBC-FL115H

DENOTES LATEST CHANGES TO THIS MATRIX

REVISION DATE 6/28/94

FIGURE 5.1 A five-cycle menu for first-class lunch service. (Courtesy of USAir)

USAIR – DINING & CABIN SERVICES
L12 / D12 - COACH - LUNCH / DINNER
ALL CITIES EXCEPT: BDA, MEX, NAS, SJU, STT & SXM
ALADDIN EQUIPMENT

36-2-2

SEP 01 94

ITEMS	CYCLE 1	CYCLE 2	CYCLE 3	CYCLE 4	CYCLE 5
TRAY SET-UP	Crunchy Salad (45-15-14/AL30) 1-01	California Salad (45-15-17/AL30) 1-01	Munich Salad (45-15-24/AL30) 1-01	Zucchini and Tomato Salad (45-15-25/AL30) 1-01	Garden Diced Salad (45-15-24/AL30) 1-01
	USAir Parmesan Pepper Lite Dressing (43-5/US27) 🕿 1-01	USAir Buttermilk Ranch Lite Dressing (43-5/US12) 1-01	USAir Thousand Island Lite Dressing (43-5/US22) 1-01	USAir Creamy Italian Lite Dressing (43-5-US24) 1-01	USAir Fat Free Honey Mustard Dressing (43-5/US37) 1-01
	Cheryl's Oatmeal Raisin Cookie (43-5/6084) 🕿 *1-01*	Fantasia Dutch Treat Brownie (43-3/FA95000) *1-01*	*Cheryl's Chocolate Chip Cookie (43-5/6094)* 🕿 *1-01*	Rachel's Cinnamon Chip Cookie (43-3/RHL7125) *1-01*	Famous Amos Chocolate Chip Cookies (43-3/FAS0018) 1-01
	Cutlery Packet (43-5/PL200) 1-01	Cutlery Packet (43-5/PL200) 1-01	Cutlery Packet (43-5/PL200) 1-01	Cutlery Packet (43-5/PL200) 1-01	Cutlery Packet (43-5/PL200) 1-01
A	MBC-LD121A	MBC-LD122A	MBC-LD123A	MBC-LD124A	MBC-LD125A
ENTREE A **B**	Chicken Honey Mustard (43-9/52547) 60% Per Chart 14-4-1	Grilled Citrus Breast of Chicken (43-14/C135) 60% Per Chart 14-4-1	Chicken, Lemon Rosemary (43-9/52436) 60% Per Chart 14-4-1	Chicken Tenders Oriental (43-9/52833) 60% Per Chart 14-4-1	Chicken Milano (43-9/52831) 60% Per Chart 14-4-1
	MBC-LD121B	MBC-LD122B	MBC-LD123B	MBC-LD124B	MBC-LD125B
ENTREE A **C**	Lasagna (43-9/52835) 40% Per Chart 14-4-1	Pasta with Three Cheese Sauce (43-11/1605) 40% Per Chart 14-4-1	Manicotti (43-17/MAN48) 40% Per Chart 14-4-1	Cheese Ravioli (43-14/C134) 40% Per Chart 14-4-1	Cappelletti Primavera (43-17/CP56) 40% Per Chart 14-4-1
	MBC-LD121C	MBC-LD122C	MBC-LD123C	MBC-LD124C	MBC-LD125C

🕿 DENOTES LATEST CHANGES TO THIS MATRIX

REVISION DATE 6/28/94

98

FIGURE 5.2   Five-cycle menu for coach-class lunch and dinner service. This menu would be used for coach service during the same service period that the lunch menu illustrated in Figure 5.1 would be used for first-class service. (Courtesy of USAir)

USAIR - DINING & CABIN SERVICES
L11 / D11 - FIRST CLASS - LUNCH / DINNER
ALL CITIES EXCEPT: MEX & SJU
MISCELLANEOUS PROVISIONING

MISC.	CYCLE 1	CYCLE 2	CYCLE 3	CYCLE 4	CYCLE 5
K	Milk, 2% - 1/2 Pint (Local/10-82) MBC-BE0023 — 1-08	Milk, 2% - 1/2 Pint (Local/10-82) MBC-BE0023 — 1-08	Milk, 2% - 1/2 Pint (Local/10-82) MBC-BE0023 — 1-08	Milk, 2% - 1/2 Pint (Local/10-82) MBC-BE0023 — 1-08	Milk, 2% - 1/2 Pint (Local/10-82) MBC-BE0023 — 1-08
L	**757 & 767 AIRCRAFT ONLY** Half and Half - 1/2 Pint (Local/10-82) MBC-MI0011 — 1-08; **ALL OTHER AIRCRAFT** Half and Half - Individual (43-5/UC10/10-82) MBC-MI0003 — 2-01	**757 & 767 AIRCRAFT ONLY** Half and Half - 1/2 Pint (Local/10-82) MBC-MI0011 — 1-08; **ALL OTHER AIRCRAFT** Half and Half - Individual (43-5/UC10/10-82) MBC-MI0003 — 2-01	**757 & 767 AIRCRAFT ONLY** Half and Half - 1/2 Pint (Local/10-82) MBC-MI0011 — 1-08; **ALL OTHER AIRCRAFT** Half and Half - Individual (43-5/UC10/10-82) MBC-MI0003 — 2-01	**757 & 767 AIRCRAFT ONLY** Half and Half - 1/2 Pint (Local/10-82) MBC-MI0011 — 1-08; **ALL OTHER AIRCRAFT** Half and Half - Individual (43-5/UC10/10-82) MBC-MI0003 — 2-01	**757 & 767 AIRCRAFT ONLY** Half and Half - 1/2 Pint (Local/10-82) MBC-MI0011 — 1-08; **ALL OTHER AIRCRAFT** Half and Half - Individual (43-5/UC10/10-82) MBC-MI0003 — 2-01
M	Heinz Steak Sauce (Local/10-83) MBC-MI0001 — 5 Per Flt	Heinz Steak Sauce (Local/10-83) MBC-MI0001 — 5 Per Flt	Heinz Steak Sauce (Local/10-83) MBC-MI0001 — 5 Per Flt	Heinz Steak Sauce (Local/10-83) MBC-MI0001 — 5 Per Flt	Heinz Steak Sauce (Local/10-83) MBC-MI0001 — 5 Per Flt
N	Entree Garnish (Local/10-81) MBC-MI0014 — 1-08	Entree Garnish (Local/10-81) MBC-MI0014 — 1-08	Entree Garnish (Local/10-81) MBC-MI0014 — 1-08	Entree Garnish (Local/10-81) MBC-MI0014 — 1-08	Entree Garnish (Local/10-81) MBC-MI0014 — 1-08
O	Beverage Condiments (Local/10-80) MBC-MI0020 — 1-08	Beverage Condiments (Local/10-80) MBC-MI0020 — 1-08	Beverage Condiments (Local/10-80) MBC-MI0020 — 1-08	Beverage Condiments (Local/10-80) MBC-MI0020 — 1-08	Beverage Condiments (Local/10-80) MBC-MI0020 — 1-08
P	Land O' Lakes Continental Butter (43-5/BU800/10-86) MBC-MI0027 — .5-01	Land O' Lakes Continental Butter (43-5/BU800/10-86) MBC-MI0027 — .5-01	Land O' Lakes Continental Butter (43-5/BU800/10-86) MBC-MI0027 — .5-01	Land O' Lakes Continental Butter (43-5/BU800/10-86) MBC-MI0027 — .5-01	Land O' Lakes Continental Butter (43-5/BU800/10-86) MBC-MI0027 — .5-01
Q	Lindor Chocolate Candy (43-5/LC85/10-72) MBC-MI0028 — 1-01	Lindor Chocolate Candy (43-5/LC85/10-72) MBC-MI0028 — 1-01	Lindor Chocolate Candy (43-5/LC85/10-72) MBC-MI0028 — 1-01	Lindor Chocolate Candy (43-5/LC85/10-72) MBC-MI0028 — 1-01	Lindor Chocolate Candy (43-5/LC85/10-72) MBC-MI0028 — 1-01
R	Hot Towels - Terry (43-5/HT400N/10-75) MBC-SC0314 — 2-08	Hot Towels - Terry (43-5/HT400N/10-75) MBC-SC0314 — 2-08	Hot Towels - Terry (43-5/HT400N/10-75) MBC-SC0314 — 2-08	Hot Towels - Terry (43-5/HT400N/10-75) MBC-SC0314 — 2-08	Hot Towels - Terry (43-5/HT400N/10-75) MBC-SC0314 — 2-08
S	**PHL - MEX ONLY** *Old El Paso Picante Sauce (43-3/PFS7501)* 🐾 *MBC-MI0023* — 1-01	**PHL - MEX ONLY** *Old El Paso Picante Sauce (43-3/PFS7501)* 🐾 *MBC-MI0023* — 1-01	**PHL - MEX ONLY** *Old El Paso Picante Sauce (43-3/PFS7501)* 🐾 *MBC-MI0023* — 1-01	**PHL - MEX ONLY** *Old El Paso Picante Sauce (43-3/PFS7501)* 🐾 *MBC-MI0023* — 1-01	**PHL - MEX ONLY** *Old El Paso Picante Sauce (43-3/PFS7501)* 🐾 *MBC-MI0023* — 1-01

🐾 *DENOTES LATEST CHANGES TO THIS MATRIX*

REVISION DATE 6/28/94

FIGURE 5.3 Miscellaneous provisioning chart for first-class lunch and dinner service. This chart would accompany the first-class service menu illustrated in Figure 5.1. (Courtesy of USAir)

USAIR - DINING & CABIN SERVICES
L11 / D11 - FIRST CLASS - LUNCH / DINNER - ALL CITIES
STANDARD EQUIPMENT

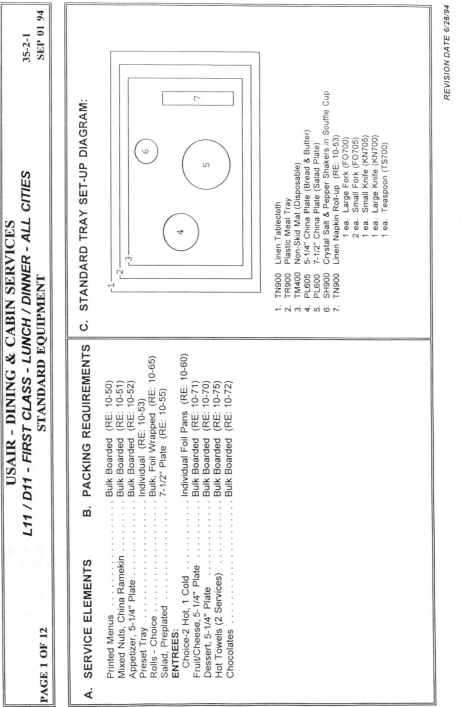

A. SERVICE ELEMENTS

Printed Menus	Bulk Boarded (RE: 10-50)
Mixed Nuts, China Ramekin	Bulk Boarded (RE: 10-51)
Appetizer, 5-1/4" Plate	Bulk Boarded (RE: 10-52)
Preset Tray	Individual (RE: 10-53)
Rolls - Choice	Bulk, Foil Wrapped (RE: 10-65)
Salad, Preplated	7-1/2" Plate (RE: 10-55)
ENTREES:	
Choice-2 Hot, 1 Cold	Individual Foil Pans (RE: 10-60)
Fruit/Cheese, 5-1/4" Plate	Bulk Boarded (RE: 10-71)
Dessert, 5-1/4" Plate	Bulk Boarded (RE: 10-70)
Hot Towels (2 Services)	Bulk Boarded (RE: 10-75)
Chocolates	Bulk Boarded (RE: 10-72)

B. PACKING REQUIREMENTS

C. STANDARD TRAY SET-UP DIAGRAM:

1. TN900   Linen Tablecloth
2. TR900   Plastic Meal Tray
3. TM400   Non-Skid Mat (Disposable)
4. PL605   5-1/4" China Plate (Bread & Butter)
5. PL600   7-1/2" China Plate (Salad Plate)
6. SH900   Crystal Salt & Pepper Shakers in Souffle Cup
7. TN900   Linen Napkin Roll-up (RE: 10-53)
                   1 ea.   Large Fork (FO700)
                   2 ea.   Small Fork (FO705)
                   1 ea.   Small Knife (KN705)
                   1 ea.   Large Knife (KN700)
                   1 ea.   Teaspoon (TS700)

REVISION DATE 6/28/94

FIGURE 5.4 Example of information provided to inflight caterers indicating equipment packing requirements and diagraming passenger meal tray setup for first-class lunch or dinner service. These equipment requirements and tray setup would be used for the lunch cycle illustrated in Figure 5.1. (Courtesy of USAir.)

USAIR - DINING & CABIN SERVICES
L12 / D12 - COACH - LUNCH / DINNER
ALL CITIES EXCEPT: MEX
MISCELLANEOUS PROVISIONING

MISC.	CYCLE 1	CYCLE 2	CYCLE 3	CYCLE 4	CYCLE 5
D	ALL CITIES EXCEPT: SJU Milk, 2% - 1/2 Pint — 1-30 (Local/10-82) MBC-BE0023 SJU ONLY Milk, 2% - Quart — 2 Per Flt (Local/10-82) MBC-BE0022	ALL CITIES EXCEPT: SJU Milk, 2% - 1/2 Pint — 1-30 (Local/10-82) MBC-BE0023 SJU ONLY Milk, 2% - Quart — 2 Per Flt (Local/10-82) MBC-BE0022	ALL CITIES EXCEPT: SJU Milk, 2% - 1/2 Pint — 1-30 (Local/10-82) MBC-BE0023 SJU ONLY Milk, 2% - Quart — 2 Per Flt (Local/10-82) MBC-BE0022	ALL CITIES EXCEPT: SJU Milk, 2% - 1/2 Pint — 1-30 (Local/10-82) MBC-BE0023 SJU ONLY Milk, 2% - Quart — 2 Per Flt (Local/10-82) MBC-BE0022	ALL CITIES EXCEPT: SJU Milk, 2% - 1/2 Pint — 1-30 (Local/10-82) MBC-BE0023 SJU ONLY Milk, 2% - Quart — 2 Per Flt (Local/10-82) MBC-BE0022
	ALL CITIES EXCEPT: BDA, NAS & SJU Half and Half - Individual — 50% Pax (43-5/UC10/10-82) MBC-MI0003 BDA, NAS & SJU ONLY Half and Half - Individual — 50% Pax (Local/10-82) MBC-MI0010	ALL CITIES EXCEPT: BDA, NAS & SJU Half and Half - Individual — 50% Pax (43-5/UC10/10-82) MBC-MI0003 BDA, NAS & SJU ONLY Half and Half - Individual — 50% Pax (Local/10-82) MBC-MI0010	ALL CITIES EXCEPT: BDA, NAS & SJU Half and Half - Individual — 50% Pax (43-5/UC10/10-82) MBC-MI0003 BDA, NAS & SJU ONLY Half and Half - Individual — 50% Pax (Local/10-82) MBC-MI0010	ALL CITIES EXCEPT: BDA, NAS & SJU Half and Half - Individual — 50% Pax (43-5/UC10/10-82) MBC-MI0003 BDA, NAS & SJU ONLY Half and Half - Individual — 50% Pax (Local/10-82) MBC-MI0010	ALL CITIES EXCEPT: BDA, NAS & SJU Half and Half - Individual — 50% Pax (43-5/UC10/10-82) MBC-MI0003 BDA, NAS & SJU ONLY Half and Half - Individual — 50% Pax (Local/10-82) MBC-MI0010
E	Beverage Condiments — 1-50 (Local/10-80) MBC-MI0020	Beverage Condiments — 1-50 (Local/10-80) MBC-MI0020	Beverage Condiments — 1-50 (Local/10-80) MBC-MI0020	Beverage Condiments — 1-50 (Local/10-80) MBC-MI0020	Beverage Condiments — 1-50 (Local/10-80) MBC-MI0020
F	Combo Cheddar Cheese — 1-01 Crackers (43-5/16374/10-93) MBC-MI0018	*Eagle Pretzels — 1-01* *(43-5/56062/10-93)* *MBC-MI0016*	Combo Pizzeria Pretzels — 1-01 (43-5/16373/10-93) MBC-MI0019	Combo Cheddar Cheese — 1-01 Crackers (43-5/16374/10-93) MBC-MI0018	Eagle Pretzels — 1-01 (43-5/56062/10-75) MBC-MI0021
G	Hot Towels - Terry — 1-40 (43-5/HC15/10-75) MBC-SC0324	Hot Towels - Terry — 1-40 (43-5/HC15/10-75) MBC-SC0324	Hot Towels - Terry — 1-40 (43-5/HC15/10-75) MBC-SC0324	Hot Towels - Terry — 1-40 (43-5/HC15/10-75) MBC-SC0324	Hot Towels - Terry — 1-40 (43-5/HC15/10-75) MBC-SC0324
H	PHL - MEX MEX ONLY ☞ *Old El Paso Picante — 1-01* *Sauce (43-3/PFS7501)* *MBC-MI0023*	PHL - MEX MEX ONLY ☞ *Old El Paso Picante — 1-01* *Sauce (43-3/PFS7501)* *MBC-MI0023*	PHL - MEX MEX ONLY ☞ *Old El Paso Picante — 1-01* *Sauce (43-3/PFS7501)* *MBC-MI0023*	PHL - MEX MEX ONLY ☞ *Old El Paso Picante — 1-01* *Sauce (43-3/PFS7501)* *MBC-MI0023*	PHL - MEX MEX ONLY ☞ *Old El Paso Picante — 1-01* *Sauce (43-3/PFS7501)* *MBC-MI0023*

☞ DENOTES LATEST CHANGES TO THIS MATRIX

REVISION DATE 6/28/94

FIGURE 5.5 Miscellaneous provisioning chart for coach-class lunch and dinner service. This chart would be used with the coach-class service menu illustrated in Figure 5.2. (Courtesy of USAir)

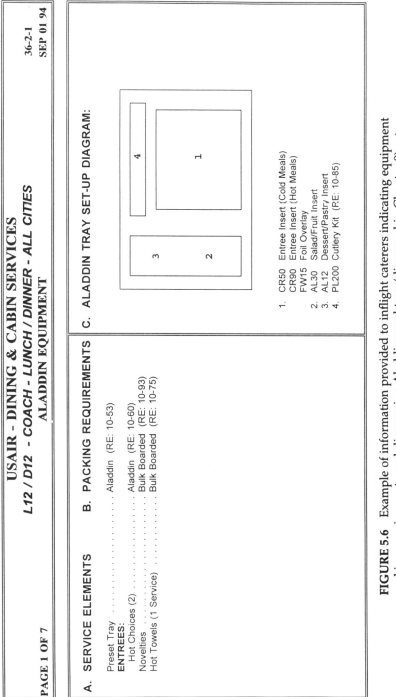

FIGURE 5.6 Example of information provided to inflight caterers indicating equipment packing requirements and diagraming Aladdin meal tray (discussed in Chapter 9) setup for coach-class lunch or dinner service. These equipment requirements and tray setup would be used for the lunch cycle illustrated in Figure 5.2. (Courtesy of USAir)

stances, specially printed menus would be developed from master cycle menus, such as the one illustrated in Figure 5.1, which would be distributed to passengers in first class and business class after takeoff so that they could make their menu selections for the meal to be served.

FIRST-CLASS AND BUSINESS-CLASS MENU DEVELOPMENT

The use of professionally designed and printed menus plays a vital role in the distinctive identity and image of an airline. They are part of its marketing strategy designed to market its flights to first-class and business passengers. This strategy incorporates promotions, amenities, and various styles of service, including food and beverage services, as a means of differentiating the airline from its competitors. Attractive menus that present mouth-watering descriptions of chefs' culinary creations, coupled with a variety of the world's premier wine selections, serve to merchandise the airline's food and beverage service, as well as to package the inflight dining experience for the first-class and business passengers.

Many airlines are committed to service excellence, including the attention to detail associated with the creation of a fine dining experience, for their first and business classes. Special glassware, china, linen, and serviceware are carefully selected to complement the gourmet foods offered for these meal services. Accordingly, the printing and use of a restaurant-style menu is an appropriate and necessary part of the passengers' experience. The airline's staff is responsible for the design, printing, and distribution of these menus to the airline's caterers who pack them into the boarding equipment for inflight distribution to the first-class and business-class passengers.

Printed menus serve several purposes, in addition to providing descriptions of meals offered on board the aircraft. These menus are used internally by airlines for promotional and sales purposes. For example, an airline's marketing department may use professionally printed menus and wine lists, along with a variety of other amenities and services such as frequent-flyer programs, hotel and rental car discounts, inflight magazines, duty-free shopping, and inflight music and video entertainment guides, as presentation pieces to attract potential customers. Customers of interest to the airline might include large corporate travel groups, members of national and international trade associations, and discriminating first-class and business travelers.

The development and printing of these menus is a complex process, and the airlines usually contract with a professional firm in the business of menu development to work with them for this project. The development process is complicated and includes many steps which may involve taking specially planned food photographs, translation of the planned menu into multiple languages, preparation of specially designed layouts, and other such considerations. Generally, the process may take anywhere from eight to sixteen weeks to complete although the time frame varies depending on a number of factors.

One of the first tasks to be accomplished is to determine the quantity and types of menus that need to be written and printed. To make this determination for any given time frame, the airline's complete flight schedule (including departure and arrival information), days and frequency of flights, aircraft configuration, (including a breakdown of seats within the cabin), yield factors, and meal codes used are considered. The menus and the number of meals and services offered on any given flight vary, depending on the destination, length of flight, and class of service, as will be discussed later in this chapter. For example, the meal schedule on a long international flight, such as traveling eastbound from Hong Kong to New York (approximately a fourteen-hour flight) would probably include several meal services. Passengers would likely receive a light snack, main entree meal, and beverages as well as a breakfast in the morning prior to their arrival. First-class and business-class service on this flight might include four- to eight-course meals accompanied by champagne and wine for each meal period.

After the airline's foodservice division has determined the meal specifications for all its flights, the printed menu development process can occur. The process begins with transforming the food specifications from the working format, as illustrated in Figure 5.1, to an attractive, accurate, well-written description detailing the type of food offered on the flight.

Once the copy is written and double-checked for culinary accuracy and proofread repeatedly until correct, it is then translated into one or several foreign languages. These translations are again proofread many times to ensure complete accuracy.

The number of languages needed is determined by the departure and arrival information on the flight schedule as well as other demographic data gathered from market research. However, once the languages have been determined, it is still necessary to translate the menus appropriately according to correct culinary terminology and regional preferences. For example, the word for potato in Spanish spoken in the western hemisphere, "papa," is different from that in Europe (patata). Only one of the two translations would be correct and appropriate depending on the particular region for which the translation is intended. Translation of culinary terms is especially difficult when describing foods and wines that are unfamiliar to a particular culture or country. Expertise in accurate culinary translation is essential in order for the international passenger to understand the menu. Generally, due to the numerous dialects that can exist in many languages, the airline will have the menus translated into the most appropriate and commonly understood form of a specific language. Figure 5.7 illustrates a menu that is written in both English and German.

When all the menu copy is written and translated for all the menus, it must then be typeset (in all appropriate languages) and prepared for printing. As soon as all printing is completed, the professionally printed menus are packaged and shipped to the airlines for appropriate distribution.

RECIPE DEVELOPMENT

The airlines also develop and document recipes for products that are to be served on their menus. Airlines either have their own staff do the recipe development (as their staff sometimes includes a chef), or they have their caterers' chefs do this development for them. The airline's foodservice staff (or sometimes their high-level executives), though, must make the final approval of the recipes that are developed. Once developed, the recipes are then specified on future menus, where appropriate.

Recipe development is an important activity of the airline's foodservice staff because it is of critical importance to the airlines that food products served on their flights be consistent, regardless of where the flights originate. Thus, airlines cannot rely on local caterers (or even the large national inflight catering firms) to develop their individual recipes for a particular product. If they adopted that practice, a product prepared and boarded in Atlanta would quite likely be very different from what is supposed to be the same product prepared and boarded in Minneapolis.

By developing specific recipes for all products served, the airlines not only ensure product consistency throughout their system, but they have a quality assurance standard available to them to evaluate the service quality provided by the inflight caterer at each of the airports from which their flights originate. They can also develop standardized cost projections for the preparation of the menu item. One criteria for evaluating the services of an inflight caterer will be the caterer's ability to accurately and consistently prepare the menu items for all classes of service from the recipes provided at the desired quality level and at the appropriate cost.

The recipes that are to be used are delivered to the inflight caterers as a part of the total menu package when new menus are to be implemented. Whenever possible each recipe should include a picture of the finished product as it should be plated or otherwise made ready for boarding on the aircraft. Figures 5.8 and 5.9 illustrate recipes that were developed by two different airlines.

Note that the recipe illustrated in Figure 5.8 requires the person preparing this cold plate to refer to other recipes in the manual to find out how to prepare the components, such as the marinated shrimp or the orange mango sauce, although the directions for slicing the squash and placing the items on the plate are indicated in the recipe. In comparison, the recipe in Figure 5.9 indicates all of the preparation steps that are necessary to prepare this sandwich, although the specifications for the items to be used are indicated elsewhere in the airline's catering manual.

TO BEGIN

Warm roasted nuts
served with your preferred
cocktail or beverage

APPETIZERS

An array of hot appetizers
including curried beef roulade,
chicken saté and crab cakes,
accompanied by a Korean barbecue sauce

SALAD

A contemporary blend of spinach, Belgian and curly endive
with a colorful garnish of red pepper strips,
yellow cherry tomato and orange and grapefruit sections

Offered with your choice
of basil vinaigrette
or Japanese ginger dressing

Freshly baked bread
and assorted rolls with butter

EXECUTIVE MEAL OPTION

If you should prefer more time to work or relax,
we suggest this complete meal presented all at once,
whenever you wish.

Steamed Maine lobster
served chilled on a bed of romaine lettuce
with a red skin potato salad seasoned with dill,
accompanied by green asparagus

Fresh fruit offered with
Gouda, Jarlsberg and cheddar cheese

Fruit cobbler

ENTREES

The Chef's Preference
The choice center cut of salmon steak
grilled to perfection and enhanced by lobster dill butter
Turned vegetables   Grilled red pepper
Couscous jardinière

Rack of Lamb
Tender rack of lamb seasoned with herbs
and complemented by a natural sauce
flavored with mint
Small green beans   Grilled red pepper
Roasted red skin potatoes

Chicken Forestière
Baked breast of free-range chicken
served with a medley of forest mushrooms
Couscous and wild rice   Buttered baby carrots

Lighter Fare
Steamed Maine lobster
served chilled on a bed of romaine lettuce
with a red skin potato salad seasoned with dill
Fresh green asparagus

FRUIT AND CHEESE

Select American and imported cheeses
accompanied by fresh seasonal fruit and assorted cheese biscuits,
served with aged port wine

DESSERT CART

Featuring a choice of decorated yogurt mousse
or Häagen-Dazs™ vanilla ice cream with a fruit topping,
offered with fresh whipped cream

INTERNATIONAL COFFEES

Freshly brewed Colombian coffee with a splash of your favorite liqueur
topped with whipped cream

Italiano with Amaretto   Royal with Cognac
Français with Grand Marnier
Mexican with Kahlúa   Scottish with Drambuie
Irish with Baileys Irish Cream

Premium international teas with a choice of milk or lemon

We apologize if occasionally your choice is not available

FIGURE 5.7 An important consideration for airlines flying international routes is having their first-class menus written in multiple languages so that most passengers may read the menu offerings. This menu is an example of one airline's BusinessFirst-class menu written in both English and German. (Courtesy of Continental Airlines)

ZU BEGINN

Warme, geröstete Nüsse
mit Ihrem Lieblingscocktail oder Getränk

VORSPEISEN

Verschiedene warme Vorspeisen
einschließlich Rinderbrustroulade mit Curry
Hühnchenspießchen und Krabbenkuchen
mit koreanischer Barbecuesauce

SALAT

Spinat, Chicorée und Friséesalat,
garniert mit roten Paprikastreifen,
einer gelben Kirschtomate, Orangen- und Pampelmusenscheiben

Basilikum-Vinaigrette
oder
japanisches Ingwerdressing

Frisch gebackenes Brot
und Auswahl von Brötchen mit Butter

EXECUTIVE MEAL OPTION

Falls Sie mehr Zeit zum Arbeiten oder Ruhen benötigen,
empfehlen wir diese vollständige Mahlzeit,
die jederzeit auf Wunsch gereicht wird.

Gedämpfter Hummer aus Maine
kalt auf römischem Salat serviert
mit rotem Kartoffelsalat mit Dill
grüner Spargel

Frische Früchte mit
Gouda, Jarlsberg und Cheddar

Fruchttorte

HAUPTSPEISEN

Empfehlung des Küchenchefs
Gegrilltes Lachsfilet
mit Hummer-Dill-Butter
Tourniertes Gemüse   Gegrillte rote Paprikaschoten
Couscous Jardinière

Lammkarree
Zartes Lammkarree gewürzt mit Kräutern
gereicht mit einem mit Minze
abgeschmeckten Bratensaft
Junge grüne Bohnen   Gegrillte rote Paprikaschoten
Rote Bratkartoffeln

Hühnchen Forestière
Gebackene Hühnchenbrust
gereicht mit einer Waldpilzmischung
Couscous und wilder Reis   Gebutterte kleine Karotten

Leichte Mahlzeit
Gedämpfter Hummer aus Maine
kalt auf römischem Salat serviert
mit rotem Kartoffelsalat mit Dill
Frischer grüner Spargel

FRÜCHTE UND KÄSE

Feine amerikanische und importierte Käsesorten,
frische Früchte, ausgewählte Käsebiscuits
und Portwein

NACHSPEISEN

Eine Wahl von
Joghurtmousse
oder Häagen-Dazs™ Vanilleeis mit Früchten
gereicht mit frischer Schlagsahne

INTERNATIONALE KAFFEESORTEN

Frisch gefilterter kolumbianischer Kaffee mit einem Schuß Ihres Lieblingslikörs
bedeckt mit Schlagsahne

Italienisch mit Amaretto   Royal mit Cognac
Französisch mit Grand Marnier
Mexikanisch mit Kahlúa   Schottisch mit Drambuie
Irisch mit Baileys Irish Cream

Vorzügliche internationale Teesorten mit Milch oder Zitrone

Wir bitten um Verständnis, falls Ihre Wahl nicht erhältlich ist

FIGURE 5.7 (Continued)

FOOD AND BEVERAGE SPECIFICATIONS

RECIPE NUMBER RC 16915

DESCRIPTION: SALAD, SOUTHWESTERN ORZO

PASTA

SALADS

EFFECTIVE DATE: 03/30/94
PRINT DATE: 03/09/94

INGREDIENT/ RECIPE NBR	DESCRIPTION	* QTY	UM	PORTION DESC	* QTY	UM	BRAND
IG 14339	CORN, FRZN, WHL KRNL, IQF	0	—		100	OUNCE	SIMPLOT
IG 102390	PEPPER, RED BELL, FRESH	0	—		40	OUNCE	LOCAL PURCHASE
RC 16974	BEANS, BLACK	0	—		80	OUNCE	
* RC 17738	CILANTRO, FRESH, CHOPPED, OUNCES/GRAMS	0	—		16	OUNCE	
RC 12356	ORZO PASTA	0	—		320	OUNCE	
RC 11916	WILD RICE	0	—		80	OUNCE	
IG 451990	SALT	0	—		2	OUNCE	NOT BRAND SPECIFIC
IG 8014	PEPPER, WHITE	0	—		1	OUNCE	NOT BRAND SPECIFIC
IG 400840	LIME JUICE	0	—		24	OUNCE	NOT BRAND SPECIFIC
IG 350540	OLIVE OIL	0	—		24	OUNCE	NOT BRAND SPECIFIC
IG 8092	RICE WINE VINEGAR	0	—		48	OUNCE	NOT BRAND SPECIFIC

INSTRUCTIONS:

- PREPARE ITEMS PER RECIPE.
- DEFROST CORN UNDER REFRIGERATION.
- SEED RED PEPPER AND CUT INTO SMALL DICE.
- CHOP CILANTRO.

```
- COMBINE ALL INGREDIENTS AND MIX WELL.
- COVER AND REFRIGERATE.

YIELD:
------
      660 OUNCES

PURCHASING SOURCE
-------------------------------------------------------------------------------
COMPONENT NUMBER   DESCRIPTION                  REFERENCE NUMBER   BRAND                SOURCE
-------------------------------------------------------------------------------
IG  14335          CORN, FRZN, WHL, KRNL, IQF   FB 0000003         SIMPLOT              FOOD & BEV. PURCHASE
IG  102390         PEPPER, RED BELL, FRESH      FB 0000003         LOCAL PURCHASE       FOOD & BEV. PURCHASE
IG  451990         SALT                         LP 0000001         NOT BRAND SPECIFIC   LOCAL PURCHASE
IG  8014           PEPPER, WHITE                LP 0000001         NOT BRAND SPECIFIC   LOCAL PURCHASE
IG  400840         OLIVE OIL                    LP 0000001         NOT BRAND SPECIFIC   LOCAL PURCHASE
IG  8092           RICE WINE VINEGAR            LP 0000001         NOT BRAND SPECIFIC   LOCAL PURCHASE
-------------------------------------------------------------------------------
```

Courtesy of American Airlines.

FIGURE 5.8 An example of a recipe (food and beverage specification) used by one airline. Note that there are two columns of codes preceding the ingredient description in the recipe. In order to prepare this recipe, the sub-recipe identified by those codes must be located and used, as well. Note also that, in some instances, the brand of product to be used is specified in the recipe.

RECIPE: TURKEY SANDWICH ON FOCCACIA ROLL   3.212.22
                 W. TOMATO AND OLIVES

YIELD: 1 ea

INGREDIENTS:	QUANTITY Or WEIGHT:	SOURCE Or PAGE REFERENCE:
Foccacia roll w. tomato and olives/sliced	1 ea	Ch 5
Turkey breast/sliced/0.9 oz ea	4 sl	Ch 5
Spinach leaves/stem removed	1/16 oz	Local
Pesto sauce	1/8 oz	Ch 5

PREPARATION STEPS:

1. Thaw Foccacia roll.
2. Remove stems from spinach.
3. Arrange spinach evenly on bottom of roll.
4. Spread pesto sauce onto spinach.
5. Fold each individual turkey slice in half.
6. Arrange on top of spinach with pesto sauce, by slightly overlapping the slices. If needed, fold turkey slices again to keep all turkey within the roll.

Notes: **This sandwich must be prepared fresh daily.**
       Leftover sandwiches cannot be used the next day.

FIGURE 5.9 An example of a different recipe format used by another airline. Note that, here too, the caterer's personnel must refer to other sections of the airline's catering manual for product specifications and other details concerning the ingredients to be used in the recipe. (Courtesy of Continental Airlines)

DEVELOPMENT OF SPECIFICATIONS FOR ALL PRODUCTS USED

An important responsibility of an airline's foodservice division is the determination of the specific products to be used, along with the specifications for all of these products. Product identification is usually quite specific (for example, see recipe in Figure 5.8). While it may be a generic specification for a product such as a fresh banana or an apple, the specification will state the size of the fruit to be served, and it may also specify a particular variety as appropriate (such as a Red Delicious or a Jonathan apple). The specification may also be by a specific brand name or product identification code for items such as cracker packets or the frozen entrees used for coach-class meals.

Figure 5.10 illustrates product specifications that may be prepared by an airline. Figure 5.10 lists a breakfast menu and not only indicates the recipe and the procedure for preparing the fresh fruit garnish to be used on the tray, but it also identifies the specific products to be used on the tray, the brand name specified for the products, and the purveyors' stock numbers for these items. Since this is a first-class menu where the passengers are offered a choice in their breakfast item selection, the load factor, or the proportion of the passenger count to be used as the count for boarding the several items, is also indicated in the far right-hand column of the specification sheet. For example, if the first-class passenger count is 10 for a flight, then 5 frozen bagels will be boarded (load factor = 0.5 or load × 0.5), and the bagels used will be plain, frozen Twin City bagels, stock number TWN0010.

Depending on the product and an airline's specific arrangement, the supplier to be used by the inflight caterer as the source of the product may also be identified, as was the case for most of the items used on the menu illustrated in Figure 5.10. The airlines may choose to specify the supplier that is to be used for two reasons: (1) to further ensure that the food items they serve are consistent from one flight to another, no matter where they originate from, and (2) to help maintain their budget constraints because they have negotiated a volume-related purchase price with a particular supplier. This purchase price would be jeopardized and probably could not be matched if each caterer purchased the product from a source of their own choosing.

Even for items seemingly as standardized as preportioned cuts of meats where wholesalers are uniformly aware of the specifications identified in the *Meat Buyers' Guide,* a particular supplier may be specified for a particular meat item. Since the *Meat Buyers' Guide* is used as the standard for meat purchase specifications throughout the United States, it would seem likely that a wholesaler in Boston would provide the same piece of meat for a particular specification number as would a wholesaler in Dallas. However, the product consistency may not be at the level required by the airline. Not only is the meat component of an entree likely to be the highest cost element of the meal, but, being the center of the plate, it is also often important to a diner's perception of meal quality. An airline, feeling that it cannot take a chance with an inconsistent meat product or the possibility that some passengers will get a substandard piece of meat will generally set very rigid purchase and source specifications.

DETERMINATION OF PACKAGING AND PRESENTATION SPECIFICATIONS

When menu items are being developed, the airline's foodservice staff must also consider how the menu will be packaged and presented to the passen-

MENU:	BB 3	Regional Revision #03-12-94	PAGE 1
CYCLE:	1		
EFFECTIVE:	08/24/94—REVISION # 1		
SUPERCEDES:	08/24/94		

MENU—COMPLETE #1

1. FRUIT	FRESH FRUIT GARNISH #1	1 EA
2. FRUIT	PETITE BANANA	1 EA
3. MILK	2% LOWFAT MILK—4 OZ	.5 EA
4. ROLL	BAGEL, PLAIN, FROZEN	.5 EA
5. ROLL	BLUEBERRY MUFFIN, UNWRAPPED	.5 EA
6. BUTTER	CLASSIC BLEND CUP	.75 EA
7. CONDIMENT	CREAM CHEESE, BREAKSTONE, SQUEEZE PAK	.5 EA
8. SANDWICH	CHEDDAR EGG CROISSANT	.8 EA
9. CEREAL	OAT SQUARE CEREAL	.4 EA
10. CEREAL	TOTAL CEREAL	.4 EA
11. YOGURT	YOGURT, NW	.5 EA

1.	FRUIT FRESH FRUIT GARNISH #1	
	LETTUCE LEAF LINER MED	1 EA
	ORANGE SLICE, 4 CUT, SEEDLESS, PEELED, 88 CT	2 EA
	STRAWBERRY, FRESH, MEDIUM, STEM ON	1 EA
	YIELD:	1 PORT

1. PLACE LETTUCE LEAF LINER ON THE LEFT SIDE OF THE 9″ PLATE. LEAVE THE RIGHT SIDE OF PLATE OPEN FOR THE ENTREE OR CEREAL.
2. FAN STRAWBERRY. PLACE STRAWBERRY ABOVE THE SHINGLED ORANGES ON THE LETTUCE LEAF LINER.
3. COVER ENTIRE PLATE WITH SARAN.

2. FRUIT   PETITE BANANA
   LOCAL PURCHASE

3. MILK   2% LOWFAT MILK—4 OZ
   LOCAL PURCHASE

4. ROLL   BAGEL, PLAIN, FROZEN
   TWN0010, TWIN CITY BAGEL

5. ROLL   BLUEBERRY MUFFIN, UNWRAPPED
   SR08607, SARA LEE

6. BUTTER   CLASSIC BLEND CUP
   LL19705, LAND O'LAKES

7. CONDIMENT   CREAM CHEESE, BREAKSTONE, SQUEEZE PAK
   MAF6594, NATIONAL DAIRY PRODUCTS

FIGURE 5.10 An example of one airline's information presentation to the inflight caterers (as included in the airline's catering manual) which consolidates the menu to be served (here a first-class breakfast) with both the specifications for the products to be used and the load factors to be used for boarding the menu onto the aircraft without incorporating codes or requiring the caterer's employees to refer to other sections of the catering manual. (Courtesy of Northwest Airlines)

ger. Details on just how each meal or snack is to be packed in the boarding equipment as well as how it is to be prepared for presentation to the passenger must be specified in written instructions that must accompany the menus when they are presented to the caterer. It is highly desirable that the airline present a picture of each menu properly packaged for boarding as well as for presentation to the passenger. In the absence of an airline-provided picture, many caterers prepare a library of their own pictures for staff reference during product preparation and assembly.

Directions must consider even the smallest detail. For example, if a snack is to be packaged in a bag as is done now by some airlines, the order in which the items are to be put in the bag must be indicated. Does the apple go in last, on top of the sandwich and the brownie because it is a pretty topping for the bag, or does it go in first so that it will not smash the sandwich and the brownie? Does the sandwich go on top of the brownie or does the brownie go on top? If the bag is to be tied with a bow, how is the bow to be tied? Or, is the top of the bag to be turned down? If so, how many turns and how wide should a turn be? It may seem to be overkill on detail, but it must be remembered that there are as many ways to prepare a package of a product (such as a snack bag) as there are individuals assembling the components and putting them into the bags all across the country. Many airlines are now using clock terminology for their specifications. For example, their specification might be for the sandwich to be placed on the tray at the 3:00 position, the coleslaw at the 11:00 position, and so on until all of the items to be placed on the tray have been given a location corresponding to a time on a clockface. It is important to remember that if even the smallest detail is not specified, it will *not* be done consistently for all flights.

Figure 5.11 illustrates a tray setup description prepared by one airline to indicate what items are to be put on each tray for a particular menu, although it does not provide a picture or other detail of exactly where each item should be placed on the tray. The use of specific brand names for products, such as Ghiradelli Mints, Cabot Cheddar, Waverly Wafer Packets, or Walkers Chocolate Chip Shortbread, should be noted. The use of the specific brand name is, in itself, a specification for the product as the brand indicates a specific product with a specific level of quality. Note that the description indicates the size or number of each item to go on the tray as part of the setup and makes reference to a recipe number or other such description that specifies what that product is composed of.

Figures 5.12 to 5.16 also illustrate different types of tray setup descriptions that might be given to an airline's caterers. Figure 5.12 represents a cold breakfast tray setup which has a picture of the expected finished product. The items to be included on the tray are listed along with product code numbers to identify the specific packaging and condiment items that are to be used for this particular meal. Note that these code numbers refer only to the equipment items or entree dish (i.e., packing) and not the food

CODE DESCRIPTION: 189

FAMIS NO: 2302SE16

TITLE: TRAY SETUP

SERVICE LEVEL: MAIN CABIN

UNIT: 1-001

ITEM	PORTION	REFERENCE
SALAD		
BASIC SALAD MIX	1.75 OZ	5022
LITE RANCH SALAD DRESSING, .75 OZ IND.	1 EA	88-3F
SLICED BREAD PACKET	1 EA	88-3F
PROMISE MARGARINE	1 EA	88-3F
CHOCOLATE MACADAMIA NUT BOX	1 EA	88-3F

CODE DESCRIPTION: 190

FAMIS NO: 2402SE28

TITLE: TRAY SET UP, CYCLE #5

SERVICE LEVEL: MAIN CABIN

UNIT: 1-001

ITEM	PORTION	REFERENCE
SALAD		
BASIC SALAD MIX	1.75 OZ	5022
LITE CAESAR DRESSING, IND. .75 OZ	1 EA	88-3F
DINNER ROLL, 1 OZ	1 EA	88-3F
BUTTER, 60 CT, LIGHTLY SALTED	1 EA	88-3F
GHIRADELLI MINT	1 EA	88-3F
CABOT CHEDDAR .75 OZ	1 EA	88-3F
WAVERLY WAFER PKT	1 EA	88-3F
WALKERS CHOCOLATE CHIP SHORTBREAD	1 EA	88-3F

FIGURE 5.11 An approach to specifying the items to be included on passenger trays (the tray setup) for two menus used for coach-class service. Note that the number of each of the items to be placed on each tray is indicated as well as reference numbers to other sections in the airline's catering manual, which the caterer will need to refer to when purchasing or preparing the tray service items. (Courtesy of United Airlines)

items associated with the equipment. Recipes or other specifications for the food products to be used are not listed on this page of a catering manual, but could be found in other narrative sections of the manual. In this example, most of the products are branded products which would be purchased according to the specifications for those products and received in the caterer's kitchen ready to serve.

Figure 5.13 represents a hot breakfast tray setup, also with a picture of the tray as it should be prepared. Here, too, the specific model of the packaging to be used is indicated along with the number of each of the items to be used and the size of the item. However, the recipes to be used for the omelette, hash-browned potatoes, and canadian bacon are not specified. The omelette could be purchased frozen as a pop-out item, in which case a recipe would not be used; rather a specification for a particular omelette would be used.

Figure 5.14 illustrates a tray setup for a cold fruit and vegetable snack pack. Here, the items to be included on the tray and the weight or count for each item is listed. The size of the cut for items such as carrot sticks and broccoli florets would be indicated on the recipe for preparing these items unless they were purchased precut to specifications. The recipe numbers for preparing the tray components are not listed in this example.

Figure 5.15 is similar to the models shown in Figures 5.13 and 5.14 in terms of the content of the tray setup sheet. However, this figure illustrates the setup for a deli platter such as might be used for executive service on private business aircraft or for a special charter service. Here, the platter would be set up to serve several persons, as requested for the particular flight. During the flight, the flight attendants would serve the individual passengers the items they wanted from the platter. Or, in the case of some wide-body flights over long distances, the platter could become part of a buffet service from which the passengers help themselves.

Figure 5.16 is an example of a photo that might accompany a menu set distributed to an airline's caterers. While there are no specifics shown on the photo other than the number of the menu (L06), the cycle on which it appears (cycle 5), and the name of the entree item represented (Chicken Sandwich), all of the specifics such as recipe numbers, amounts to be served (i.e., 2 tomato slices), or product specifications are detailed on the documents included in the menu cycle set. The caterer would plan the production and tray setup schedule using the information sheets incorporated into the menu cycle. Then, during the actual tray setup or other product preparation activities, such as plating or garnishing, this photo would be made available to the personnel involved so that they could see what the finished product should be.

FOOD AND BEVERAGE SPECIFICATIONS
GRAPHICS MANUAL

DOM/CRB/MEX/HNL
BREAKFAST
TRAY SETUP
PG. Y-3

TSU - YC BRK CEREAL CAR - U.S.
EFFECTIVE: SEP 01-94
DOM/CRB/MEX/HNL REVISION: AUG 08-94   PG. Y-3

Touch of Butter	
Muffin	
Orange Juice	
Milk	
Entree Dish	DI-95
Napkin	
Flatware Pack With:	BA-60
Knife	KN-21
Spoon	SP-70
Meal Tray:	
727/S80/DC10-30/	TR-84
AB6	MA-108
767/DC10	TR-67
	MA-107

FIGURE 5.12   An example of an airline's use of graphics to illustrate their desired tray setup while also listing the items to be included on the tray and a code number referencing the specification for those items. (Courtesy of American Airline)

FBO CATERING SERVICES

Breakfast Standard Tray Set Up and Entree
Page: FB-04-03
Date: 3/92

Meal Tray ....1 each
Cutlery Pack 6 In 1 ....1 each
Side Dish ....1 each
Cup Bon Faire ....1 each
Entree Dish Aluminum 7800 Bon Faire ....1 each
Meal Mate Cracker ....1 each
Butter , P/C ....1 each
Muffin ....1 each
Orange Juice ....1 each

Setup - Fruit Starter
    Lettuce Liner ....1 each
    Cantaloupe ....1 each
    Pineapple Section ....1 each
    Strawberry ....1 each
    Parsley Sprig ....1 each

Entree #1   Cheese Omelette ....4 oz.
            Hash Browned Potatoes.. 2 oz.
            Canadian Bacon ....1.5 oz.

FIGURE 5.13 Another example of an illustrated tray-setup specification used by a caterer. (Courtesy of CA One Services, Inc.)

FBO CATERING SERVICES

Fruit & Vegetable Snack Pack
Page: FB-03-23
Date: 3/92

Green Grapes ....2 ounces
Red Grapes ....2 ounces
Apples Wedges, Red Delicious,88 ct., 10 cut....................................3 each
Celery Sticks ....3 each
Carrot Sticks ....3 each
Broccoli Floret, 1 oz. ea. ....1 each
Cauliflower Floret, 1 oz. ea. ....1 each
Lettuce Leaf Liner..1 each
Estes Mint ....1 each
Sour Cream & Chives Dip ....2 ounces
Parsley Sprig ....1 each
Plastic Cup with lid .... 1 each
Snack Tray - 3200 Bon Faire .... 1 each

FIGURE 5.14 An example of a fruit and vegetable snack tray setup specification with an illustration of the finished tray. (Courtesy of CA One Service, Inc.)

DETERMINATION OF CREW MEALS AND SPECIFICATIONS

At first glance, providing meals for the crew (pilots, flight officers, and flight attendants) seems simple enough. The flight attendants could simply give the flight deck crew (pilots and flight officers) a tray to eat at the same

FBO CATERING SERVICES

Deli Platter
Page: FB-03-04
Date: 3/92

Cure 81 Ham, slices ....5 ounces
Swiss Cheese, slice ....5 ounces
Corned Beef, slice ....5 ounces
Roasted Turkey Breast, slices ....5 ounces
Salami, Genoa, slices ....5 ounces
German Potato Salad ....10 ounces
Sweet Gerkin, midget ....5 each
Stuffed Olive ....5 each
Black Olive, medium, pitted ....5 each
Lettuce Leaf Liner ....5 each
Parsley Sprigs ....5 each
Mustard P/C ....5 each
Mayonnaise P/C ....5 each
Oval Rye Bread ....5 each
Oval Pumpernickel Bread ....5 each
Lace Doily ....3 each
Silver Disposable Tray, large, oval ....1 each
Silver Disposable Tray, small, oval ....1 each

Trays available for 1-6 passengers - quantity and arrangement for 5
passengers shown.

FIGURE 5.15 An example of a deli platter specification for a platter that might be used on private business aircraft or for charter service. (Courtesy of CA One Services, Inc.)

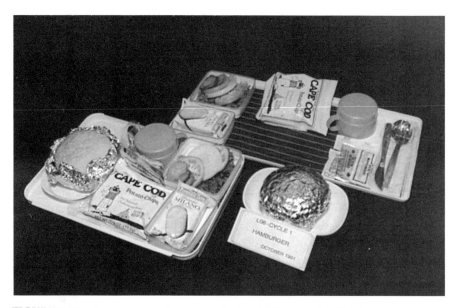

FIGURE 5.16 An example of a photo that an airline might distribute to caterers along with its cycle menu set to illustrate how the finished tray for each menu should look when it is boarded onto an aircraft. (Courtesy of CA One Services, Inc.)

time they are serving the passengers—the only decision being whether it should be a first-class or coach-class tray, or more likely, which of the first-class entrees should be served to the flight deck crew. Then, after they have served the passengers, the flight attendants could just eat whatever entrees or other tray components are left over since it seems likely there would be some spare trays on board every flight as a result of passenger refusals of the meals offered. However, the process is not as simple as it seems, and all airlines have very specific crew meal policies and specifications which caterers must adhere to. Whether an airline has special crew meals or not is generally a matter of its labor agreements. Flight deck and cabin crews may have different contractual provisions regarding their meals.

Generally, when crew meals are scheduled or ordered, their requirements are factored into the choices offered in first class, business class, or coach (depending on the airline's policy) to be sure that there are choices available to all of the passengers seated in these classes of service. If a flight is fully booked, there may not be space to board additional meals that are specially prepared for the flight crew. However, it is common practice when crew meals are provided to board a specially prepared captain's meal that is composed of foods different from the other meals as a safety precaution against an outbreak of food-borne illness that might otherwise affect all of the flight deck crew, jeopardizing their ability to control the flight of the aircraft.

This approach may be fine unless you are a member of the flight crew flying the same flights over and over again. How many identical trays of lasagna or chicken salad or even first-class roast beef can people eat before they start to complain about the working conditions of their job? This is the situation faced by the flight crews on commercial passenger flights.

To avoid this problem, some airlines provide special meals for their flight crews. Inflight caterers may be provided with a special menu cycle for crew meals, but frequently the crew meals consist of the foods prepared for first-class service that are packaged in the coach-class reusable plastic serviceware. In many cases, provisions in the flight and cabin crews' union contract may address criteria for meals to be provided to flight crews while they are on board aircraft.

On extended flights, the physiological needs of the flight crew members, particularly those on the flight deck, becomes a factor in crew meal specifications. Crew members must be provided with meals and snacks not only to alleviate hunger, but also to provide them with the energy required to maintain alertness for the extended flight period. In this situation, the crew needs meals and snacks similar in composition to meals designed to meet the energy needs of an athlete participating in a competitive event, that is, meals high in carbohydrates and low in fat content.

If there is a separate menu cycle for crew meals, it too is prepared by the airline's foodservice division. While the product specifications for the crew menus may not be as precise as those for the passenger menus (if there is a separate cycle menu)—after all, variety to break the monotony is the objective here—the caterer is expected to provide the foods indicated on the menus and to insure that these meals are of top quality. Depending on the airline's attitude toward its flight crews and the presence or absence of language regarding crew inflight meals in union contracts, the quality of these meals may be equally or even more important, than the quality of any of the other meals boarded on an aircraft. An unhappy flight crew complaining about poor meals does not contribute to a smoothly running airline that provides positive, high-quality service to its passengers.

Figure 5.17 illustrates a crew lunch or dinner menu that has been used by one airline for its crew meal service. This menu would also be served to business-class passengers on flights longer than six hours.

In addition to hot crew menus, airlines may also have shelf-stable crew menus which are used to provide crew sustenance on flights where there is no scheduled meal service but the crew has been in flight long enough to be entitled to it. These meals might also be used to provide flight crews with meals from airports where the airline is providing only commissary service and no hot food preparation facilities are available. A shelf-stable breakfast menu might be a prepackaged donut or sweet roll, a snack-pack can of fruit, cheese-and-cracker packets, a snack-size box of raisins, and

The crew would have four entree choices:

ENTREE #1

NEW YORK STRIP STEAK
Wild Mushroom Mix with Cafe d'Paris Butter
Wild Rice Pancakes
Vegetable Medley
(Baby Zucchini, Baby Carrots/Green Onions
and Turned Yellow Squash)

ENTREE #2

FILLET OF SOLE, Stuffed
Lobster Sauce with Tarragon/Sherry & Dill
Oven Roasted Turned Potatoes
Vegetable Medley
(Baby Zucchini, Baby Carrots/Green Onions
and Turned Yellow Squash)

ENTREE #3

RANGE CHICKEN BREAST, Sauteed
Riesling Sauce & Garnish
Buttered Fresh Fettucini with Red Pepper
Turned Carrots and Baby Zucchini

ENTREE #4 (Lighter Fare)

BLACKENED SALMON COLD PLATE

Each entree is accompanied by:

Coach class **SALAD**: on Cycle 1, Rotation B, Domestic Flights
(or similar salad)

Coach class **SALAD DRESSING**: on Cycle 1,
Rotation A

Coach class **DESSERT**: on Cycle 1, Rotation C
(or similar dessert)
Coach class **ROLL**: on cycle 1, rotation B
BUTTER: according to Airline's specification

FIGURE 5.17 Example of a crew lunch/dinner menu for an international flight. (Note that the same menu would be served to business-class passengers on this flight as it exceeds six hours in length.) (Courtesy of Continental Airlines.)

an individual box of cereal. A shelf-stable lunch or dinner might consist of a 3.5-ounce can of tuna, a mayonnaise packet, a packet of crackers, a snack-pack can of fruit, a snack-size box of raisins, a prepackaged dessert item, and an instant soup pack. These shelf-stable crew meals would be packed into snack boxes for the crew to carry onto the plane.

AIRLINE NEGOTIATION OF PURCHASING CONTRACTS WITH SUPPLIERS

The responsibility for procurement of the foods, beverages, and supplies is divided between the airline and its caterers. Responsibilities of the airline's foodservice division include the negotiation of purchase contracts with suppliers for many of the products to be used on the planned menus. In some instances, the airline believes that it can obtain better pricing (thus reduce the cost of its inflight foodservices) by purchasing products directly from the manufacturer (the supplier) of the product. Sometimes the airline works with the supplier to develop products specifically designed to meet the airline's needs. When such products are developed, the airline usually commits to the purchase of a specified minimum quantity of the product for its food and beverage services. Without such a purchase commitment, the supplier would generally be unwilling to commit the resource necessary to develop a specialized product for the airline.

Direct Purchases by the Airlines

In instances such as these just noted, the airline contracts directly with the supplier to purchase the specified product for use on its flights' meal or beverage service. Generally, these products are then delivered directly to the caterer's facilities, either by the supplier or through a distributor with whom the supplier works. Distributors that focus on the airline industry and provide a significant amount of the distribution service to inflight caterers include Sage Enterprises, Inc. and the Michael Lewis Company, both headquartered near Chicago, Illinois, as well as Bunzl Distributors USA, headquartered in Edison, New Jersey. While these distributors are national in scope, others such as Air Stream Foods in Oceanside, New York focus on niche markets within the airline industry. Air Stream, for example, focuses on the New York area while also serving some other East Coast markets.

At the inflight kitchen, the caterer is responsible for (1) documenting receipt of the foods, (2) storing the products, and (3) seeing that they are properly used only for that particular airline's catering. Usually, the caterer maintains a par stock level of these products and orders new deliveries of them from the supplier (or distributor) when stocks run down to a predetermined order point. The caterer uses the airline's open purchase order number when the order is placed. Thus the supplier (or the distributor) bills the airline directly for the purchase, although the order is placed by the caterer, and the products are delivered to the caterer's kitchen.

The airline's foodservice division, in conjunction with its purchasing department, is responsible for negotiating and monitoring any contracts that may be developed for these direct purchase items. The airline's inflight foodservice division determines the specifications for the products desired—whether it is a product that already exists on the market or one that is to be developed specifically for the airline. The airline's purchasing department then puts the product specifications out for bid. Interested suppliers prepare competitive bid proposals, and the bids received are evaluated on the basis of how well they fit the product specifications, the price quoted for the product, and the services provided. The bid is awarded to the supplier best meeting the specifications at the best price.

When the airlines purchase products directly, the products so purchased are always the property of the airline. Even though they are delivered to the inflight caterer's warehouse, the caterer is *never* the owner of these items. However, the caterer is responsible for accounting for and safekeeping any such products delivered directly to the caterer's kitchen facilities.

Thus, a challenge faced by the inflight caterer is finding appropriate storage space for the items purchased by the airline and shipped to the caterer. Because these products are the property of the individual airlines served by the caterer, products belonging to one airline cannot be used for another, even if the two airlines use identical products (such as cans of the same brand of soft drinks). Therefore the caterer must provide separate storage areas for these products to insure that inventories are properly maintained and the products are used as they should be. If a product was not the property of the airline but was the property of the caterer, when airline specifications allowed the use of a common product the caterer would need to hold only one stock of the product in storage, reducing its storage needs.

When products are used that are purchased directly by the airline, caterers do not charge the airline for the cost of the product as that cost was paid directly to the supplier by the airline. However, they *do* charge a handling and storage fee for the product, as it is used, to offset the operating costs that they incur for the product.

Purchasing by the Caterer

Other items are sourced and purchased directly by the caterer for use on the meals provided to one or more airlines. In this situation, the caterer prepares the specification for the product (multiuse items) or uses the specification provided by the airline. Just as the airline purchasing department did, the caterer's purchasing department requests bids for the desired products based on the product specifications, reviews the bids received, and purchases from the most cost-effective suppliers.

Usually, the caterer needs to separate the storage of the products that are purchased and owned by the catering firm from those products that belong to the airline, for the purposes of inventory management and product accountability. As they are needed, the caterer-owned products are used in the preparation and packaging of the airlines' meals. Since the products belong to the caterer and not the airline, the airline is charged for the products, whether they are components of a meal or expendable supplies sold to the airline. Here, detail is important. Even if the product is a small item, such as a soufflé cup, the items used for a flight must be counted, and an appropriate price charged to the airline for the product issues.

Purchasing of Liquor Supplies

Liquor purchasing is somewhat different from the purchasing of food products and supplies. The airlines write the specifications for the liquor products to be boarded on their flight, just as they do for food and all other products used. However, the inflight caterer does *not* purchase the beer, wine, or spirits used on flights as most caterers do not have a liquor license, a requirement for any firm to purchase any type of liquor products wholesale. Depending on the state's liquor regulations, a caterer may have to have a warehouse license to be able to store liquor for the airlines.

Thus, all liquor products must be purchased by the airline, either through a prepaid arrangement with the distributor or through an arrangement whereby the charges are directly invoiced to the airline. Because of the strict legal controls associated with liquor sales and distribution, if a liquor delivery came to an inflight caterer's facility as a C.O.D. purchase or if it came directed to the caterer rather than to the airline (the purchasing entity), the caterer must refuse the delivery. The caterer is only a holding and distribution facility for liquor products, just as it is for any other type of products purchased directly by the airline. However, as noted, depending on the state regulations, the caterer may have to maintain a warehouse license to fulfill their holding and distribution responsibilities.

Another unique consideration regarding the purchasing of liquor for flights is that some states require that all liquor boarded in that state be purchased in that state while other states allow the airlines to fly their liquor supplies in from other states. For example, if states allow liquor purchased elsewhere to be flown in for boarding purposes, an airline might be able to make an arrangement with a distributor near their corporate office or some other convenient location which would provide them with discounted pricing for large-quantity purchases. The airline would then fly the liquor needed at the different catering facilities to those facilities as company freight on flights going to those destinations and deliver the liquor to the caterer there.

On the other hand, if a state required that all liquor boarded on flights in that state be purchased there, the airline would have to originate a purchase order for liquor supplies in its home office. This purchase order would be sent to a liquor distributor in the state in which the liquor was to be used. On receipt of the purchase order, the distributor would deliver the liquor supplies to the in-state caterer(s) and then invoice the airline for the charges, after the caterer okayed the invoice for payment (i.e., indicated that the liquor supplies charged on the invoice had indeed been received).

DETERMINATION OF MEAL AND SNACK SERVICE POLICIES

Airline staff responsibilities include the development of the service schedule for the meals. This schedule indicates which menus should be served on which flights and the rotation in which the menus should be served. Generally, the decision about the type of meal to be served on a particular flight is a function of the time of day that the flight originates, the distance the flight is going (a determinate of the time the passengers are on board the aircraft), the direction in which the flight is going when time zones are crossed during the flight, and the class of service.

Generally, the airlines will try to structure meal service patterns that will help passengers get adjusted to the time zone of their destination. For example, passengers boarding a direct flight to New York which leaves San Francisco at 6:00 P.M. and has a short stopover in Salt Lake City would probably not receive a meal on this flight. At most, they might be served a small snack during the fairly short San Francisco to Salt Lake City leg. However, Salt Lake City is in the Mountain time zone while San Francisco is in the pacific time zone. It was already 7:00 P.M. in Salt Lake by the time the flight left, and well beyond mealtime by the time the flight touched down there. The longer flight leg, from Salt Lake City to New York, occurred well within a nonmeal time period.

In comparison, passengers on a direct flight to San Francisco, leaving from New York City at 6:00 P.M. (Eastern time zone) with a short stopover in Salt Lake City would quite likely receive dinner on their flight. Although it is 6:00 P.M. in New York when they leave, it is only 4:00 P.M. in Salt Lake City and 3:00 P.M. in San Francisco. Thus, the flight would arrive in Salt Lake City, probably sometime between 7:00 and 8:00 P.M., and a dinner would probably be served to all classes of passengers enroute from New York as that leg of the flight occurred during a normal dinner service period, based on Salt Lake City time. It is also a long flight leg with ample time for a full meal service. Since the leg from Salt Lake City to San Francisco would be outside of a meal period (as well as being a rather short flight), passengers would probably receive only beverage service here. Thus, because of time zone considerations, two flights leaving their point of origin at exactly the same time would have completely different meal service patterns.

To further illustrate this concept, on a flight departing at 6:00 A.M. going only 100 to 200 miles, first-class passengers might be given only beverages/cocktail service and orange juice. Some airlines would not serve cocktails this early in the day and would offer only coffee, soft drinks, and juices. Coach-class passengers on the same flight would definitely not get any liquor service and may or may not get any beverage service at all because of the limited flight time for this distance.

However, according to some airlines' meal policies, first-class passengers leaving at 6:00 A.M. on a flight going 1,400 miles would get a tray service breakfast with a choice between hot entrees and one cold entree. Coach-class passengers on that same flight might also get a tray service breakfast, but there would generally be no choice. These passengers would all receive a cold entree breakfast. In some cases, coach-class passengers may have to be on a flight of at least 1,600 miles before they are offered a choice in breakfast entrees, if they receive any choice at all. This type of meal service pattern is similar for other time periods throughout the day.

The inflight caterer is responsible for following the meal service schedule defined by the individual airline when preparing and boarding meals for a particular flight. Boarding a full meal when only a snack is specified will result in excess costs for the caterer, as the airline will pay only for the specified snack. Boarding errors will be disruptive for the flight crews, as well. They may be expecting a particular type of meal for service on a particular flight. Errors may lead to the flight attendants' having insufficient time or staff to serve the incorrect food supplies put on the aircraft or may lead to dissatisfied passengers if only a snack is boarded when a full meal should have been provided, according to the airline's meal schedule pattern.

DETERMINATION OF MEAL SERVICE PROCEDURES

The procedures that the flight attendants will use to serve the meal, snack, or beverages scheduled for a particular type of flight are also determined by the airline's foodservice division. The inflight caterer, however, may be less concerned with the actual service procedures than with many of the other aspects of the total menu planning and meal service process. The actual service of the meal on board the aircraft is done by the airline's flight attendants. The airline provides them with very specific procedures regarding the service sequence, the handling of the food, arrangement of the trays, and sometimes the plating of the food if that is a component of

APPETIZER:
Assorted Hot Appetizers with Pesto (PEH-stoh) Dipping Sauce
Boarded in large ceramic dish, 1 unit for 4 customers.
Crab Claw Gratin with Portuguese Sauce and dipped in Parmesan Cheese.
Chicken Brochette (broh-SHEHT) - mini-kebab, tikka.

<u>Special Instructions:</u> Dip is boarded separately in a butter ramekin (do not heat),
place on medium plate with choice of appetizers. Customer serving is 3 items and
1 dipping sauce.

Recommended Wines: White - Labouré-Roi Chassagne-Montrachet 1990
                             Red - Carruades de Château Lafite Rothschild Pauillac 1986
Salad Dressing: herb vinaigrette or red pepper

360°/5-8 min.

ENTREE: Chef's Preference - **Medallions of Venison**
With a flavorful mustard and fruit sauce.
Basmati (bahs-MAH tee) and Wild Rice - a variety from India with a nutty,
buttery aroma.
Vegetable Stir-Fry

<u>Special Instructions:</u> Place veal medallions on lower half of plate. Arrange
vegetable stir-fry on top left of plate and rice on top right. Pour mustard fruit
sauce over half of meat. Garnish with parsley.

Recommended Wines: Red - E. Guigal 1990 Châteauneuf du Pape Côtes-du-Rhone
                             1991 Franciscan Napa Valley Cabernet Sauvignon

360°/15-18 min.

ENTREE: **Chicken Supreme**
Grilled boneless breast of corn-fed chicken complemented by a black currant sauce.
William Potatoes
Baby Turnip, Carrot and Fennel

<u>Special Instructions:</u> Spoon a small portion of sauce in the lower center of plate,
placing the chicken on top. Arrange the potatoes and the vegetables clockwise from
the top left of plate. Garnish center with parsley.

Recommended Wines: White - 1992 Lyeth Sonoma Chardonnay
                             Red - Carruades de Château Lafite Rothschild Pauillac 1986

360°/12-15 min.

ENTREE: **Herbed Trout**
Fillet of Trout in an herb sauce with Maître d'Hôtel (MAY-truh doh-TELL) butter.
Red Cabbage Parcel
Baby Carrots
Turned Zucchini (zoo-KEE-nee)
Potatoes Parisienne (Puh-ree zee EHN) - small, turned round potatoes.
<u>Special Instructions:</u> Place the fillet in the lower center of plate; top with the maître
d'hôtel butter. Arrange the potatoes, carrots, zucchini and cabbage parcel clockwise
above fillet. Serve with wrapped lemon-half on plate. Garnish with dill sprig and
puff pastry.
Recommended Wines: White - Labouré-Roi Chassagne-Montrachet 1990
                             1992 Lyeth Sonoma Chardonnay

360°/12-15 min.

ENTREE: Executive Meal/Lighter Fare - **Roasted Tenderloin of Beef**
Served chilled on a bed of garden greens with creamed horseradish and garnished
with a yellow cherry tomato, radish and asparagus tips.
Grilled Artichoke
Cucumber Crown - with Cumberland sauce, a red currant and port wine sauce.

<u>Special Instructions:</u> No preparation needed.

Recommended Wines: Red - E. Guigal 1990 Châteauneuf du Pape Côtes-du-Rhone
                             1991 Franciscan Napa Valley Cabernet Sauvignon

FIGURE 5.18   This galley attendant briefing sheet (GABS) has the dual function
of providing meal preparation and service directions to the flight attendants and

CHEESES: Carriebyrne, Blue Shropshire, Cheddar, Stilton crock.

DESSERTS: Chocolate layer gâteau (ga-TOE) or fruits of the Forest Mirror; whipped cream.
Between Movie Treat: LGW-IAH/DEN only:
Ice cream sundae with chocolate and butterscotch sauce.
Special Instructions: Warm chocolate sauce, bring butterscotch to room temperature.

INFLIGHT CHAMPAGNE:
Lanson Brut 1988 (lahn-sown broot). Lanson's grapes are cultivated in the very best vineyards of Champagne. A harmonious blend of Pinot Noir and Chardonnay grapes yields a well balanced wine of straw-yellow color with a delicate froth and fine, vivacious bubbles. Exuding aromas of sweet spices and fresh fennel, this classic Champagne has great body and a sharp finish.
WHITE WINES:
Labouré-Roi Chassagne-Montrachet 1990 (Lah-boo-ray rwah Sha-san-yuh mon-trah-shay). This very rich but balanced French Chardonnay is golden in color and has toasted hazelnut aromas that perfectly compliment citrus and pineapple flavors.
1992 Lyeth Sonoma Chardonnay (LYE-eth soh-NOH-ma shar-duh-NAY) - This wine has a fine nose of fruit and a light vanilla tone with a rich and round body. Fine "lies," the light yeasts remaining with the wine after fermentation, bring complexity, fullness, body, and good balance to the wine.
RED WINES:
Carruades de Château Lafite Rothschild Pauillac 1986 (Kahr-wahd duh sha-toh la-feet rott-sheeld Poh-yak). This elegant ruby red-colored French wine is characterized by ripe soft currant aromas, spicy oak scents and soft tannins.
1991 Franciscan Napa Valley Cabernet Sauvignon - This cabernet has good complexity and harmony among tannin, cherry, and plum flavors, with aromas of vanilla derived from aging in oak barrels. The 1991 vintage is excellent to drink today, especially in-flight, where young wines are at their best.
E. Guigal 1990 Châteauneuf du Pape Côtes-du-Rhone (Shah-tow-nuhff doo pahp Coat doo rohn). Guigal's deep red-colored French wine, loaded with black cherry fruit, is aged in oak barrels for two to three years before its release. It is full-bodied with an aromatic complexity, and it rests long and rich on the palate.
PORT WINE:

CONTINENTAL
BUSINESSFIRST/TRANSCON
CATERING SURVEY WORKSHEET

FLT # _____   FROM_____
DATE _____   TO _____
ZONE _____(A/B/U-D)   # CUSTOMERS _____
WORKED   IN YOUR ZONE

ENTREES	**#BOARDED**	**#REQUESTED**	**+/-**	**COMMENTS**
LUNCH/DINNER (as applicable)				
BEEF/RED MEAT	_____	_____	_____	_____
POULTRY	_____	_____	_____	_____
SEAFOOD	_____	_____	_____	_____
COLD PLATE	_____	_____	_____	_____
EXECUTIVE MEAL	_____	_____	_____	_____
JAPANESE MEAL	_____	_____	_____	_____
(HNL/NRT only)				
BREAKFAST/BRUNCH (as applicable)				
HOT EGGS	_____	_____	_____	_____
COLD PLATE	_____	_____	_____	_____
CEREAL/FRUIT	_____	_____	_____	_____
HOT FRENCH TOAST	_____	_____	_____	_____
HOT BRUNCH ITEMS	_____	_____	_____	_____
RED EYE SNACKS				
HOT ENTREE	_____	_____	_____	_____
COLD PLATE	_____	_____	_____	_____
PRE ARRIVAL 2ND SERVICES (as applicable)				
SANDWICH TRAYS	_____	_____	_____	_____
CHEESE/GRAPE TRAYS	_____	_____	_____	_____

Please list any other items you run short of, have excess of, or any comments:
_____
_____
_____
_____
_____
_____

Thanks for filling out this form to better our services. Deposit completed form with Base IPM.

(IPM - Please forward to Dining Services/GTWDS)

providing them with a form for comments regarding the food and the inflight caterer's services. This GABS is for first-class service on an international flight. (Courtesy of Continental Airlines)

the service provided to first-class passengers (as when cart service is called for).

Still, it is preferable for the inflight caterer to know what these service procedures are. The caterer must be sure that all required items are packed in the right quantity and location on the aircraft, and must be sure that the tray setup that it is doing matches that indicated to the flight attendants in their service procedures.

It is particularly important for the caterer to be aware of the service procedures specified for first-class service where plating and other enhancements may require special items to be packed as part of the boarding complement. Sometimes, the inflight caterer may be provided copies of the specified service procedures to be included in the boarding equipment with the meal components, again particularly for specialized first-class service. Sometimes airlines require that these directions be included. Including these directions with the meal service items means that the flight attendants have a how-to reference at their fingertips during the flight. Having this reference available may help them avoid service errors which could later be reported to the airline as problems for which the caterer may be held accountable even though the errors were not the caterer's fault. Figure 5.18 illustrates one such form which provides service directions for the flight attendants as well as providing them with space to comment about the products and equipment boarded for their use during the flight.

It is sometimes easy to forget that the flight attendants are not, first and foremost, in the foodservice business. They have limited training in food handling and service, with the bulk of their training focused on passenger management, safety procedures, handling of emergencies, and so on. Thus, the more caterers are aware of the service requirements, the more they are able to do to be sure that the flight attendants are able to complete the service as expeditiously as possible in the desired manner. After all, the way the service is done affects passengers' perception of the food and beverage service offered by the airline which, in turn, affects the airline's perception of the inflight caterer and its willingness to continue to do business with the caterer.

SUMMARY

The provision of high-quality inflight food and beverage services is contingent upon a close, positive working relationship between the airline and its inflight caterer. To achieve that relationship, it is important for each party to understand the needs and concerns of the other and how they can work together for their mutual benefit. Today, there is an increased sense of partnership between the airline, the inflight caterer, and the suppliers of products needed for inflight foodservices. Each member of this group has specific responsibilities which it must fulfill. All members of the group must recognize the contributions of the others, and must help each other to fulfill these responsibilities to the best of their ability. Only in this way will the airline realize good value for its money.

Each airline has a foodservice department in its organizational structure, although this department may have many different titles and be structured many ways. This department is responsible for developing menus, recipes, product specifications, purchasing specifications, serving directions and other such matters. It also determines the meal service schedule for different types of flights. All of the information and materials that the foodservice department develops must be carefully and clearly communicated to all of the caterers servicing that airline if product consistency and quality is to be maintained. The increased emphasis on partnership among all parties concerned with an airlines' inflight foodservice is a positive step toward facilitating this needed communication.

REFERENCES

National Association of Meat Purveyors. *The Meat Buyers Guide.* McLean, VA: National Association of Meat Purveyors, first printed in 1988.

KEY TERMS

Burn Off Supplies	Forward Cabin
Count	Load Factor
Cycle	Pre-Lim (Count)
Flight Deck	Shelf Stable

DISCUSSION QUESTIONS

1. Identify responsibilities of an airline's foodservice department.
2. Why do most airlines plan their own menu cycles? In addition to the food items to be served, what else is specified by an airline in its menu cycle development?
3. Why does an airline do extensive recipe development in support of its menus? To whom are these recipes distributed? Why is this distribution made?
4. For what types of products does the airline develop specifications? To whom does the airline distribute these specifications?
5. Why does the airline go to such lengths in describing even the smallest details in the specifications that are developed for products, meal packaging, tray setup, and so on?

6. Why are pictures often an important part of an airline's specifications? Where might pictures best be used?

7. Does the airline crew eat the same meals as the passengers do in the cabin they service? If not, why not? What do they eat?

8. Does the caterer purchase any products for use in servicing its airline contracts? If so, what type of storage is necessary for these products? How are the airlines charged when these products are used to service their flights?

9. Why would an airline want to negotiate a purchasing contract directly with a supplier rather than let its caterer make the supplier decision in accord with the airline's specifications?

10. Who owns products purchased directly by the airlines and distributed to a caterer's facility by a supplier's distributor? What is the caterer's responsibility in regard to these products? Are there any charges to the airlines when these products are used by the caterer to service the airline?

11. What factors does an airline consider when determining its meal and snack service policies for its flights?

12. Why might passengers on a flight traveling from east to west get a meal service while those on a flight at the same time, traveling from west to east, might not?

13. Why would an inflight caterer be concerned with the on-board service procedures that the flight attendants use for the meals?

14. Why would there be instances when not all foods to be served on board an aircraft are individually portioned and plated in the flight kitchens?

6

Inflight Caterers' Managerial Responsibilities

Contract and Financial Interfaces with the Airlines

LEARNING OBJECTIVES

After studying this chapter, the student should be able to:

1. Describe the organizational structure of a typical inflight foodservice kitchen.
2. Identify at least three areas of managerial responsibility within an inflight kitchen.
3. Discuss the process by which airlines contract for services from inflight caterers.
4. Identify at least eight types of provisions that would usually be in a catering agreement between an inflight caterer and an airline.
5. Explain the impact of deregulation on airline inflight foodservice budgets.
6. Discuss the current trends in airline budgets and costs for inflight foodservices.
7. Discuss how charges and selling prices are established by inflight caterers.
8. Explain why airlines would be doing cost analyses of inflight caterers' billings to them.

ORGANIZATION OF AN INFLIGHT CATERING FIRM

The organizational structures of inflight caterers are quite varied as the size, scope of operations, and management philosophies of the different catering firms impact on each firm's approach to the management of its flight kitchens. Catering firms range in size from small, local firms that may handle only a limited number of contracts at a small airport to large firms such as Caterair, Dobbs International, or Ogden, with central corporate headquarters and large inflight kitchens at multiple airports.

Even though a corporation, as a whole, may be large, it operates kitchens of all sizes. For example, McCarren Airport in Las Vegas, Nevada is one of the ten busiest airports in the United States, but the two flight kitchens serving that airport are considered to be medium-sized kitchens (with approximately 40,000 to 60,000 square feet compared with square footage of 125,000 to 200,000 for large kitchens). It is not only the number of flights arriving and departing from an airport that determines the catering load of that airport, but other key factors are the types of foodservice requirements for those flights and the number of flight kitchens serving the airport. In the case of McCarren Airport, a large number of flights depart at night (requiring only beverage service supplies and equipment) and many more depart early in the morning (requiring only breakfast service). Thus, the overall catering requirements are less than would be the case if most of the flights were from east to west, rather than west to east and if most departed during the day (during hours that lunch and dinner would normally be served).

Generally, an inflight kitchen is divided into five primary areas: (1) administration; (2) purchasing; (3) food production; (4) equipment sanitation and control; and (5) transport. Each of these areas may have a supervisor or coordinator responsible for that particular area, and all areas are under the overall direction of a general manager. An organization structure typical of that which may be found in an inflight kitchen is sketched in Figure 6.1.

This figure represents the possible organizational structure of a medium or large inflight catering kitchen. Smaller kitchens would have to perform all of the functions indicated in Figure 6.1; however, they would consolidate responsibilities so that one person may be responsible for both food production and purchasing, for example, while another might be responsible for all aspects of human resources, including training, and the operations manager may also be responsible for the financial operations. As has been mentioned, a particular kitchen's organizational structure is tailored to its specific needs and will be unique for each firm and for each of the different-sized kitchens operated by that firm.

As can be seen from Figure 6.1, some of the basic functions of the inflight caterer's organization for which managers may have responsibility include: (1) production of the food products; (2) employee recruitment,

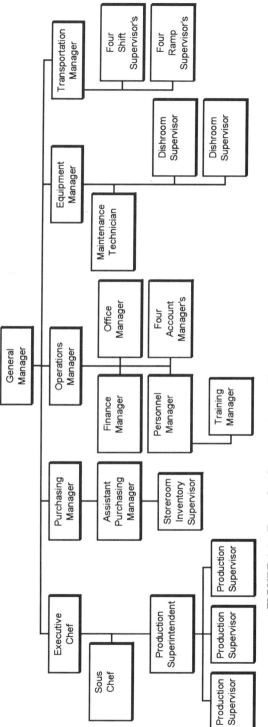

FIGURE 6.1 Example of an organizational structure typical of an inflight catering operation. Note the five primary areas within the kitchen structure which are characteristic of inflight kitchens.

retention, and training; (3) financial management of the catering operations; (4) purchasing of food products and supplies; (5) coordinating the flow of airline equipment through the kitchen; (6) accounting for the products and supplies owned by the airlines; (7) transportation of products and equipment to and from the aircraft; and (8) general operation and maintenance of the catering facility. Managing the general operations, then, entails responsibility for managing several subareas, including the exterior transport of the food products, equipment, and supplies from the inflight kitchen facilities to and from the aircraft, maintenance of relations with the several airline clients served by the inflight kitchen, and the overall production and packaging of the food and beverage products so that they are ready for transport to the aircraft.

While account maintenance (or client interface and communication) is shown on this chart as part of the facility manager's responsibility, there is no indication here of anyone responsible for contract sales. While the general manager might be involved in some aspect of contract sales to airlines, there is quite likely to be someone at the corporate level or located in a kitchen facility close to an airline's corporate headquarters who is responsible for selling the inflight caterer's services to the airline and, once sold, retaining that account. In a small, local facility, though, contract sales may very well also be a responsibility handled by the flight kitchen's general manager.

In some instances the inflight caterer may also have the contract for the operation of the foodservices inside the airport terminal. Figure 6.2 illustrates an organization structure representing this situation. As can be noted from Figure 6.2, the basic structure of the flight kitchen operations is similar to that illustrated in Figure 6.1. However, the total structure of the overall operation is expanded to incorporate management staff for the other operational components of the caterer at that particular airport site.

CONTRACTING FOR SERVICES FROM INFLIGHT CATERERS

For a true partnership to develop between an airline and the caterers who service its flights, there must be a good understanding between the two organizations and their personnel of the expectations the airline has of its catering partners and of the responsibilities that the caterer has toward meeting the service needs and performance standards of the airline. Occasionally, when the two organizations have been working together for some time, this understanding can be achieved through nothing more than a handshake between representatives of the two firms. However, since the provision of inflight foodservices is a very competitive business, a written contract between the two parties is desirable.

Inflight caterers compete for the right to provide these services to the airlines, particularly for the right to service major scheduled carriers. The

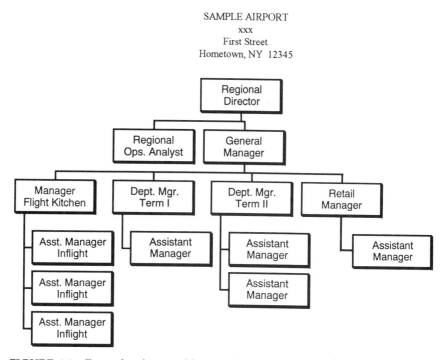

FIGURE 6.2 Example of a possible organization structure of an inflight caterer's operations where the caterer is also operating the airport terminal foodservices. (Courtesy CA One Services, Inc.)

airline's foodservice division or purchasing group is responsible for accepting bid proposals for the provision of inflight foodservices, evaluating the proposals received from competing caterers, selecting the caterers to be used at particular airports, and negotiating the service provisions with the caterer.

Interestingly, in contrast to most segments of the noncommercial foodservice industry, contracts between airlines and inflight caterers are very informal. Sometimes only an open purchase order is used to formalize the purchasing arrangements. However, such a document, when used, seldom has as many service, or performance, details as would be covered in a contract. One inflight kitchen operated by one of the major caterers, for example, indicated that it had no contract at all with one of the major airlines it serviced while it had a multiyear contract with another. In the case where there was no contract, there was simply a letter indicating that it was to provide the food and beverage services to that airline. Regardless of the level of formality of the contract between the caterer and an airline, there are always price lists for the meals and services to be provided that are agreed upon by the two parties. These lists at least formalize the caterer's selling prices and the airline's costs.

No matter what the paperwork underlying the servicing agreement or the terms incorporated into that paperwork—whether a letter of agreement or a formal contract—typically, an airline can make a change in the inflight caterer it uses at any time by simply giving its current caterer thirty days' notice. Thus, from the inflight caterer's perspective, the contracts it has are only as good as the level of service it provides. As long as it provides the quality of service expected by an airline it services, it will continue to service that airline. When it does not, another caterer will make a counteroffer, and the airline will take its business elsewhere in thirty days.

Winning the right to service a particular airline at a particular airport (or losing an existing right) can be a function of many considerations. Not the least of these considerations is the pricing structure offered by the caterer (which would be the cost to the airline for a firm's services). The extent to which the caterer's proposal is responsive to the airline's needs and interests is another important consideration in the decision process. However, other factors such as how the caterer is performing at other airports where it provides inflight services to this airline, how well the caterer handles an unusual emergency that may have occurred in the past, or the personality mesh between the local management staff of the caterer and the airlines' representative servicing the area in which the airport is located are quite likely to also be significant decision factors. However, it should be noted that airlines infrequently charge their caterers at the major airports serving large metropolitan areas because of the costs involved to transfer their account to a new caterer.

Table 6.1 indicates some of the provisional areas commonly covered by a catering agreement between an airline and an inflight caterer. In addition to the areas outlined in Table 6.1, other provisions or clauses can be added to the contract at any time by attaching a memorandum of agreement indicating what change has been made. Changes can be made to existing clauses in the same manner, and such changes are quite common for meal and service price lists.

AIRLINE BUDGETS FOR INFLIGHT FOODSERVICES

In order to forecast expense and maintain control of food and beverage costs, most airlines establish catering budgets. These operating budgets are monitored closely with adjustments in food and beverage requirements being made, as necessary, to meet the budget parameters. Generally the budget levels are based and measured on a targeted per-meal cost for each category of passenger meals to be served (for example, first, business, and economy class). The three methods most often used to establish and measure catering costs are

TABLE 6.1
Provisions Commonly Included in a Catering Agreement

PARTIES INVOLVED: Identifies the name of the airline and the name of the caterer, the two parties to the agreement.

LOCATION: Identifies the name of the airport where this catering service is to be provided and what its location is.

TERM: Identifies the beginning date of the contract and the period for which it is effective.

PRICING: Identifies the pricing formula and the fixed service charges to be used by the caterer to calculate the billings to the airline. Also identifies the unit charges for various types of items. If the agreement is a multiyear agreement, the time period for which the initial pricing structure is firm and the procedure for changing prices is also identified.

INVOICING AND PAYMENT: Identifies the frequency of invoicing by the caterer to the airline and the documentation required from the caterer to support the invoiced amount. Also identifies the conditions under which the airline will make payment on the invoice.

SUPERVISION: Identifies the caterer's responsibilities for proper supervision of the catering operations.

WORKER ASSISTANCE: Identifies conditions under which the caterer would be required to pay employees of the airline for work done for the caterer by those employees.

STANDARDS OF SERVICE: Specifies the menu, product, and service standards expected from the caterer. Identifies how the caterer can get questions answered regarding service standards. Also identifies the minimum time that the caterer's kitchen facility must be open to service the airline and remedies that the airline has should the caterer fail to perform its services in accord with the airline's standards.

EQUIPMENT CLEANING: Identifies caterer's obligations for cleaning equipment owned by the airline.

ORDERS AND DELIVERIES: Identifies airline's obligations for notification to the caterer regarding any flight schedule changes. Specifically identifies the minimum time for cancellation of meal orders without the airline having to pay the charges that would normally be made for those meals. It also identifies products that are exempt from these charges, such as canned sodas that would be reused. Also considered here is the caterer's obligations to deadhead equipment on outbound flights and the caterer's responsibilities for vehicle transportation of the airline's equipment and property after off-loading a flight and when boarding a flight.

SERVICES AND MATERIALS TO BE FURNISHED BY THE AIRLINE: Identifies the items that the airline will loan or otherwise supply to the caterer and how the caterer acquires those items. It also identifies the caterer's obligations regarding the care, use, and securing of these items.

SANITATION: Identifies the caterer's responsibility to abide by and maintain the health, sanitation, and food handling requirements specified by the U.S. Food and Drug Administration and other regulatory agencies.

COMPLIANCE WITH LAWS: LICENSES, PERMITS, AND CERTIFICATES: Indicates the obligation of the caterer to conform to all applicable laws and regulations. Also indicates caterer's responsibility for obtaining all necessary licenses and the right of the airline to immediately terminate the agreement should a necessary license not be obtained or be lost by the caterer.

SALVAGE: Indicates that caterer will not salvage perishable food products from inbound flights. Also indicates caterer's obligations to salvage reusable nonperishable items from inbound flights.

TABLE 6.1 *(Continued)*

WARRANTY: Indicates that the caterer warrants that all foods and beverages delivered to the airline under the agreement will be wholesome and fit for human consumption.

CHANGE OF MANAGEMENT/OWNERSHIP OR SUBCONTRACTING: Identifies caterer's obligation to notify the airline should a change in management occur. Also identifies caterer's obligation to notify the airline prior to subcontracting any part of the inflight services to be provided.

INDEMNITY: Indicates caterer's obligation to indemnify the airline, or hold it harmless, against any liabilities incurred by the caterer.

INABILITY TO PERFORM: Identifies conditions of notification to the airline if the caterer is unable to perform as specified in the terms of the agreement. Also indicates nonliability of both parties to each other in cases of inability to perform due to acts of God.

ASSIGNMENT: Indicates that neither party has the right of assignment of any of their rights and obligations under the contract without the prior written consent of the other party. Indicates that violation of this clause can nullify the agreement.

BANKRUPTCY: Indicates that the airline has the right to terminate the contract if the caterer goes into bankruptcy and must suspend operations.

DEFAULT OF CATERER: Indicates the conditions under which the airline can terminate the contract should the caterer refuse, neglect, or fail to perform as agreed in the catering agreement.

COMPUTER EQUIPMENT TO BE FURNISHED BY THE AIRLINE, IF ANY: Indicates what computer equipment would be placed with the caterer and all of the terms and conditions associated with such placement.

NOTICES: Indicates that procedure whereby either party can give notices to the other.

INSURANCE: Indicates the type and amount of insurance coverage that the caterer will maintain while the agreement is in effect.

INDEPENDENT CONTRACTOR: Indicates that each party to the agreement is an independent contractor.

GOVERNING LAW: Indicates the state whose laws will govern the agreement.

1. Catering Cost per Passenger
2. Catering Cost per Revenue Passenger Mile (RPM)
3. Catering Cost per Available Scat Mile (ASM)

Catering cost per passenger is total catering costs (actual or projected) for a given period divided by total number of passengers flown (actual or projected) for the same period (including passengers flying free such as airline employees or passengers using free tickets as a result of redeeming frequent flyer miles).

$$\text{Catering Cost/Passenger} = \frac{\text{Total Catering Costs for the Period}}{\text{Total Number of Passengers Flown During the Period }(\textit{Including}\text{ Passengers Flying Free})}$$

Catering cost per RPM is total catering costs (actual or projected) for a period divided by the revenue passenger miles (actual or projected) flown for that period. A revenue passenger mile (RPM) is defined as one revenue passenger flown one mile. In general, passengers flying free are not included in RPM figures for the purpose of determining a catering cost per RPM. RPM is generally calculated on a system-wide basis rather than on a segment by-segment basis. Thus RPM is total passengers times total miles flown within the airline system.

$$\text{RPM} = \text{Total Number of Passengers Flown} \times \text{Total Miles Flown}$$
(Within the Airline's System, *Excluding* Passengers Flying Free)
$$\text{Catering Cost Per RPM} = \frac{\text{Total Catering Costs for the Period}}{\text{RPM for the Period}}$$

Catering cost per ASM is total catering costs (actual or projected) for a period divided by the available seat miles (actual or projected) for a period. An available seat mile (ASM) is one seat in an aircraft flown one mile. ASM, like RPM, is also calculated on a system-wide basis for the period. Since ASMs are a more fixed unit of measure, this method of developing and/or projecting catering costs does not recognize the effect of changes in the number of passengers flown.

$$\text{ASM} = 2 \, (\text{Number of Seats in an Aircraft})(\text{Number of Miles in}$$
a Flight Segment)
For all the Flights Flown by the Airline for the Period
$$\text{Catering Cost per ASM} = \frac{\text{Total Catering Costs for the Period}}{\text{ASM for the Period}}$$

In the past, there have been times when inflight foodservice budgets were quite liberal as these costs were built into the regulated air fares set by the government and other regulating authorities, such as the Civil Aeronautics Board (CAB) and the International Air Transport Association (IATA). From 1918 to 1978, the U.S. federal government controlled, or regulated, all facets of the airline industry. Among other things, government agencies determined airline routes, how often planes could fly, and the number of seats that could be flown between destinations and airfares. During this period, the CAB was the agency responsible for setting fares that the airlines could charge.

Since international air travel is still regulated by IATA while domestic flights, fares, and landing rights in the United States are not, budget allowances are more liberal on international flights where higher food costs are built into the regulated flight fares. Since many international flights cross the borders of multiple countries, it is still necessary to have an agency, such as IATA, establish fares for international flights. For example, a flight originating in New York might first land in Paris, France and then continue on to Cairo, Egypt. Since three different governmental bodies have jurisdiction over the airports involved in this flight, some neutral party (such as IATA) is needed to establish an equitable fare structure. Also, some international airlines are subsidized by the country they represent. Without IATA to level the playing field, the subsidized airlines would be able to charge fares that would be less than their costs incurred, relying on their governmental subsidies to pay their full operational costs.

Impact of Deregulation on Airline Foodservice Budgets

In the late 1970s and early 1980s, U.S. airlines became deregulated. This deregulation was a gradual process that began with the passage of the Airline Deregulation Act in 1978. The first of the CAB's many functions to be eliminated was their authority over the specific routes to be flown by airlines. In accord with the provisions of the 1978 Deregulation Act, CAB regulation of domestic fares, flight schedules, mergers, and acquisitions ended in 1983, five years after the passage of the act. The CAB was dissolved in 1984.

In the first year of deregulation, average air travel costs were cut, and airline service was expanded. However, by the early 1990s, deregulation was blamed, at least in part, for the increasing number of commercial air carriers that were declaring bankruptcy. Now, although the Federal Aviation Administration (FAA) still approves routes and fares charged by an airline, it is a rubber-stamp approval. The only real federal regulations applicable to the airlines are the strong safety controls imposed by the FAA.

In this deregulated operating environment, airlines are free to fly to any destination they choose as long as they can gain landing rights at the airport from the local airport authority, and are able to negotiate the use of a gate for deplaning and boarding passengers. They can begin or stop service to a destination at any time. Airlines are also free to charge whatever fare they want for the flight and put whatever conditions they want on passengers qualifying for the fare (as long as people will pay the fare charged). They can, and do, use yield management programs to decide how many seats on a particular flight to sell at a particular fare. In other words, the U.S. airline industry became a competitive marketplace. Some airlines thrived in this new competitive environment (Southwest Airlines, for example) while others were unable to survive (Eastern Airlines, for example). Still others have had to make significant changes in the way the airline is operated, and many major airlines are currently operating at a loss.

Current Airline Foodservice Budgets and Their Impact on Foodservices Offered

While domestic deregulation of the airlines has lowered fares on many flights, it has also meant that airlines have fewer dollars per passenger to invest in inflight food and beverage services, and budgets for these services have been significantly curtailed. Table 6.2 indicates the changes in per-passenger meal expenditures by major domestic airlines from 1993 to 1994. Overall, there has been an average decrease of approximately 10 percent in airline foodservice per-passenger expenditures in spite of United's 8 percent increase.

As a result, fewer full meals are served, particularly in coach class. More snacks are served in lieu of full meals; cold, lighter meals are being served in lieu of hot meals; and more flight segments receive no meal or snack service at all, again particularly in coach class. An example of the changes that are occurring is that in early 1994 one major airline indicated that they had overhauled their entire foodservice system and had eliminated hot food service for flights less than 90 minutes in duration. However, there were some exceptions to this limitation based on the time of day and connecting flight parameters to make sure that passengers did not go for excessive amounts of time (six to eight hours) without a meal. Other airlines are reducing the number of menu options as a means of reducing costs. Another major airline has announced that, no matter the time of day that the flight is flown, they are not going to be serving any meals on any flight that is less than 2.5 hours in duration. Generally, most airlines feel that their passengers have responded positively to their changes, indicating to them that the people who are buying coach-class tickets are most interested in price and flight availability—not a hot meal. Note that this perspective is very different from that governing the expansion of first-class seats and meal services provided there (Chapter 3).

Many airlines are replacing hot meals with cold selections or branded snacks. The use of branded items is becoming very popular as meal service patterns are reviewed by the airlines. The use of branded items reduces labor costs for all parties as they are usually purchased prepackaged and

TABLE 6.2
Comparison of Airline Per-Passenger Meal Expenditures, 1993 and 1994

Airline	1st Quarter 1993	1st Quarter 1994	Percent Change
AMERICAN	$8.07	$8.03	−0.5%
UNITED	$7.10	$7.67	+8.0%
TWA	$5.74	$5.77	+0.5%
NORTHWEST	$6.27	$5.68	−9.4%
DELTA	$5.79	$5.32	−8.1%
CONTINENTAL	$6.44	$3.59	−44.3%
USAIR	$4.62	$3.56	−22.9%
AMERICA WEST	$2.20	$2.04	−7.3%
SOUTHWEST	$0.14	$0.12	−14.3%
AVERAGE	**$5.83**	**$5.25**	**−9.9%**

Source: "Airlines' Food Budget Takes Bite in Cutbacks," July 26, 1994. *USA Today*, 12(144):8B.

ready for placement on the tray or for direct service to the passengers. As will be discussed in Chapter 16, branded items also help meet passengers' service expectations by providing familiar name brands and choice as a part of the food service in an environment where people have little control. No matter what course of action they are taking, all domestic airlines are reviewing their foodservice operations with the objectives of decreasing costs. Most want to do so while keeping their passengers satisfied with their service.

The cost per individual meal is quite modest (ranging from just over $2.00 to just over $8.00 per passenger in 1994—see Table 6.2). However, because of the many meals served the cost of inflight food and beverage services does represent a significant cost to the airlines. Although the average food cost per passenger declined for most major airlines in 1994, the total cost incurred by the airlines for food and beverage services generally increased because of increased passenger counts. This cost is currently considered to be the fifth-highest-cost item in an airline's total budget, with the highest being fuel and personnel salaries.

AIRLINES' VIEW OF FOOD COSTS

Airlines view food costs as being more than the fees paid to caterers or suppliers for food products and services. For the airlines, reduction in, or elimination of, food services can mean reductions in labor hours (their second-highest-cost category) as fewer flight attendants are needed on flights that offer only beverage service. Federal regulations stipulate the minimum number of flight attendants that an airline must have on board a flight. That number is a function of the number of seats on the aircraft as the flight attendants' first priority is passenger safety and the handling of emergencies. This required number of flight attendants is adequate to handle beverage services, but additional attendants must be staffed on flights with meal services because of the additional work load.

Another cost of full meal service is slower turn time for aircraft. When equipment and provisions for full meal service must be boarded, a turn for an aircraft may take 1 to 1.5 hours compared with Southwest Airline's turn time goal of twenty minutes. Since an airline earns revenue only when its aircraft (fixed costs to the airline) are flying, shortened turn times can help increase the revenue generated from the airline's capital investment.

Although these costs are a significant component of an airline's budget, they are not a major consideration in establishing passenger fares as are fuel costs and fluctuations in fuel prices that the airlines must pay. Thus, since food and beverage costs have little impact on ticket prices for a particular airline's flights and they are an important marketing tool, airlines can sometimes be "penny wise and pound foolish" when economies in food and beverage service are carried too far.

Whenever an aircraft takes off for a flight, fixed costs (fuel, crew salaries, depreciation, insurance, etc.) are incurred. If there are not enough passengers aboard to cover these fixed costs, much less the variable costs of the flight such as the cost for food and beverage services, the airline loses money from that flight. If food and beverage services are an important component of a flight for passengers and a consideration when they select an airline to fly, then incurring a variable cost for these services may be an important factor in helping fill seats at the fare structure desired by the airline—a structure that will cover both fixed and incremental, variable costs and perhaps even create a profit for the flight. There is some concern at the present time that at least some airlines, responding to the red ink resulting from their overall operations, are trying to find short-term economies through curtailment of their food and beverage services. As a result, they may be eliminating an effective long-term marketing tool for the airline, and their passengers may soon be finding other airlines to fly on.

IMPACT OF AIRLINE FOODSERVICE BUDGET REDUCTIONS ON INFLIGHT CATERERS

This reduction in the number of flight segments on which food is served is a concern for inflight caterers. It is particularly significant for the caterers as the greatest reduction is in foodservice for coach class. Coach-class products are the high-volume products that can be readily produced and assembled using efficient, production-line methods characteristic of a food factory.

In comparison, far fewer first-class and business-class meals are required for any one flight, and these meals are much more labor intensive for caterers to prepare. Therefore, as inflight caterers lose significant sales volume through the curtailment of food service to coach-class passengers, they also lose the ability to profitably service the needs of airlines for other types of meals and services without: (1) increasing prices and charges (which makes them less competitive); (2) decreasing operating costs; or (3) finding new sources of revenue through sales of food products to other customers. Sales to new customers would enable caterers to efficiently use their assembly-line production capacity. The increasing diversification of inflight caterers into new markets has already been discussed in this text. The driving force behind this diversification is the curtailment of airlines' purchase of coach-class meals as a result of the current budget limitations for inflight food and beverage services for passengers.

ESTABLISHING CHARGES AND SELLING PRICES

Pricing processes vary, depending on what type of service is being priced. At one time, pricing was primarily predicated on food cost plus a markup for labor and overhead. (This approach to pricing is still done for some local charter flights or other such onetime services that the caterer might contract for.) However, as competition increased and profit margins decreased for the caterers, the markup approach was no longer desirable.

Shortcomings of the Price Markup Approach to Pricing

To understand why this change occurred, it is necessary to consider the shortcomings of the food cost markup system for the airline industry. There are important differences between airline pricing and restaurant pricing as the restaurant menu can be adjusted in the event of anticipated price fluctuations while such adjustments to the inflight menu cannot be so readily made. There are several adjustments that the restaurateur can easily do: (1) The entire menu can be repriced, if needed. The only restriction is market competition and the printing costs for the menu. (2) Portion sizes can be adjusted downward to keep the overall menu price consistent, as specific item weights or measures are not listed on the menu; (3) Menu items, other than the main entree item, can be changed to an alternate selection, if necessary, to keep the menu cost in line. In contrast, the inflight caterer's prices are locked in for a predetermined time period, usually for one or more years. Additionally, the menu items and the portion sizes to be served are also locked in by contract and can be changed only in the event of dramatic price fluctuations.

Because of the restrictions in menu and portion flexibility faced by the inflight caterer, there were significant problems with the markup formula for both the airline and the caterer. Some of the problems encountered by the caterer were:

1. Because of the fixed nature of the contract, it was necessary to project pricing trends for a wide variety of commodity products for an extended period of time. However, as actual market prices changed over the duration of the contract, the caterer was sometimes unable to make timely pricing adjustments to reflect the new market prices.
2. The nature of the food-cost-based pricing made a kitchen's profit performance directly dependent upon the menu items the client airline chose to place on its menus. Since profit was determined by the markup on the food cost price, menu items with higher food costs tended to produce larger profits per meal. Thus, when high-cost menu items, such as filet steak, were replaced by boneless chicken thighs (a low-cost item), the kitchen's profit level suffered.
3. Since the trend over the past six years or so has been for airlines to reduce their foodservice costs, the reciprocal (or food-cost markup) method of menu pricing tended to reduce a kitchen's profit performance even though there was no reduction in the kitchen's efficiencies.

4. Prices quoted in the bid to the airline could not be inflated sufficiently to cover all the eventualities because of the intense competition applied by competitors for the airline's business. Therefore, a kitchen's profit potential was significantly determined by whether or not agricultural product growing conditions and other market forces cooperated with the kitchen's long-term price projections.

Similarly, problems encountered by the airlines included:

1. Because of the caterers' restrictions, airlines were required to pay higher prices on commodity items than the actual market prices would otherwise demand.
2. There was increased incentive for certain caterers to cheat (that is, to substitute lower cost items which might not conform exactly to the airline's specifications) on airline menu specifications in order to meet their profit projections when any major commodity market disruptions occurred. The airlines were affected by this problem through increased demands on their foodservice departments to police specifications and by possible customer dissatisfaction.
3. The airlines were severely penalized by the food-cost markup system in that they were restricted in what products could be used on any given menu. The markup approach tended to inflate price variations between competing products; therefore product price increases exaggerated the menu price increase. For example, a price differential of only $0.80 between a chicken breast and a chicken thigh would be reflected in a selling price differential of $2.00 under a 40 percent food-cost pricing policy. If the chicken thigh was changed to a filet steak with a cost differential of $5.50, the selling price differential increased by an incredible $13.75 per meal.

Current Pricing System Based on Labor Efficiencies

Now, a more sophisticated (and complicated) pricing approach, which eliminates many of these problems, is used for meals. This approach incorporates the food cost, a labor cost factor, and a calculated overhead recovery charge. The overhead and profit margin that used to be incorporated into the markup over the food cost are now incorporated into the cost of a man minute (or work value point). Pricing for meals is now based on the cost of a defined number of man minutes (or work value points) that are estimated to produce that meal plus the profit required. This method requires the caterer to know: (1) the menu's labor requirements; (2) the kitchen's mean labor rates, by department; and (3) the anticipated profit requirement.

In general, the advantages of this approach for the caterer are: (1) The kitchen's profit performance is no longer held hostage by agricultural growing conditions or other commodity price influences; (2) Budget projections are less dependent upon customer specifications; (3) The need to misstate price projections is reduced, although not eliminated; (4) Caterers no longer have to guide their airline clients toward high-priced menu items to maintain profitability; (5) Kitchen managers no longer see their profit margins (and their bonuses) destroyed by changes in menu specifications; and (6) Management has greater control over profitability, which can now be directly increased by controlling the labor force.

The airlines also realize advantages from this pricing approach, such as: (1) They pay only the difference in product cost to upgrade services without the previous price exaggerations; (2) It simplifies menu planning even though labor intensity now takes on more meaning; (3) It reduces the likelihood of cheating on specifications; (4) It gives the airlines first-hand knowledge of the profit level each caterer is looking to make from its account; and (5) They are likely to pay less per product as the product cost influence on the caterer is greatly reduced.

Table 6.3 illustrates the calculation of pricing to the airlines using this new approach. As profits are no longer impacted by the price of any selected menu item, caterers no longer have reason to fear the cheapening of menus through product cost reduction. Conversely, the airlines are no longer penalized by selecting high-priced menu items as they were under the cost markup system. Although all parties benefit under this labor-based model, the most satisfied person may be the kitchen's general manager, who is no longer subject to the fear of the destruction of his kitchen's profit margin every time a new menu is introduced.

Differences between Food Product and Service Pricing

Separate labor rates are determined for both food and services. When calculating the selling price of food products, only the food labor rate is used. Similarly, only the service labor rate is used to calculate service charges. When items are already the property of the airline, then the only charge to the airline is the service charge for the storage and handling that the caterer does for these products for the airline plus a charge for overhead recovery. The overhead charge also includes a profit margin for the caterer. If they are not the airline's property, then they are priced on the basis of their cost plus a markup for the overhead and labor involved in product storage and handling.

It is important to note that there are many different ways to calculate and apply numbers in these types of pricing scenarios, and different caterers use different variations of this approach to pricing. The example of meal pricing shown in Table 6.3 assigns a gross overhead recovery charge to each passenger meal. However, another approach to recovering overhead charges would be to assign a percentage to each menu item. This approach

TABLE 6.3
Pricing Structure Formulas and Pricing Procedures

MENU PRICING FORMULA:

Raw Food Cost + [Assigned MM (or WVP) × MM Rate (or WVP Rate)]
+ Overhead Costs = Selling Price
where MM = Man Minutes (WVP = Work Value Points)

SERVICE PRICING FORMULA:

[Assigned MM (or WVP) × MM Rate (or WVP Rate)]
+ Overhead Costs = Service Charge Price
where MM = Man Minutes (WVP = Work Value Points)

MISCELLANEOUS ITEM PRICING:

The handling of miscellaneous items by the caterer's commissary is assessed for labor requirements in terms of Man Minutes or Work Value Points. Once the Work Value Points have been determined for these items, their handling is charged to the airline using the Menu Pricing Formula.

CALCULATION OF MAN MINUTE (WORK VALUE POINT) RATE:

1. Determine the labor requirements for a task or series of tasks.

   For example, assume 20 hours were determined to be the required labor time to prepare and pack a particular menu for every 50 passengers served.

2. Divide the associated labor into work classifications (e.g., food preparation, plating, storeroom operations, or packing, etc.).

   For example, the required labor can be divided as follows:

   chef's time—1 hour
   cook's time—4 hours
   storeroom time—2 hours
   pantry (preparation, plating, etc.) time—10 hours
   packing time—3 hours

3. Determine the average hourly wage for each work classification.

   For example, the wage rates associated with the identified classifications are:

   chef = $25.00 per hour
   cook = $9.00 per hour
   storeroom worker = $7.50 per hour
   pantry worker = $6.50 per hour
   packer = $6.50 per hour

TABLE 6.3 *(Continued)*

4. Determine the percentages for management allocation, fringe benefits, and overtime for each work classification.

For example, the benefits, etc. percentages for the several work classifications are:

> chef = 28%
>
> cook = 25%
>
> storeroom worker, pantry worker, and packer = 20%

5. Multiply base labor rate of the kitchen (step 3) by 100% plus the percentages from step 4 to determine the true labor cost per hour for the several work classifications.

For example,

> chef—$25 × 1.28 (128%) = $32.00 per hour
>
> cook—$9.00 × 1.25 (125%) = $11.25
>
> storeroom worker—$7.50 × 1.20 (120%) = $9.00
>
> pantry worker—$6.50 × 1.20 (120%) = $7.80
>
> packer—$6.50 × 1.20 (120%) = 7.80

6. Multiply the hours required from each work classification (step 2) by the actual cost of labor per hour including benefit and overtime allocations (step 5). Sum the cost of all of the work classifications to find the total labor cost required to prepare the menu or complete the other activity.

For example,

> chef—1 hour × $32.00/hour = $32.00
>
> cook—4 hours × $11.25 = $45.00
>
> storeroom worker—2 hours × $9.00 = $18.00
>
> pantry worker—10 hours × $7.80 = $78.00
>
> packer—3 hours × $7.80 = $23.40
> _____
>
> Total adjusted cost of labor = $196.40

7. Divide the total adjusted labor cost by the total hours required for the meal or other task to determine the average adjusted wage rate per hour, or the Work Value Points to be assigned to that menu. Divide the average adjusted wage rate per hour by 60 minutes to determine the adjusted wage rate per minute (i.e., the Man Minute Rate).

For example,

> $196.40 (total adjusted labor cost)/20 hours =
> $9.82 as the average adjusted wage rate per hour
> and $9.82/60 minutes = $0.164 as the adjusted wage rate per minute (the Man Minute Rate).

Also, based on the preparation of 50 meals, the work point value per meal would be based on 2.5 meals prepared/hour for an hourly adjusted wage rate (or work point value) per meal of $3.93. Based on

TABLE 6.3 *(Continued)*

these figures, it is estimated that 24 man minutes would be required per meal to prepare this menu.

CALCULATION OF OVERHEAD RECOVERY RATE:

The components of the Overhead Recovery Allocation (or the Overhead Costs included in the pricing formulas) are: (1) Direct operation expenses; (2) Fixed depreciation of capital investments; (3) Corporate general and administrative expenses; and (4) A profit factor.

All menu and service Man Minutes (or Work Value Points) will be allocated an overhead rate. Once assigned, the overhead recovery rate can be converted to a per-passenger-per-meal charge for overhead.

FOR EXAMPLE:

(A) Assume that a coach-class meal had a raw food cost of $3.00; labor requirements as calculated above ($3.93 average adjusted wage cost or $0.164 for 24 Man Minutes per meal); and the overhead cost per passenger (coach class) was $1.00. Then, using the menu price formula, the price of the meal quoted to the airline would be:

Raw Food Cost + [Assigned MM × MM Rate] + Overhead
Costs = Selling Price

Substituting in the formula, then, the price would be:

$3.00 + (24 × $0.164) + $1.00 =
$3.00 + $3.93 + $1.00 = $7.93

or approximately $8.00 as the price of the snack to the airline.

(B) A can of soda that was already owned by the airline would be similarly priced using the service pricing formula. Assume here that there is no production labor required; that transportation labor per 100 cans is 10 minutes; ware washing and equipment handling labor is 15 minutes; the average labor rate per Man Minute for the wage classifications involved is $0.134; and the overhead cost is $0.31 (calculated on a percentage basis per item).

Then the service charge to the airline for handling and boarding the can of soda would be:

[Assigned MM × MM Rate] + Overhead Costs = Service Charge Price
[(10 × $0.134) + (15 × $0.134)]/100 + $0.35 =
($1.34 + $2.01)/100 + $0.35 = $3.35/100 + $0.35
=$0.034 + $0.35 = $0.384 per can

would be more applicable to pricing individual snack or beverage items. While it could be used when pricing complete meals, the use of the gross overhead charge to cover to labor, and so forth, involved in the total meal preparation is easier to work with than assigning percentages of the total overhead charge to individual items listed on the menu.

Generally, menu item prices are quoted to the airlines separately from the service charges. Thus, charges for transportation, ware washing, and so on would be quoted as separate charges, distinct from the food products that might be purchased as no matter which food products were chosen for service, the same transportation or ware washing would be required. Table 6.4 illustrates a typical listing of prices that might be submitted to an airline.

Regardless of the pricing methods used, the caterer's charges are still regulated by the airlines. Airline foodservice personnel know food and labor costs within each regional area. They prefer to have the same prices from all their caterers within a region, if not within the total United States, if at all possible. However, service charges, such as the storage and handling charges for airline-owned products, are still set at the discretion of each caterer, and caterers at a particular airport can still compete with each other on the basis of their service charge rates. Because of this very consistent pricing structure among caterers, the quality of the caterer's service and the quality of the products provided to the passengers on the airline's flights are the critical factors in gaining and retaining a contract with an airline.

COST ANALYSIS OF INFLIGHT FOOD AND BEVERAGE SERVICES

Of course, good management mandates careful control of food and beverage service costs if budget goals are to be met. However, the key word here is *control*. Control implies a plan for and recognition of costs relative to the planned value the airline gains from its food and beverage services. The objective is to optimize the perceived value that the passengers place on the inflight foodservices received on a particular flight while also making the best possible use of the airline's investment in inflight foodservices.

Cost analyses are required on the billings and any other performance data received from the caterers to determine any cost variances that may have occurred. Part of the responsibility of the several on-site airline representatives and quality assurance teams is verification of accurate billings for the products and services provided to the airline by the inflight caterer. Where deviations are noted, airline representatives work with the caterer to identify the causes of such variances and possible corrective actions that might be taken, if appropriate. Inflight caterers need to maintain adequate records to support their billings to the airlines and should be prepared to work with airline representatives to reconcile differences when appropriate.

TABLE 6.4
Sample Pricing Typical of Pricing Submitted to Airlines by Caterers

FIRST CLASS*

Tray setup	$ 1.50	@100%
Entree #1	10.50	@ 60%
Entree #2	7.50	@ 60%
Dessert	2.45	@100%
Appetizer	4.95	@100%
Overhead Recovery	6.45	
Total Price per Passenger	$26.15	

ECONOMY CLASS

Tray setup	$1.13	@100%
Entree	4.98	@100%
Dessert	0.45	@100%
Overhead recovery	1.23	
Total Price per Passenger	$7.79	

SERVICE**

Transportation/Loading	$375.00
Sanitation	65.00
International Trash	40.00
Airline Inventories	N/C
Storage Space	N/C
Etc.	

* First-class costs may not be extended on the submitted price list on the basis of the item prices and the boarding ratios as shown here. First-class pricing is often provided in the form of a matrix as the price per passenger may change as the passenger count changes because of the dependency of the per-passenger price on the first-class boarding ratios. For example, a presentation tray may serve from 1 to 12 passengers or a loaf of special bread may serve from 1 to 4 passengers. However, a whole tray or one or more whole loaves of bread will be boarded even if the first-class count is less than 12. Thus, the actual price (or airline cost) per passenger varies, as the cost of these items is divided among a different number of passengers on board a flight.

** The charges indicated here reflect the charges that would be made to the airline per aircraft serviced. A charge, such as International Trash, would apply only to international flights.

SUMMARY

The organizational structures of inflight catering firms vary widely, but the basic structure of most firms represents the functions that are common to all inflight kitchens—administration, purchasing, food production, management of airline equipment and supplies, and transportation. It is important that the structure of the caterer's organization be related to the expectations that the airline has of the caterer. Generally, these expectations are identified in a contract, or catering agreement, between the caterer and the airline it is serving. While there are a number of provisions common to most catering agreements, any number of provisions specifically tailored to a specific relationship can be included in the agreement.

One of the challenges that inflight caterers are facing today is the reduction in the airlines' food and beverage service budgets. Because of operating losses, airlines are looking closely at their food and beverage service practices and policies. In many instances they are completely revising their services to better fit today's competitive operating environment.

In this environment, setting prices for their services becomes a challenge for the inflight caterers who must also streamline and economize their operations. The traditional food-cost markup approach to pricing has many problems when applied to inflight foodservices. A new pricing approach, based on the caterer's labor requirements, appears to resolve many of the problems associated with the cost markup method, and is finding wide usage throughout the inflight foodservice industry. No matter what approach is used, though, airlines still have a responsibility to conduct cost analyses of the charges received for the inflight foodservices provided to them by their caterers.

REFERENCES

"Airlines' Food Budget Takes Bite in Cutbacks." (July 26, 1994). *USA Today*, 12(144): 8B.

Allen, R.L. (Feb. 7, 1994). "Preparing for Takeoff: Fine-Tuning Inflight Food." *Nation's Restaurant News*, 28(6): 39–40.

KEY TERMS

Available Seat Mile (ASM)	Revenue per Passenger Mile (RPM)
Contract	Turn
Letter of Agreement	Turn Time
Man Minute	Work Value Point
Man Minute Rate	Work Value Point Rate
Regulated Air Fares	

DISCUSSION QUESTIONS

1. Describe the structure of an inflight catering facility. What are the five major areas of managerial responsibility within an inflight kitchen?

2. Describe the contract process between an airline and a caterer. Are inflight catering contracts long-term or short-term agreements? Can they be canceled? If so, how? What length of notice is required?

3. What are some of the provisions that would usually be found in a catering agreement between an inflight caterer and an airline?

4. What has the impact of deregulation been on domestic inflight foodservices since the late 1970s?

5. What has the recent trend been in airline budgets for inflight foodservices? In the costs of providing these services? In the types of services provided? Is this trend expected to continue?

6. How does the food-cost markup pricing system work for inflight foodservice charges to the airlines? What problems are associated with this pricing methodology—for the caterer and for the airline?

7. How is labor cost now being incorporated into the pricing of inflight foodservices to the airlines?

8. What is meant by the terms Work Value Point, Work Value Point Rate, and Man Minute?

9. How are prices to the airlines calculated using the new labor-cost-based approach to pricing for inflight foodservices?

10. Why should airlines conduct cost analyses of the billings that they receive from their caterers?

7

Airline and Caterer Interfaces

LEARNING OBJECTIVES

1. Discuss airlines' expectations from their caterers in regard to the packing and boarding of products and equipment on the aircraft.
2. Discuss the rationale for an airline's development of loading diagrams and the need for the inflight caterer to follow these loading diagrams closely.
3. Identify the meaning of the terms *weight*, *balance*, and *cube* and the importance of these terms to the caterer and the airline.
4. Discuss the need for effective employee training.
5. Describe the rationale for airlines' having representatives regularly visit and work with their caterers.
6. Discuss why catering firms sometimes locate representatives near airlines' corporate offices.
7. Identify what is meant by *electronic data interchange*.
8. Discuss how EDI can facilitate the development of partnerships among airlines, their caterers, and their suppliers.

PRECISION IN FOLLOWING SPECIFICATION DETAILS

Caterers are expected to follow the specifications of the airlines in *precise* detail. Yet, because airlines are continually changing their operations and no two flights are exactly the same, the management of an inflight catering facility is a job for someone who thrives on creativity, problem solving, and constant change in the services provided. Airlines' specifications are quite detailed, and the caterer is expected to carefully note the detail. Each airline is using its food and beverage services to distinguish its flight services from those of its competitors.

It is very important to the airline that there be no variance in the food products from one airport to another. It is because the airline is constantly getting food and beverage products that are supposed to be identical from so many different sources that no variance from the established specifications can be tolerated. Because of the detail provided to the caterer for the services to be rendered to an airline, it may seem as though there is little creativity involved in the management of an inflight kitchen. However, a flight kitchen is a very dynamic operation, and much creativity is required if the caterer is going to be able to precisely meet the catering requirements of the several airlines served by the kitchen.

The contract established between the airline and the caterer defines the general expectations that the airline has of the caterer and the official lines of communication that will exist between the two parties. However, once the contract is in effect, the airline provides materials to the caterer defining the changing specifics of the foods and beverages to be provided.

DOCUMENTATION FOR EQUIPMENT PACKING AND LOADING

Documentation provided to the caterer by the airline includes sketches of the different types of drawers or bins, tray carts, carrier boxes, and oven inserts which indicate the specific items that are supposed to be loaded in these transport units. The inflight caterer is responsible for seeing that all of the items specified in the diagram are, in fact, packed in the drawers as they should be, and that there are no items in the drawers other than those specified. Figures 7.1 and 7.2 illustrate some of these patterns.

As these figures show, each different configuration for packing a carrier box or a tray cart or other piece of equipment is given a name or a number. The airline uses these names or numbers to specify the equipment and supplies to be loaded for a particular flight on a particular type of aircraft. Not only are these names or numbers used to refer to a drawer, carrier, or trolley with particular contents, they also refer to specific locations in the aircraft's galleys where that item is to be placed in the boarding process. For example, a flight may be specified as requiring carrier boxes numbers 410 through 414, or beer/wine drawers #2 and #3, tray carts numbers 104 through 106, or 1/2-size meal cart, and so on until all of the necessary foods, beverages, and supplies had been included by specifying the standard equipment component numbers. Figure 7.3 lists all the equipment needed on some aircraft of one airline.

Figures 7.4 and 7.5 illustrate two airlines' layouts of their galleys. Figure 7.4 shows the galley layouts the airline uses for its Boeing 737 aircraft. Figure 7.4 (a) illustrates the galley supporting the first-class section and Figure 7.4 (b) diagrams the rear galley, or the galley supporting the coach-class section. As can be seen, the support cart diagramed in Figure 7.1(a) goes into space 1-5 in galley #1, the first-class galley [Figure 7.4(a)]. Figure 7.5 (a-c) is a similar illustration of a Boeing 757 galley layout from a different airline. By using this system, airlines are able to ensure that a particular type of aircraft being used for a flight of a particular length serving a particular menu will have exactly what is needed for that service, no matter where the supplies are boarded. It is all standardized following the airline's detailed study of exactly what is needed.

AIRCRAFT LOADING DIAGRAMS

Each particular type of aircraft has a different loading diagram for the equipment required for that flight's food and beverage service. It is essential that the caterer's transport crew follow the loading diagram and place the correct piece of equipment in the correct space. The flight attendants' service procedures are based on the prescribed loading pattern, and they expect to be able to go directly to a cart or a carrier and find just what they are looking for. Failure to follow the specified loading diagram is a good way to get complaints from the airline's flight attendants about the caterer's service.

Weight and balance, as well as cube, are very important considerations for aircraft flights and are the reason that the airlines give such serious consideration to exactly what is needed for their food and beverage services. The terms *weight* and *balance* refer to the total weight of the products to be loaded on the plane (including both the particular piece of boarding equipment and its contents) and how that weight is distributed throughout the plane's structure. The term *cube* refers to the total volume required to place the boarding equipment and its contents on the plane.

Aircraft have a maximum weight which they cannot exceed if they are to have sufficient lift to actually take off. The aircraft's weight must include the plane and *everything* in it, including fuel, baggage, freight, people, food, beverages, and so on. The weight allocated to food and beverage service products and equipment is always calculated into the *zero fuel weight* (the weight of the aircraft with everything loaded except fuel) at the maximum weight that would be incurred if the equipment was fully loaded to support a full passenger load. However, it is important to the airline to minimize the weight allocation for their food and beverage services because (1) excess weight used there could be better used by the airline to generate revenue through carrying more air freight and (2) a reduction in the total weight of the aircraft can result in less fuel used per flight and a savings in fuel costs.

Each type of aircraft has a limited volume of space. The available space must be used to its maximum capacity. There must be a space allocated for every item that comes aboard the aircraft, and that item must fit into that space or it cannot be taken on the flight. The available space must be

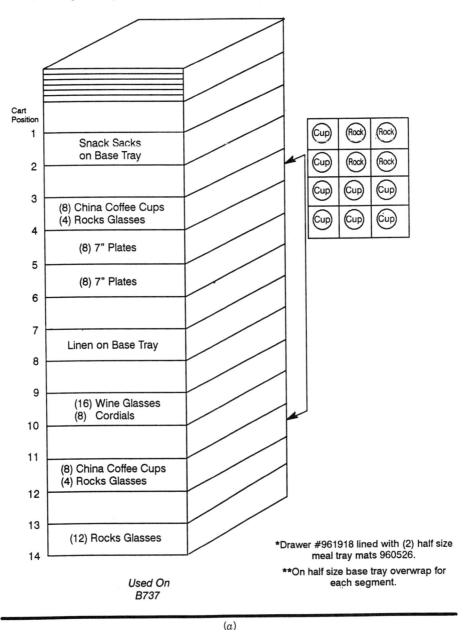

Half Size, First Class, Double Provisioned Rotable Support Cart
For FS1/FS3 Flights Only

Cart Position

1	Snack Sacks on Base Tray
2	
3	(8) China Coffee Cups (4) Rocks Glasses
4	(8) 7" Plates
5	(8) 7" Plates
6	
7	Linen on Base Tray
8	
9	(16) Wine Glasses (8) Cordials
10	
11	(8) China Coffee Cups (4) Rocks Glasses
12	
13	(12) Rocks Glasses
14	

*Drawer #961918 lined with (2) half size meal tray mats 960526.

**On half size base tray overwrap for each segment.

Used On
B737

(a)

FIGURE 7.1 (a) Packing diagram for B737 first-class support cart; (b) packing diagram for B737 main cabin beverage cart. (Courtesy of America West Airlines)

Two—Thirds Size, Main Cabin, Beverage Cart #1, Packing Specification

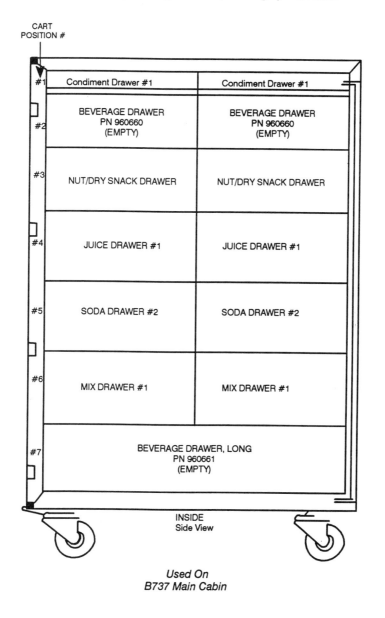

(b)

FIGURE 7.1 (*Continued*)

FC CART 142 EQUIPMENT SUPPORT CART - ALL SERVICES OR AS DESIGNATED

UTENSIL DRAWER*
DR

CREAM SERVER / GLASS
CR4 / GL7 (INSULATE TO PREVENT BREAKAGE)
CARAFES
(BRK SNK / CONTL BRK/ BASC BRK ONLY)
DR

CORDIAL GLASSES
(ONLY WHEN LIQUOR SCHED.)
12 GL52/RA68

SOUP MUGS* MU2
(SAME PROVISIONING RATE AS SOUP WHEN SHCED.)

SERVING TRAYS
2 TR83 / 2 TR84
TR83

LARGE PLATES
12 PL68
(FOIL WRAPED IN STACKS OF 4 WHEN
ENTREES ARE BULK PACKED ONLY)
DR

LINED BASKET
BA117/LA55
(ONLY WHEN BREADS/CANDIES ARE SCHED.)
DBL. SOS DR*
LINEN / HOT TOWELS*
DR

(EXTRA) LARGE PLATES
4 PL68 (FOIL WRAPED) TR83

WINE GLASSES
RA67

BLUE COFFEE SERVERS / LIDS
2 SE54 / 2 LI67
ICE SCOOP 1 SC40
PITCHER
PI15
DR

NUT DISHES - 12 DI87
(ONLY WHEN BULK NUTS SCHEDULED)
SML. PLATES 12 PL69
(FOR COOKIES OR ICE CREAM)
(SNACK 1 / LT LUNCH / DLX L / D ONLY)
BEVERAGE ACCOMP* (1ST /2ND LEG)
(PLACE ON GALLEY COUNTER IF NO ROOM)
DR

PRE DEPARTURE
COFFEE MUGS / SPOONS
14 CU58 / 14 SP70
DR

MILK / CREAM / JUICE* (QTS)
BEVERAGE GARNISHES*
PRE ARRIVAL CANDIES*
(1ST LEG)
DR

FRONT — REAR

FC CART 143 LIQUOR CART (FOR 1ST AND 2ND LEG)

1ST LEG FRONT SIDE OF CART	2ND LEG REAR SIDE OF CART
(PACK 1ST) SODA / MIX / JUICE* — PRIMARY DR — AM OR PM SERVICES	(PACK 1ST) SODA / MIX / JUICE* — PRIMARY DR — AM OR PM SERVICES
(PACK 1ST) SODA / MIX / JUICE* — SECONDARY DR — AM OR PM SERVICE	(PACK 1ST) SODA / MIX / JUICE* — SECONDARY DR — AM OR PM SERVICE
LIQUOR MINIS* — DR	LIQUOR MINIS* — DR
RED WINE* — DR	RED WINE* — DR
WHITE WINE* — DR	WHITE WINE* — DR
BEER* CHAMPAGNE* — DR	BEER* CHAMPAGNE* — DR

FRONT — REAR

*PROVISION WHEN SCHEDULED IN FISS

727-200 (12/138)
DOMESTIC/CARIB/MEX
DOUBLE PROVISIONED SERVICES

SECTION 130-25
P. 7
JUN 30-94

FIGURE 7.2 Packing diagram for 727-200 first-class equipment support cart and beverage cart. (Courtesy of American Airlines)

B2 B737–300, N150, N151, N160, N306 – N309, N311, Equipment Requirements

ITEM DESCRIPTION	AWA PART #	SERVICE LEVEL		QTY ONBD
		F/C	M/C	
Cart, Liquor, 2/3 Size	960929	1	2	3
Cart, Meal, 1/2 Size	961373	1		1
Cart, Meal, 2/3 Size	960930		2	2
Drawer, Beer/Wine #2	960661	1		1
Drawer, Beer/Wine #3	960661		2	2
Drawer, Condiment #1	960654	2	4	6
Insert, Condiment	960327	2	4	6
Drawer, Juice #1	960660	2	4	6
Drawer, Liquor #2	960656	2	4	6
Insert, Liquor	960645	2	4	6
Drawer, Mix #1	960660	2	4	6
Drawer, Soda #2	960660	2	4	6
Drawer, Supply #1	960660	1		1
Drawer, Supply #3	960660	1	2	3
Ice Container, Aft, Dark Blue	961778		4	4
Ice Container, Fwd/Lower	961776	1		1
Ice Container, Fwd/Upper	961775	1		1
Pallet Serving Tray (White)	960328		2	2
Pot, Coffee	961772	2	4	6
Waste Bin, Aft, Blue	961777		2	2
Waste Bin, Fwd Liquid, Green	961774	1		1

B2 B737 300

FIGURE 7.3 Example of a listing of all equipment needed on certain 737-300 aircraft of one airline. (Courtesy of America West Airlines)

B2 B737–300 Galley #1

N150AW, N151AW
N160AW
N306AW – N309AW
N311AW

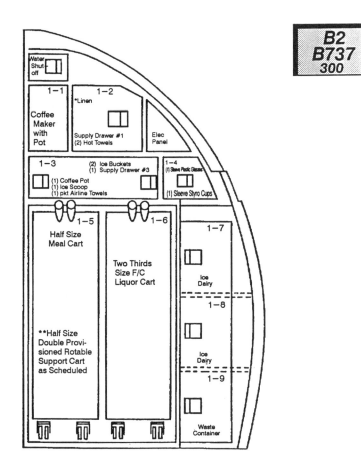

*   Linen boarded on First Class meal flights only.
** Used on double provisioned flights.

(a)

FIGURE 7.4 Galley diagrams for Galleys #1 #2 and #3 for same aircraft for which the equipment list in Figure 7.3 was prepared. Diagrams are to be used by inflight caterer's staff to place equipment into the aircraft's galley structure. All of the equipment indicated in Figure 7.3 should have a placement location indicated in one of these galleys. (Courtesy of America West Airlines)

B2 B737–300 Galleys #2 & #3

N150AW, N151AW
N160AW
N306AW – N309AW
N311AW

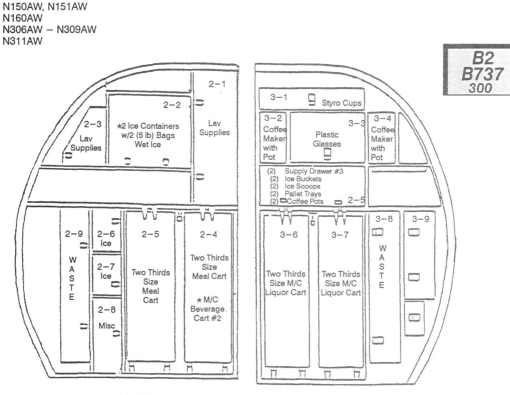

GALLEY #2   *GALLEY #3*

★ Provisioned on round trip beverage flights only.

FIGURE 7.4 *(Continued)*

divided among several uses, such as galleys for the storage of food and beverage supplies and for the preparation of coffee, passenger seating, or baggage storage. The airline generates revenue through seating passengers and carrying freight. Thus, if galley space can be minimized, perhaps an extra row of seats can be inserted into the aircraft's seating plan. Since the galleys are structured for maximum utilization of available space, failure to follow the loading diagram for the particular aircraft may mean problems in boarding all the required equipment and products for the flight.

The loading diagram also controls the balance of the weight of the equipment and products that must be loaded onto the aircraft. Each aircraft

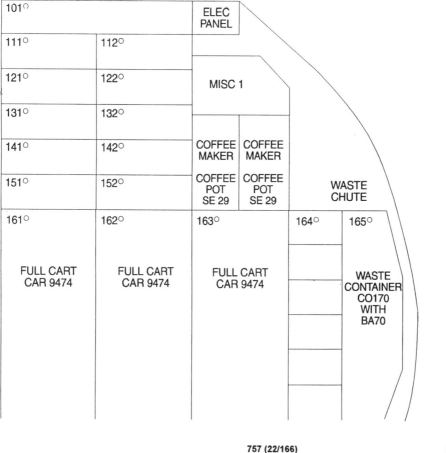

757 (22/166)
GALLEY CHARACTERISTICS
GALLEY G1

SECTION 140-05
P. 9
JAN 11-93

FIGURE 7.5 Galley diagrams for four galleys on a 757 aircraft. The small circles next to galley position numbers indicate how many drawers are in that position. The small circles beside the position numbers at the cart locations indicate if the cart position is refrigerated or not. An empty circle means that it is nonrefrigerated. A solid circle indicates a refrigerated position. In this example, none of the cart positions are refrigerated (i.e., all carts would have to be chilled with dry ice). (Courtesy of American Airlines)

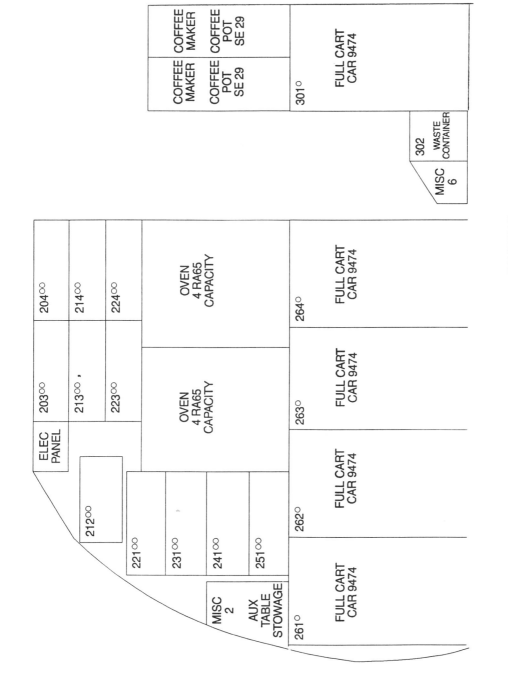

757 (22/166)
GALLEY CHARACTERISTICS
GALLEYS G2 & G3

FIGURE 7.5 (*Continued*)

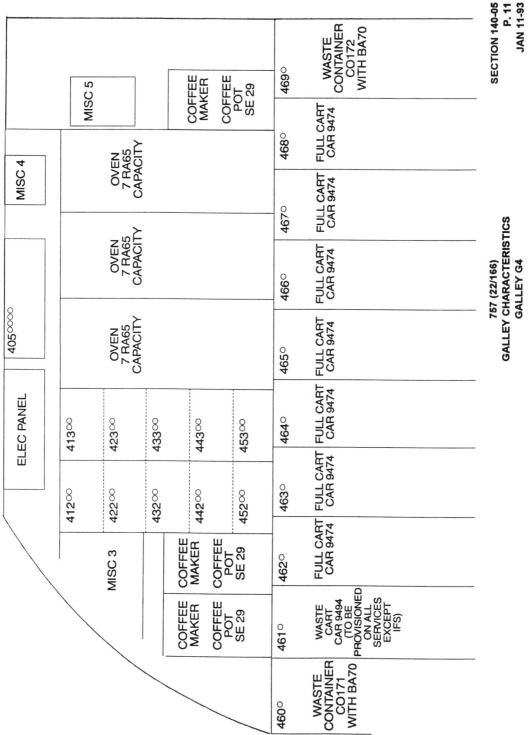

757 (22/166)
GALLEY CHARACTERISTICS
GALLEY G4

FIGURE 7.5 (*Continued*)

has a specific *weight and balance envelope* certified by the FAA. Generally, the command pilot will prefer loading the aircraft so that the heavier weight is toward the rear of the aircraft, but within the parameters of this approved envelope. Since the loading diagram is calculated on the maximum weight for the food and beverage equipment, if the different pieces of equipment are properly placed in the designated compartments there should be no problems in the plane's balance. However, it is important to assure that the maximum placarded weight limits have not been exceeded for any one compartment.

The only time that it should be important for a caterer to talk with the airline about the weight and balance of the aircraft is when equipment, dishes, and other such supplies that have accumulated at the caterer's kitchen are being shipped to another kitchen as freight on the aircraft. China and glassware are very heavy items, and a sizable shipment packed together could exceed the maximum deck stress limit of the forward baggage compartment. When such shipments are to be made, they are documented similarly to any other air freight shipment. That is, they are given a bill of lading number which includes the number of pieces (or boxes) to be shipped and the weight of each piece (box). The airline's baggage crew uses this information to know what is being shipped so all shipments can be properly distributed in the baggage compartments.

TRAINING EMPLOYEES TO MEET AIRLINE EXPECTATIONS

Having well-trained, motivated employees is an important consideration for inflight caterers. Because of the precision required in their work, the production efficiencies that must be realized, and the potential for loss that exists should employees make errors or become careless in their work, employee commitment to their jobs and to the interests of the catering firm is very important. In the past, most employee training in many organizations has been minimal—often just enough to get the employee started on the job, where they learn the rest of their needed skills from watching and working with the other employees doing the same type of job.

However, many firms including inflight caterers, are now recognizing that such an approach to training is inadequate to meet current employee performance requirements. Some of the leading caterers, such as Dobbs International (the first airline caterer to use such a system) are implementing total quality management programs to improve the skill level, productivity, and commitment of their employees. These total quality management programs utilize a quality improvement process which is based on employee involvement and customer/supplier partnerships. It also involves a decentralized system of teamwork and additional responsibility for employees.

When initiating the program, one of the lessons that Dobbs learned was that it was necessary to initiate a training system for employees to self-train. Their system, known as the Training and Productivity (TAP) system, was based on the concept that all employees should be involved in the training process. Effective training starts at the top and cascades throughout the organization via a train-the-trainer approach. Such an approach not only makes effective use of the reservoir of employee talent available in any organization, but it also helps ensure employee buy-in and commitment to training as a critical and never-ending process as well as to the goals and objectives of the firm.

Effective training is closely linked to a company's work processes, and it provides a way for employees to learn how to make improvements. As process improvements are made, they can be quickly incorporated into existing training programs to ensure that employees throughout a firm are taught the latest and best methods and techniques. In this process, training needs are continually being assessed, and training is delivered on a *just-in-time* basis by subject-matter experts who are certified to train in a particular functional area. By delivering training when and where it is needed, a company is able to effectively address specific knowledge and skill deficits. Such an approach helps ensure that a company's human resource investment provides a return on investment in the form of improved employee productivity and better job performance.

THE AIRLINES' INTERFACE WITH INFLIGHT CATERERS

The airline's foodservice division is the line interface with the inflight caterer at each airport. The airline has representatives who are responsible for working with each inflight catering site to: (1) see that the caterer is providing the required food and beverage services for the flights passing through that airport; (2) assure that the airline's quality standards are met; (3) help resolve any problems that the caterer may encounter in servicing the airline's needs; and (4) engage in other such interactions that may be necessary to establish and maintain a smooth working relationship with the inflight caterer. The airline's catering representative could be assigned to one specific caterer at a particular airport, to a catering firm handling several contracts with the airline at different kitchens, or to all the kitchens run by several contractors in a geographical area—depending on the scope of the airline's operations at a particular airport, with a particular caterer, or in a particular region.

In addition to their on-site catering representative, airlines usually have a representative or teams of representatives who conduct periodic inspections of all inflight catering facilities providing services for the airline. This rep or team of reps is responsible for insuring that the caterer is meeting all quality standards established by the airline, including standards for facility sanitation, food safety, product quality assurance, equipment maintenance, and for the use of airline property and equipment as well as for administrative tasks (inventories, billing, or updating of manuals). These inspection teams are very influential in terms of the airline's decision to continue to contract with the caterer, and it is quite important for the caterer to be prepared to have these teams on-site at any time. It is equally important for the caterer to welcome the teams, on their arrival, and work with them positively while they are on site to alleviate any problems that may be observed by the team and to be sure that the caterer has a clear understanding of the airline's expectations regarding its food and beverage services.

Airlines may sometimes send a representative or a training team to the caterer's facility to provide on-site training. Such training might cover a new menu cycle that they have prepared, any problems that may have arisen regarding the menus, or small menu changes that the airline desires (as opposed to a totally new menu set). Such training, or menu meetings, helps the caterer's facility manager and key staff members gain a clear perception of the menu, the food products specified, and the service procedures that are anticipated. The airlines that conduct this type of on-site menu training feel that this first-hand contact with the caterer gives them greater assurance of achieving the consistency and quality level that is desired throughout their system of flights.

Generally, there is much interaction between airline staff and the staff of the inflight caterer. Since the working relationship between the airline and the caterer is very close—and one is quite dependent on the other—positive interaction between the two organizations at all levels is quite important to facilitate the successful achievement of both firms' objectives—the provision of quality food and beverage services, as specified by the particular airline, on all flights.

INFLIGHT CATERERS' REPRESENTATION TO THE AIRLINES

Major inflight caterers are increasingly placing representatives in cities where airlines have their corporate offices. These representatives are responsible for maintaining close contact with the airline's corporate office to help with timely and effective communications on service and performance issues. As a spinoff of such closeness, the inflight caterer may be able to bid more effectively on catering contracts with the airline and to be more responsive to the airline and its concerns as an important means of facilitating the retention of contracts already in existence.

In years past, some airlines have ignored suggestions from caterers regarding ways to improve their foodservices. Instead, they assumed the attitude that they determined what was best for their food and beverage services and that the only responsibility the caterer had was to deliver the products as specified. However, inflight caterers are knowledgeable about foods, food production, and food products. They are often able to see what foods are not well accepted by passengers (waste from inbound flights), know about production efficiencies that might save both the caterer and the airline costs, and could make suggestions which would improve the airlines' food and beverage services, reduce costs for all parties, or both.

Airlines are becoming more receptive to recommendations from their caterers. They are taking a new, positive partnership approach in working with the inflight catering firms. As a result, inflight catering managers have new opportunities for creativity and for forging new cooperative relationships with the airlines with whom they are working. This partnership philosophy, which is extending to suppliers for both the airline and the caterer, is expected to smooth working relationships among all parties involved in inflight foodservices, and to be a key factor in improving service quality, efficiency, and cost effectiveness.

ELECTRONIC DATA INTERCHANGE

Electronic data interchange (EDI) is a term that has been coined to identify and define the exchange of routine business transactions in a computer-processable format. Examples of such business transactions include requests for quotations, purchase orders, planning schedules and material releases, shipping schedules, order status inquiries, receiving advice, and invoices. EDI is part of the move toward the information superhighway and the concepts of *electronic commerce* and *paperless society*.

The Need for EDI

Traditionally business transactions have been exchanged using paper such as preprinted business forms sent through the mail services. However, with the increased complexity of the business process and the exponential increase in the data needed for businesses (including airlines, inflight caterers, and foodservice product suppliers) to function, a more cost-effective method of communication and data interchange had to be found. The answer has been in the increasingly widespread use of the computer and computer telecommunications for commercial business applications.

Originally, individual companies developed bilateral electronic interchanges to minimize the paper load. However, this concept was found to be unwieldy and costly as each arrangement required the creation of a different version of each transaction, similar to the variety of forms received in the paper systems. Out of these early beginnings, industry groups were formed that began cooperative efforts to develop a single standard for each business transaction (i.e., purchase orders, invoices, and so on). In North America, this effort is coordinated under the American National Standards Institute. The EDI committee is known as ANSIX12, and it has published over 100 standards for individual business transactions to be communicated electronically.

Efforts are also being made on a worldwide basis to take this process one step further and create a truly international standard. This effort is being administered under the auspices of the United Nations. The standard is known as UNEDIFACT, and a number of standard transactions have been published by this group.

What is EDI and How Does it Work?

Electronic data interchange is the electronically automated flow of business transactions in a *standard* format between two companies. These business transactions are created, received, and acted on by the companies' internal computer-based business management system. The key point here is *electronically automated*, meaning that a business transaction is created, moves from one company to another, and is actioned by the other company *without human intervention*. This is the ultimate application of the EDI concept.

For example, consider a case of lettuce that would be carried by almost any produce supplier and how EDI can assist in the order and invoice processing of this item for the inflight caterer. The basis of this discussion requries the assumption that both the produce wholesaler's office and the inflight caterer's kitchen have internal computer systems that manage their business functions and that they have programmed their systems to communicate using EDI transactions instead of paper. Each time a case of lettuce is sold, the arrival of an electronic purchase order at the wholesaler's office causes the wholesaler's internal computer system to reduce the quantity of the lettuce on hand by the sales quantity. After each sale, the system checks to see if the inventory quantity has been reduced to a predetermined number called the order (or reorder) point. When this point is reached, the system automatically generates a purchase order for the predetermined replenishment quantity to bring the wholesaler's inventory level back up to the stipulated par stock level.

Prior to the use of EDI, even with this degree of sophistication in the internal computer system the result of this transaction would have been the printing of a caterer's purchase order on preprinted paper. This order would then have to be mailed to the produce wholesaler. At the wholesaler's facility, it would require several human interventions before the information on the order form would be rekeyed into its business system to start the sales process at the wholesaler's site.

Now, with EDI, the data is generated into the EDI standard for a purchase order and then transmitted over a computer telecommunications network to the supplier. On arrival at the supplier's computer system, the transaction is immediately recognized and actioned without human intervention. The next thing that is seen is the creation of a shipping advice in the warehouse to dispatch the required lettuce. Behind the scenes, the computer has automatically sent back an EDI standard acknowledgment to the caterer confirming receipt of the order and advising when it will be shipped and the pricing. After the shipment is made and the warehouse person confirms this action, the system will again automatically send an EDI shipping advice and an EDI invoice to the customer. The final action is another EDI transaction. This time a payment advice is sent from the caterer to the produce wholesaler when the payment is made. The payment, too, could have been made by means of an electronic bank transfer.

In this simple transaction, EDI has eliminated six paper transactions that would have been limited by the time it took to mail, receive, and interpret them. With EDI, they are sent instantaneously, and are recorded and acted upon immediately by the computer systems with no human intervention unless there is an exception. The produce wholesaler can repeat this same process with all of his foodservice clients without any computer redesign, if they use EDI; thus, the advantage of creating universal standards rather than being limited to bilateral agreements that have no flexibility is reinforced.

What EDI Is Not

It is important to differentiate EDI from other electronic data transmissions that may seem to be EDI, but are not. Facsimile (fax) is an electronic transmission of a paper document. However, it needs human intervention to translate the data contained in it and then to act on it. If data or information on the paper is needed for the business system, it must be rekeyed into the computer system. Electronic mail (e-mail) eliminates the paper output associated with a fax, but again it requires human interpretation before it can be rekeyed into a computer system. Bilateral arrangements between two companies to transmit and receive business transactions are called *proprietary EDI.* These arrangements yield some of the benefits of EDI, but they cannot be extended to other companies because the transactions are nonstandard, and they have to be redesigned for each new bilateral agreement.

How EDI Is Being Used in the Inflight Catering Industry

The major use of EDI in the airline industry has been restricted to the implementation of proprietary EDI systems that have been developed by the airlines in their endeavor to control costs. As such, no true EDI standards have yet been established within the industry. On the supplier side, a number of companies are working with both caterers and airlines on the control and administration of supplies. In these endeavors, they are using EDI standard transactions for purchasing, schedule management, and invoicing.

At this time, one major American airline is in the process of redesigning its entire computer-based inflight management system and has indicated that it will adopt the ANSIX12 standards for all its external transactions with suppliers and caterers. This system implementation will be a major breakthrough regarding the use of EDI in the inflight catering industry. Hopefully, once this system is in place, it can become a model for the industry. Transactions through this system could be used as a basis to develop true standards that all participants in the industry can accept and adopt.

SUMMARY

To maintain their contractual relationship with the airline, it is essential for caterers to follow all of each airline's specifications precisely. One area where precision is important is in packing products and supplies in transport equipment and in boarding that equipment. The airline's specifications reflect their study of the most effective use of each aircraft's space while also minimizing the weight of the aircraft and having the load weight properly balanced throughout the plane's structure.

To meet the precision level required by the airlines, inflight caterers are having to rethink how they train their employees and focus on the development of new total quality management programs which are designed to enhance employee training and commitment to their jobs. Both the airlines and the caterers are finding that increased involvement of their employees in problem identification, problem solution discussions, and work skills training provides a high return to them in terms of overall employee productivity and job satisfaction.

At all times, there is a strong interface between an airline and its caterers. This interface occurs in many ways ranging from visits from an airline site manager to inspections of a caterer's kitchen by an airline inspection team to co-location of a caterer's corporate representatives near corporate headquarters of the airline. Whenever this interface occurs, there is a new emphasis on communication between the airline, the caterer, and the suppliers to both the airline and the caterer.

One way that the airline–caterer interface could be strengthened and the overall inflight foodservice system made more efficient would be through the development of electronic data interchange systems. While many standards have been developed which could be used by the inflight industry, to date only very limited use of this technology has been made. One airline is currently experimenting with the adoption of an EDI protocol, and it will be of interest to see how well this system performs as it could potentially become a model EDI system to improve communications between the airlines, their caterers, and their suppliers.

REFERENCES

For more information regarding EDI and the potential for this concept, contact:

The Inflight Food Service Association, 304 W. Liberty Street, Suite 201, Louisville, KY 40202. Phone: (502) 583–3783.

Data Interchange Standards Association, Inc., 1800 Diagonal Road, Suite 355, Alexandria, VA 22314-2852. Phone: (703) 548–7005.

KEY TERMS

Balance	Lift
Carrier	Load Plan
Cube	Placarded Weight Limit
Deck Stress Limits	Weight
Electronic Data Interchange	Zero Fuel Weight

DISCUSSION QUESTIONS

1. What are the airlines' expectations from the caterers in regard to their product and service specifications? In regard to the airline's equipment loading diagrams?
2. What is meant by the terms *weight*, *balance*, and *cube* when loading an aircraft? Why are these terms important to both an airline and an inflight caterer?
3. What actions are the larger catering firms currently taking to increase their visibility and responsiveness to the airlines and their inflight service needs?
4. What is meant by partnering or the new partnership approach between an airline, its inflight caterers, and its suppliers?
5. How might this partnership arrangement help improve the quality and economic feasibility of inflight food and beverage services in the future?
6. How might electronic data interchange contribute to this partnering concept?
7. What is the airline's purpose in having representatives assigned in the field to work with their caterers? In sending inspection teams to the caterer's kitchens?
8. What types of training programs are being developed by some inflight caterers?
9. Why should training programs improve employee skill levels while also improving their understanding of and commitment to their jobs and the objectives of the catering firm?
10. What is electonic data interchange? How has business been transacted prior to the development of EDI?
11. What distinguishes EDI from other types of electronic information exchange, such as faxes?
12. How might EDI be applied to the inflight foodservice industry?

8

Airline Galley Structure

LEARNING OBJECTIVES

After studying this chapter, the student should be able to:

1. Recognize the importance of having the right amount of the right equipment on the right aircraft at the right time.
2. Discuss factors limiting the interchangeability of equipment from one aircraft to another.
3. Recognize the necessity of keeping each airline's equipment carefully separated from that of other airlines.
4. Recognize the need for the inflight caterer to be familiar with the interior structure of the galleys of different types of aircraft.
5. Describe a galley structure typical of that which might be found on today's newer aircraft.
6. Discuss the rationale for modular construction of aircraft galley structures and components.
7. Discuss construction weight and durability considerations for aircraft galley structures and components.
8. Explain why quality construction of the locking mechanisms in galley structures is very important for flight safety.

One of the challenges facing firms providing inflight catering services is that they are always working with someone else's equipment. Not only does the airline own the food and beverage product storage and preparation equipment on the aircraft, but it also owns the boarding equipment, the serving equipment, and the serviceware that is used on its flights. Thus, most of the boarding equipment and serviceware that inflight caterers have to work with has been provided to them by the airlines.

HAVING THE RIGHT AMOUNT OF THE RIGHT EQUIPMENT AND SERVICEWARE IN THE RIGHT PLACE AT THE RIGHT TIME

Caterers must always be concerned that the equipment that they have available to them is proper for the type of aircraft scheduled for a flight. They must also be sure that they have a sufficient quantity of all required equipment and serviceware available in their facility. Since the equipment and serviceware arriving on a flight does not always match the equipment and serviceware leaving on that same aircraft's outbound flight, there is a constant need to transfer equipment and serviceware among caterers servicing that airline or among different facilities of one catering firm if the inflight caterer has contracts with the same airline at more than one airport.

For example, the equipment and serviceware that arrived on an inbound flight that originated on the east coast at 7:00 P.M. and served only beverages on a nonstop flight enroute to the west coast will not be the same equipment and serviceware required for that aircraft's return flight to the east coast, departing at 6:00 A.M. and serving breakfast and a snack enroute. If enough of this type of differential occurs, at some point the east and west coast caterers must exchange some of the airline's equipment and serviceware in order to have proper quantities on hand in their respective facilities to continue properly servicing the airline's flights.

On the other hand, an inbound flight that originated on the east coast at 6:00 A.M. on a nonstop flight enroute to the west coast that served breakfast and a snack enroute would have the necessary equipment and serviceware on board to service the same aircraft returning to the east coast at 2:00 P.M. and serving dinner and a snack enroute. To help reduce the equipment balance problems that invariably arise, almost all airlines plan all services (by level) to use the same equipment. Thus, a hot meal served in the coach-class cabin would generally use the same equipment and serviceware regardless of whether it was a breakfast, a lunch, or a dinner. Similarly, a cold snack served in the first-class cabin would use the same equipment regardless of what time of day it was served.

Managing the flow of its equipment can be a major concern for an airline's foodservice division as it requires constant attention. As airlines downsize to become more cost efficient, there is potential for the airlines to outsource, or contract for, the management of their equipment. Should an airline decide to take this action, it offers a new potential revenue source for an inflight catering firm that might choose to bid for this type of contract.

LIMITS ON THE INTERCHANGEABILITY OF EQUIPMENT AND SERVICEWARE

Much of the equipment used to provide inflight foodservices is quite similar on all airlines. There are many requirements that equipment usable for inflight foodservice has to meet, such as durability standards, size, or shape in order to fit onto the aircraft and meet Federal Aviation Administration (FAA) standards. Many of these requirements are the same for all airlines flying the same type of aircraft. However, there are still a number of differences among the equipment used by the different airlines. Some of these differences may be as simple as the airlines' logos. There are also differences in the equipment used for different types of aircraft. The inflight caterer's management and staff must be familiar with the equipment of each airline they are servicing and with the equipment configuration of each type of aircraft if they are to be error free in their packing and boarding responsibilities.

Table 8.1 lists the different types of aircraft in use today and notes any unique features about each aircraft that impacts on the equipment that can or must be used on it. The aircraft are also categorized as either wide body or narrow body, and the number and location of the galleys on the aircraft are noted.

OWNERSHIP LIMITATIONS

Again, although many of the pieces of boarding equipment for the different airlines and the different aircraft are very similar (or even identical), there are important limits on the extent to which they are interchangeable. Equipment and serviceware belonging to one airline can be used *only* on that airline. It is inappropriate to use one airline's equipment to service a flight for another airline, and most catering agreements prohibit such equipment interchange. Caterers doing so will soon find themselves in serious trouble—and probably without their former clients if the practice were to continue. Since most serviceware is now imprinted with the name or the logo of the owning airline (or both), interchanging these items among airlines can be quite embarrassing for all concerned.

One of the most important responsibilities of the inflight caterer is keeping each airline's equipment and serviceware separate from that of the other airlines serviced by the caterer. Accomplishing this task requires careful kitchen space organization, well-defined policies and procedures regarding the handling and storage of each airline's equipment, and well-trained catering facility staff who clearly understand their equipment- and serviceware-handling responsibilities.

TABLE 8.1
Aircraft Configuration Summary[*]

Aircraft Type	First-Class Seats	Coach-Class Seats	Total Seats
Wide-Body Aircraft			
747-100 (Boeing)	18/70[**]-44	305-348	392-393
747-200	18/79[**]-44	272-348	369-393
747-400	18/80[**]-36/126[**]	184-320	346-418
DC10-10 (McDonnell-Douglas)	22-28	259-262	284-287
DC10-30	38-44	185-260	229-287
Narrow-Body Aircraft			
A300 (Airbus)	24	233	257
A320-200	12	132	144
727-200 (Boeing)	12-14	135-139	147-153
737-100	0-8	113-86	94-113
737-200	8-10	92-101	109-118
737-300	8-10	118-120	126-130
737-500	8-10	94-100	104-108
757-200	24	164	188
767-200	10/32[**]	126	168
767-300	15/42[**]	154	211
DC9-30 (McDonnell-Douglas)	8	95-100	103-108
MD80	14	125-130	139-144

[*] The seat counts indicated here are only approximations. Airlines configure their aircraft differently, and even the same model aircraft used by the same airline may have multiple seat configurations. The configurations used are the result of a number of factors such as what type of passenger the airline thinks will usually fly the route(s) the aircraft is used for; the type of passenger the airline caters to; the airline's policy for space between seats; the different galley and lavatory configurations built into the aircraft; and how the airline acquired the aircraft (purchased new and the airline specified the configuration, or purchased from another airline, for example). Since there is more space allowed for first-class passengers than for business or coach-class passengers, the higher the first-class/business-class seat ratio, the lower the total seat count possible on the aircraft.

[**] xx/xx = approximate number of first-class seats/approximate number of business-class seats

GALLEY STRUCTURE LIMITATIONS

Another limit on the interchangeability of equipment is the configuration of the galley structure within each type of aircraft and the service procedures required by the aircraft's interior structure or defined by the airline. It is possible that each type of plane could have different galley configurations and available interior space in which galley structures might be placed or in which the flight attendants can work.

The successful inflight caterer must know the different galley configurations of the different types of planes flown by the various airlines serviced (or in some cases by the same airline). Some pieces of equipment are interchangeable within the different types of equipment used by an airline; some are not. If caterers do not know the galley configurations and what is interchangeable and what is not, they will not be able to make decisions regarding alternative pieces of equipment to use, should they be short a particular equipment piece.

The caterer's staff should always check the aircraft tail number listed for a particular flight. The tail number identifies the aircraft that will be used for the flight. This number can be compared to a list provided by the airline that identifies the galley type for each of its aircraft. Many inflight caterers have a complete listing of aircraft tail numbers and the type of plane that has each tail number for each airline they service. Sometimes even different aircraft of the same type have different galley configurations. It is very common for an airline to implement a galley modification program. When it does so, it uses the aircraft tail number to identify those aircraft that have received the modification (the "mod"). The airline updates its aircraft listing as frequently as needed until the project is completed. The tail number is the *only* way to identify each individual plane. By checking the designated tail number for a flight, the staff packing the boarding equipment for that flight can be sure that they are using the correct equipment.

Also, if an airline changes the aircraft that it is going to use for a flight (as happens quite often), it is important for the inflight caterer to know whether the foods and beverages already packed for boarding that flight have to be repacked in different boarding equipment or not. When they are notified of an aircraft change, the caterer should check the new tail number to see whether it is the same type of equipment (or compatible equipment) as was originally scheduled for the flight.

Errors either way are costly. If the caterer repacks products and supplies unnecessarily, the products have been handled an additional time, and increased handling is always undesirable from the perspective of product quality and potential sanitation hazards. Also, the caterer has wasted labor that could have been more effectively used. On the other hand, if the caterer does not repack the products and the packed boarding equipment is incompatible with the new aircraft to be used for the flight, the caterer's boarding team will be unable to board the products and supplies for the flight when they get to the aircraft. They will normally have little choice but to return to the caterer's production facilities to repack and then redeliver the correctly loaded boarding equipment. To do so will likely cause the caterer to be late getting the food and beverage supplies on board the aircraft for the flight, possibly delaying the flight's takeoff and potentially leading to a fine against the caterer by the airline.

THE INTERIOR OF THE AIRCRAFT

An important component of each airline's equipment to be taken into account by the inflight caterer is that of the interior of the aircraft and the galley structure found there. No food or beverage products can be served on a flight that cannot be stored, prepared, or otherwise handled as needed in the aircraft's galley. Since different types of aircraft differ in their interior configurations and galley structures, the services that can be provided on different types of aircraft may vary as well.

As noted above, even the same type of aircraft being flown by the same airline can have different galley structures. One of the reasons that this situation occurs is that as airlines have gone out of business their fleets of aircraft have been sold to other airlines. When the planes were manufactured, their galley structures were configured to the specifications of the original owning airline. It is not always cost effective for the airline purchasing the used planes to reconfigure the galley structure to their specifications. An airline that has purchased used aircraft from several different airlines can often have wide variance in galley structures on their aircraft.

VARIATIONS IN INTERIOR STRUCTURE

When an aircraft manufacturer builds an aircraft, it essentially builds an airframe structure with an empty interior that can be equipped in any way that the purchaser of the airplane desires. For example, the DC-10, one of the wide-body aircraft flown by several airlines, is the same aircraft that is used by the military as a tanker for air-to-air refueling of fighter jets. The difference is not in the basic structure of the aircraft—the two were both built by Douglas Aircraft Corporation (now McDonnell-Douglas) on the same assembly line. The difference is in the equipment placed in the interior of the planes. The airline equips the interior with nice (but removable) interior walls, seats, coat closets, lavatories, and galleys whereas the military equips the interior of the same aircraft with fuel tanks and the necessary equipment to accomplish refueling activities.

The same principle applies to airlines' decisions on the interior of the planes they are using for passenger flights. For example, many airlines now use Boeing 737 aircraft. However, each airline decides how many seats it will have, how many will be in first class, whether there will be a business class, and so on. In the cabin configuration, each airline also determines the actual structure of its galleys, although it will probably use modular structures to configure them. It is this flexibility in the configuration of the hollow shell of the aircraft body that leads to a lot of variance in the interiors of passenger aircraft galleys.

In some cases, however, this flexibility may increase the cost of the plane to the airline. Often, when a new model aircraft is being developed to meet the specifications of an airline or a group of airlines, the model which is finally developed and sold to the leader (or developing) airline or group of airlines will be the base model airplane. Subsequent purchasers who want to modify the base model with changes, such as a different galley location or configuration or a different number of lavatories, will have to pay a premium price over the base model.

GALLEY STRUCTURES

Each galley area is composed of a fixed galley structure. Fixed galley structures are the framework, plumbing, panels (such as the power panels) and work surfaces, countertops, shelves, and so on into which carts (trolleys), ovens, liquid containers (equipment used to transport food products, beverages, serving equipment and supplies from the inflight caterers kitchen to the aircraft), and any built-in equipment such as coffeemakers fit into. Figure 8.1 illustrates a galley structure fully loaded with trolleys, ovens, carriers, and other equipment. It is only the *framework* in the unit shown in Figure 8.1 that constitutes the galley structure. All of the remaining components are carriers, inserts, or modules that an airline can select to use in the structure compartments.

While these galley structures are generally built in modular sizes that can be configured to fit into many aircraft bodies, an airline outfitting multiple aircraft (or even a few aircraft for a higher price per unit) can specify the configuration of the galley structure units so that it is customized to accommodate the specific equipment components desired by the airline for its inflight foodservice specifications. In any condition, the airline will choose the specific model of coffeemaker, oven, and other pieces of equipment that it wants placed in the appropriate galley structure spaces. All of this equipment, even the built-in coffeemaker, is *plug-in* modular equipment that can readily be placed in or removed from the basic galley structure.

It is important that this galley equipment be constructed by reliable manufacturers knowledgeable about the airline industry as not just any equipment built in just any way will be functional on an aircraft or will meet aircraft equipment standards. For example, an airline could not just plug in a household coffeemaker or a toaster oven into its galley structure. All of the equipment used must be thoroughly tested and awarded a Standard Type Certificate (STC). No equipment can be used in an aircraft galley that has not been STC'd.

CONCERNS WITH CONSTRUCTION WEIGHT

Two areas of concern for any structures used on aircraft are weight and durability for weight. The weight of anything that goes on board an aircraft—whether it is people, freight, engines, or galley structures—is always a concern. There is a maximum weight that any equipped and loaded aircraft can have and still be able to become airborne with the lift provided by the engine power, the lift surfaces of the particular aircraft model, and

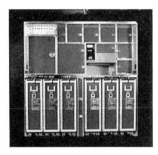

GALLEY STRUCTURES

CONSTRUCTION:
- Composite panels with mortise and tenon intersections
- CAM manufactured subassemblies and components
- Ultimate strength and light weight

ELECTRICAL:
- 115/200 volt AC, 400-hertz, 3-phase
- Approved bonding provision

OPTIONS:
- Fiberglass or carbon graphite panel structures
- Stainless steel or hard anodized aluminum work decks
- Composite panel or machined solid aluminum alloy doors

DESIGN:
- CAD designed to ATLAS, KSSU, or customer specifications

FEATURES:
- Complete interchangeability of like parts
- Integral lip on work decks
- Sealed panel joints and intersections
- Corrosion resistant

CERTIFICATION:
Fully meets FAR 25.853 (a-1) 65/65/200 flammability rule and all other higher certification standards

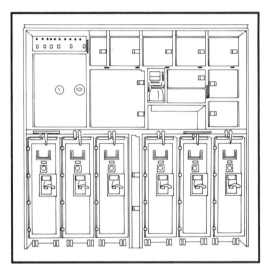

FIGURE 8.1 An illustration of an aircraft galley structure with equipment loaded into the structure. The galley structure provides the framework for the boarding equipment used for a flight's food and beverage service. (Courtesy of Aircraft Products Company)

the specified runway length. A plane should never be loaded beyond its maximum certified weight, and safety margins in weight allowances and takeoff distances are always maintained.

As has been noted, commercial airlines earn revenue by carrying passengers, freight, mail, and other such cargo. The more of the total weight allowance that is available for revenue-generating cargo, the more revenue (and hopefully profit) the airline can earn. Therefore, it is important that fixed equipment, such as galley structures (or seats, lavatory components, and so on) be made of materials that are as lightweight as possible while also being structurally strong. Some of the new composite materials now available for equipment construction, which are both lightweight and stronger than many metals, have made the manufacture of improved galley structures possible in recent years.

THE DURABILITY OF GALLEY STRUCTURES

The durability of interior structures, such as the galley structures, is also quite important. During takeoffs and landings, especially, as well as in weather problems such as turbulence or other conditions which can cause sudden movements of the aircraft, the body of the aircraft and all attached structural components are subjected to very high stress. The galley must be able to maintain its structural integrity, no matter what the stress on it or on the aircraft frame.

Equipment that is used for aircraft galleys and galley components must be in accord with Federal Aviation Regulation (FAR) 25.853. This regulation is concerned with the materials used in the construction of aircraft interior components and with the durability of component construction design. Equipment not in compliance with this regulation may not be sufficiently sturdy, relative to its weight, to withstand the stress placed on it during flight operations. Therefore, although lower-cost bids may be submitted for galley structures, galley components, or other boarding equipment, only equipment constructed in accord with FAR 25.853 can be considered for use on board passenger aircraft.

While it is not pleasant to think about, the ability of the galley to retain its structural configuration is also a crash consideration. A disintegrating galley, and the release of many pieces of heavy equipment, could be the cause of passenger injuries or deaths that might not otherwise occur if the galley retained its integrity on sudden impact. This is much the same principle that applies to research on automobile structural integrity in crash situations. Equally important is the fact that, on most aircraft, the galley structures are adjacent to the exit doors. Having the galley retain its structural configuration on impact may mean that passengers are able to escape through the exits.

Another concern with the durability of the galley structure is its locking mechanisms. These locking mechanisms are there to hold all of the components (ovens, trolleys, etc.) in place during stress periods or periods when the aircraft is climbing to or descending from its flight altitude (takeoffs, landings, turbulence, and so on). During these times, all the equipment in the galley must be *securely* locked into place with locking mechanisms that will *not* fail.

If the locking mechanisms should fail, the laws of gravity will prevail, and the free-falling equipment piece can become a flying missile or rolling truck which can cause injury to both the flight attendants and passengers as well as damage other equipment or passenger property. Since equipment such as loaded ovens or fully loaded trolleys can easily weight 100 to 200 pounds or more, the injury or damage that could be done by such free equipment could be substantial and could expose the airline and the inflight caterer to substantial risk.

SUMMARY

Generally, airlines have control over the galley structures on the planes that they use for their flights. Since galley structures are very modular, as is the equipment used in them (to be discussed in the next chapter), customizing the galleys to meet the particular needs of the airline is quite possible.

All equipment used for inflight food and beverage services, whether it is located permanently in the aircraft or is boarded equipment, must be well constructed of lightweight materials. It must meet all of the construction standards of any other equipment used on an aircraft. The modular nature of the equipment further contributes to the need for its precision construction.

KEY TERMS

Maximum Certified Weight
Modular Equipment

Serviceware
Standard Type Certificate (STC'd)

DISCUSSION QUESTIONS

1. Who owns the boarding equipment used for inflight food and beverage services? Why is this so?

2. Does it matter which pieces of equipment go on which aircraft? Explain your answer.
3. Can equipment owned by one airline be used to service the boarding needs of a different airline?
4. How important is it for the right amount of the right equipment to be boarded on a flight? Why is this so?
5. Does it make any difference to the inflight caterer if an airline changes the aircraft assigned to a particular flight? Explain why or why not.
6. What is meant by the term *galley structure*?
7. Why is it necessary for an inflight caterer to know the different configurations of aircraft galley structures? Why are the galley structures not the same in all passenger aircraft?
8. Why are galley structures and their inserts built in modular configurations?
9. Why is there concern about the weight and durability of galley structures used on aircraft? Discuss how new materials now available are leading to improvements in weight and durability.
10. What are some factors that should be taken into consideration when evaluating galley structures and equipment for possible use on aircraft? Why are these factors important?
11. Explain why it does not work for an inflight caterer to take equipment and serviceware off an inbound flight, clean and/or wash it, and then simply reload it with the foods and beverages needed on that particular aircraft's outbound flight.

9

Airline Galley Equipment

LEARNING OBJECTIVES

After studying this chapter, the student should be able to:

1. Identify reasons for replacement of modular units within a galley structure.
2. Identify features of an aircraft beverage system that distinguish it from a traditional coffee-making system that might be found in a commercial foodservice facility.
3. Describe at least two different types of rethermalization equipment that might be on board an aircraft.
4. Discuss how hot meals are boarded onto aircraft when the rethermalization ovens are part of the equipment built into the galley structure.
5. Identify at least four uses of trolleys (or carts) in inflight food and beverage services.
6. Describe the features of a typical trolley used in inflight foodservices.
7. Explain why the casters on a trolley and the trolley's brakes are significant cart construction components.
8. Discuss the responsibility for and the procedures to be used in the repair and replacement of airline-owned boarding equipment.
9. Discuss concerns associated with equipment balance and actions that an inflight caterer might take to acquire necessary boarding equipment.
10. Describe the acquisition process of small wares, such as trays, china, glassware, flatware, and linens and the inflight caterer's role in this process.

The galley structure of an aircraft must be equipped with different pieces of equipment to make it functional for passenger food and beverage service. There are a number of different types of equipment that fit into the galley structures of most aircraft. Some of these equipment pieces remain on board most aircraft at all times while others are components of the equipment that is used to board the required foods, beverages, and serviceware.

FIXED GALLEY STRUCTURE EQUIPMENT

Fixed galley structure equipment consists of items such as coffee makers, service counters, some types of ovens or other rethermalization equipment that are not readily removable and do not serve a dual role as boarding equipment, and storage compartments for the boarding equipment containing the food products, beverages, and supplies. Such equipment is not removed from the aircraft by the inflight caterer when they off-load the aircraft on its arrival at an airport. It is generally the airline's responsibility to clean and maintain all galley structure equipment. However, the caterer's boarding crew is sometimes responsible for cleaning and sanitizing the galley work surfaces and sometimes the galley floors when they are servicing the aircraft.

Modular Structure of Galley Equipment

It is important to remember, though, that galley structures and the equipment placed in those structures are modular and highly varied among airlines and among different aircraft for the same airline. Because the galley is constructed of a frame into which modular equipment is inserted—and that equipment may be frequently changed—the importance of high-quality, precision construction of the galley structure is underscored. A number of manufacturers construct equipment which might be used in any one galley. It is essential that all equipment be compatible with the basic framework of the galley if the manufacturers want to continue to service the airline industry.

Even though some galley equipment may not be part of the boarding equipment, this equipment is still modular and readily removable from the galley structure. In some instances, such equipment is constructed as *plug-in* units, which precisely fit into a designated compartment in the galley structure. That compartment has the appropriate power or water source lines built into it, or provided to it through a rail unit on which the piece of equipment can be mounted, so that all that has to be done to install the particular piece of equipment is to mount it into the space and plug it in.

416-0201/62-0101
RAIL
ASSEMBLY

OVERALL DIMENSIONS:
Height . . . . 2.687 inches (68.25 mm)
Width . . . . 5.825 inches (147.96 mm)
Depth . . . . 11.718 inches (297.64 mm)

WEIGHT:
2.60 pounds maximum

CONSTRUCTION:
Anodized aluminum casting

ELECTRICAL:
• Electrical current from aircraft power supplied to the unit through the connector on the rail is 115 VAC, 3-Phase, 400 Hz

OPTIONS:
• Rear or sump drain for unit server base

PERFORMANCE:
• Rail assembly serves as a quick disconnect for electrical power, fresh water, and optional drain system
• Permits unit to be easily removed or re-installed in or out of the rail assembly, facilitates maintenance
• No tools required to remove/re-install unit on the rail

SAFETY:
• Equipped with isolated AC return and dual static grounds

SPECIAL FEATURES:
• Rugged construction
• Precision guide pin ensures proper engagement of water and electrical connections

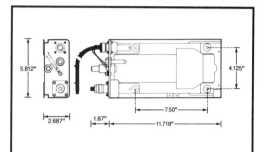

FIGURE 9.1   Rail assembly that is installed in aircraft galley structures to provide "plug in" power and fresh water source and an optional drain system for galley equipment. (Courtesy of Aircraft Products Company)

Figure 9.1 illustrates a rail assembly that provides the connection into the aircraft's power and water and drainage systems needed by the piece of equipment to be mounted to the rail unit. Figure 9.2 illustrates a coffee maker that can be mounted on the rail assembly and readily installed in the modular space allocated for coffee or beverage makers in the galley structure.

Other equipment that may be used in a galley configuration, such as the high-heat oven shown in Figure 9.3 or the water boiler shown in Figure 9.4, are permanently mounted into the designated spaces in the galley structure and connected directly to the aircraft's power, water, and draining systems. However, because they are still modular units that are mounted into the galley structure, and are not constructed as an integral part of the galley structure, they could be removed at any time with a minimum of effort and replaced by other structures of the same modular size.

Reasons for Replacement of Modular Units

Some reasons for possible replacement of these modular units (either installed on rail assemblies or installed directly into the modular space) would be: (1) to make repairs to a unit needing maintenance; (2) to install a new, improved model of the same type of equipment; or (3) to make a change in the type of system or products used by the airline for its inflight food and beverage services. This modular type of construction for galley structure equipment is an important advantage for the airlines as it enables them to replace components in need of maintenance or repair with equipment that can be operational in a very short time. This short repair time is essential to keep an aircraft flying on schedule. While aircraft systems are generally redundant, there is no spare space in aircraft galleys, and all equipment must be operational for all flights.

The life of a particular aircraft may exceed that of the galley equipment used on it, or new developments in galley equipment may be made more frequently than aircraft are replaced. Thus, modular construction enables airlines to upgrade their galley equipment at any time while still keeping an aircraft operational. The same concept applies to a change in the type of food products or in the system that an airline might choose to use for its inflight food and beverage services. Such a change may mean new equipment requirements. As long as the new equipment is constructed in accord with the modular configurations of the existing galley structures, the old equipment is readily replaced with the new, and the airline is able to change its inflight foodservices.

416-0001/416-1001
COFFEE MAKER
(Mechanical/Touch Switch)

OVERALL DIMENSIONS:

Height . . . . 12.00 inches (304.80 mm)
Width . . . . 6.32 inches (160.53 mm)
Depth . . . . 14.89 inches (378.21 mm)

WEIGHT:

19 pounds (8.6 Kg) maximum (empty)

CONSTRUCTION:

Primarily of cast anodized aluminum alloy

ELECTRICAL:

- 115 Volts AC, 3-Phase, 400 Hz
- 2785 Watts TOTAL
  - 2700 Watts (Tank heaters)
  - 60 Watts (Heater pad)
  - 25 Watts (Control circuit)

OPTIONS:

- Mechanical switches or membrane touch panel
- Extended standard faucet/tap
- Swivel faucet
- Rear or sump drain on server base

PERFORMANCE:

The unit will brew 54 ounces (1.6 L) of coffee in 2 minutes 45 seconds ± 15 seconds with a recovery to repeat in approximately one minute.

SAFETY:

- Hot water to brew head will stop should the brew lockdown be inadvertently raised.
- Should the water tank sidewall temperature become excessive, power to the heaters will automatically be removed by three manually resettable overheat switches.
- Dual server level sensors prohibit the start of brew cycle if there is a full server.
- Control circuit will prevent operation when the internal tank temperature is below 32°F (0°C) or above 212°F (100°C).
- Low water sensor prevents heaters from operating when water level drops below the sensor.
- Over pressure relief valve is designed to relieve at 80 PSI.
- COLD WATER light will illuminate red should there not be enough water in the tank.

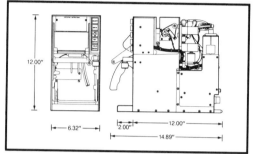

SPECIAL FEATURES:

- Rugged, easy to operate
- Uses "pillow pack" (filter paper packaged) coffee
- Unmonitored operation, frees flight attendant to other duties
- Easy to clean stainless steel server base
- Standard rail mounted unit
- HOT WATER and COLD WATER push button operated faucet/tap

OPERATION:

To begin brewing, server and brew cup (with pillow pack) must be in place, the brew handle locked down and the ON/OFF and BREW switches activated. Once the water in the tank reaches the correct brewing temperature, 195°F (91°C), the HOT WATER light will illuminate and the brew cycle will begin. Brew cycle will end when coffee or liquid in the server reaches the sensor probes in the server. BREW light will de-energize approximately 15 seconds after completion of brew cycle. The HOT PLATE switch will allow the brewed coffee/liquid in the server to be maintained at 170°F to 190°F (77°C to 88°C) for approximately half an hour.

APC OFFICES — Manufacturing Facilities: Delray Beach, Florida • APC Headquarters • P.O. Drawer 130 • Delray Beach, FL 33447 • Tel: (407) 276-6083/Fax: (407) 278-8031/Telex: 497-5073 • Jacksonville, Florida • Manufacturing (Structures) • 11710 Central Parkway • Jacksonville, FL 32216 • Tel: (904) 641-4900/Fax: (904) 646-0281 • Regional Offices: Long Beach, California • Western Regional Office • 3780 Kilroy Airport Way • Suite 200 • Long Beach, CA 90806 • Tel: (213) 988-6556/Fax: (213) 988-1920 • Minneapolis, Minnesota • Midwest Regional Office • 1 Appletree Square • Suite 202D • Bloomington, MN 55425 • Tel: (612) 854-2745/Fax: (612) 854-4505 • Seattle, Washington • Northwest Regional Office • 10900 N.E. 8th Street • Suite 1038 • Bellevue, WA 98004 • Tel: (206) 455-2685/Fax: (206) 454-4383 • Germany • European Regional Office • Tiroler StraBe 531 • 6000 Frankfurt/Main 70 • Germany • Tel: (069) 637-053/Fax: (069) 631-1113 • Taiwan • Far East Regional Office • Chung Hsiao E. Road, Section 4 • 12th Floor, Suite 1, No. 512 • Taipei, Taiwan, Republic of China • Tel: (02) 755-7577-80/Fax: (02) 704-8821

FIGURE 9.2 Typical coffee maker that might be installed into a rail assembly such as the one shown in Figure 9.1. (Courtesy of Aircraft Products Company)

2510-0003
HIGH HEAT OVEN

OVERALL DIMENSIONS:
Height . . . . 27.50 inches (698.50 mm)
Width . . . . 14.68 inches (372.87 mm)
Depth . . . . 35.63 inches (905.00 mm)

WEIGHT:
121 pounds (54.89 Kg) maximum (empty)

CONSTRUCTION:
• Stainless steel base and inner liner
• Clear anodized aluminum outer case

ELECTRICAL:
• 115/200 Volts AC, 3-Phase, 400 Hz
• 7300 Watts
• Blower wheel 7500 RPM

OPTIONS:
• Right or left hand hinge
• Door trim color

CONTROLS:
• Operates by using 2 controls on front face, timer and temperature setting
• Mechanical timer (1 to 120 minutes with 10 minute soak cycle)
• Temperature settings of 155°F (68°C) HOLD, 275°F (135°C) MEDIUM, 375°F (191°C)

OVEN CAVITY:
Height . . . . 20.25 inches (514.35 mm)
Width . . . . 11.25 inches (285.75 mm)
Depth . . . . 31.50 inches (800.10 mm)

PERFORMANCE:
• Will reconstitute 70 typical in-flight meals
• Will maintain cooked meals at approximately 155°F (68°C) serving temperature

SAFETY:
• Vent flap on oven door vents water vapor prior to opening oven door
• Indicator light illuminates when oven is in operation
• Manually resettable overheat thermostat 450°F (232°C)
• Overtemp indicator light

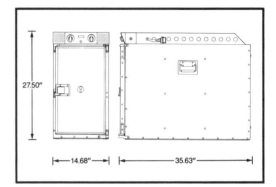

SPECIAL FEATURES:
• Combination rack slide baffles mounted to each sidewall (remove without tools)
• Recessed carrying handles each side
• Coated door latch and laminated door trim provide a comfortable touch temperature
• Detented hinges hold door open during loading and unloading
• Ceiling mounted blower wheel optimizes heat distribution
• Fully meets FAR 25.853 (a-1) 65/65/200 rule

FIGURE 9.3 One model of a high-heat oven commonly used in aircraft galleys to rethermalize entrees for passenger meal service. (Courtesy of Aircraft Products Company)

400-0001
WATER BOILER

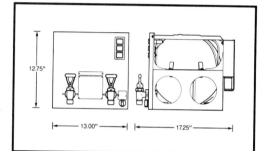

OVERALL DIMENSIONS:
Height . . . . 12.75 inches (323.85 mm)
Width . . . . 13.00 inches (330.20 mm)
Depth . . . . 17.25 inches (438.15 mm)

WEIGHT:
30 pounds (13.7 Kg) maximum (empty)

CONSTRUCTION:
- Cast anodized aluminum frame
- All stainless steel tank and front face
- All plumbing and fittings are stainless steel, except for the chrome plated brass pressure relief valve and faucets/taps

ELECTRICAL:
- 115 Volts AC, 3-Phase, 400 Hz
- 6030 Watts TOTAL
  6000 Watts (Tank heaters)
  30 Watts (Control circuit)

OPTIONS:
- Water temperature thermometer

PERFORMANCE:
The unit will heat 4 gallons (15 L) of water to 195°F (91°C) in approximately 11 minutes.

SAFETY:
- Should the water tank sidewall temperature become excessive, power to the heaters will automatically be removed by six manually resettable overheat switches
- Control circuit will prevent operation when the internal tank temperature is below 32°F (0°C) or above 212°F (100°C)
- Low water sensor prevents heaters from operating when water level drops below the sensor
- Over pressure relief valves are designed to relieve at 80 PSI.
- NO WATER light will illuminate should there not be enough water in the tank

SPECIAL FEATURES:
- Rugged, easy to operate
- Self-closing manually operated hot water faucets/taps
- Front mounted drain valve facilitates complete drainage of water tank without removing the unit from the galley
- Unit will preheat water to 195°F (91°C) in 15 minutes
- After an initial draw off of 1.5 gallons (5.68 L) at 195°F (91°C), recovery to 195°F (91°C) will not exceed 4 minutes, 30 seconds

OPERATION:
To begin heating water, the ON/OFF and HOT WATER switches must be activated. Once the water in the tank reaches 195°F (91°C), the WATER HOT light will illuminate (normally 15 minutes from a cold start). Following an initial draw off of 1.5 gallons (5.68 L) in one minute, recovery to 195°F (91°C) will not exceed 4 minutes, 30 seconds.

FIGURE 9.4 A water boiler that might be found in an aircraft galley to rapidly heat water. Unit contains sensors as a safety feature to cut off power to the unit in case of low water level or excessive heat in the tank sidewall. (Courtesy of Aircraft Products Company)

BEVERAGE EQUIPMENT

There are several types of beverage equipment that might be found in aircraft galleys. Such equipment might include: coffee makers, water boilers, combination coffee makers and water boilers (combi-units), hot and cold jugs, and hot cups.

Coffee makers are just that—drip coffee makers that brew coffee one pot at a time. They differ from coffee makers that might be found in other foodservice operations in that they have self-contained boilers which heat the water drawn from the aircraft's water system to the proper brewing temperature. That temperature will be around 180°F on an aircraft. An aircraft cabin is pressurized to a level approximately equivalent to the air pressure at an altitude of 8,000 feet (about the altitude of Aspen, Colorado), and water boils at a lower temperature at higher altitudes.

Another important feature that would not be found on any other type of commercial coffee brewing equipment is the locking mechanism that locks the pot into place in the coffee maker. The brew mechanism of the coffee maker will not operate unless the pot is properly locked into place. This locking mechanism is an important safety feature as it prevents the pot with hot coffee (or hot water if the mechanism is a water boiler or a combination unit) from falling out of the brewer or being thrown out as a result of a sudden movement of the aircraft.

Another safety feature on this type of equipment is the automatic sensor controls which prevent its operation should the water tank overheat or the water temperature go below the freezing point. Because the outside air temperature is so cold at high altitudes (e.g., at an altitude of 30,000 feet, it could be as low as −55°F), it is possible to freeze the water in the aircraft's holding tanks. This type of equipment will not operate when sensors indicate that the water level is too low in the water tank. When the water level is low, not only will the pots not brew, but the tank heaters will not operate either.

Generally, these coffee makers (and the water boilers and combination units as well) are high-speed units with the capability of brewing a pot of coffee (approximately 1.5 quarts in volume) in 2.5 to 3.5 minutes with a recovery time between brew cycles of approximately one minute. Once brewed, most coffee makers (or beverage holding units) will maintain the temperature of the coffee in the pot at a temperature of 170°F to 190°F (77°C to 88°C)—depending on the altitude. This high-speed brewing capacity is necessary to enable the flight attendants to service all the passengers on a fully loaded flight in the serving time that is available, particularly on some of the shorter flights.

Water Boilers/Combination Units

Water boilers and combination units are similar to coffee makers. Water boilers heat water to the boiling point for brewing tea or coffee. Combination units can either brew coffee or just heat water, depending on whether a coffee packet is put into the machine or not or depending on what option is selected on switch settings.

Hot and Cold Jugs

Hot and cold jugs are the modern thermos jugs of early inflight foodservice. They are insulated containers that will hold cold beverages cold and hot beverages hot for a limited time period. The hot jugs have heating elements which will plug into outlets in the galley structure. The heating elements help keep the contents hot until they are served during the flight. There are no similar units in the cold jugs as cold items can be chilled with ice for longer holding periods.

The most common capacity of these jugs is two gallons, but they can sometimes be obtained in a one- or three-gallon size. A feature that may be found in these jugs is that the inner tank is designed on an angle sloped toward the faucet to facilitate emptying the jug while it is mounted in place in the galley.

A hot cup is a two-quart unit which is used to rapidly heat water on the aircraft. Similar to the hot pot found on the retail market, it plugs into an outlet in the galley structure and immediately begins heating. The thermostat automatically shuts off the heating unit when the container reaches a temperature of 221°F (105°C). It turns on again when the container temperature cools to 203°F (95°C). Having a hot cup available means that flight attendants always have hot water ready to meet requests for tea or hot chocolate or other beverages that have to be individually brewed in the passenger's cup.

RETHERMALIZATION EQUIPMENT

Convection Ovens

The workhorse among rethermalization options available is, and has been for some time, the convection oven. As previously noted, the convection oven was first developed by Pan American Airways in 1945 and manufactured by the Maxson Company. Since then, the convection oven has been modified and improved, but it is still the basic rethermalization unit used for inflight foodservices (and many other types of foodservices, as well).

Generally, the convection oven modular units are mounted into the galley structure in the space designated in the airline's galley configuration. In most cases, the oven units themselves are not removed from the aircraft when it is serviced by the inflight caterer. However, there are exceptions in some types of galleys, most notably those for the L-1011. Here, the ovens sit on top of the trolleys for off-loading from the aircraft and for boarding meal service provisions. The entrees to be heated are loaded into the ovens while they are on the trolleys in the caterer's kitchen. Once on board, the ovens are taken off the trolleys and plugged into the aircraft.

Holding Ovens

Other aircraft where the ovens are removed from the planes and taken to the caterers' kitchens are some Boeing 727s. Here modular galleys are actually removed from the aircraft and taken to the inflight kitchens. Because of the size and weight of these units, special handling equipment is required for their movement. The entrees to be served are heated in the caterer's kitchen and packed straight from the caterer's ovens into the modular galleys. The galleys are then transported to the aircraft and plugged into the galley area on board the airplane.

This type of galley structure is one of the few remaining situations where the food is heated in the caterer's kitchen and transported to the aircraft already heated to the appropriate serving temperature. Because the 727 galleys have temperature control units built into the transport equipment which help insure temperature maintenance above 140°F, these galleys have survived increasing concern with food protection standards. However, it is anticipated that the overall life of these galley units is short as the 727s are gradually being phased out and replaced by the more fuel-efficient 757s (that also have a lower noise pollution level).

Oven Inserts/Racks

In the general situation where the ovens are not removed from the aircraft galleys, there are racks which fit inside the oven units which actually hold the meals that are being heated. In the inflight kitchen, the entree dishes are placed on glides (or trays) that slide into the racks. These racks, then, are the transport equipment for boarding the entrees that are to be heated for a particular meal service. However, since these are open racks, U.S. Food and Drug Administration (FDA) regulations required that they either be covered with plastic during the transport process or placed into carry boxes for transport and boarding onto the aircraft. Covering the meals also prevents any dust or dirt particles from collecting on the foil covering the entrees which could possibly fall into the entrees when the covers are removed for service to the passengers.

When they are boarded, the racks with the meals are placed inside the galley ovens on the aircraft where they will be heated for meal service. Figure 9.3 illustrates a convection oven with a capacity for heating 70 entrees at one time. Figure 9.5 illustrates a different model of a convection oven that has a capacity of 32 entrees. Figure 9.6 illustrates an oven insert and racks that could be used to board the meal entrees as well as become the racks used in the convection oven when the entrees are heated.

Loading Ovens on Aircraft

Several oven units are required for a typical commercial aircraft since one oven unit has a capacity for only 32 to 70 meals depending on the model used. The ovens are distributed among the different galley spaces on the aircraft according to airline galley configurations and galley loading specifications. The ovens have optional temperature settings which enable the flight attendants to vary the heating periods to best meet the serving periods of a particular flight. Usually these ovens also have a holding temperature setting that will maintain the entrees at a serving temperature of approximately 155°F (68°C) until they are served.

All of these ovens have carry handles; they are mobile and can be readily transported from place to place. However, they are not light, weighing from 45 to 121 pounds, empty. With the added weight of the meals, fully loaded, two persons would generally be required to lift and move them. A typical coach entree weight is 9 to 10 ounces plus the weight of the dish or casserole. The dish or casserole weight would vary, depending on whether it was plastic or ceramic. At an estimated 12 ounces per entree, the entree weight for an oven with a 40-meal capacity would be 15 pounds added to the empty weight of the oven. In comparison, the carry boxes are made of lightweight sheet metal, and they are not insulated. Therefore, they are much lighter to carry, especially when fully loaded with the meal entrees.

High-Technology Heating Systems

Although convection ovens are by far the most common rethermalization equipment in use on commercial aircraft today, they are not the only systems available. There are now some high-technology carts available that function as transport and boarding equipment, as well as heating and chilling equipment for all components of the meal once they are boarded onto the aircraft. Drawing on technological developments of the space industry, these carts usually have imbedded heating elements, either on the rack holding the entree or in the entree plate, as the means of heating the entree while the rest of the cart remains chilled. Figure 9.7 illustrates a high-technology system with the heating elements imbedded in the entree plate while Figure 9.8 illustrates a system which requires the entree container to be placed on the small contact pads on the left-hand side of the cart just above each tray rack.

2510-0032 ATLAS HIGH HEAT OVEN

OVERALL DIMENSIONS:
Height . . . . 22.09 inches (560.83 mm)
Width . . . . 11.22 inches (284.99 mm)
Depth . . . . 22.04 inches (583.44 mm)

REMOTE CONTROLLER DIMENSIONS:
Height . . . . 4.39 inches (115.51 mm)
Width . . . . 4.00 inches (101.60 mm)
Depth . . . . 7.69 inches (195.33 mm)

WEIGHT:
45 pounds (20.45 Kg) maximum (empty) (**oven**)
2 pounds (.91 Kg) maximum (**controller**)

CONSTRUCTION:
• Stainless steel base, inner liner
• Clear anodized aluminum outer case

ELECTRICAL:
• 115/200 Volts AC, 3-Phase, 400 Hz, 3850 Watts
• Blower wheel 7500 RPM

OPTIONS:
• Adjustable temperature control
• Audible chime when cook cycle is complete
• Overtemperature indicator
• Door hinging, right or left side
• High impact plastic door or stainless steel

CONTROLS:
• Modular, slide-out design facilitates maintenance
• ON/OFF switch and mechanical timer (1 to 60 minutes, 10 minute soak cycle)

OR:
• **Remote flush mounted oven controller** will operate either KSSU or ATLAS standard high heat ovens
• Preset cooking temperature settings LOW (225°F, 107°C), MED (335°F, 168°C) and HI (400°F, 204°C)
• One hour timer with 10 minute soak mode to provide a uniform entree temperature
• Automatic hold mode and soak cycle

OVEN CAVITY:
Height . . . . 19.00 inches (482.60 mm)
Width . . . . 10.45 inches (265.43 mm)
Depth . . . . 19.50 inches (495.30 mm)

PERFORMANCE:
• Will reconstitute in-flight meals, 32 per cavity
• Low exterior temperature during operation

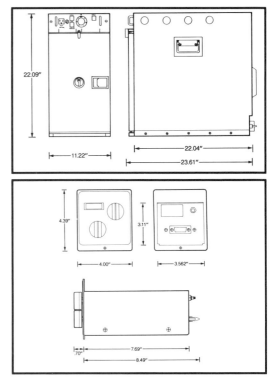

SAFETY:
• Door vent flap vents oven prior to opening oven door
• Manually resettable overheat thermostat 450°F (232°C)

SPECIAL FEATURES:
• Accepts ATLAS standard casserole carrier
• Slide-out removable control module (no tools required)
• Recessed carrying handles each side
• Polished stainless steel inner liner facilitates cleaning
• Symmetrical door allows hinging on right or left side
• Quick disconnect rear mounted electrical connector
• Rear mounted blower wheel optimizes heat distribution
• Fully meets FAR 25.853 (a-1) 65/65/200 rule

FIGURE 9.5 A different rethermalization oven model than the one illustrated in Figure 9.3. This oven is much lighter in weight, even when fully loaded, as it has only about $\frac{1}{2}$ the capacity of the oven in Figure 9.3. (Courtesy of Aircraft Products Company)

- Aluminum extrusion frame attached to a one piece aluminum body
- Aluminum angle runners
- Body perforated to meet oven heating requirements
- Anodized or mill finish
- Lightweight and durable
- Racks to match insert, made of perforated aluminum (optional)
- Inserts and racks custom designed to customer dimensions and specifications

FIGURE 9.6 An oven insert and racks that would be used to transport meal entrees to the aircraft. When boarded, the insert would be placed into an oven mounted in the aircraft's galley structure so that the entrees could be rethermalized during the flight for service to the passengers. (Courtesy of Lermer Corporation)

In either case, since the heating principle for these ovens is conduction rather than convection, the entree has to be carefully placed to insure that contact is made between the entree dish and the heating elements for proper heating to occur when the elements are activated during the flight. In at least some of these systems, there is also a significant restriction on the configuration of the containers that can be put on the passenger's tray because of the size and placement constraints required for the heating unit contacts.

These newer rethermalization systems incorporate some of the latest technological developments available, and they can save galley space as

CHAMPION

FLITE FARE
MEAL SYSTEM

The Flite Fare Meal System is like an executive chef for executive aircraft. It's a versatile system that enables you to serve a variety of high-quality meals —quickly and easily. Meals are prepared and portioned in advance, then thermalized later on board.

The key is Flite Fare's unique heating/serving dishes. They contain individual sensors which detect when proper serving temperatures are reached— then automatically switch to a holding mode to keep meals at proper serving temperature.

The dishes are designed to hold hot food hot, yet the outside remains cool for safe handling. They are dishwasher-safe. Dishcover is reusable clear polycarbonate.

A variety of heating cabinets are available. Each is compact, lightweight, rugged and dependable.

The Flite Fare Meal System. It's designed for ease, convenience and the perfect degree of meal quality for your executive aircraft.

Master Switch

Shelf Cut-Off Switches allow for heating control of individual shelves

Interior Light Switch

Digital Timer and Controller provides variable control for flexibility in prep time (0-60 minutes)

Removable Shelves for easy cleaning. Shelves also lock dishes in securely to maintain good contact when heating.

Individual Shelf Lights

Interlock Safety Switch automatically cuts power when door is opened.

Ceramic inner dish with insulating plastic outer shell.

Entire system removable for simple cleaning and servicing.

Tinted, see-through door.

FIGURE 9.7 One type of high-technology heating system for entree rethermalization which has heating elements embedded in the entree plate. (Courtesy of Champion Products Inc.)

HIGH CUISINE MEAL SYSTEM

CONSTRUCTION:
- Light weight composite panel sidewalls and doors
- Stainless top
- Injection molded heater pad shelves

ELECTRICAL:
- 115 VAC, 3-phase, 400 Hz

OPTIONS:
- Mechanical or Touch Switch Controller
- Cooling—dry ice or chiller system
- Decorative trim
- Brushed or hard anodized aluminum extrusions
- Cart dimensions and capacity correspond to customer requirements

SPECIAL FEATURES:
- Eliminates oven requirement
- Facilitates passenger inflight service
- Creates additional galley storage space or passenger seating
- Fully meets FAR 25.853 (a-1) 65/65/200 flammability rule and all FDA requirements

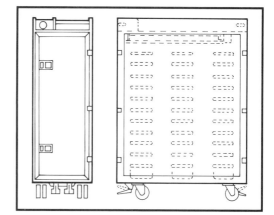

FIGURE 9.8 A different type of high-technology meal heating system which eliminates the requirement for an oven in the galley structure by having entree heating pads that heat only the entree dish built into the tray boarding carts. The pads allow the remainder of the tray to remain chilled. (Courtesy of Aircraft Products Company)

they use refrigerated carts as the rethermalization equipment as well as the boarding equipment for the meal trays and entrees. The space saved could be significant and could allow more seats to be added to the aircraft cabin. However, they have met with only limited airline acceptance because of the additional constraints on meal packaging that are encountered and the additional costs incurred without an increased level of product quality or passenger satisfaction. Other problems encountered with the entree heating carts have included butter and dessert icing melting and salads being warm because of heat transfer that has occurred. Indeed, there is some question regarding the continuing viability of these products in the inflight foodservice market.

Radiant Heat Units

There are other, smaller warming ovens (radiant heat as opposed to heating by conduction or convection air flow) that are sometimes used in aircraft. These smaller ovens might be used for purposes such as heating rolls or hot towels in first-class service or for heating a small number of entrees on a charter flight, private business aircraft flight, or any flight where there are only a small number of entrees required. Such units plug into the galley structure and heat products much as an oven in a standard electric range would. Figure 9.9 illustrates these small ovens.

Insulated Trays

In the past, some airlines used insulated trays, such as the trays manufactured by Aladdin Synergetics, Inc., which are used quite a lot in health care foodservice systems, in lieu of on-board ovens to serve hot meals. Now, while smaller airlines may use this system in a few instances, only one major airline still uses this system.

When the Aladdin system is used, the hot entrees are heated in the caterer's ovens in the flight kitchen. Then, the trays are assembled on the caterer's tray line. The insulated trays have compartments made to hold the several dishes of hot and cold items required for the meal. All of the items required for the meal, including both the cold foods and the hot entree, are placed on the tray in the specified compartments. The tray lids (also insulated) have inserts cut out to exactly fit over the tray compartments.

When the trays are stacked, cold items fit over cold items and hot items fit over hot items in vertical thermal columns which help each of the compartments retain the proper temperatures. The system has been refined and improved over the years it has been in use, and is quite effective at retaining proper food product temperatures over an extended period of

ATLAS High Heat Oven

This ATLAS high heat oven is state-of-the-art in reliability, maintenance and safety, will re-constitute 32 meals in 30 minutes while maintaining a low exteri-or temperature on all exposed surfaces. Models available with modular or remote type controller. Its optional high impact plastic door is symmetrical and may be hinged from the right or left hand side. Options include an audible chime and overtemp indicator. Fully meets FAR 25.853 (a-1) 65/65/200 flammability rule.

Oven Controller, ATLAS/KSSU

This versatile remote controller is equipped with a 1-hour timer and can operate both ATLAS or KSSU ovens. It has 3 preset temperature settings (Low/Medium/High) with a built-in 10 minute soak cycle and an automatic hold mode upon completion of cook cycle.

FIGURE 9.9 Small high-heat oven that can plug into an aircraft's galley structure. (Courtesy of Lermer Corporation)

time (approximately four hours). However, for this system to be effective, it is essential that hot foods be at 185°F to 190°F at the time they are packed into the trays. An important consideration prompting some airlines to continue the use of this system is that the trays eliminate the use of heavy heating ovens that require quite a lot of electrical power from the plane's power system. The reduced power demand can have an impact on an aircraft's fuel usage.

Microwave Ovens

Contrary to popular belief, microwave ovens are very infrequently used on aircraft. Indeed, there are few modern aircraft used by the major airlines even equipped with such ovens. Today, they are used primarily on small corporate or private aircraft where only a few meals have to be heated (or to pop popcorn). Microwave ovens are really not practical on large passenger aircraft due to the limited oven capacity of microwaves, the individual handling involved, and the large number of meals to heat.

Despite those restrictions, TWA actually introduced microwave ovens, which had been developed and tested in conjunction with Litton Industries, in the 1968–1970 period. The ovens were designed for the first-class galley in their fleet of international 707 aircraft, with one microwave added to augment the convection ovens. The international first-class configuration was just 16 seats, and menus were designed to incorporate items that could be heated in the microwave and served in a timely manner. This included crab imperial appetizers and baked potatoes, heated from scratch.

In a classic example of the kinds of challenges airline foodservice staffs sometimes face, at that time TWA's marketing department decided at the last minute that the microwave ovens should be installed on the fleet of domestic 707 aircraft because there was a greater competitive need in the transcontinental market. Instead of the carefully orchestrated service for 16 passengers, the domestic 707s had 28 first-class seats and menus could not really be designed around the microwave capabilities. The idea was to offer a theme of "service on request," but the idea never worked as well for 28 passengers as the concept had for 16. Eventually, when 747s were introduced, the microwaves were removed from 707s and incorporated into the 747—one in first class and one in coach. The intended use was limited, such as food that needed additional heating or for warming hot towels; eventually they just became too much of a luxury and were replaced by more important galley and service requirements.

CARTS (TROLLEYS)

Carts of all types make up the bulk of the boarding equipment. They are versatile pieces of equipment for both the airline and the inflight caterer. Because carts are a modular size, regardless of their purpose the configuration of carts boarded on a particular aircraft can be readily customized to the specific needs of that flight. Carts are used for boarding almost everything for the flight's food and beverage services except that they are seldom used to tranport the hot entrees for a meal.

Some uses of these carts include:

1. *Boarding beverages*—liquor, beer, wine, and soft drinks, as well as the nut packets (or other snack packets), cups, napkins, garnishes, and other supplies needed for beverage service.
2. *Boarding serving utensils, linens, china, glassware, and other such serving equipment and supplies*—particularly for first-class and business-class service.
3. *Boarding the trays set with the tray service items and the cold food items for the meal service.* Generally, these carts are chilled with dry ice placed in dry ice drawers with vents designed to maximize the flow of chilled air throughout the cart. There are only a limited number of electrically powered refrigeration units on board an aircraft. Dry ice is the primary cooling medium that is used for most chilled food products.
4. *Boarding duty-free products on international flights.* While these items are not food and beverage items, their bonded storage is often handled by the inflight caterer servicing the airline. The flight attendants are responsible for their sale, and the products are stored in the galley areas on the aircraft.
5. *Boarding trash containers and, as waste management programs expand, boarding trash compactors.* Trash handling is a major concern of airlines and inflight caterers, as will be discussed in Chapter 14. Carts provide the wastebaskets for the aircraft for all types of waste associated with food and beverage services, as well as any other trash generated by the passengers.

Tray Carriers

Often there is insufficient capacity on the carts for all of the passenger trays. Additional trays are boarded through the use of tray carriers which are also refrigerated by dry ice. Figure 9.10 illustrates these carriers and a standard drawer that fits into these carriers (often used for boarding milk or other such products that are not preset on trays but need to be kept under refrigeration).

Sometimes it is still necessary to double-stack, or piggyback, trays in the carts or carriers to have enough trays boarded for the passenger count for the flight. When trays are double-stacked, a full tray with two sets of components is placed over an empty tray before it is loaded into the cart of the carrier.

Galley Refrigerated Units

In some instances, there are electrical refrigerator or freezer units installed in the galley structures of the aircraft (particularly in first-class galleys).

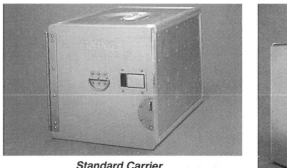

Standard Carrier

Meal Container

Standard Drawer with Lid

FIGURE 9.10 Standard carriers are used to board many items onto an aircraft, ranging from chilled entrees to serviceware and condiments. The drawer can be stocked according to the airline's specifications. It can then be placed into a carrier or into a cart. (Courtesy of Lermer Corporation)

Here, trays or other food products that need to be refrigerated or frozen are packed into carriers that are put directly into the refrigerator or freezer units which are electrically powered from the aircraft's power system, just as are the convection ovens or other types of heating equipment. The most efficient refrigerator and freezer units use forced air systems for improved circulation of the chilled air throughout the unit. Figure 9.11 illustrates a forced air refrigerator unit that might be found on board an aircraft.

Cart Dimensions

Most of these carts come in either the original full size or the newer half-size dimensions. The difference in size between the two models is in the depth (or length) of the cart. Whereas a full-size cart would be 12 inches wide, 40.5 inches high and 31.75 inches deep (or in length), a half-size cart would still be 12 inches wide and 40.5 inches high, but it would be only 15.95 inches deep (or in length). As their name indicates, the half-size carts have about half the capacity of the full-size carts. For example, a full-size

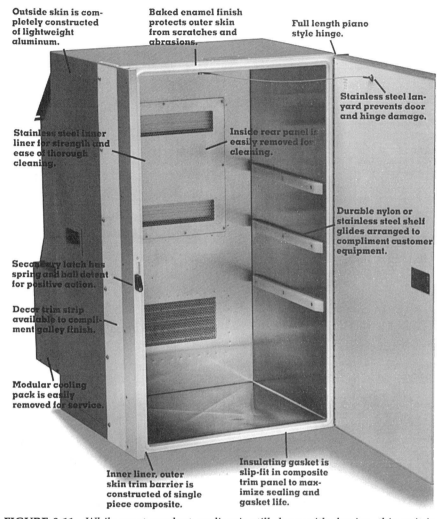

Outside skin is completely constructed of lightweight aluminum.

Baked enamel finish protects outer skin from scratches and abrasions.

Full length piano style hinge.

Stainless steel lanyard prevents door and hinge damage.

Stainless steel inner liner for strength and ease of thorough cleaning.

Inside rear panel is easily removed for cleaning.

Durable nylon or stainless steel shelf glides arranged to compliment customer equipment.

Secondary latch has spring and ball detent for positive action.

Decor trim strip available to compliment galley finish.

Modular cooling pack is easily removed for service.

Inner liner, outer skin trim barrier is constructed of single piece composite.

Insulating gasket is slip-fit in composite trim panel to maximize sealing and gasket life.

FIGURE 9.11   While most product cooling is still done with dry ice, this unit is an electrically powered refrigeration unit incorporating new construction technology that might be used for cold food storage in an aircraft galley. (Courtesy of Acurex Corporation)

tray cart stores two trays per shelf, or runner, while a half-size cart would store only one tray per shelf. However, there would be the same number of shelves in both carts as they are the same height.

The half-size carts have been developed to fit into some of the galley structures that have been designed for several of the newer, more fuel-efficient aircraft that many airlines are now flying whenever possible. Figure 9.12 illustrates a half-size cart configured to board passenger trays, and Figure 9.13 illustrates a full-size cart with the same configuration.

FIGURE 9.12 Half-size standard cart (trolley) for transport and storage of meal trays, drawers, and other products and supplies on board passenger aircraft. (Courtesy of Iacobucci S.p.A.)

Service Carts

Another type of cart that is found on board the aircraft, but with which the inflight caterer has little direct contact is a folding, or service, cart. This type is most frequently used in first class to provide cart service. Although the caterer has little contact with this cart, the caterer's staff must be aware of

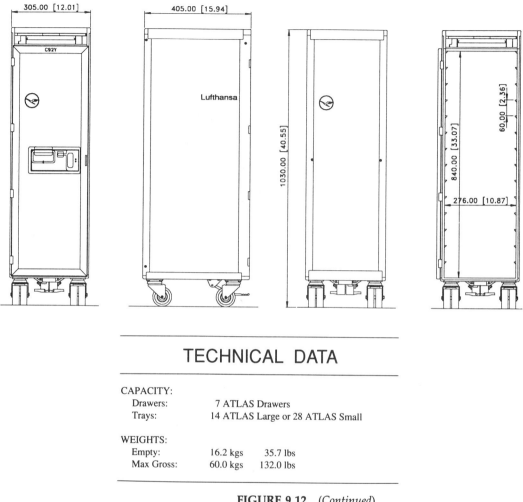

TECHNICAL DATA

CAPACITY:
Drawers: 7 ATLAS Drawers
Trays: 14 ATLAS Large or 28 ATLAS Small

WEIGHTS:
Empty: 16.2 kgs   35.7 lbs
Max Gross: 60.0 kgs   132.0 lbs

FIGURE 9.12   (*Continued*)

the cart and its dimensions when working with the airline to develop food products and serving procedures for which this type of cart will be used.

Casters and Brakes

Two very important components of all carts which are not always given a lot of consideration are the casters and the brakes. Both of these components must be very durably constructed to withstand the constant handling that the carts are subjected to.

The casters have to be strong enough to adequately support the weight of the cart (fully loaded carts are quite heavy) swivel freely, and roll

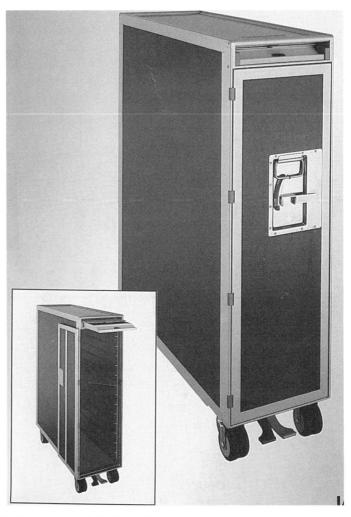

FIGURE 9.13 Standard full-size trolley used for the transport and storage of meal trays and other products and supplies on board passenger aircraft. (Courtesy of Iacobucci S.p.A.)

smoothly. It must be remembered that one flight attendant is probably going to need to be able to roll many of the carts up or down the aisle of the aircraft without undue effort. Because of the demands placed on them, cart casters are heavy duty dual casters, rather than the single wheel casters commonly used on foodservice carts. The quality of the casters used can have an important effect on how well the cart rolls and the extent of the maintenance that is required on the casters over the life of the cart. After all, if the casters do not work and the cart does not roll, it is essentially useless.

The quality of the brakes on the cart and their ease of use are just as important as the quality of the casters. Unless the cart is locked into its

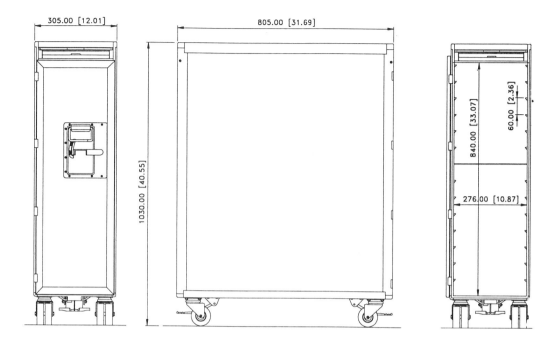

TECHNICAL DATA

CAPACITY:
Drawers: 14 ATLAS Drawers
Trays: 28 ATLAS Large or 56 ATLAS Small

WEIGHTS:
Empty: 29.0 kgs   64.0 lbs
Max Gross: 100.0 kgs 220.5 lbs

FIGURE 9.13 *(Continued)*

storage compartment in the galley structure, it is the cart brakes that keep the cart from moving when it is not being rolled to a new position. On board an aircraft where the aisle or the galley floor is usually not level (a plane typically flies 4° to 5° nose high) or could be subjected to sudden movements, quality brakes that will hold the heavy weight of the cart can be critical to avoid possible accidents.

As an added inflight safety feature, many aircraft have cart hold down devices built into the floor of the aircraft especially in galley and door areas where a number of carts may be staged during service. These devices or "mushrooms" as they are called are designed to grab hold of the under-cart brake device to provide additional inflight security and stability when carts are not actually in use during service. Some of these mushrooms are retractable to floor level (those in passenger or crew traffic areas) so as not to impede foot traffic. Caterers generally do not use these mushrooms during their loading or unloading process except those that may be part of a fixed galley floor assembly.

Equally important is the ease with which the brakes are set and released. Flight attendants must often work quickly and must move a cart from which they are providing beverage or meal service frequently. They do not have the time (or the patience) to struggle with the brakes on the carts. Since the brakes are usually set and released with the attendant's toe, the brake control mechanisms should be designed in such a way that the flight attendants can set and release them without constantly scuffing the toe of their shoes. Continual scuffing can ruin their uniform shoes and result in additional uniform expense for them.

EQUIPMENT REPAIRS AND REPLACEMENT

The airline is responsible for keeping all of the inflight boarding, galley, and service equipment in good repair and stocked at the caterers' in amounts adequate to service the airline's needs. Of course, purchasing stocks of this equipment requires an investment of capital, which the airlines do not necessarily see as profitable. Therefore, most airlines prefer to keep their equipment investment as low as possible. Because the supply of equipment is limited, an important concern of each inflight kitchen is having an adequate supply of all the equipment required to board a particular flight for a particular airline.

When a caterer finds a piece of equipment that needs repair, it is put aside and not used. To get it repaired, the caterer first rates the priority of the equipment problem on a three-level scale of "now," "urgent," or "delayed." The equipment is then tagged to indicate the problem and the determined priority level, and the airline is notified about the problem. The caterer retains the piece of equipment until notification is received from the airline regarding the action to be taken.

The airline may determine that the equipment is to be repaired locally at the airline's repair shop on the airport premises, or the piece of equipment may be shipped to a central point designated by the airline for equipment repair, depending on the piece of equipment, the problem, and the policies of the airline involved. In some situations, though, the caterer does assume responsibility for equipment repair.

Once the equipment is repaired, it is placed back into service by the airline, but it will probably not return to the caterer who took it out of service and submitted it for repair. It will be put back into service either at the caterer's facility which is nearest the repair point or at a facility requesting an additional amount of that type of equipment at that particular time.

The airline also makes the decision regarding the amount of equipment needed in the inflight catering system to support its flights and their service needs. The airline may or may not discuss its perception of boarding equipment needs with the caterers servicing its flights. When caterers find that they are having problems locating an adequate amount of equipment to service an airline's flights, they must discuss those problems and their recommendations for equipment replacements with that airline's representative with whom they work. In the partnership relations that are developing now between the airlines and their inflight caterers, it is anticipated that when equipment shortages are called to the attention of the airline they will take appropriate actions to provide the equipment needed by the caterers to service the airline to the standards desired.

No matter what actions are taken by the airlines, equipment balance (or the appropriate distribution of equipment to caterers within an airline's system) is a major problem for inflight caterers and likely to continue to be so. As has been indicated, all airlines maintain different levels, or quantities, of equipment and supplies. However, they all have an inventory management system that their caterers report to on a daily, weekly, or monthly basis so that each airline knows where its equipment is, and collectively, how much they have within the system.

TRAYS, CHINA, GLASSWARE, FLATWARE, AND LINENS

The serving trays, reusable plastic dishes, and flatware used for all classes of service and the china, glassware, and linens used for first-class service are also all provided to the inflight caterer by the airline. Generally, they are purchased by the airline from the supplier of their choice and shipped to the inflight caterers. Since the airline is the purchasing agent for this equipment, it is purchased by the airline on its purchase order through its purchase agreement with the supplier. The supplier in turn bills the airline, not the caterer, for the purchase, even though it may ship the products to a designated address other than the airline's office which originated the purchase order.

Most airlines have their logo or their name or both on their trays, linens, and serviceware. Such use of their name and logo is one means of marketing an airline to its passengers as it keeps the airline's name and logo in front of the passenger while they eat or drink.

An important responsibility of the caterer is keeping all of these trays, linens, and small wares accounted for and separated by airline served in their production kitchen facilities. Generally, the caterer turns over the stock of these items that it recovers from in-bound flights daily and does not have a large backup stock of these items to work with. Therefore, accountability for and efficiency in organizing and using these items is very important to the caterer's ability to meet its service responsibilities to the several airlines it is working with.

SUMMARY

This chapter has discussed the galley equpiment placed into the galley structure on passenger aircraft serviced by the inflight caterer, as well as equipment owned by the airline but used by the caterer to pack and board the necessary food products, beverages, and supplies. Since galley structures are very modular, as is the equipment used in them, an airline can configure the galleys to meet its particular needs.

All equipment used for inflight food and beverage services, whether it is located permanently in the aircraft or is boarded equipment, must be well constructed of lightweight materials. It must meet all of the construction standards of any other equipment, whether seats, bulkheads, or closets, used on an aircraft. The modular nature of the equipment further contributes to the need for its precision construction.

A variety of equipment pieces are used to provide inflight foodservices. Generally, the equipment is tailored to specific uses, but must be as adaptable as possible to make the very best use of the space available. The airline is responsible for all inflight equipment supply, repair, and maintenance.

The airline is also responsible for supplying its caterers with small wares such as the passenger service trays, linens, plastic dishware used in coach class, flatware, china, and glassware. The caterer is responsible for storing, cleaning, and resetting trays with these small wares (or packing them into the appropriate boarding cart for first-class service) and for keeping the wares of all the airlines serviced by the caterer separated and accounted for. Because of the volume of meals prepared by an individual caterer, this accountability is no small task.

The bottom line is that there is much equipment associated with the provision of inflight food and beverage services which is the property of the individual airline. Equipment and small wares belonging to one airline cannot be used on another. The logistics involved with tracking all of this equipment and the small wares as they pass through the caterer's production facility enroute to being returned to the right aircraft of the right airline in the right amount at the right time is a real challenge to the inflight caterer.

KEY TERMS

Double Stacking (Piggybacking) Trays

Equipment Balance

Folding Cart (Service Cart)

Oven Rack

Redundant Aircraft Systems

Tray Runner (Shelf)

DISCUSSION QUESTIONS

1. Cite some examples of galley equipment. Discuss why this equipment can just slide in and out of the galley structures (or at least be fairly easily replaced).

2. Why would an airline want to replace a piece of galley equipment in its aircraft? Why is the modularity of this equipment a significant advantage when replacement is desired?

3. What are some unique features of beverage equipment found in aircraft galleys? Why are these features important on board an aircraft?

4. What piece of equipment is the workhorse for rethermalization on board an aircraft? Why is this so? What other types of rethermalization equipment are available?

5. How are entrees for hot meals boarded when the ovens are not removed from the aircraft for boarding? Why is it more practical to board the entrees this way than to always remove the ovens from the aircraft (even if they did just slide in and out)?

6. Describe how some of the newer high-technology carts work to rethermalize entrees while keeping the rest of the tray chilled.

7. How are trolleys, or carts, used during the boarding and serving of foods and beverages on board an aircraft?

8. Describe a typical full-size trolley. How is a half-size one different?

9. Why are the casters and the brakes of a trolley very important? What are some caster or brake features to consider when selecting a trolley for use on board an aircraft?

10. Who is responsible for all inflight boarding equipment, galley and service equipment repair and replacement?

11. What is the procedure that the inflight caterer must follow when a piece of equipment is in need of repair?

12. How does an inflight caterer acquire more boarding equipment and serviceware for an airline's inflight foodservice needs? Or can the caterer acquire such equipment? Who makes the decision to replace equipment or to increase the stock in circulation?

13. What is meant by the term *equipment balance*? Why is equipment balance such an important problem for the inflight caterer?

14. How does an airline know where its equipment is at any point in time? What is the inflight caterer's responsibility in this regard?

15. Why would an inflight caterer heat entrees to their proper serving temperature in the inflight kitchen rather than board them chilled? What equipment would facilitate the handling and heating of these meals? What airlines are using insulated tray systems?

10

Inflight Caterers' Equipment and Facilities
Refrigeration, Ice Production, and Food Preparation

LEARNING OBJECTIVES

After studying this chapter, the student should be able to:

1. Explain the cook–chill (freeze) system that is used for the production and transport of most inflight meals today.
2. Discuss the importance of having proper equipment and storage facilities if a cook–chill (freeze) production system is to be used.
3. Discuss why new refrigerants meeting the environmental protection regulations are now being used, and the potential implications of these new regulations for inflight caterers.
4. Discuss actions that inflight caterers may need to take to modify their refrigerations, freezing, and icemaking equipment to comply with environmental impact laws regarding refrigerants and their impact on the ozone layer.
5. Explain why ice machines and a large ice production capacity are essential for an inflight catering kitchen.
6. Describe the different types of ice that might be produced by ice machines and the suitability of the different types for different inflight food and beverage service applications.
7. Explain why most inflight caterers cure ice and keep a stock of bagged ice on hand at all times.
8. Discuss why an inflight caterer might want an automated icemaking system if the usage volume were adequate to support investment in this type of system.

9. Discuss equipment available to facilitate the handling of the high volumes of fresh produce typically used by inflight caterers.
10. Identify other high-volume production equipment (other than produce-handling equipment) that might be found in an inflight kitchen.
11. Describe how coach-class entrees are now typically acquired and handled in an inflight kitchen.
12. Describe equipment often used in inflight kitchens to facilitate the handling and packaging of serviceware and the tray-set process.

Many activities of the inflight caterer are accomplished through the use of equipment that is the property of the airlines. However, the caterer also has a kitchen facility which is used for the production and packaging of the meals for transport to the aircraft, and the equipment in that facility as well as the transport equipment is the property of the inflight catering firm. The design and layout of the caterer's facilities and the equipment available in it to accomplish the work that must be done are important considerations in this logistics- and capital-intensive industry. No less important is the specialized delivery equipment required to service the aircraft.

INFLIGHT FOODSERVICES AS COOK–CHILL SYSTEMS

Most inflight foodservices are cook–chill (freeze) foodservice systems. In this type of system, all food products, including those products that are to be served hot, are cooked prior to the day of service and are either chilled or frozen. If the products are frozen, they are then tempered (or completely or partially defrosted) for 24 to 48 hours prior to boarding on the aircraft. On most airlines, all the products, whether they are to be served chilled or hot—whether they were initially frozen or initially chilled—are boarded on the aircraft in the chilled state. (The exceptions here, as noted previously are some of the 727s still in use today and planes using the Aladdin insulated tray system.) Of course, if it is something like ice cream or other food product that is to be served frozen, it is boarded frozen.

Although once quite commonplace, in today's inflight systems it is rare for products to be boarded already hot in insulated containers. However, it should be noted that the use of the insulated tray system, or any other system that requires hot foods to be rethermalized in the caterer's kitchen, means that hot foods are retained at high temperatures for fairly extended periods of time (approximately 2 to 3 hours with no flight delays). Such extended holding times can contribute to product quality deterioration as a result of excess cooking time.

These long holding times also mean that departure delays or changes in flight schedules are more critical for these meals than for those boarded in the chilled state as there is a finite time period for which these trays or other systems are capable of maintaining the hot entree temperatures. If a holding time of approximately four hours is exceeded or the entree temperatures fall below 140°F before they are served to the passengers, the meals must be replated and the original meal is destroyed. It is anticipated that, as aircraft are replaced, the practice of boarding entrees at serving temperatures will gradually completely disappear.

Chilled products, such as the entree, that are to be served hot are then rethermalized on board the aircraft in rethermalization equipment such as that discussed in Chapter 9. Depending on the product, the length of the flight, and the anticipated time that meal service is to start after the flight departs, the rethermalization process may begin just as soon as the meals are loaded on board the aircraft, or the flight attendants may begin the process after the aircraft is underway.

Anytime that a cook–chill (or cook–freeze) system is used, it is essential that the production kitchen be well equipped with adequate refrigeration and freezer space and that equipment capable of rapidly chilling or freezing the prepared products be part of the facility's refrigeration or freezing equipment. Food safety requirements mandate that hot, prepared foods to be used in a cook–chill or a cook–freeze system be cooled to an internal temperature of less than 70°F in less than two hours and to below 45°F in an additional four hours. Depending on the product to be chilled and the volume of new product added to the refrigerator per hour, achieving appropriate chill times may require a special refrigerator with a very-high-velocity airflow, or in the case of cook–freeze systems, a blast freezer may be required.

Generally, the food products that are produced in the inflight caterer's production facility are portioned into individual servings as part of the initial production process, then put into the refrigerator to chill. Because the products are chilled as individual portions, the mass of each unit is small, which facilitates the rapid chilling of the products.

Exceptions to items being chilled as individual portions would be products to be used in first-class service where the flight attendants are portioning the product on board, often as a part of first-class cart service. An example of this type of situation would be a chateau or sirloin roast that is to be carved on board in front of the passengers as they are served. However, the number of first-class passengers on any one flight is relatively small (compared with the number of coach-class passengers); so, the total quantity of any product to be chilled in bulk for first-class service is still relatively small. Thus, it can be chilled quite rapidly. In most instances, even though the flight attendants may be plating the entree components on board the aircraft, the components are preportioned during the production process and chilled and boarded as individual portions.

REFRIGERANT ISSUES FACING INFLIGHT CATERERS

Because of their high reliance on extensive refrigerator and freezer units, as well as on ice production equipment, inflight caterers need to be concerned with the recent laws regarding the use of refrigerants. These laws have been developed on a worldwide basis as a result of the concern with the depletion of the ozone layer and global warming. As a member of the global community, the United States has promulgated laws and regulations in accord with the international agreements in regard to the refrigerant issues.

The U.S. Clean Air Act was passed in November 1990. This legislation contained comprehensive regulations for the production and use of ozone threatening compounds, such as the chlorofluorocarbons (CFCs), including the refrigerants R-12 (Freon) and R-502 commonly used for commercial refrigerators and freezers. Among the regulations in this act were (1) phase-out schedules for the use of CFCs in the United States; (2) mandates for recycling and recovery of refrigerants in auto-air-conditioning units as well as in stationary refrigeration equipment such as commercial walk-in or reach-in refrigerators or freezers; and (3) dictates concerning safe alternatives that might be developed and used. Alternative refrigerants must meet criteria such as being inflammable, nontoxic, and environmentally acceptable.

Under these regulations, U.S. production of CFCs must end by December 31, 1995. Dupont, one of the largest U.S. manufacturers of refrigerants, decided to end their CFC production by December 31, 1994. It should be noted that this ban is on the *production* of CFCs, not the *consumption*. Therefore, it will still be legal to purchase and use CFCs as refrigerants until the supply runs out. Of course, the price of these refrigerants has already risen markedly, and will continue to escalate as the supply declines. Anyone who has had to service the air conditioner in their car recently can certainly verify the marked price increase for refrigerants that has occurred since the passage of the Clean Air Act.

Options Available

As a result, inflight caterers have three possible options regarding their refrigeration and freezing equipment. These options are: (1) stockpile CFCs currently used in their equipment and continue to use them until the supply is depleted; (2) wait for their equipment to break down and then replace it with a system that uses the new refrigerants being developed; or (3) convert their equipment to an alternative system now. One factor that will help extend the supply of CFCs is that the current laws make it illegal to vent CFCs into the atmosphere when equipment is being serviced.

All CFCs must be recovered, and they can be sold back to refrigerant manufacturers for recycling. The fine for anyone found venting CFCs to the atmosphere is severe—$25,000 per day per violation.

Ultimately, all caterers will have to consider either retrofitting (or converting) their equipment to make it operable with the new refrigerants or replacing the compressors for their equipment or even the complete refrigeration or freezer unit. However, that decision should not be made hastily. If a system is not leaking refrigerant to the atmosphere and is operating properly, there is no technical reason to replace the CFC refrigerant the system is using. Indeed, retrofitting the equipment to change the refrigerant under these conditions may void the U.L. listing of the unit.

The decision to retrofit equipment currently using R-12 and R-502 should be based on a number of factors, including the following:

1. The system's age: Retrofitting is not recommended for equipment purchased prior to 1973 because different materials were used in motor insulation then. These insulation materials have not been evaluated for compatability with the new refrigerants and the lubricants required for them to work.
2. The retrofit cost: Current costs to retrofit a small reach-in refrigerator is $300—about half the cost of a new one; costs for larger systems are higher.
3. Reclaimed CFC availability.
4. Aversion of technical risk: Many of the new alternative refrigerants are just being developed, and there is much ongoing research in regard to this problem.
5. Public relations concerns: If retrofitting is not appropriate and a supply of CFCs is not available, then when compressor servicing or replacement is needed, there may be no alternative to investing in new equipment.

Use of HCFCs

Most newer equipment is now being manufactured to use R-22 as the refrigerant in compressors. R-22 is a hydrochloroflurocarbon (HCFC). HCFCs are a class of refrigerants that can be used on an intermediary basis as transitional products between the CFCs and the development and use of refrigerants which have no impact on the ozone layer. R-22 is now being widely used as the refrigerant of choice for most new equipment as it has a low first cost and an ozone depletion potential (ODP) of only 0.05 (compared with 1.0 for R-12 and 0.37 for R-502). R-22 and other HCFCs will also ultimately be phased out of use, but the phase-out period is much longer than for CFCs. R-22 can no longer be produced for new equipment after the year 2010, and in 2020, R-22 production will cease entirely (under the current regulations).

One of the most important things that inflight caterers should do now is learn as much as possible about refrigerants and the new rules governing their usage. There is little question that the Environmental Protection Agency (EPA) will be watching all types of foodservice operations more closely to be sure that violations, such as venting refrigerants to the atmosphere, are not occurring. Caterers need to be proactive about this issue and begin planning ahead to avoid potentially high unanticipated costs in the future just to maintain the refrigeration and freezing systems that they need to operate their facility.

ICE MACHINES

In addition to refrigerators and freezers, another very important piece of equipment for most caterers is the ice machine. The demands for ice are very high in inflight foodservices. The inflight caterer is expected to provide all of the ice needed on all of the flights serviced by the caterer. Often, the very high volume of ice required means that the caterer is in the ice-production business. Indeed it may be difficult for the caterer's facilities to keep up with the ice demand, particularly in the summer when both ice usage and melt is higher than in the winter. If the caterer should run low on ice and the facility's machines are working at maximum capacity, there is no alternative other than purchasing additional ice from an outside ice-house (or ice manufacturer).

Having to purchase ice from an outside supplier, as opposed to making all needed ice in-house, is very expensive for most caterers in the United States. Since the markup on ice charged to the airlines is minimal, having to purchase ice outside to supply airline clients essentially reduces the caterer's profit on ice sales to nothing. Thus, some of the most important equipment in the inflight caterer's production facility is for icemaking, ice packaging, and ice storing/handling.

Internationally, though, not all inflight caterers are in the ice-production business. While most major caterers in Europe do make their own ice as the U.S. caterers do, major caterers in Japan make no ice. They find it more economical to purchase ice for all of their needs from an outside ice contractor.

Types of Ice

The inflight caterer does not just make ice; a caterer makes *several kinds of ice* for different uses. Ice is much more than frozen water, and the mechanics of producing it are not as simple as most people think when they reach into their refrigerator's freezer unit and get a few cubes from their automatic icemaker's storage bin. Ice can vary in terms of size, shape, clarity, consistency, and sanitation. The kinds of machines used and the total ice production system available in an inflight caterer's facility is an important determinant of the type and quality of available ice.

One type of ice that is usually made is called *tube* ice. This is the round, barrel-like ice with the hollow center that is used for beverage service on the aircraft. This type is used for few other purposes as it tends to melt rapidly because the hollow center decreases the total mass of the cube and allows greater ice-to-ambient-air contact.

Other types of ice that are produced by the in-flight caterer include crushed, flakes, and cubes. Crushed and flake ice also melt rapidly because of their low mass, but they are best for icing areas such as a salad or dessert bar that might be used for first-class service on international flights. Because it is a solid mass, cube ice has the slowest melt time. It is used on board the aircraft for beverage service. Indeed, cube ice and tube ice are used interchangeably on domestic flights, depending on the ice machines that the caterer who is servicing the aircraft has in its kitchen.

Ice Production

An inflight caterer is generally going to have multiple ice machines which are well maintained and serviced to keep them at optimum operating efficiency. The discussion earlier in this chapter regarding refrigerants and the need to make changes in equipment using refrigerants in compliance with the Clean Air Act and the regulations derived from this act applies to ice machines as well as to refrigerators and freezers.

Generally, the ice machines used by inflight caterers will be high-volume machines. Depending on the temperature of the water when it enters the ice machine and the power level supplied to the compressor, a large-capacity tube machine could produce from 2,500 to 3,400 pounds of ice per 24-hour period. The colder the water is at the point of entry into the machine, the less it must be chilled to reach the freezing point, and the less time it takes to make a piece of ice—thus, more ice can be produced per day. A high-volume cube or flake machine could produce from 3,000 to 5,000 pounds of ice per 24-hour period.

Because there are peaks and lows in air traffic during a 24-hour period, personnel transporting foods and beverages to the aircraft cannot just go to the ice machine and bag ice for transport as they need it unless their machines' icemaking capacity is quite large relative to the number of flights serviced by the kitchen. If that were the practice, there would be times when the machines were full and no longer producing any ice and other times when the ice would be all used up when more was needed for other flights. So the caterer usually bags ice from the machines throughout the day and stores it, ready for transport, in a freezer so that the machines will keep producing ice throughout each 24-hour period.

Bagging ice ahead of time and storing it in the freezer may also be a requirement of some airlines. These airlines require that all ice boarded on their aircraft be *cured*, or hard-frozen in the bags (as opposed to bagged from the machine and loaded directly onto the transport truck for delivery to the aircraft) prior to boarding. The reason that these airlines request only cured ice is to slow ice melt during the transport and service periods. Also, dry ice is used to keep the ice frozen during the boarding process and while the ice is being held on board the aircraft. When dry ice is used to keep ice frozen, it is likely that partially melted, watery ice will be refrozen into a solid mass. It would be very difficult, if not impossible, for the flight attendants to break up such a mass into usable pieces while trying to serve beverages on the flight.

Anyone who has bagged and handled full bags of ice that weight four to five pounds or more knows that bagging and handling 5,000 pounds of ice per machine per day is a lot of work. Here, too, automation is a help to the inflight caterer. Equipment is available for bagging ice automatically as well as for closing and tying the bags shut. Figures 10.1 and 10.2 illustrate machines that can perform these functions.

Some inflight production facilities, such as several of the very large European flight kitchens, are such high-volume operations that they have fully automated ice-production, bagging, and storage systems. Figure 10.3 illustrates such a system. These fully automated systems are similar to those used in commercial ice production. They are highly efficient systems that can substantially reduce the costs of energy, water, and maintenance when compared with conventional type ice-production and handling equipment. In addition, there is a marked reduction in the labor costs required to supply the ice needed to meet the inflight caterer's service obligations. For example, industry studies indicate that it takes an average of twenty seconds to manually fill, tie, and store a bag of ice by conventional means. In this same time period, a fully automated system can fill, tie, and store thirteen bags—a productivity increase of 92 percent.

Even more important is the enhanced sanitation level that is possible with a fully automated system. Ice is considered to be a critical control item in terms of food safety because of the opportunities for ice to become contaminated through contact with human hands and dirty surfaces (floors, scoops, bag surfaces that have been in contact with the floor, and so on). In an automated system, the ice contacts only stainless steel or FDA-approved high-density polyethylene surfaces from the time it is produced until the bags are opened for use. As long as the system is properly maintained and the contact surfaces are regularly sanitized, the opportunity for ice contamination declines markedly.

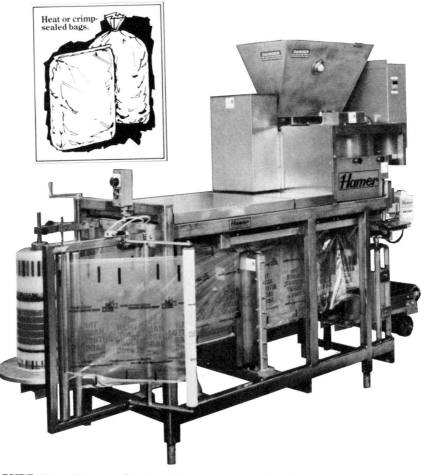

FIGURE 10.1 Automated ice bagging machines such as this one can save inflight caterers many hours of labor. (Courtesy of Automated Ice Systems, Inc.)

FOOD PRODUCTION EQUIPMENT

Food production equipment found in an inflight caterer's kitchen is similar to that found in other high-volume kitchens. The exact configuration of the equipment pieces and the volume capacity of the equipment is unique to each kitchen and is generally a function of (1) the resources available for equipping the kitchen, (2) the number of flights serviced by the kitchen, (3) the total number of meals served from the kitchen, and (4) the type of meal service requested by the airlines serviced. Production equipment such as grills, ranges, ovens, broilers, steamers, steam-jacketed kettles, mixers, and so on would likely be a part of most kitchens' equipment. However,

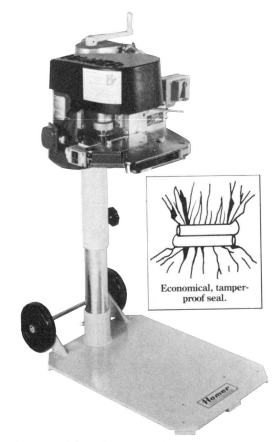

Economical, tamper-proof seal.

FIGURE 10.2 Automated bag closing machines such as the one illustrated here are an important component of an automated ice production system that an inflight caterer might use. (Courtesy of Automated Ice Systems, Inc.)

there are a few equipment considerations that are somewhat unique for inflight kitchens that will be discussed here.

Equipment for Handling Fresh Produce

An important consideration regarding the equipment for most inflight kitchens would be the focus on high-volume equipment to wash, prep, and finally prepare fresh produce items and any other such items that cannot be purchased for a particular use in a shelf-stable or frozen form. For example, most inflight lunch and dinner meals have some type of fresh vegetable salad as a component of the meal. Thus, salad greens of varied

Automated Wet Ice System Schematic

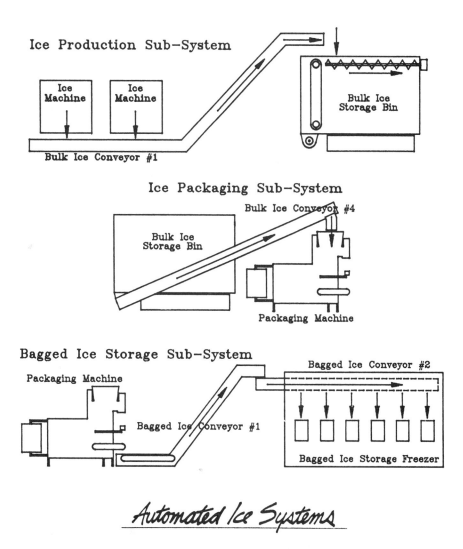

FIGURE 10.3 Schematic model of a fully automated wet ice production system. (Courtesy of Automated Ice Systems, Inc.)

types and other fresh vegetables, such as carrots, celery, or cherry tomatoes, have to be received, washed, and prepared for use in the salads, and the salads have to be made, generally in very large quantities unless the inflight kitchen is quite small. Therefore, equipment that would be appropriate to an inflight production kitchen would be machines that would facilitate the washing, handling, and cutting or chopping of large volumes of produce into salad-size pieces.

Examples of such high-volume vegetable-handling equipment would be a continuous-cycle vegetable washer such as that shown in Figure 10.4. A machine such as this, in the largest model made, could wash up to 1,500 pounds (or 0.75 ton) of light vegetables, such as salad greens or green peppers, per hour, and up to 4,400 pounds (2.2 tons) of heavy vegetables or fruit, such as carrots, potatoes, or apples, per hour. While such a machine would be appropriate only in very-high-volume inflight kitchens, smaller versions, such as the machine shown in Figure 10.5, would have application in almost any flight kitchen.

Machines such as these vegetable washers can be of great value to inflight caterers in terms of labor cost savings; in some very-high-volume kitchens, they may be what makes it possible to meet the production requirements of the many flights serviced. In other kitchens, the labor cost for washing produce has become so high that caterers are now finding that it is more cost effective to use prewashed produce.

Careful produce washing is also important for food safety. While the produce-washing machines can be very helpful in getting the products as clean as possible, they cannot sanitize the produce. Microbiological washes using sanitizers can be particularly critical for reducing microbial counts and ensuring the safety of raw fruits and vegetables served to airline passengers.

Once washed, an important concern for quality salads is drying the leaves, because excess moisture left on them will cause salad dressings to

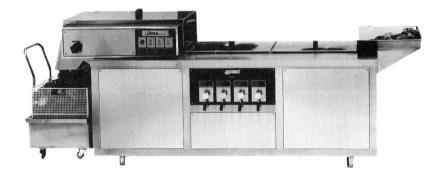

FIGURE 10.4 A very high volume automatic continuous washer for vegetables and fruits. (Courtesy of Nilma S.p.A., Parma, Italy)

FIGURE 10.5 A smaller capacity, universal vegetable and fruit washer that could be used in many inflight catering kitchens. (Courtesy of Nilma S.p.A., Parma, Italy)

run and could lead to deterioration of the refrigerated salad product. Again, automation can help with what is otherwise a very time-consuming task. Figure 10.6 illustrates an automated vegetable dryer that could dry up to eleven pounds of raw vegetables in a one-minute drying cycle.

Not only must the salad greens be washed and dried; they must be shredded into specified-size salad pieces as well. Figure 10.7 illustrates an automated shredding machine which, in the large-size model, has the capacity for shredding up to 1,540 pounds of leaf vegetables per hour.

Other Production Equipment

Some types of equipment that would help inflight kitchens handle a very-high-production volume are shown in Figure 10.8; a variety of other such equipment is available as well.

Although many tasks can be done manually or with equipment more traditionally found in production kitchens of all types, rising labor costs and the large number of meals required creates a need to develop and use equipment that is more automated (thus reducing overall labor requirements for the inflight kitchen) and capable of producing the

FIGURE 10.6 An automated dryer used to dry fresh produce in large volume food production operations, such as inflight kitchens. (Courtesy of Nilma S.p.A., Parma, Italy)

product volume that is required in the available production time. The incorporation of a particular piece of equipment would depend, as noted previously, on the resources available for equipment purchase, the labor savings possible, the demand for certain types of products by the airlines serviced, and the overall volume of the different types of products prepared by the kitchen.

The Use of Frozen Entrees

Much of the equipment discussed so far in this section is equipment that would be used by an inflight caterer to accomplish in-house production. However, the majority of the inflight caterers in the United States now

FIGURE 10.7 A shredding machine such as this one has the capacity for shredding high volumes of salad vegetables efficiently. (Courtesy of Nilma S.p.A., Parma, Italy)

confine a large portion of their in-house production to all of the foods required for first class and most of the items for business class and to uncooked items for all classes, such as the salad production discussed above. Many of their coach-class entrees are purchased frozen and ready to use—the cook–freeze component of most inflight foodservice systems. These frozen entrees are prepared by commercial manufacturers of frozen food products according to airline specifications. It should be noted that the manufacturers of these entrees are firms that primarily specialize in the unique custom requirements of airline meals, and not frozen food manufacturers who mass-produce frozen meals for the retail market. If an airline's usage volume is sufficient, its entrees will be prepared according to its particular specifications while smaller airlines or charter airlines may simply use whatever products a manufacturer or inflight caterer has available as a result of its production for the larger airlines.

However, even though these entrees arrive at the inflight caterer's facilities ready to use, they must still be stored until they are needed for service (requiring extensive freezer space to support a high-volume kitchen). They must also be made ready to use for the airline meals. As has been noted previously, there are two alternatives possible. The first is to heat the meals to an appropriate serving temperature in the inflight

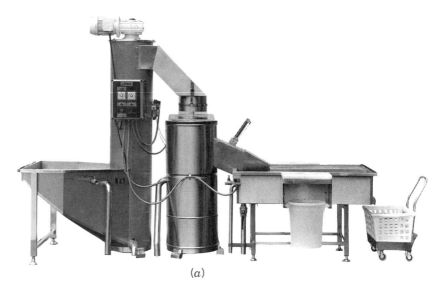

(a)

FIGURE 10.8(a) Many different types of high-volume food processing and production equipment are gradually being incorporated into inflight kitchens to help caterers produce large volumes of food products more efficiently. Examples of such equipment include: (a) automated line for potato peeling, mono-directional product flow; (b) a 75-gallon-capacity tilting braising pan; (c) a continuous fryer; (d) a double deep fat fryer with an automated oil pump (20-gallon capacity, each basin); (e) a double pasta cooker; and (f) automated very large capacity steam cooker. (Courtesy of Nilma S.p.A., Parma, Italy)

caterer's facility, package them hot for transfer, and hold them hot during the transport period and on board the aircraft until time for service.

The other alternative is to temper the meals in the inflight caterer's refrigerators so that they are partially thawed and transport them to the aircraft in this chilled state. There are two reasons for tempering the frozen entrees before boarding them onto the aircraft. One is to reduce the time required to rethermalize them on board the aircraft. The other is to assure that the temperature at the beginning of the onboard rethermalization process is a constant temperature (usually about 38°F) so that the rethermalization time can be standardized for the flight attendants. If the boarding temperature for the frozen entrees was not relatively constant, the flight attendants would have no idea how to gauge the pace of the rethermalization process or to estimate the serving time of their meals.

It should be noted, though, that not all coach-class entrees are the pop-out frozen meals. Some airlines still specify freshly prepared entrees that are produced in-house in the caterer's kitchen. Some charters, corporate planes, and contracts for military flights also still want the caterer to prepare their meals in-house.

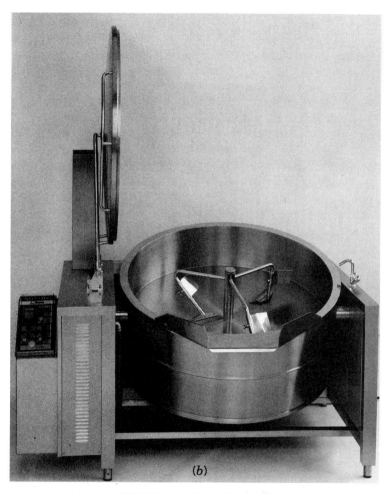

(b)

FIGURE 10.8(b) *(Continued)*

PACKAGING EQUIPMENT AND FACILITIES

Packaging the components for the inflight meals and packing the boarding equipment with all of the components also requires the use of specialized equipment in the inflight caterer's kitchen. One of the logistical considerations faced by the inflight caterer is keeping the individual airlines' flatware separated and packaged into the plastic packets to be placed on each passenger's tray. As with many food production processes, the high volume of flatware being used makes flatware packaging by hand economically unfeasible because of the very high labor investment that would be involved.

Generally flatware and condiments are packaged together into one packet that can be quickly placed on passenger trays during the tray assem-

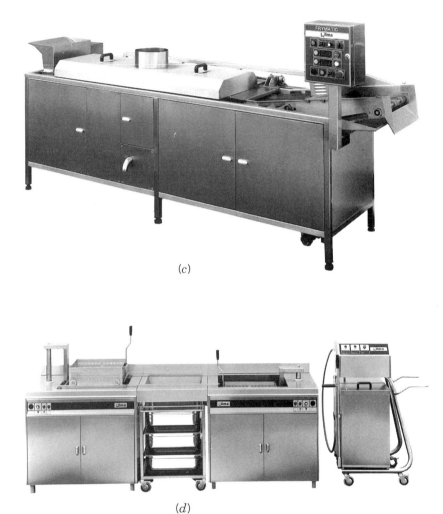

(c)

(d)

FIGURE 10.8(c) and (d)   *(Continued)*

bly process. This packaging is now done automatically by machines that can feed one of each item desired in the packet on a conveyor belt; the items are then automatically packaged together and sealed into a plastic packet. Such a machine is illustrated in Figure 10.9.

This machine can be operated by one person, but operations are much more efficient with two or three operators. It is capable of producing from 5 to 60 packets per minute, according to the manual specifications. The

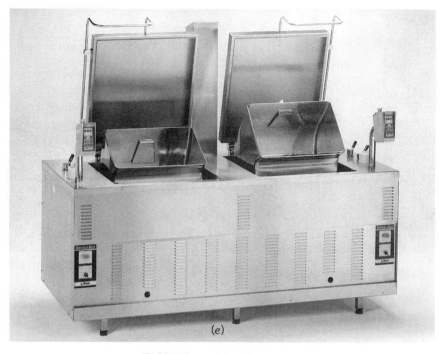

(e)

FIGURE 10.8(e) *(Continued)*

usual production rate is from 20 to 30 per minute, depending on the number of components being packaged and what those components are. For example, when napkins are included in the packet, it takes longer to package a packet than if there is no napkin. Unfortunately (from the viewpoint of production efficiency), first-class flatware packets must still be rolled and banded by hand. Stainless or silver-plate flatware and linen napkins are generally used for this class of service, and the linen napkin cannot be handled by the machine.

The passenger trays are set up with the required flatware, condiments (usually packaged together), cup, and any cold food items and then put into the airline's trolleys or other boarding equipment for transport to the aircraft. As has been discussed in Chapter 4, usually an automated tray line is used for this purpose. The configuration of the tray line varies from kitchen to kitchen, depending on the space available for it, the number of personnel available to work on it, and the total number of trays to be set in one day.

The operating principle, however, is the same for all tray lines, regardless of their size or configuration. The efficiency of such tray lines can be measured in the number of trays prepared per minute, or the number of trays prepared per hour in large operations where many identical trays must be prepared.

(f)

FIGURE 10.8(f)   (Continued)

SUMMARY

Most inflight foodservice kitchens are operated as cook–chill systems. Thus, refrigerators and freezers are some of the most important equipment in the caterer's facility. Generally, most inflight caterers have a large refrigerator and freezer capacity in order to accommodate the extensive flow of products that is required.

Because of the importance of refrigerators and freezers to the inflight caterer, the new laws and regulations regarding the use of refrigerants, promulgated worldwide in an effort to protect the earth's ozone layer, potentially have a signficant impact on the caterer's operating costs. It is important for inflight caterers to learn as much as they can about the new refrigerants and how the laws and regulations governing refrigerant usage will affect their particular operation. Making cost-effective decisions regard-

FIGURE 10.9 Automated packaging machines are used to package utensils, condiments, and napkins in accord with each airline's specifications, efficiently using a minimum amount of labor. (Courtesy of Ogden Aviation Service)

ing refrigerant usage and equipment retrofitting or replacement requires planning ahead.

Many inflight caterers are also in the ice-production business, a further reason for them to be concerned about the changes in refrigerant usage requirements. Caterers are responsible for providing the airlines with all of their ice requirements, which means that most caterers are handling very large volumes of ice on a daily basis. In the United States and most European countries, it is not profitable to purchase ice from an outside source. Thus, large-capacity ice machines are necessary equipment for the caterer's flight kitchen.

Generally, the inflight kitchen has equipment similar to that found in any other large food-production facility. However, special production equipment is often needed to accommodate the very large volume of meals prepared by many inflight catering facilities. There is generally a need for equipment to wash, dry, and shred or cut large volumes of produce as almost all meals or snacks served on an airline have some type of fresh fruit or vegetable as a component. Specialized production equipment used in inflight kitchens is becoming more automated, and this equipment has increasing production capabilities as technological developments and computerization of equipment continues. Not only does the increased automation enlarge the production capacity of the equipment, it also increases the productivity of the caterer's employees as fewer employees are required to do greater amounts of production when automated equipment is used.

Another area where specialized equipment is needed is in the handling and packaging of serviceware and condiments. Manually wrapping and sealing these items into the plastic bags used to insure their cleanliness for the passengers would be a very labor-intensive task for most inflight caterers, although there are many smaller kitchens where this is still done. Many now use automated packaging equipment that wraps and seals the serviceware and the condiments for a particular type of meal or snack, which makes this part of their production highly efficient.

REFERENCES

Dupont SUVA HP Refrigerants. (April 1993). Technical Pamphlet, Wilmington, DE: DuPont Chemicals, 16 pps.

Introduction to Refrigerant Mixtures. (February 1993). Technical Pamphlet, Sidney, OH: Copeland Corporation, 18 pps.

Knipe, T. (April, 1990). "Chemistry in a Frozen Sky: The Ozone Hole." *Calypso Log*, 17(2):6–8.

Refrigerant Changeover Guidelines R-502 to SUVA HP80. (July 1993). Technical Pamphlet, Sidney, OH: Copeland Corporation, 6 pps.

The CFC Report: Leading the Way Into a New Age. (October 1993). Technical Pamphlet, Sidney, OH: Copeland Corporation, 12 pps.

Winchester, S. H. (May 1994). "Keeping Your Cool." *Restaurants USA*, 14(5):10–13.

KEY TERMS

Ambient Air	Hydrochloroflurocarbons (HCFCs)
Chlorofluorocarbons (CFCs)	Ozone Depletion Potential
Cured Ice	Retrofit

DISCUSSION QUESTIONS

1. Describe a cook–chill (freeze) foodservice system. Why are extensive refrigeration or freezer facilities necessary to support this type of system? What special equipment is necessary?

2. Why must frozen products usually be tempered prior to being boarded on an aircraft?

3. How does the inflight caterer portion products prepared in the inflight kitchen for boarding on the aircraft?

4. What types of refrigerants are now being used in refrigerator, freezer, and ice machine compressors? Why is R-12 no longer being used?

5. What changes are inflight caterers having to make in existing equipment to comply with current environmental protection laws? What criteria should they consider in the selection of a refrigerant if they have to make modifications to their existing equipment?

6. Describe a fully automated ice production facility. What are the advantages of a fully automated system? When would it be appropriate for an inflight caterer to invest in such a facility?

7. Why would an inflight caterer usually have large-capacity ice-production capability? What type(s) of ice would usually be produced? How would this ice be used on the aircraft?

8. What is meant by *curing* the ice before it is boarded? Why do the airlines want the ice they use to be cured?

9. Why does an inflight catering kitchen often have equipment for handling and preparing large volumes of produce? Describe equipment that might be used for handling and preparing produce—what the equipment does and the purpose it serves.

10. Why does an airline or an inflight caterer usually purchase coach-class entrees already prepared and frozen? How are these entrees handled and prepared for use on a flight once they are in the caterer's kitchen?

11. Describe at least two pieces of equipment that might be found in an inflight caterer's kitchen to help accomplish the equipment packing and the tray-set functions.

11

Inflight Caterers' Equipment and Facilities
Ware Washing, Storage, and Transport

LEARNING OBJECTIVES

After studying this chapter, the student should be able to:

1. Discuss characteristics and alternative features of ware washing equipment commonly used in inflight kitchens.
2. Identify modifications being made to ware washing equipment to reduce the energy consumption of these machines.
3. Describe layouts that are efficient for ware washing systems appropriate for different sizes of inflight catering operations.
4. Discuss ergonomic considerations applicable to the development of ware washing equipment and ware washing areas in flight kitchens.
5. Describe the types of dry storage and equipment storage areas that must be included in an inflight kitchen and features or characteristics of these areas.
6. Discuss the transport equipment used by the inflight caterer to transport foods, beverages, and equipment from the caterer's kitchen to the aircraft and to board these items onto the aircraft.
7. Discuss the need for a standby meal cart or a service room in the passenger terminal to make last-minute adjustments to the meals boarded on a flight.

In addition to refrigeration and production equipment, some of the most important elements of an inflight caterer's facility are the ware washing equipment, storage areas, and transport equipment. All inflight catering operations need to focus considerable attention on these areas.

WARE WASHING EQUIPMENT

One of the most critical pieces of equipment for any inflight catering firm is its ware washing equipment. An inflight catering operation is predicated on the concept that equipment comes in and is washed, repacked, and used to supply flights going out. Generally, many airlines plan on a four- to six-hour equipment turnaround time, and they build their equipment inventory par levels accordingly. There is very little excess serviceware stock kept by any inflight caterer for any airline. There is certainly an inadequate quantity to service the flights on the caterer's daily schedule without the incoming equipment being washed and reused. Thus, ware washing is one of the most central processes of the inflight kitchen. The caterer's ware washing equipment must always be operational and adequate in capacity to handle the caterer's ware washing requirements.

To gain some perspective on the ware washing needs of the inflight caterer, a single fully loaded wide-body aircraft could generate as many as 30,000 individual items (dishes, glasses, flatware, containers, meal carts, and other utensils) that need to be off-loaded from the aircraft, delivered to the caterer's facilities, *and washed* as soon as possible. Generally, inflight caterers are operating their ware washing equipment anywhere from 16 to 22 hours per day. The downtime hours are used to break down and clean the machines and the total ware washing area.

Use of Flight-Type Dish Machines

Ware washing in the inflight foodservice industry is highly automated. Indeed, the flight-type dish machines widely used in the foodservice industry today are a result of efforts to improve the capacity and efficiency of dish machines, as well as to increase staff productivity, to service the inflight industry. Some of the technological advances now impacting the development of ware washing systems for inflight foodservices include dual rinsing systems, low-temperature drying, new belt structures, and fully electronic machine controls.

The concern with energy usage has led to the development of low-water-volume, heat-recycling, low-humidity drying of the serviceware washed. Outcomes of these developments are drastic reductions in energy costs and reduced heat and humidity in the ware washing area, making it a more pleasant working environment. New heat pumps that recycle heated air, working in conjunction with waste air heat-recovery devices, are an integral part of this development and the primary source of the energy savings realized. Fully electronic controls with keyboard displays are making it simpler to monitor the operations of the machine and are increasing the flexibility of the machines' ware washing capabilities. Figures 11.1 and 11.2 illustrate the functioning of these new drying systems and the accompanying heat recovery systems.

Because of the high labor usage associated with ware washing, the more that this equipment can be automated (particularly in the larger inflight kitchens), the lower the labor costs of this mandatory area of operations. Also, increased automation can make a traditionally unpleasant work area a more desirable place to work.

However, not all inflight kitchens use the highly automated flight-type dish machines. Some of the caterer's facilities are too small to use these machines to their capacity, and it would be very costly to them to try to do so. Not only would they have to invest excessive capital to purchase the machine, as a flight-type ware washing machine is one of the most expensive pieces of equipment in a kitchen of any type, but they would also incur excessive ware washing costs because of the excessive usage of

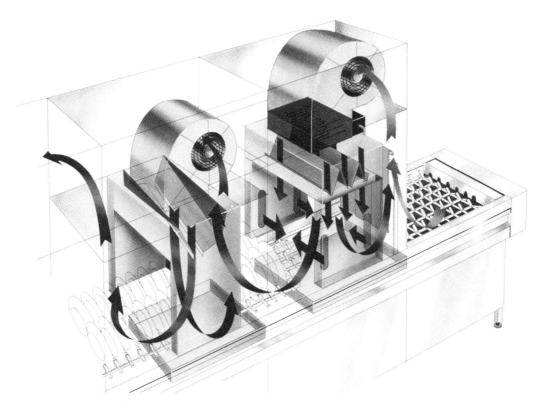

FIGURE 11.1 New developments in ware washing equipment have high-velocity drying systems. (Courtesy of Meiko USA)

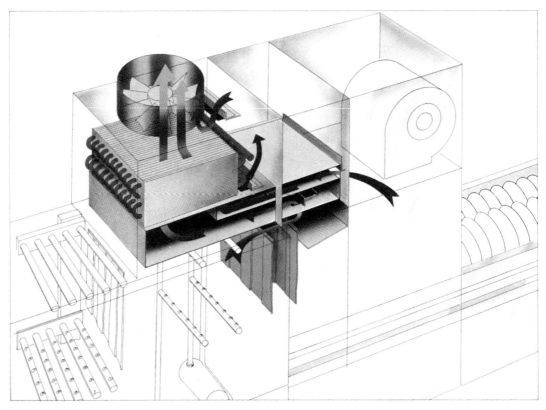

FIGURE 11.2 Heat recovery systems are important new developments that help reduce a flight kitchen's energy usage as well as improve the working environment for employees in the ware washing area. (Courtesy of Meiko USA)

water, chemicals, and labor that would be required to make the machine operable for only a small amount of ware washing. Thus, many of the smaller flight kitchens still use the single- or double-tank rack-type dish machines, such as those commonly found in restaurants.

Ware Washing Area Layout

Not only is automation important to achieve labor efficiency, but the layout of the ware washing area and the flow of the products through the system can have a significant impact on system efficiency. The layout of the ware washing area must be tailored to the space available and the washing needs of each inflight caterer. Most manufacturers of ware washing equipment recognize the uniqueness of each individual facility's capacity requirements and can customize their equipment to meet a specific caterer's needs. Some examples of ware washing area layouts are shown in Figures 11.3 and 11.4.

Figure 11.3 illustrates a possible layout that might be installed for a smaller catering operation located in a new building with limited available space. This system would have a capacity of 1,500 complete tray sets per hour. In comparison, Figure 11.4 illustrates a possible layout for a very large operation that has been expanding and needs to refurbish, modernize, and expand its ware washing facilities. This layout would have a capacity for 4,500 complete tray sets/hour. It gives special emphasis on the processing of long-haul casseroles without presoaking (a problem for caterers serving international airports). It also has an integrated pot, pan, and sheet pan washing area.

Some of the considerations in the design of ware washing equipment and areas are the type of conveyor belt to be used (finger or basket conveyor), the location and layout of the stripping and sorting areas for the

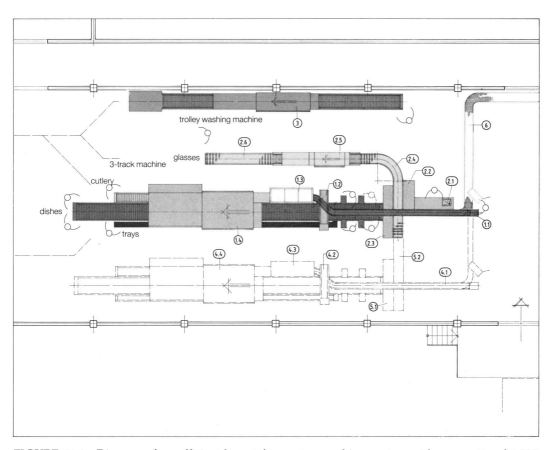

FIGURE 11.3 Diagram of an efficient layout for a ware washing system with a capacity of 1,500 complete tray sets per hour. (Courtesy of Meiko USA)

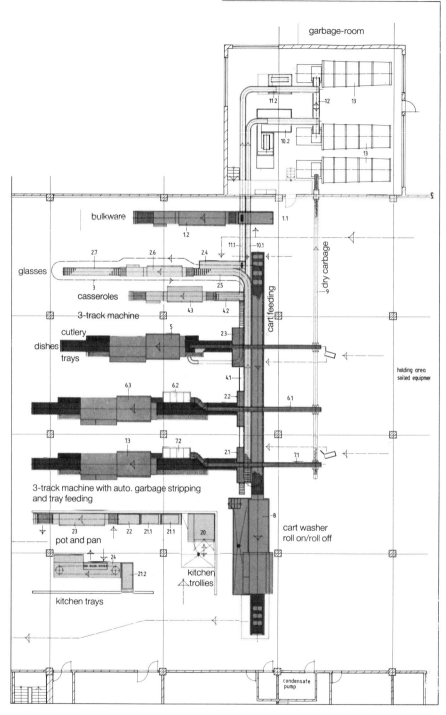

FIGURE 11.4 Diagram of an efficient layout for a ware washing area with a capacity of 4,500 complete tray sets per hour. (Courtesy of Meiko USA)

different pieces of china, glassware, and flatware as they are taken off the trays, the means of stripping the trays of trash and garbage (manual or automated), the garbage flushing and disposal system, and off-loading, sorting, and stacking equipment (manual or automated). When considering options in the development of ware washing areas, it should be remembered that it is not only the service wares that have to be washed whenever a flight lands. The boarding equipment also has to be thoroughly cleaned and sanitized. Although this equipment is often washed and cleaned with high-pressure steam hoses or other types of high-pressure washing equipment, there are now automatic conveyor washing machines for trolleys and other types of transport equipment which are in use in some of the high-volume inflight catering facilities.

Ware Washing Machine Capacity and Construction

While the capacity of a total inflight ware washing system is usually measured in terms of the number of complete tray sets that can be washed per hour, the capacity of a particular ware washing machine is generally measured in terms of plates per hour (finger-type belts) or racks per hour (basket transport belts). The capacity is given as a range for most machines as the conveyor belt speed is usually adjustable. When the belt is set at a slower speed, the wash period for the dishes will be longer—a necessity when the dishes, such as casseroles with baked-on food particles, are harder to clean.

Examples of the capacities of flight-type machines with finger belts that would be appropriate for an inflight catering facility might range from 1,300 to 1,900 plates per hour to 5,100 to 8,800 plates per hour. Basket conveyor capacities might range from 100 to 150 racks per hour to 180 to 270 racks per hour. Although it may sometimes seem that the finger-belt machines have a greater capacity than a comparably sized basket conveyor machine, the two types of machines are really equal in hourly throughput capacity. Some advantages of basket conveyor machines over the finger-belt conveyors include longer wash periods for hard-to-wash crockery items with many small parts, and smaller areas required for installation compared with what would be needed for a finger-belt machine of comparable capacity.

Large inflight operations may have a special machine for washing the casseroles (or entire dishes) used for lunch and dinner entrees if their casserole volume is large enough to justify a unique machine for this purpose. Entree casseroles are essential pieces of serviceware for inflight meals, but they are always among the most difficult pieces to wash because of the dried-on and burned-on food residues in these dishes. These casseroles usually cannot be washed through a regular ware washing machine without presoaking in a soak tank, (and sometimes being scoured by hand) a task which is labor intensive and not very pleasant. A separate machine for this task that is designed for casserole washing with special presoak cycles

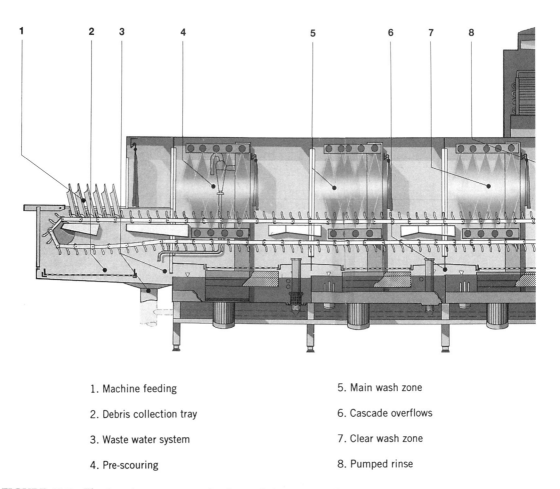

1. Machine feeding

2. Debris collection tray

3. Waste water system

4. Pre-scouring

5. Main wash zone

6. Cascade overflows

7. Clear wash zone

8. Pumped rinse

FIGURE 11.5 The interior structure of a finger belt ware washing machine, the type of machine particularly suitable for the ware washing needs of mid- to large-size inflight catering operations. (Courtesy of Meiko USA)

and very-high-pressure water jets in the wash areas can help simplify the difficult and undesirable casserole-washing process.

The interior operations of a finger-belt (flight-type) and a basket (rack) conveyor machine are somewhat different. Figure 11.5 illustrates the operating sequence of a finger-belt machine and Figure 11.6 illustrates the functional sequence of a basket conveyor machine.

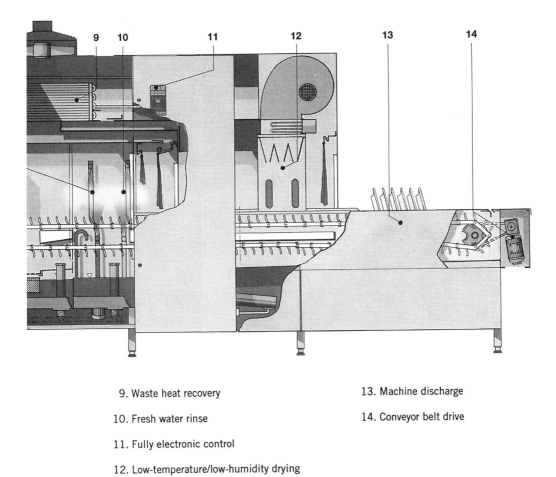

9. Waste heat recovery

10. Fresh water rinse

11. Fully electronic control

12. Low-temperature/low-humidity drying

13. Machine discharge

14. Conveyor belt drive

FIGURE 11.5 *(Continued)*

Ergonomic Considerations

When considering any type of ware washing system, ergonomic features are very important (Figure 11.7). The machine feeding and off-loading ends of the machines should be built in accord with ergonomic considerations to be comfortable for the average-height employee standing beside the machine. Sorting racks and other ancillary parts of the system should also

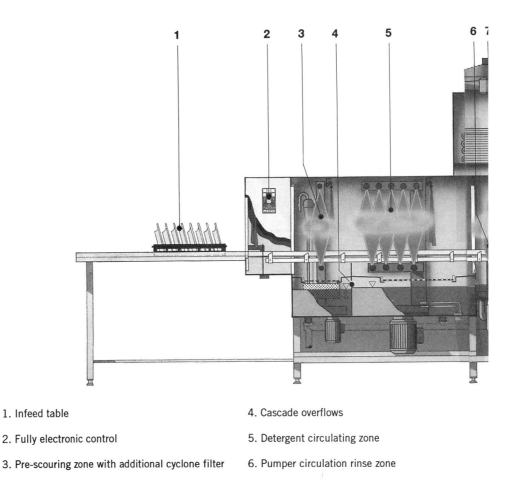

1. Infeed table

2. Fully electronic control

3. Pre-scouring zone with additional cyclone filter

4. Cascade overflows

5. Detergent circulating zone

6. Pumper circulation rinse zone

FIGURE 11.6 The interior structure of a ware washing machine with a basket conveyor belt system. (Courtesy of Meiko)

be located at comfortable reaching heights within arm's length of where the person doing the sorting is standing.

If necessary, platforms should be constructed adjacent to the machine or sorting areas so that employees can stand at an elevated height to make reaching more comfortable. Some kitchens now use lowerators or

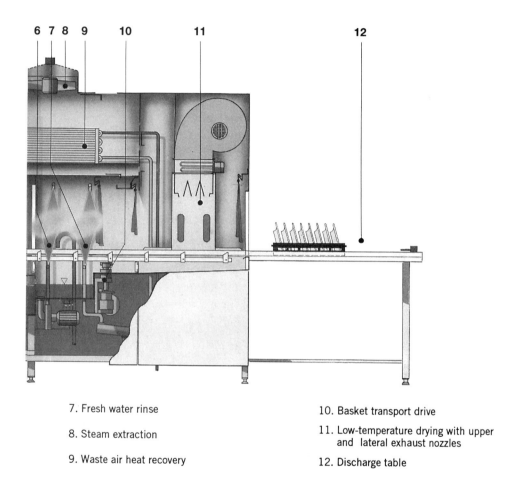

7. Fresh water rinse

8. Steam extraction

9. Waste air heat recovery

10. Basket transport drive

11. Low-temperature drying with upper and lateral exhaust nozzles

12. Discharge table

FIGURE 11.6 *(Continued)*

hydraulic lifts to bring inbound carts and carriers to optimum work heights for their dishwashing staff. Ware washing is a fast-paced operation in any inflight production facility. The more that the facilities can be designed to provide a comfortable working environment, the more the employees assigned to that area will be able to be productive in their jobs.

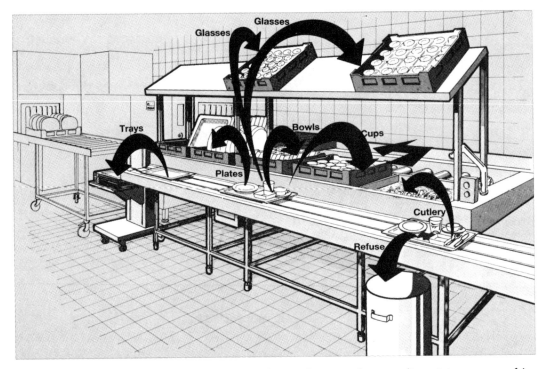

FIGURE 11.7 An example of a well-planned layout for a work area adjacent to ware washing machine which considers the ergonomic needs of employees. (Courtesy of Meiko USA)

STORAGE AREA CONSIDERATIONS

Not only must an inflight production kitchen have adequate space for producing and packaging food products, for refrigerating and freezing both prepared products and products received for future production needs, and for large-scale ware washing, it must also serve as a warehouse for the airlines serviced as well as for its own supplies.

Storage of Airline Equipment and Serviceware

As has been noted, much of the equipment and serviceware used by inflight caterers belongs to the airlines serviced. This equipment and serviceware flows through the caterer's facility in a never-ending cycle, but it is a cycle with peaks and lows. There are periods during a 24-hour day when the inflow of equipment and serviceware exceeds the outflow, and the equipment must be stored somewhere while it is in the caterer's facility.

Once this equipment has been washed and is ready to reuse, it must be organized by airline as it is stored. It is essential that the equipment of the different airlines not be mixed together in storage. One airline's equipment *cannot* be used on another airline. Packing and transporting the boarding equipment for an airline is a very fast-paced operation in a busy inflight kitchen. There is no time to sort through equipment in a storage area to try to find the right equipment for the right airline. Such a process offers far too many opportunities for mistakes and misuse of an airline's equipment. Depending on the number of flights served and the pattern of equipment flow, the square footage required for this equipment and serviceware storage may be substantial.

Repacking cart drawers and compartments with serviceware as soon as possible after both the serviceware and the carts are washed is one way to help reduce the square footage requirements for this equipment storage. The china, glassware, linen, service utensils and so on must be stored somewhere. The most efficient use of both labor and space is to use the boarding equipment as the storage cabinets for this serviceware as much as possible and repack the carts as quickly as possible after they are washed. This is especially true for equipment that is not further processed, or is basically used "as is" on an outbound flight.

Airlines estimate how much of the various types of equipment and serviceware are needed by each of their caterers on the basis of the number of flights serviced by the caterer and the type of food and beverage service scheduled for both inbound and outbound flights. Airlines have regularly scheduled inventories that caterers must complete at a date and time specified by the airline. These inventories enable the airline to track its equipment as it is disbursed throughout its system (including enroute aircraft, caterers, warehouses, and so on). From these inventories, equipment excesses and shortages at different caterers are noted, and shipments of surplus equipment from one caterer's facility to another catering operation where it is needed are triggered.

However, sometimes there is still a buildup of some type of serviceware in a particular caterer's facility or a shortage of some type of ware occurs in another caterer's facility. If a caterer accumulates an excess of a particular type of serviceware, it is the caterer's responsibility to let the airline know. It is then the caterer's responsibility to pack the excess serviceware for shipment either to the airline's central warehouse or to another caterer. The airline ships the packed serviceware via a specialized distributor as discussed below or on its flights as COMAT (company-owned materials) when there is baggage space available. Sometimes it may take a while for the airline to accomplish this shipping if it should occur at a time when the airline's freight loads are heavy. In that case, the caterer has yet another need for storage space. There must be somewhere to hold the packed boxes of serviceware which have not yet been picked up for shipping by the airline.

The issue of equipment balance is a continuing, complex problem for the airlines. A contributing factor is some kitchens' or airport operations' at times hoard or stockpile, equipment to be sure they will not run short. As a result, some locations do not have what they need to properly provision flights. The impact on the airlines is unnecessary equipment purchases and excessive staff time spent administering equipment balance issues. Because of the problems in this area, airlines closely monitor equipment flow whenever they visit or inspect a caterer's facility.

Some airlines now feel that the staff time (and the corresponding labor cost) required to maintain and manage their foodservice equipment and serviceware themselves is excessive and they are now looking to outsource, or contract for, this service. When they do so, they are looking for a firm that will handle both the procurement and repair of the equipment and serviceware as well as manage the flow of equipment to the caterers. Firms that handle the distribution of food products and supplies to the inflight caterers have been the firms most involved with the airlines, to date, as contractors for this type of service.

Storage of Products Owned by the Airlines

Another warehouse requirement which is part of the inflight caterer's responsibility is the storage of products that are purchased by an airline (and therefore are the property of the airline) and delivered directly to the caterer's facility for use on that airline's flights. Examples of such products range from liquor and soft drinks to peanut packets to boxes of disposable containers for meal components. Special U.S. customs requirements for the storage of bonded goods, as discussed in Chapter 4, must also be considered when planning storage requirements. Anything that an airline may feel is in its advantage to purchase directly from the supplier could fall into this product category. While such items are generally dry stores, they could also be perishable products, such as frozen meal entrees, particular cuts of meat, or baked goods.

Products that are the property of the airlines must be stored in separate areas from those that are purchased by, and are the property of, the inflight caterer. Not only must these storage areas be separate from those of the caterer, in many cases they must be secured areas. Products such as soft drinks or liquor may be very generic items that are the same for several of the airlines served by the caterer. Keeping each airline's supply separate from another's usually means having locked areas, often caged areas, for each airline's supplies. It is particularly important to keep products such as liquor, that could readily "walk away" from the caterer's facility, in well-secured storage areas that are separate for each airline serviced.

Here, too, labor can be used efficiently and storage space can be more effectively used if the drawers of the beverage service trollies are packed as soon as they are available for reuse. That way, the drawers are always ready and any last-minute panic can be avoided.

If some of the products owned by the airlines are perishables, they need to be kept in a freezer or refrigerator separate from that storing the products belonging to the caterer to insure that there will be no misuse of one airline's product for another or any misbilling for the use of the caterer's product when the airline already owned the product used. Here, too, depending on the products involved, it may be necessary to have the refrigerators or freezers in which they are stored locked for product security.

Storage of the Caterer's Supplies

Inflight caterers have their own products and supplies that need to be stored. To be sure that these products are kept separate from those owned by the airline, a separate dry storage area is needed. These products are used in general food preparation and packaging whenever a particular airline does not already have a directly purchased product available for that purpose. Most food-production products fall into this category of supplies as most of the items purchased directly by the airlines are beverages and packaging materials prepared to their specifications or printed with their name and/or logo.

The inflight caterer needs to have personnel assigned to the responsibilities of purchasing, receiving, and managing these dry food and refrigerated stores and their inventory flow. The costs of these items are charged to the airline by the inflight caterer through: (1) the prices charged for meals or snacks prepared and boarded for the airline; and (2) through fees charged for the cost plus a profit margin on packaging supplies. For goods owned by an airline, caterers normally charge only for handling. Charges to an airline for goods owned by a caterer are a derivative of the product's cost plus the caterer's profit margin (see Chapter 6). These differential treatments of how charges are handled is an important reason for keeping the two types of products separated—in addition to the caterer's stewardship obligation for the products owned by the airlines.

A final storage area requirement for the inflight caterer's facilities is for a staging area for the boarding equipment being prepared for transport. The boarding equipment for a flight must be gathered together from several different areas—ranging from the refrigerators holding the equipment packed with the preset trays to the ice freezer for bags of ice to storage areas for carts packed with beverage service items or serviceware and utensils. All the equipment required for a flight must be gathered together before any of it is loaded onto a truck for transport. If several flights are being prepared for transport at similar times (which is quite common), a fairly sizable staging area may be required for this function.

By gathering everything for one flight in a single location, checkers are able to make one last check of the pack to make sure that all is as it should be, based on the latest passenger count received from the airline. None of the equipment can be loaded until this check is completed. This final check is a critical function in any flight kitchen. Staff assigned this responsibility must be knowledgeable of every airline's flights, the foods and beverages to be served on those flights, and the airline's food and beverage service policies.

TRANSPORT EQUIPMENT AND FACILITIES

Probably the most important piece of equipment that the catering firm has for its transport obligations is the high-lift truck. Most commercial aircraft are too high for the service doorways to be reached any other way. The lift trucks have beds that can be raised to the level of the doorway into the aircraft so that the boarding equipment can be rolled or carried directly from the bed of the truck into the aircraft. One concern of the transport operation is to make the most efficient use of the transport personnel's labor to make the delivery as fast as possible while minimizing the fatigue level of these employees since handling the transport equipment can be fairly heavy work, particularly if the aircraft is a wide-body plane.

High-lift trucks come in different sizes, and the equipment that a particular caterer would own would be a function of purchase resources available, the number of flights serviced in a particular time period, and the type of aircraft serviced. The time period would be a function of the turnaround time between when the caterer starts to load a truck for a flight and when it comes back, is off-loaded, cleaned, and ready for reloading for another flight. Different types of aircraft are different heights, and require different amounts and types of boarding equipment. Some of the smaller trucks do not have the carrying capacity (in terms of either weight or cube) to handle the load that would be required for wide-body aircraft, and they cannot rise to the height level of the doorways for these very large aircraft.

Proper operation of the high-lift trucks is an important function of the inflight caterer's operation as these trucks can be quite dangerous if operated improperly. Mishandling of these trucks can cause personnel injuries, damage to expensive aircraft and to the truck, and lead to possible fines for the caterer. Generally, personnel authorized to drive these trucks are some of the caterer's most reliable and senior employees. Some common safety precautions that are of concern when operating these trucks are listed in Table 11.1. Some airlines will assist the caterers in promoting employee awareness of the need for safety on the ramp area and of procedures to use when approaching and leaving aircraft by including diagrams such as those in Figure 11.8 in their catering manuals.

Inflight caterers need to be aware of U.S. Department of Transportation (DOT) regulations that may apply to their truck drivers and the driver testing they pass, particularly if the trucks are newer than 1984 models. Recent regulations published by the Department of Transportation specify that drivers of trucks that are newer than 1984 models and have a gross weight of more than 26,000 pounds must have a class B driver's license. However, this regulation is applicable only if the trucks are driven on a public road, and it does not apply if a caterer's trucks never leave the airport grounds. In some cases, if the caterer's trucks are limited to use *only* on airport grounds, they may not even have to be registered with the Department of Motor Vehicles in the state where the kitchen is located. In addition to, or in the absence of, DOT requirements, many airports have their own regulations which include written, oral, and practical driving tests to ascertain the skill and knowledge levels of drivers relative to the unique circumstances of airport driving.

Depending on the type of aircraft serviced by the caterer, special equipment may be needed to load and unload the transport equipment. Certain DC-10s pose a particular problem in this respect. Items to be loaded onto these DC-10s must be containerized into large container units that are very heavy. They can only be moved, loaded onto the trucks, and off-loaded onto the plane through the use of rollers and other special equipment. The containers are loaded into the lower lobe level (cargo level) of the aircraft, and after storage there, the trolleys and other containers of foods, beverages, and serving utensils are taken to the upper level, or main deck, where the passenger seats are located.

On aircraft such as some 747s, DC-10s, and L-1011s, where the carts and carriers are loaded into the aircraft in the lower lobe level, the carts are taken up to the main deck on lifts (or elevators). These lifts are located in different areas on each type of aircraft and are of two types: personnel lifts which can be used for either personnel or carts and cart lifts which are about 1/2 the height of the personnel lifts and can be used for carts only. Catering transport employees should be fully trained on the operation of these lifts on all types of aircraft serviced by the caterer to avoid injuries to personnel or possible damage to the aircraft.

Servicing the DC-10s, or most any aircraft, is made even more difficult by the airlines themselves as aircraft are configured differently for every airline, which makes it hard for an inflight caterer to develop a boarding

TABLE 11.1
Safety Precautions Commonly Required for the Operation of High-Lift Trucks

1. Smoking is strictly forbidden in the truck or anywhere on the ramp area.
2. A safety pretrip inspection should always be done before operating any truck for the first time on a shift.
3. All equipment and supplies must be secured in the truck with the proper tie-down straps (for both loading and off-loading the aircraft).
4. Truck body overhead doors must be securely closed and latched before moving the truck.
5. Drivers must not be allowed to drive these trucks until they have been approved or licensed in accord with state and local regulations applicable to the particular airport location.
6. Drivers should drive defensively and follow their companies' rules as well as airport driving rules.
7. All road markings and warning signs must be obeyed.
8. The right-of-way must always be given to moving aircraft.
9. Drivers should be aware of aircraft around them and take care to not get caught in jet blast.
10. Speed limits should be carefully observed, particularly within the circle of safety (an imaginary ring that extends ten feet out from the wing tips, nose, and tail section of the plane).
11. The truck should never be left unattended with the engine running.
12. All accidents, no matter how small, should be immediately reported to the caterer's shift supervisor.
13. Proper hearing protection must be worn when working around jet engines. Wearing hearing protection is a federal requirement.
14. Drivers and guides must be very familiar with the hand signals used to guide the trucks into positions.
15. Guides must be used at all times inside the circle of safety when positioning the truck at the aircraft and when leaving the aircraft.
16. Drivers should not approach the aircraft until it has been secured with engines shut down and wheels chocked.
17. The truck should be stopped four to twelve inches away from the bottom of the aircraft's catering door to be sure there is no contact with the aircraft's exterior surface which may cause damage.
18. The truck's wheels must be chocked whenever it is parked at the aircraft to service the aircraft.
19. The truck's stabilizers must be lowered prior to raising the truck's body to the level of the aircraft's catering doorway.
20. Personnel must always knock on the aircraft's door before opening it to alert the crew inside that they are there and to be sure the emergency slide attached to the door is disarmed.
21. The safety guardrail must always be extended during the service period.
22. The correct loading ramp must be installed between the truck and the aircraft galley.
23. Drivers must be knowledgeable about all of the special positioning requirements for the several different types of aircraft used by the airlines.

24. All ramps and guardrails must be retracted and all containers and equipment must be secured in the truck before the truck body is lowered when the aircraft servicing is completed.
25. The aircraft's galley door should be securely closed prior to lowering the truck body and moving the truck away from the aircraft.
26. Before lowering the truck body after the plane is serviced, both sides of the platform must be checked carefully to be sure no personnel or equipment are underneath the truck.
27. Before retracting the stabilizers, both sides of the vehicle must be checked to be sure there are no personnel or equipment in the way.
28. The driver must always be able to see the guide fully in the rear view mirror when the guide is providing directions and the truck is moving.
29. The wheel chocks are not removed until the truck is clear of the aircraft. Then they should be picked up and stowed in the truck by the guide.
30. High-lift trucks should never be driven under an aircraft wing or directly between an aircraft and the terminal.
31. Airport security is a critical concern. Transport personnel must always wear their airport identification cards and not hesitate to question strangers or anyone acting suspiciously around their truck.

---

procedure for the aircraft and train personnel involved in the boarding process. Indeed, there are often different interior configurations of the same model aircraft within any one airline's fleet, which makes this task even more difficult for the caterer. Such differences only add to the transport challenge facing the inflight caterer.

STAND-BY (BANK) MEALS

Another type of transport equipment is the standby (or bank) meal cart, which might be used by some airlines in busy terminals where a caterer is serving a number of flights for one airline. Passenger loads on aircraft are always changing until the very last minute when the door of the plane is closed. The inflight caterer has to be able to adjust the food supply on the plane up until the very last minute as the caterer (or in some cases, the airline's passenger service staff) is responsible for making sure that there are sufficient meals on board the aircraft to serve all of the passengers a meal. This procedure also enables the airline and the caterer to control waste by not overboarding meals in excess of the passenger load.

If the delivery truck had to make one or more runs back to the production facility to make an adjustment to the boarded meals, it would be a very time-consuming effort that would quite likely delay the aircraft beyond the scheduled takeoff time (and be the possible cause of a penalty fine for the catering firm). One way to resolve this problem is

RIGHT FRONT GALLEY
B737, A320 AND B757 APPROACH PROCEDURE

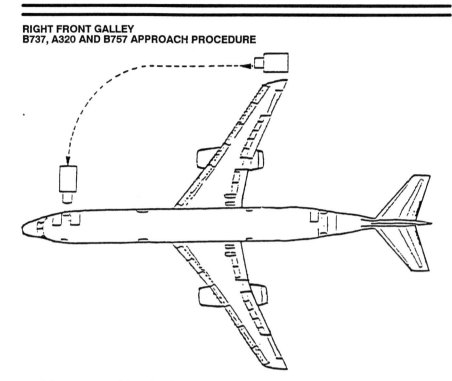

- Driver stops parallel to aircraft at a distance equal to the width of the wing tip.
    - Tests brakes.
    - Guide leaves truck to direct approach to aircraft.
- Guide directs truck toward aircraft at walking speed, takes position under galley door and directs driver throughout final approach to aircraft.
- Following guide's directions, driver moves truck slowly into position and comes to a complete stop eight feet from aircraft and in line with galley door and tests brakes.
- Following guide's directions, driver stops truck one foot from aircraft.
- Guide places chock securely under right front wheel and rear wheel.
- Driver sets all brakes.
- Truck body is raised to catering position. Safety rails are moved in place. Platform should be no closer than four inches from galley door.

(a)

FIGURE 11.8 (a) Diagram illustrating the proper procedure for approaching the front galley door of an aircraft; (b) diagram illustrating how to back off from the front galley door of the same aircraft. Directions that the drivers and guides should follow are included with the diagrams. (Courtesy of America West Airlines)

RIGHT FRONT GALLEY
B737, A320 AND B757 BACK–OFF PROCEDURE

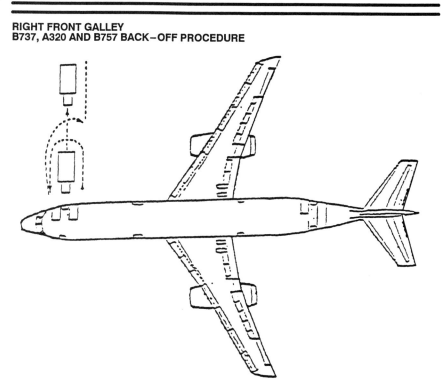

- Close galley doors to cracked position.

- After closing galley door, driver and guide look to right and left of truck to ensure there are no people or equipment on the ground under truck body as it is lowered.

- Guide makes complete walk around truck to check for obstructions to safe backing of truck and removes rear wheel chocks and replaces on bumper hanger.

- Guide maintains position approximately 15 feet to the left rear of truck. Guide must always be in full view of the driver's rear view mirror. Guide signals driver to start back–out pattern.

- Guide stops truck when clear of aircraft.

- Guide replaces wheel chock on bumper hanger and reboards truck.

- Driver and guide carefully maneuver truck around aircraft and ground equipment as they move to their next assignment.

(b)

FIGURE 11.8 (Continued)

for the caterer to prepare standby meals that are loaded into a cart or carrier that is transported to the aircraft boarding area with the regular boarding equipment for a particular flight. These meals are also sometimes referred to as bank meals. This standby cart or bank meal carrier is prepared with a supply of all items that might be needed on a flight at the last minute. If extra supplies are needed, they can quickly be taken from this standby supply and loaded onto the aircraft. Depending on the number of flights departing at or near similar times and the meal or snack pattern on these flights, one standby cart may be able to service more than one flight.

An alternative to a standby meal cart or carrier that is used by some caterers in some locations is a service room in the terminal. The service room is used the same way that the cart might be used in other locations. Another alternative is to have the standby meals held in one of the caterer's trucks on the ramp area. The truck is then able to service multiple flights as meals are needed. Other approaches that airlines have looked at are the use of shelf-stable meals, or one "commonized" meal that could be used for all lunch and dinner flights.

The airlines specify bank meal procedures that they want their caterers to follow for their flights. Figure 11.9 illustrates such bank meal specifications. These specifications are provided to the inflight caterers in the airline's catering manual.

SUMMARY

Even though inflight caterers use a lot of equipment and serviceware that is the property of the airlines, they also have extensive equipment and facility holdings of their own. They are responsible for having a production facility which is adequate in size to accommodate all of the production, storage, packaging, ware washing, and transport needs of the caterer. Because of the logistical orientation of inflight foodservices, large storage spaces which can be divided between space for airline equipment and servicewares, airline-owned products, and caterer-owned products is essential.

A critical equipment area for an inflight caterer is the ware washing area. The ware washing demand of airline foodservices is so substantial that no caterer operates without some type of ware washing machine. In many ways, the ware washing area is the heart of the inflight catering operations as the operations would cease if incoming serviceware and equipment could not be quickly and thoroughly washed so that it could immediately be reused to service outgoing flights. From that perspective, it is in the caterer's interest to invest in high-quality, automated ware washing equipment, keep it well maintained, and have it operated by

Bank Meals

B737

The caterer will bank up to (10) meals maximum.

B737–B2, B737–AV, A320, B757

First Class

The caterer will bank up to (6) meals maximum at a 50/50 ratio of the two hot breakfast choices and beef and chicken entrees for lunch/dinner flights.

Main Cabin

The caterer will bank up to (10) meals maximum at a 50/50 ratio if two choices are offered. The trays should be set with all accompaniments. Overwrap tray set–up and place foil wrapped entree on top for easy access.

All Aircraft

Meals boarded should be the same as on scheduled service.

The caterer will stand by with bank meals until directed to board by local America West management or representative.

In no case are bank meals to be included in meal orders at any time.

All meals should be dated.

Bank Meal Packing Specification, B737–B2, B737AV, A320 AND B757

FIRST CLASS	MAIN CABIN
Dry Ice	Dry Ice
(1) TSU	(2) TSU
(1) TSU	(2) TSU
(1) TSU	(2) TSU
(3) Appetizers*	(2) TSU
(3) Desserts*	(2) TSU

2 STCs = 6 bank meals   1 STC = 10 bank meals

*Appetizers and Desserts where applicable.

FIGURE 11.9 Procedures for the handling of bank meals by the caterer as specified by an airline. (Courtesy of America West Airlines)

competent personnel as a means of insuring minimal problems from the ware washing area.

The inflight caterer also owns the transport equipment used to board the food and beverage products on the aircraft. This equipment is highly specialized because of the need to have lifts for the truck beds which will raise them to the height of the doorways of the aircraft.

Overall, an inflight caterer has a substantial investment in equipment and facilities. To continue in business, the caterer must be able to recover the costs of this investment over a reasonable time as well as make a profit from the operations.

KEY TERMS

Checker (Flight Checker)
Circle of Safety
COMAT
Ergonomics
Finger Belt
Guide

Outsourcing
Ramp
Setup Area
Tarmac
Turnaround Time

DISCUSSION QUESTIONS

1. How important is ware washing equipment to an inflight catering operation? Why is this important (or unimportant)?
2. Describe ware washing equipment that would be appropriate for use in a large inflight kitchen.
3. What developments are being made in ware washing equipment to help reduce the energy consumption level of these machines? Why is there a concern with these machines' energy usage?
4. What are some important ergonomic considerations for the design of ware washing equipment and ware washing areas in inflight kitchens? Why should an inflight caterer be concerned with ergonomics in the ware washing area?
5. Describe some ware washing layouts that might be appropriate for different sizes of inflight catering facilities.
6. Discuss some of the new developments in ware washing equipment.
7. How is the capacity of ware washing equipment measured? What capacity level is appropriate for very large inflight kitchens? For medium kitchens? For small kitchens?
8. Identify all the different types of equipment and dry storage areas that an inflight caterer's kitchen must have. Why are all of these different storage areas neces-

sary? How can an inflight caterer divide space to meet all of these storage requirements?

9. Describe a high-lift truck. What is this type of truck used for? Why is it a necessary piece of equipment for an inflight caterer?

10. Are there other pieces of transport equipment used? If so, what are they and for what purposes are they used?

12

Inflight Catering Operations and Quality Assurance

There are many operational constraints which an inflight caterer faces daily when providing services to the airlines. All of these constraints must be taken into consideration when the caterer plans for and provides the required food and beverage services. Some of these operational constraints include: (1) the aircraft galley structures and the limitations on the equipment that can be used and the space that is available on the aircraft; (2) the time available for the flight attendants to accomplish the required food and beverage services on a flight (particularly on shorter domestic flights); (3) the service requirements established by each airline; (4) the service expectations of the catering operations itself; (5) flight attendant considerations; and (6) the capability of the caterer's kitchen facilities.

To provide effective inflight foodservices on their flights, airlines must work in partnership with their caterers and the industry suppliers. Together, they must address each of these constraint areas and devise products and procedures which will enable the partnership to prepare, handle, transport, and serve quality food and beverage products which meet or exceed each passenger's expectations. Caterers incorporate quality assurance processes within their operations to assure that operational activities are being done as they should which, in turn, will assure that the inflight caterer has met or exceeded both the airlines' and the airlines' passengers' expectations.

THE AIRLINES' CATERING MANUALS

It has already been noted in Chapter 5 that the airlines send their caterers comprehensive manuals regarding the food and beverage products that they want served on their flights. These materials include items such as the menu cycles, recipes, product specifications, and sometimes pictures of the finished products as they are to be served or the tray setup desired. However, no matter how many materials are provided to the caterer by the airlines, the level of service that they desire and the product consistency that they want will not always be attained unless the inflight caterer's employees receive and understand the communications the airlines send to the caterer.

These information and policy manuals from the airlines are the heart of the caterer's operations as they outline specifically what is required and provide the standard by which the inflight caterer's operations will be evaluated. The specifications, recipes, and other such directives contained in the manuals determine the activities of all of the inflight caterer's personnel. The information here tells the purchasing area what to purchase and from whom, as well as what to expect the airline to provide. That information then guides the development and organization of the caterer's storage areas. It also tells the production area what to prepare, what products should be used in the preparation process, and how to portion, package, or setup the products. The equipment and transport area can see what equipment will be inbound to them compared to what they will need for outbound flights, and it indicates the timing of that flow. It also indicates what boarding equipment, food products, and support supplies should go to each plane they are serving for that airline. Once one day's cycle is completed, the caterer then looks to the menu developed for the next day and begins the cycle again.

Often, the information in these manuals that the inflight caterers receive from the airlines is quite complex, and much of the information is in code format. Each airline has developed its own code, and no two codes are alike, or even similar. The caterer's staff must become familiar with the codes and the manual formats of *each* of the airlines serviced by the caterer.

The manuals that any one caterer receives usually contains information that is applicable to *all* the caterers servicing that airline's flights. Generally, there are many items in the manual which are never applicable to a specific caterer. For example, in some cases that airline may not have any flights departing from a particular airport on which a hot breakfast is served to the coach-class passengers. All the flights from that airport may leave after breakfast service hours or those that do leave early may be too short in duration to warrant hot breakfast service. In this case, anything in the airline's manual concerning the preparation and service of hot breakfasts to coach-class passengers is not relevant to that particular caterer's operation.

Because of this complexity and the possibility of sections not being applicable to a particular caterer, it is highly desirable for a caterer to develop a system for simplifying the extensive manual information for its employees even though it may make the whole manual available to all employees for a reference that they can use at any time. Also, the manuals are always prepared in English. Yet, more and more inflight caterering employees may not read English (or even speak it as their primary language). This employee language limitation is yet another reason why inflight caterers need to simplify the materials from the airlines' manuals for their employees.

MENU CYCLES AND RECIPES

Some of the most important information in the airlines' manuals are the menu cycles that are to be used for their flights and the recipes that support the planned menus. The cycle menu information given in the manual will indicate the specific dates for each cycle and each menu within a cycle. It will also indicate how each item on the menu is to be plated or served. Even the specific packaging to be used and the serviceware and condiments to be provided will be indicated. However, it is no simple task to incorporate all that information in a user friendly format on a readily referenced single page. Thus, there is a chaining of information to other sections of the manual. The complexity of the information that must be provided and the need to chain that information is an important reason for the airlines' development of the many codes they use.

Figures 12.1 and 12.2 are examples of some menu and recipe pages from the manuals that two different airlines provide their caterers. Figure 12.1 illustrates a first-class menu and some related manual components. Here, if this menu were to be served on flights "tomorrow," an employee assigned to prepare the first-class and crew entrees to be served would have to first find the cycle menu page with the next day's (tomorrow's) date at the top. Then, he or she would have to look at the "F" class of service to see what the entrees were to be. Note that the entrees for "Y" class of service are different from those listed for the "F" class. ("F" = first class; "Y" = coach class.)

However, the menu only gives the names of the entrees, and there are no directions for the preparation of these products. So, the employee would next have to find the directions for these entrees. This would be done using the item number (in this case 18481 for the Greek salad with feta cheese, spinach plate entree) to first find the specifications for that item which are in another section of the manual. The specifications, once found, indicate that the product is to be made according to the recipe provided, and the recipe number is given. In this case, the Greek salad with feta cheese, spinach plate entree is listed as recipe number 18481. Again, the employee must go to a different section of the manual to find the recipe. Once that recipe is found, it indicates that there are several subrecipes to be used for this item, such as number 18547 for preparing tomatoes, Roma fresh, .50 inch dice, and number 18546 for preparing the diced seeded cucumbers for the plate.

Figure 12.2 illustrates a different airline's approach to providing essentially the same information to the caterer as was shown in Figure 12.1. Here, a code sheet is provided which indicates when a menu in the cycle is to be served on each scheduled flight. To plan production and set up for a particular flight, the caterer's employees must first refer to this code sheet. Then, having determined which menu is to be used, they must find the menu in the menu section.

For example, flight number 1043 arriving in Denver had dinner DC served to the first-class passengers sometime during the flight. Since this is an inbound flight to Denver, the caterer there would not be interested in what foods to prepare for this flight, but it would be interested in the arrival time and the equipment that would need to be stripped, washed, and made available for boarding meals and beverages on an outbound flight that they were serving. This same aircraft then leaves Denver for Dallas/Fort Worth as flight number 1082. First-class passengers on this flight will be served meal SD which must be prepared and boarded by the Denver caterer.

The menu for the DK meal on menu cycle 1 for this same airline is also shown in Figure 12.2. The menu, as written, indicates the portion to be used and how it is to be plated. However, the recipes for the items are in the recipe section, and that section would have to be referenced were the

AMERICAN AIRLINES — FOOD AND BEVERAGE SPECIFICATIONS — ITEM NUMBER IT Q 2128

DESCRIPTION: TSU-FC BSC DIN DOM/CAR/MEX CY3

EFFECTIVE DATE: 09/28/94
PRINT DATE: 09/12/94

	INGREDIENT/ RECIPE NBR	DESCRIPTION	PORTION QTY	PORTION UM	PORTION DESC	PORTION QTY	PORTION UM	BRAND
RC	9546	SHRIMP APPETIZER		-		1	PORTION	
RC	18481	GREEK SALAD W/FETA CHEESE,SPINACH		-		1	EACH	
IG	50020	CONTINENTAL BUTTER, UNSALTED, 47 CT		-		1	EACH	BREAKSTONE
IG	16224	GLASS, WINE		-		2	EACH	
RC	16872	TRAY, LARGE W/MAT & LINEN COVER		-		1	EACH	
RC	16852	ROLL-UP, LINEN, DK/2DF		-		1	EACH	
RC	16845	SOUFFLE CUP W/S&P SHAKERS		-		1	EACH	
* RC	18641	APPLE COBBLER PASTRY,PL-69		-		1	PORTION	

INSTRUCTIONS:

- PREPARE ITEMS PER RECIPES.
- PORTION APPETIZER ONTO PLATE, PL-69.
- PORTION SALAD ONTO BOWL, BO-124.
- PORTION DESSERT ONTO PLATE, PL-69.
- PRESET ITEMS ON A LINEN-LINED MEAL TRAY PER GRAPHICS MANUAL PHOTO AND COVER WITH ONE SHEET OF PLASTIC WRAP.

YIELD:

1 UNIT

	PURCHASING SOURCE COMPONENT NUMBER	DESCRIPTION	REFERENCE NUMBER	BRAND	SOURCE
IG	50020	CONTINENTAL BUTTER, UNSALTED, 47 CT	FB 0000002	BREAKSTONE	FOOD & BEV. PURCHASE
IG	16224	GLASS, WINE	AA 0000001		AA PURCHASE

FIGURE 12.1 Series of recipes from an airline's catering manual illustrates the "chaining" of recipes that is generally required to produce the necessary food products for a meal's menu. (Courtesy of American Airlines)

AMERICAN AIRLINES   FOOD AND BEVERAGE SPECIFICATIONS   RECIPE NUMBER RC   9546

DESCRIPTION: SHRIMP APPETIZER   EFFECTIVE DATE: 09/28/94
APPETIZERS AND HORS D OEVRES   SEAFOOD   PRINT DATE: 09/12/94

----
                                                       *-------PORTION------   *------
INGREDIENT/   QTY   UM   DESC   QTY   UM   BRAND
RECIPE NBR/   DESCRIPTION

IG   151670   SHRIMP,CKD,PDQ,TAIL ON,41/50,FROZEN   0   -   4   EACH   GOLDEN PACIFIC
IG   15642   COCKTAIL SAUCE   0   -   0.75   OUNCE   NATURALLY FRESH
IG   16221   RAMEKIN/CRUET,CHINA   0   -   1   EACH
IG   16214   PLATE,CHINA,SMALL   0   -   1   EACH
* RC 17127   LEMON,FRESH,200 CT,WEDGE,8 CUT   0   -   1   WEDGE

INSTRUCTIONS:

   - PREPARE ITEM PER RECIPE.
   - THAW SHRIMP UNDER REFRIGERATION. RINSE WELL UNDER COLD RUNNING WATER
     AND ALLOW TO DRAIN.
   - PORTION COCKTAIL SAUCE INTO RAMEKIN, RA-38, AND PLACE AT THE 12
     O'CLOCK POSITION ON PLATE, PL-69.
   - SHINGLE SHRIMP WITH TAILS TOWARD RAMEKIN FROM THE 2 TO 6 O'CLOCK
     POSITIONS.
   - PLACE THE LEMON WEDGE NEXT TO THE RAMEKIN FROM THE 10 TO 8
     O'CLOCK POSITIONS.
   - COVER AND REFRIGERATE.

YIELD:
------
   1 PORTION

PURCHASING SOURCE

COMPONENT NUMBER   DESCRIPTION   REFERENCE NUMBER   BRAND   SOURCE

IG   151670   SHRIMP,CKD,PDQ,TAIL ON,41/50,FROZEN   FB 0000004   FOOD & BEV. PURCHASE
IG   15642   COCKTAIL SAUCE   EA 0000001   GOLDEN PACIFIC   EASTERN FOODS
IG   16221   RAMEKIN/CRUET, CHINA   AA 0000001   NATURALLY FRESH   AA PURCHASE
IG   16214   PLATE, CHINA, SMALL   AA 0000001   AA PURCHASE

FIGURE 12.1 (Continued)

AMERICAN AIRLINES   FOOD AND BEVERAGE SPECIFICATIONS   RECIPE NUMBER RC   18481

DESCRIPTION: GREEK SALAD W/FETA CHEESE,SPINACH   EFFECTIVE DATE: 09/28/94
SALADS   LEAFY GREEN   PRINT DATE: 09/12/94

INGREDIENT/ RECIPE NBR	DESCRIPTION	* QTY	UM	PORTION DESC	QTY	* UM	BRAND
RC 18546	CUCUMBER,SEEDED,SKIN ON,.50 IN CUBE,OZ/G	0	—		0.5	OUNCE	
RC 18480	ROMAINE/SPINACH SALAD MIX	0	—		1.5	OUNCE	
* RC 19275	OLIVES,KALAMATA,PITTED,EACH	0	—		2	EACH	
IG 15867	FETA CHEESE,CRUMBLED,1,LB,PKG	0	—		0.25	OUNCE	CHURNEY
IG 16220	BOWL,GLASS	0	—		1	EACH	
RC 18547	TOMATO,ROMA,FRESH,.50 INCH DICE,OZ/GM	0	—		0.5	OUNCE	

INSTRUCTIONS:
- - - - - - - - - - - -
- PREPARE ITEMS PER RECIPES.
- PORTION ROMAINE/SPINACH MIX INTO BOWL,BO-124.
- PORTION TOMATOES,CUCUMBER, OLIVES AND FETA CHEESE OVER LETTUCE MIX.
- COVER AND REFRIGERATE.

YIELD:
- - - - -
 1 EACH

PURCHASING SOURCE
- - - - - - - - - - - - - - - -

COMPONENT NUMBER	DESCRIPTION	REFERENCE NUMBER	BRAND	SOURCE
IG 15867	FETA CHEESE,CRUMBLED,1,LB,PKG	FB 0000002	CHURNEY	FOOD & BEV. PURCHASE
IG 16220	BOWL, GLASS	AA 0000001		AA PURCHASE

FIGURE 12.1 (*Continued*)

AMERICAN AIRLINES   FOOD AND BEVERAGE SPECIFICATIONS   RECIPE NUMBER RC   16872

DESCRIPTION: TRAY, LARGE W/MAT & LINEN COVER
EQUIPMENT   TRAY/MAT

EFFECTIVE DATE: 09/28/94
PRINT DATE: 09/12/94

INGREDIENT/ RECIPE NBR	DESCRIPTION	*QTY	UM	PORTION-- DESC	QTY	* UM	BRAND
IG 16241	EQUIP, TRAY, PLASTIC, LARGE	0	-		1	EACH	
IG 16246	EQUIP, TRAY MAT, LARGE	0	-		1	EACH	
IG 16239	EQUIP, LINEN, TRAY LINER	0	-		1	EACH	

INSTRUCTIONS:
- LINE TRAY WITH MAT.
- LAY LINEN OVER MAT COVERING TRAY EDGES.

YIELD:
-----
* 1 EACH

PURCHASING SOURCE

COMPONENT NUMBER	DESCRIPTION	REFERENCE NUMBER	BRAND	SOURCE
IG 16241	EQUIP, TRAY, PLASTIC, LARGE	AA 0000001		AA PURCHASE
IG 16246	EQUIP, TRAY MAT, LARGE	AA 0000001		AA PURCHASE
IG 16239	EQUIP, LINEN, TRAY LINER	AA 0000001		AA PURCHASE

AMERICAN AIRLINES   FOOD AND BEVERAGE SPECIFICATIONS   RECIPE NUMBER RC   16852

DESCRIPTION: ROLL-UP, LINEN, DK/2DF
EQUIPMENT   ROLLUPS/SILVERWARE

EFFECTIVE DATE: 09/28/94
PRINT DATE: 09/12/94

INGREDIENT/ RECIPE NBR	DESCRIPTION	*QTY	UM	PORTION-- DESC	QTY	* UM	BRAND
IG 16205	KNIFE, DINNER	0	-		1	EACH	
IG 16208	FORK, DINNER	0	-		2	EACH	
IG 16240	EQUIP, LINEN, NAPKIN, WHITE	0	-		1	EACH	

INSTRUCTIONS:
- ROLL FLATWARE IN LINEN PER AA INSTRUCTIONS.

YIELD:
-----
* 1 EACH

FIGURE 12.1 (*Continued*)

276

COMPONENT NUMBER	DESCRIPTION	REFERENCE NUMBER	BRAND	SOURCE
IG 16205	KNIFE, DINNER	AA 0000001		AA PURCHASE
IG 16208	FORK, DINNER	AA 0000001		AA PURCHASE
IG 16240	EQUIP, LINEN, NAPKIN, WHITE	AA 0000001		AA PURCHASE

AMERICAN AIRLINES   FOOD AND BEVERAGE SPECIFICATIONS   RECIPE NUMBER RC 16845

DESCRIPTION: SOUFFLE CUP W/S&P SHAKERS   SALT/PEPPER   EFFECTIVE DATE: 09/28/94
EQUIPMENT   PRINT DATE: 09/12/94

INGREDIENT/ RECIPE NBR	DESCRIPTION	* QTY	UM	PORTION DESC	QTY	* UM	BRAND
IG 500130	CUP, SOUFFLE, 5.5 OZ.	0	-		1	EACH	
IG 16250	SHAKERS, SALT/PEPPER	0	-		1	EACH	NOT BRAND SPECIFIC

INSTRUCTIONS:
- PLACE FILLED SHAKERS IN A SOUFFLE CUP.

YIELD:
* 1 EACH

PURCHASING SOURCE

COMPONENT NUMBER	DESCRIPTION	REFERENCE NUMBER	BRAND	SOURCE
IG 500130	CUP, SOUFFLE, 5.5 OZ.	LP 0000001	NOT BRAND SPECIFIC	LOCAL PURCHASE
IG 16250	SHAKERS, SALT/PEPPER	AA 0000001		AA PURCHASE

FIGURE 12.1 (Continued)

AMERICAN AIRLINES

FOOD AND BEVERAGE SPECIFICATIONS

RECIPE NUMBER RC 18641

DESCRIPTION: APPLE COBBLER PASTRY,PL-69
DESSERTS

PASTRY

EFFECTIVE DATE: 09/28/94
PRINT DATE: 09/12/94

INGREDIENT/ RECIPE NBR	DESCRIPTION	QTY	UM	---PORTION--- DESC	QTY	* UM	BRAND
IG 16562	APPLE COBBLER CAKE, 12 CUT WEDGE	0			1	EACH	LOVE AND QUICHES

INSTRUCTIONS:

- PREPARE ITEMS PER RECIPE.
- THAW CAKE.
- PLACE WEDGE OF CAKE ON PLATE, PL-69.
- COVER AND REFRIGERATE UNTIL USED.

YIELD:
----
1 PORTION

PURCHASING SOURCE

COMPONENT NUMBER	DESCRIPTION	REFERENCE NUMBER	BRAND	SOURCE
IG 16562	APPLE COBBLER CAKE, 12 CUT WEDGE	FB 0000006	LOVE AND QUICHES	FOOD & BEV. PURCHASE

FIGURE 12.1 (*Continued*)

278

Dining Service
Individual Station Equipment/Service Rotation Chart

CITY ___ DENVER ___   EFFECTIVE DATE ___

	Inbound			Outbound		Min/Max EC Codes
Flight	Service	Flight	Dest	Service		
274	F RM2 Y RM2 I G8A G06	274	ATL	F SD G8G Y TL I G09 RR5 EC8 ED8		0/11
343	F BC Y BL I G06 RRI G8A	656	DFW	F DC Y DL I G8W G8A G12 RR3 EC8 EB8		Constant 21
721	F BC G8G Y BL I G09 RR1	721	SLC	F SD Y TM I G8B G06 RR5 EC8		0/9
349	F RM2 G8G Y RM2 I G8A G12	216	DFW	F DC G8G Y DL I G8A G8W G12 RR3 EC8 EB8		0/21
1049	F DC G4G HC Y DL I G4W RR3 G24	1010	ATL	F SD Y TL I RR5 G4A G18 EC4 ED4		Constant 12
1043	F DC Y DL I G4A G4W G18 RR3	1082	DFW	F SD Y TM I G4A RR5 G18 EC4 ED4		Constant 12
262	F SD Y TM R10 I G8A G06 RR5	262	CVG	F DC HC G8G Y DL I G8W RR3 G12 EC8 EB8		0/21

FIGURE 12.2(a) Code sheet from an airline catering manual illustrating how the menus planned for a cycle have code numbers that are used to identify each menu and indicate the particular menu to be served for a particular flight and class of service on that flight. (Courtesy of Delta Airlines)

279

209	150	DFW		9/21
F SD G8G Y TM G6Y I GBN G09 RR5			F DC G8G Y DL GB3 I G8A G12 RR3 G8W EC8 EB8	
F Maximum beer/ Y wine/champagne I Beer (REG) 117 each (LITE) 123 each			F Y I	
F Wine Fifths Y (WHITE) 11 each I (RED) 11 each			F Y I	
F Wine Splits Y (WHITE) 151 each I (RED) 24 each (CHAMPAGNE) 2 each			F LONG HAUL − 0 Y MEDIUM HAUL − 0 I SHORT HAUL − 4 SNACK − 4	
F Y I			F Y I	

THROUGH FLIGHTS—Number of carriers/carts is dependent on menu code boarded on outbound flight.
ORIGINATING FLIGHTS—Number of carriers/carts is dependent on the menu codes inbound or outbound, whichever is greater. (NOTE: All previous segments of inbound flight must be considered when determining "greatest service.")
Copies to Local Kitchen Manager; Regional Manager—Catering

FIGURE 12.2(a) (*Continued*)

Dinner—DK1
Medium Haul—Tourist Class

SALAD:

Tourist Class Dinner Salad #1 (Section 15—Salads)—One each.

DRESSING:

Caesar (Section 15—Sundries)—One each. Place on meal tray.

*ENTREE CHOICE #1 - BOARD AT 60%:

MEAT:

Chicken Breast—Roasted (Section 15—Entrees)—Four ounces each. Place in center of entree casserole.

SAUCE:

Tarragon Butter Sauce (Section 15—Sauces)—.5 ounces each. Portion over chicken.

VEGETABLES:

Orzo Pasta with Herbs (Section 15—Vegetables)—2 ounces each. Place in one end of casserole.

Cut Green Beans (Section 15—Vegetables)—2 ounces each. Place in other end of casserole.

*ENTREE CHOICE #2 - BOARD AT 40%:

PASTA:

Garden Vegetable Lasagna (Section 15—Entrees)—One portion each. Place in one end of entree casserole.

MEAT:

Italian Sausage Link, 2 ounce (c.w.) (Section 15—Vegetables)—1 each. Place in other end of casserole.

BREAD:

Roll—Sesame Twist (Section 15—Sundries)—One each. Place on meal tray.

BUTTER:

Classic Blend (Section 15—Sundries)—One each. Place on meal tray.

DESSERT:

Chocolate Sheet Cake (Section 15—Desserts)—One each. Place on dessert plate.

CONDIMENTS:

Salt and Pepper Packets (Section 15—Sundries)—One each. Wrap with silverware.

* On 737-300 aircraft, board entree in plastic casserole.

FIGURE 12.2(b) A dinner menu for this airline and the loading factor that would be used by the caterer to board the meal. (Courtesy of Delta Airlines)

items to be prepared in the particular caterer's kitchen. Note too that the menu indicates meal provisioning information, or the proportion of the total passenger count to be used as the count for each entree (as was also the case for the menu shown in Figure 12.1). A footnote indicates that the entrees should be boarded in plastic casseroles when the equipment for the flight is a Boeing 737-300 aircraft as opposed to the ceramic casseroles that should be used for all other types of equipment.

Production Work Sheets

This process is tedious and cumbersome for employees, to say nothing of the valuable production time that would be used for this type of activity if all employees individually had to locate this information from the airlines' manuals to complete their daily assignments (presuming that they could read the pages and understand the codes used by each airline). To make these manuals operational in a practical sense, it is highly desirable to have someone who is well versed in all the different airlines' manuals who can research them for the necessary operational details and then prepare simplified worksheets for the employees to use as a guideline for their work on a daily basis. Figures 12.3 and 12.4 illustrate sample worksheets typical of what might be used in a catering operation.

Figure 12.3 indicates the passenger count to be prepared for each flight serviced by the kitchen. It also indicates any special meals, including crew meals, that are needed for each flight. Note that these meals are being prepared the day prior to the day they will be used. However, this production sheet does *not* list the food items to be prepared. Rather, it only indicates the codes for the menus to be used. For example, for United Airlines flight 1412, menu C09 is to be used for first class (8 meals needed) and menu V06 is to be used for coach class (118 meals needed). However, since two crew meals are also needed, the production staff will need to prepare 10, rather than 8, first-class meals. Or, Northwest's flight 1190 will need 10 first-class meals prepared using menu B13B and 127 coach-class meals prepared using menu BB63. In addition, there are three special meals needed for coach class—a KSML (or Kosher meal) for passenger Summers, a VLML (Lacto-ovo vegetarian plate) for passenger Viafora, and a CHML (child's meal) for passenger Cappadenia. While this type of production sheet provides a total overview of the work that needs to be done on a particular production shift, it does require the production personnel to be familiar with the menu and recipe sections of the airlines' manuals that are generally available on most kitchens' production floor so that they can see the specific production tasks that must be done.

Figure 12.4 illustrates an alternate approach. These sheets indicate the

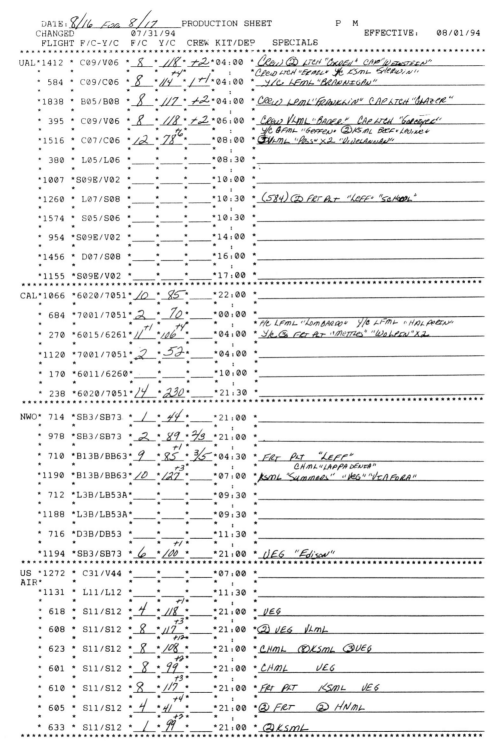

FIGURE 12.3 Sample production sheet used by one caterer that is typical of the production sheets prepared by inflight kitchens as a means of "translating" the airlines' catering manuals into daily work activities to be completed by the caterers' employees. Production sheet indicates all of the meals to be prepared on a shift. (Courtesy of Ogden Aviation Services)

CYCLE 4   EFF:09/01/94

FIRST CLASS SERVICE

FLT. 270 72X 14/139

6015-4 SHORT HAUL SNACK AM   BULK SERVICE

100%	BREAKFAST COLD PLATE	1 EA.
LE80311	BIG AND CRUSTY PLAIN BAGEL, 3 OZ. (LENDERS)	1 EA.
KF01120	CREAM CHEESE POUCH, 1 OZ. (KRAFT)	1 EA.
SM80767	STRAWBERRY PRESERVES, 1/2 OZ. (SMUCKERS)	2 OZ.
YOP6666	ASST. FRUIT YOGURT IN NUT RAMEKIN (YOPLAIT)	.1 EA.
LOCAL	BANANA, 150 CT	14 EA.

NOTE: ARRANGE ALL ITEMS ON LARGE PLATE AND OVERWRAP W/SARAN. BULK BOARD
2 EA. COLD PLATES AND LINEN ROLL-UPS IN WINE GLASSES ON LARGE F/C TRAY.
BULK BOARD ADDITIONAL TRAYS TO 50% PAX. CT. TRAYS TO EQUAL F/C PAX CT.

FLT. 170 AB3 24/233

6011-4-SHORT HAUL SNACK PM   BULK SERVICE

100% SANDWICH AND FRUIT & CHEESE COLD PLATE
TURKEY SANDWICH ON FOCCACIA ROLL SANDWICH PLATE

USV8000	FOCCACIA ROLL W/TOMATO AND OLIVES, SLICED (US FOODSERVICE)	1 EA.
JNO8483	TURKEY BREAST, SLICED (JENNIE'O)	4 SL.
VD03736	PESTO SAUCE (VIE DE FRANCE)	1/8 OZ.
HLL8951	DIJONNAISE PKT., 1/4 OZ. (BEST FOODS)	1 EA.
KFO6526	MAYONNAISE PKT., 7/16 OZ. (KRAFT)	1 EA.
CAL	SALT AND PEPPER PKT. (P/N 8-9878)	1 EA.
BY4Z712	BRISTOL WAFERS PKT. (BURRY'S)	1 EA.
KLO9536	CHEDDAR CHEESE WDG., 7/8 OZ. (KOLB LENA)	1 EA.
LOCAL	RED GRAPES, STEM ON	3 OZ.
FA90804	CAPPUCCINO DESSERT BAR (FANTASIA)	1 EA.
		24 EA.

NOTE: ASSEMBLE ALL ITEMS ON LARGE PLATE AND OVERWRAP W/SARAN. BULK BOARD
2 EA. COLD PLATES AND LINEN ROLL-UPS IN WINE GLASSES ON LARGE F/C TRAY.
BULK BOARD ADDITIONAL TRAYS TO 50% PAX CT. TRAYS TO EQUAL F/C PAX CT.

FIGURE 12.4(a)   A production worksheet where the caterer annotates production directions on the airlines menu sheet. This approach indicates the detail of one particular production assignment as opposed to providing an overview (but not the detail) of the total production responsibilities of the shift (as shown in Figure 12.3). (a) Indicates the first-class portion of the worksheet for a flight. (b) Indicates the coach-class portion for the same flight. (Courtesy of Continental Airlines and Ogden Aviation Services)

<u>CYCLE 4 EFF::09/01/94</u>

COACH CLASS SERVICE

FLT. 270 72X 14/139

<u>6261-4 - COLD BREAKFAST SNACK</u>   **CARDBOARD WINDOW BOX, 100%**

SMA5840	RAISINS PKT., 1 OZ. (SUN MAID)	1 EA.
LE80073	CINNAMON RAISIN BAGEL (LENDERS)	1 EA.
KFO1120	CREAM CHEESE POUCH, 1 OZ. (KRAFT)	1 EA.
CAL	CARDBOARD WINDOW BOX (P/N 8-9677)	1 EA.
CAL	SMALL PLASTIC KNIFE (P/N 8-9413)	1 EA.
CAL	DINNER NAPKIN (P/N 8-9125)	1 EA.
APS	COLOR CODE ROTATION CIRCLE (SAGE)	139 EA.

FLT. 170 AB3 24/233

<u>6260-4- COLD SHORT HAUL SNACK</u>   **CARDBOARD WINDOW BOX, 100%**

BUL6660	NATURES CANDY CARROT STICKS, 1 OZ. (BUNNY LUV)	1 EA.
#348	SOUR CREAM & HERB DIP, 1 OZ. (NATURALLY FRESH)	1 EA.
	VINEYARD CHEESE WEDGE, .5 OZ. (STAUFFERS)	1 EA.
BY43712	BRISTOL WAFER CRACKERS (BURRY'S)	1 EA.
PP07409	PRETZEL GOLDFISH CRACKERS, .5 OZ. (PEP. FARM)	1 EA.
RHL4444	COOKIE PKT., .5 OZ. (RACHEL'S)	1 EA.
CAL	CARDBOARD WINDOW BOX (P/N 8-9677)	1 EA.
CAL	SMALL PLASTIC KNIFE (P/N 8-9413)	1 EA.
CAL	DINNER NAPKIN (P/N 8-9125)	1 EA.
APS	COLOR CODE ROTATION CIRCLE (SAGE)	233 EA.

FIGURE 12.4(b)

specific tasks that need to be done to prepare the snacks for flight 270 which will use aircraft type 72X in the morning and flight 170 which will use aircraft type AB3 in the afternoon. The passenger count is indicated as 14 in first class and 139 in coach class for Flight 270; for flight 170 it is 24 in first class and 233 in coach class. The two pages of the worksheet indicate the specification number of the item to be used, the amount to be used for the plates, and directions for arranging the plate. However, it does not contain directions for boxing the coach-class snacks. The directions for preparing the boxes would be at the tray/box assembly area. While sheets such as these give personnel the specifics on the tasks to be done, they do not provide an overall picture of the total work to be accomplished on a shift. Ideally, both types of sheets would be available to production personnel so that they could see the big picture and plan their work accordingly as well as having task specifics readily at hand.

THE AIRLINE COMMUNICATIONS CHALLENGE

When considering the complexity of this communication challenge for the inflight caterer, it must be remembered that most inflight kitchens service several different airlines. Each airline has different menus, different recipes, and different service requirements. Each of them provides a different set of manuals to the caterer. Every day, the inflight caterer is dealing with information from several different manuals, each written in a different format and using different codes for different purposes.

In addition, to make this communications task even more challenging, the airlines frequently send changes to the manuals. Each change must be carefully reviewed when it is received in the caterer's kitchen. The change will indicate an effective date as well as the change to be made. Generally, the new page must be put into the airline's manual as a replacement for an existing page which must be removed and destroyed. The change's effective date must be carefully noted as it cannot be made prior to that date, but it must not be forgotten; it must be made on the date indicated.

Sometimes these change notices are received well in advance of the desired change date, giving the flight kitchen's management staff ample time to circulate the change notice to all persons concerned. However, many times the change notice will be received by fax or meter (an electronically printed message or memo similar to teletype). Such a notice often indicates that the change is to be effective immediately upon receipt. This situation requires immediate action by management staff on duty to see that the notice is promptly circulated and the appropriate change in procedures or menu items is made instantaneously.

Because of the complexity of the airlines' manuals and the need for prompt, consistent action in regard to change notices received, it is usually better to centralize the responsibility for inserting change sheets, as well as for communicating the change to the kitchen employees. Fewer communication problems are likely to occur if only one (or a very few) person(s) handle this responsibility as a primary duty to be sure that these updates are given priority consideration and that the manuals are corrected and updated in a timely, organized manner. Sometimes in a kitchen with multiple airlines, this task is spread among several key staff management with each having the responsibility for one airline. This allows one or two persons to specialize on one airline and be the principal source of information and detailed knowledge about that airline.

AIRLINE MENU CHANGES

The airlines also change their cycle menus frequently. Some change their cycles weekly while others change monthly or on other time periods. These changes are made to provide variety to passengers, especially frequent travelers, including substantial numbers of commuters (e.g., passengers that take the same flight pattern on a very regular basis). When the change is monthly, the change date is not necessarily the first of the month. The change date is set by the airline. An airline's cycles change nationwide at approximately the same time. Although menu changes can be disruptive to production routines and staff familiarity, it is important that not all airlines change on the same date. In a facility with many airlines, it would be a monumental task to assimilate and execute so many changes at once, although it is not unusual for two or three airlines to make menu cycle changes on the same date.

These frequent changes, especially where the menus are changed weekly, add to the challenges faced by the inflight caterer. Whenever the menu cycle changes, all employees have to learn new specifications and a new set of products must be available for production personnel to work with. If the change is weekly, then both the learning and the change in inventory stock levels is weekly. There are a number of reasons prompting the airlines to make changes to their menu cycle. Some of these reasons include: (1) competition from other airlines; (2) trends in food consumption patterns; (3) economic changes (what the airline can afford to serve); (4) changes in equipment (both the type of aircraft used on flights and equipment for boarding and providing the inflight service); and (5) the need to have the proper equipment in the right place at the right time.

The frequent menu changes present a complex challenge for the purchasing and storage areas as the mix of products needed can change weekly. Some items which may have been used heavily this week may not be needed at all next week. This situation makes it very difficult for the caterer's purchasing department to have just the right amount of an item on hand so that it is used up at the time the cycle changes; yet, there are no product shortages either.

The inflight caterer's purchasing agent tries to purchase exactly what will be needed for the menus during a particular menu cycle period. However, products must be ordered in advance so that delivery is assured in time for usage. An order lead time of three to four weeks is not unusual. The amounts of the different items purchased are based on airline passenger count estimates and the caterer's records of previous meal service on the flights. However, if passenger counts are low for some reason, then it is possible that there will be items that the caterer will have to carry in storage for perhaps an eight- to ten-week period until the menu cycle with that item is again served. Because of the number of airlines served and the number of cycles used by each airline, it is possible for the caterer to tie up a considerable amount of funds (and inventory storage space) in such items. Unlike other types of foodservice operations, the inflight caterer cannot readily use up these excess items by making menu substitutions as the menus served must always be exactly what is specified for that day by the airline unless the caterer requests and receives permission from the airline to burn off on-hand stock. While a caterer can make such a request occasionally, to do so often may make the airline concerned about the quality of the caterer's services. Further, some airlines permit only one or two early-start or burn off days on either side of a cycle change date to facilitate such fluctuations in planning.

There is, though, some latitude that the caterer has in regard to the menu if problems are encountered with vendors. For example, if a particular fruit is specified on the menu as part of a salad plate, but it is out of season and unavailable in the local market, then an alternative available fruit can be substituted. However, caterers cannot just make substitutions at will. They must first call the airline and explain the situation, and get the airline's permission to make the substitution.

Such menu changes, particularly when a complete new cycle menu is introduced, may be cause for adjusting the caterer's pricing for that airline. Changing the foods on a menu changes the cost of the menu to the caterer. It is not only the cost of food that may change, but the amount of labor required may also vary. Thus, the caterer may feel that it is appropriate to renegotiate the prices charged for the different meals served, or if the initial contract allows price adjustments based on menu cost, then the caterer may need only to calculate the new meal production costs and notify the airline of an adjustment in the meal-pricing structure.

AIRLINE PROVISIONING STANDARDS

Although there is considerable attention given to provisioning, it may not always seem so to a passenger who is asking for an item on board an aircraft that is no longer available because the flight attendants just ran out of it. The stocking, or provisioning, patterns and the amounts of the different items that are boarded on an aircraft are determined after very serious consideration of consumption patterns on flights, space available to stock different types of items, trends observed, changing demand patterns, and other such considerations. The airlines develop provisioning guidelines which tell their caterers how much of each item to board on a particular flight. These guidelines indicate how much or how many of the different items stocked should be boarded relative to the number of passengers to be served.

Figures 12.5 and 12.6 illustrate typical provisioning charts used by one airline. As can be noted from these charts, even somethig as seemingly small as creamers for the coffee are boarded in accord with a provisioning chart that has been developed. When costs need to be controlled and space and weight are premium commodities, as is the case on passenger aircraft, nothing is too small to consider. Figure 12.7 illustrates a provisioning chart from a different airline that shows the proportion of the passenger count to be used to board menu items.

Milk Provisioning

Code	Quantity Domestic	Quantity Mexico	Flight
RR1	1 for ea 4 psgrs	1 for ea 16 psgrs	Breakfast Flights (Selected)
RR2	1 for ea 6 psgrs	1 for ea 20 psgrs	Breakfast/Brunch Flights
RR3	1 for ea 8 psgrs	1 for ea 32 psgrs	Lunch/Dinner Flights
RR5	1 for ea 10 psgrs	1 for ea 40 psgrs	Snack Flights
RM1	1 half pint	-	Supplemental and Beverage Flights
RM2	2 half pints	-	Supplemental and Beverage Flights
RM4	4 half pints	-	Supplemental and Beverage Flights
RM6	6 half pints	-	Supplemental and Beverage Flights
R10	10 half pints	-	Supplemental and Beverage Flights
R15	15 half pints	-	Supplemental and Beverage Flights
R20	20 half pints	-	Supplemental and Beverage Flights
R30	30 half pints	-	Supplemental and Beverage Flights
R40	40 half pints	-	Supplemental and Beverage Flights

NOTE: • RR codes in "I Class" apply to entire aircraft. Quantities are to be computed individually for each class (F-Y). The F-Y quantities are then added together for the total boarded.
• Milk is to be boarded at 50% whole and 50% 2 percent.
• Board in Half Pints, Except Mexico - Board in Liters

Half & Half/Creamer Provisioning

Code	Item	Quantity
RCM	Half and Half Coffee Cream	1 Pint (1/2 liter) for ea. 15 psgrs
RC5	Individual creamers	10 creamers
RC6	Individual creamers	15 creamers
RC7	Individual creamers	20 creamers
RC8	Individual creamers	25 creamers
per menu spec	Half and Half Coffee Creamers Section 15 - Sundries	F/C - B/C ONLY (individual creamers) Breakfast/Breakfast Snack/Brunch - 50% of Pax Count Lunch/Dinner - 25% of Pax Count Deluxe Snack/Snack - 25% of Pax Count
per menu spec	Liquid Non-Dairy Creamer Section 15 - Sundries	T/C ONLY (individual creamers) Breakfast/Breakfast Snack/Brunch - 50% of Pax Count Lunch/Dinner - 25% of Pax Count Deluxe Snack/Snack - 25% of Pax Count

FIGURE 12.5 Provisioning chart typical of those used in the inflight foodservice industry. (Courtesy of Delta Airlines)

Wine and Bulk Board Wine Glass Provisioning

Code	Class	Description	Ratio	Quantity	Wine Glasses P/N 0442-01556
G2W	F F	White Fifths Red Fifths	1:6 1:8	-	4
G3W	F F	White Fifths Red Fifths	1:6 1:8	-	4
G4W	F F	White Fifths Red Fifths	1:6 1:8	-	10
G5W	F F	White Fifths Red Fifths	1:6 1:8	-	10
G6W	F F	White Fifths Red Fifths	1:6 1:8	-	6
G7W	F F	White Fifths Red Fifths	1:6 1:8	-	10
G8W	F F	White Fifths Red Fifths	1:6 1:8	-	4
G9W	F F	White Fifths Red Fifths	1:6 1:8	-	4
GDW	F F	White Fifths Red Fifths	1:6 1:8	-	4 F/C 10 B/C
GJW	F F	White Fifths Red Fifths	1:6 1:8	-	4
GRW GAW GBW GEW	F & C	White Fifths Red Fifths	1:6 1:8	-	4 F/C 10 B/C
GW1	F	White Wine Fifths	-	1 Ea.	-
GW2	F	Red Wine Fifths	-	1 Ea.	-
GW3	F	White Wine Fifths	-	2 Ea.	-
GW4	F	Red Wine Fifths	-	2 Ea.	-
GWY	F or Y	White Wine Splits Red Wine Splits	-	4 Ea. 4 Ea.	-
G1Y	F or Y	Red Splits	-	5 Ea.	-
G2Y	F or Y	Red Splits	-	10 Ea.	-

FIGURE 12.6 Another example of a typical provisioning chart. (Courtesy of Delta Airlines).

G4Y	F or Y	Red Splits	-	20 Ea.	-
G5Y	F or Y	White Splits	-	5 Ea.	-
G6Y	F or Y	White Splits	-	10 Ea.	-
G8Y	F or Y	White Splits	-	20 Ea.	-
GWW	F	ATL/DFW-HNL (L1011-250 ships 737/724 ONLY) 8 Ea. White Wine Fifths 6 Ea. Red Wine Fifths 6 Ea. Champagne Fifths 18 Ea. Beer (regular) 18 Ea. Beer (lite)			
	Y	48 Ea. White Wine Splits 24 Ea. Red Wine Splits 24 Ea. Champagne Splits 24 Ea. Beer (regular) 24 Ea. Beer (lite)	-	-	-

NOTE: For wine glass provisioning use glass tray P/N 0442-02229. Place on meal tray and saran wrap. Place in F/C support carrier or cart as applicable.

FIGURE 12.6 Another example of a typical provisioning chart. (Courtesy of Delta Airlines).

Once the provisioning chart has been determined, then space in the boarding equipment and in the galley area is allocated to the items. Other charts or diagrams are prepared by the airline and distributed to the caterers which show specifically what the content of boarding carts should be and where the carts go in the galley. Figures 12.8 and 12.9 illustrate the diagrams that are issued to the caterer to show how two different trolleys should be loaded for a flight.

Figure 12.8 illustrates a support cart for first-class service (note the allocation of space for creamers in the front of the bottom drawer) while Figure 12.9 illustrates a liquor cart packed for coach-class service. It is up to the caterer to have copies of these diagrams readily available for their employees to use to prepare the carts for the airline's flights. The person assigned the responsibility for checking the pack prior to loading it onto the trucks for transport to the planes will also certainly need to be familiar with these diagrams, not for just one airline, but for all of the airlines serviced by the caterer. Caterers often pack copies of these diagrams in the carts for the flight attendants' reference as well.

Changes in Provisioning Standards

The airlines do not change their provisioning estimates without a great deal of forethought as making even the most simple change is a complex

FLT.622(22) 1988(12)	F/C LIGHT LUNCH I	CYCLE1

60%   TRAY SETUP (IT14377)

40%   TRAY SETUP (IT2100)

60%   FACCICIO CHICKEN SANDWICH (IT14915)   1 EACH
　　　　　　　FACCOCIO BREAD (3015)　　　　　　　　1 EA.
　　　　　　　ROASTED CHICKEN BREAST, 3 OZ　　　1 EA.
　　　　　　　　　(WRAP UP TO 2 PIECES OF CHICKEN IN FOIL SHEET)
　　　　　　　　　(WRAP BREAD IN FOIL SHEET)
　　　　　　　　　(PORTION UP TO 2 UNITS IN FOIL PAN-NO LID)

60%   TOMATO BASIL SOUP (IT14320)   1 EACH
　　　　　　　(1 UNIT = 8 oz. SOUP, 2 4oz. FOIL CUPS, 2 LIDS.)
　　　　　　　(PLACE IN BULK FOIL PANS)

60%   COLD PLATE SET-UP (IT15207) (RC15936)   1 EACH
　　　　　　　ROMAINE LETTUCE-JULIENNE CUT 1/4″　　　1/2 OZ.
　　　　　　　GREEN CHILE MAYONAISE-RAMEKIN (RC16238)　3/4 OZ.
　　　　　　　TOMATO SLICE, 6 CUT　　　　　　　　　　2 EA.

40%   SHRIMP AND VERMICELLI COLD PLATE (IT11462) (RC13552)   1 EACH
　　　　　　　MARINATED SHRIMP 41/50 TAIL-ON (RC16906)　　5 EA.
　　　　　　　ZESTY ORANGE MANGO SAUCE (RC12355)　　　　1 OZ.
　　　　　　　VERMICELLI STIR-FRY (RC13002)　　　　　　　4 OZ.
　　　　　　　SNOW PEA PODS BLANCHED (RC11247)　　　　　3 EA.
　　　　　　　TOMATO WEDGE 6 CUT (RC16983)　　　　　　　2 EA.
　　　　　　　YELLOW SQUASH CUT LENGTHWISE SLICED　　　3 EA.

1 UNIT PER 4 PAX: 1 UNIT
100% CHOC. CHUNK MACADAMIAN NUT COOKIE
　　　　(PACK 6 COOKIES IN FOIL PAN W/LID = 1 UNIT)

40% BUTTER 47 CT. UNSALTED MID-AMERICA FARMS (IT2100)   1 EACH

1 UNIT PER 3 PAX.　　　ASSORTED BREADSTICKS　　　(IT13669)

　　PARMESAN BREADSTICK　　　　　　　　USD6500　　2 EA.
　　ROSEMARY/GARLIC BREADSTICK　　　　USD6502　　2 EA.

DK/2DF/S

FIGURE 12.7(a) Example of a provisioning chart that shows the load factor to be used to board the menu items. (a) First-Class Chart. (b) Coach-class chart for the above flight.

FLT.622 (166). 1988 (130)	C/C LIGHTER FARE II	CYCLE1

100%	HOT TURKEY AND CHEESE KNOT ROLL (IT15021)	1 EACH

          (PC16741)
                WHOLE WHEAT KNOT ROLL   #6810 1 EA.
                TURKEY BREAST (THIN SLICED)   1.75 OZ.
                MILD CHEDDAR CHEESE 1/2 OZ. SLICE 1 EA.   (AA)
                FOIL SANDWICH BAG   1 EA.

BASKET (IT 15016)
POTATO CHIPS, RUFFLES   1 EACH
MAYONNAISE PACKET, BEST FOODS   1 EACH
CREAMY DIJON MUSTARD, BEST FOODS   1 EACH
LITE WIGHT KNIFE, 5″   1 EACH
RED CHECKERED NAPKIN   1 EACH
DINNER NAPKIN   1 EACH
DISPOSABLE BASKET   1 EACH
WHITE CHOCOLATE W/PECAN COOKIE #8710   1 EACH

FIGURE 12.7(b)

process. Should an airline decide to change the amount of a particular item that is to be boarded per passenger or to change the mix of a class of items (such as more diet and less regular soda than they had been using previously), there are many steps that must be taken to make that change happen. Not the least of those steps is determining the *cost impact* (if any) of such a change. Once the cost impact has been determined and the change is found to be cost effective (hopefully it is a cost savings) for the airline, some of the steps that must occur include (1) preparing a change sheet indicating the desired change and distributing the sheet to all of the caterers used by the airline; (2) determining an effective date for the change; (3) reconsidering the cart pack to accommodate the change; (4) once the revised cart pack has been determined, preparing a change sheet and new cart diagram and distributing these items to all the caterers; (5) allowing time for the caterers to make adjustments in their stock levels to accommodate the change; (6) if an item is being eliminated, allowing time for the caterers to use up existing stock; (7) retraining the caterer's personnel in regard to the items to be stocked and where they go; and (8) reorienting the flight attendants regarding their supply of this item and where they are located in the galley(s). Accomplishing all the steps that are required to make a provisioning change is both costly and time consuming for the airline and the caterer.

L1011-250
FIRST CLASS SUPPORT CART

POSITION: CART STOWAGE POSITION #8 GALLEY G1
EQUIPMENT: BEVERAGE CART P/N 0443 03649
6 DRAWERS P/N 0441 02918

SIDE A	SIDE B
DRAWER #1 12 soup spoons 60 B&B knives 60 salad forks 60 teaspoons 36 ea. dinner knives/forks	12 Base Plates – saran wrapped
DRAWER #2 2 sauce ladles, 9 tongs, 2 cake servers, 14 serving spoons, 4 serving forks	*12 2nd service silverware packs (linen-folded)
DRAWER #3 1 soup tureen w/lid, soup ladle 12 ea. salt and pepper shakers	15 china coffee cups
DRAWER #4 1 silver coffee pot 1 silver sugar bowl 1 silver tea pot 2 silver creamers 1 silver tong, 1 box sugar cubes 1 pepper mill	Thermos Jugs
DRAWER #5 21 china coffee cups	12 B&J Dishes 6 ea. soup bowls w/soup spoons 2 baskets P/N 0442-02306
DRAWER #6 12 dinner plates (foiled wrapped) 6 ramekins	12 dinner plates (foiled wrapped) 6 ramekins

*FC Silverware Pack (2nd Service) consists of:

DINNER NAPKIN FC DAMASK	P/N 0442-03895
FC DINNER FORK	0442-03872
FC SALAD FORK	0442-03873
FC DINNER KNIFE	0442-03874
FC B&B KNIFE	0442-03875
FC TEASPOON	0444-03876

FIGURE 12.8 Loading diagram for first-class support cart which also indicates the stowage position and the galley number in which the cart is to be placed when it is boarded onto the aircraft. (Courtesy of Delta Airlines)

L1011-250
L1011-500 (Ships 751-756, 764-769)
B767-332ER, A310-300 (Ships 035-043)

TOURIST CLASS BEVERAGE CART

CART EQUIPMENT:	PART NUMBER:
L1011/B767- 3 CARTS	0443-03649
A310 - 2 CARTS	0443-03649
6 DRAWERS (EACH CART)	0441-02918

SIDE A	SIDE B
1A 2 – Liquor Units – 48 Miniatures	1B 2 – Liqueur Units – 48 Miniatures
2A 6 – Champagne Splits 10 – Beer	2B 20 – Beverages/Mixes 5 – Coke 5 – 7-Up 3 – Diet Coke 2 – Diet 7-UP 2 – Orange Juice 2 – Apple Juice 1 – Tomato Juice
3A Beverage/Juice Drawer	3B Beverage/Juice Drawer
4B Beverage/Juice Drawer	4A Beverage/Juice Drawer
5A 18 – White Wine Splits	5B 18 – Beer
6A 1 – Liquor Unit – 24 Miniatures 1 – Liqueur Unit – 24 Miniatures	6B 18 – Red Wine Splits

FIGURE 12.9 Loading diagram for full-size coach-class beverage cart. (Courtesy of Delta Airlines)

Sometimes airlines make provisioning changes which contain a lot of detail regarding different types of aircraft, different flight times, different flight time lengths, and so on. For example, one airline recently redesigned their provisioning standards for the soft drinks served on their flights. Originally, the airline used two different packs for their soda drawers. After the change, there were five different packs for their soda drawers which were designated for specific types of flights.

As a result of this change, the caterers serving this airline had to acquire more equipment (spare drawers for the trolleys) so that they could now pack and maintain an inventory of five, rather than two, different drawer configurations packed, ready to board. The caterer's employees preparing the drawers had to learn the new packs, and the employees preparing the trolleys for transport had to learn which types of flights got what type of drawer. Further, if the time was changed on the flight for some reason and the new flight time required a different drawer pack, the drawers originally loaded into the trolleys had to be taken out and replaced with new drawers packed for the new flight departure time. Not only did this change increase the complexity of the system for all concerned and cause the inflight caterer to focus new emphasis on quality assurance for the beverage pack for this airline, the additional stocking and checking requirements added to the caterer's cost of service to the airline.

How the airlines buy items, such as soft drinks, and how unused product is accounted for is an important consideration underlying many of the airlines' decisions on the provisioning requirements. The airline that made the change in the beverage pack noted here buys its soda from the caterer's stock (as opposed to directly purchasing the soda and having it delivered to the caterer for exclusive use on its flights). Once the soda is boarded on the airline's aircraft, it is effectively purchased by that airline. Thus, any unused soda (even though the cans may be reused as the drawers are repacked at another caterer's facility) is an expense to the airline. As a part of their effort to reduce their inflight foodservice costs, the airline was trying to more closely tailor the actual amount of soda boarded per flight to the actual consumption on that flight. The objective was to reduce the number of unused sodas that for them was a loss—or, in some cases, that they purchased more than once from different caterers. The airline, in effect, purchased some sodas multiple times because the sodas that the caterer received when it stripped the inbound flights of this particular airline were salvaged and returned to the caterer's inventory. They were then resold to the same or another airline as the caterer assembled the beverage carts for the outbound flight per the airline's provisioning chart. While such "reselling" may seem to be a tremendous revenue generation for caterers, under such programs airlines moderate their costs by including a salvage factor in their pricing agreements with their caterers. For example, if an airline knows its typical rate of inbound unused (and therefore salvaged) sodas is 20% of the amount originally boarded, then the selling price of the outbound soda is factored downward by the 20% salvage rate.

GALLEY LOADING

The galleys must be loaded in accord with the airline's plans. Their plans are made to accommodate all of the provisions that they have determined to be necessary for the flights using a particular type of equipment. Sample diagrams used by some airlines are shown in Figures 12.10 and 12.11. Figure 12.10 indicates the equipment to be boarded onto the aircraft while figure 12.11 (a–d) illustrates the placement of that equipment into the four galleys on the plane. The galley-loading diagrams indicate the location of the different pieces of boarding equipment in the galleys, which both facilitates loading the equipment into the plane and helps the flight attendants see at a glance where the different items needed for meal and beverage services are to be found. Indeed some airlines require the caterer to board menus, provisioning sheets, and/or pictorial diagrams with the boarding equipment because they are so helpful to the flight attendants who may not be familiar with a particular galley configuration and just what is packed where. It should be noted that an airline's multiple aircraft and galleys are likely to be more confusing to flight attendants than to the caterers. Figure 12.12 illustrates one such diagram.

Since the galleys are all different in terms of their configuration and what is loaded into them, they are numbered so that the caterer's boarding crew knows which diagram to use for which galley and the flight attendants know which galley to go to for certain items. The numbering system used goes from front to back with galley number one (Figure 12.11a) being the forward one or the one on the *right* as the boarding crew goes through the front galley service door. Number 2 (Figure 12.11b) would be in the aft position of the front galley or on the *left*, and so on progressing toward the galleys in the rear of the plane. Smaller aircraft have only front and rear galleys, so they would have no more than four galleys—a right and left front and a right and left rear. The larger, wide-body aircraft may also have a midcabin galley that would be galleys three and four with the rear galleys being numbers five and six. In the case of the B757-200 illustrated here, there is only one midcabin galley (Figure 12.11c) and a large back galley that extends across the rear of the aircraft (Figure 12.11d).

Sometimes the flight attendants will ask the caterer's boarding personnel to put items in places other than the space designated in the galley diagram. If they do make such a request, the caterer's personnel explain that they are required to board very specific equipment and supplies in very specific locations on the aircraft and to deviate from those directives would jeopardize their job. This is because complaints received later on about missing supplies could be the result of such variances in boarding. Drivers and loaders are discouraged from responding to such requests, and catering companies, in general, are specifically told by airline dining service departments to make no service or packing deviations.

QUALITY ASSURANCE IN THE INFLIGHT KITCHEN

The use of the information from the airlines for the caterer's quality assurance efforts cannot be over emphasized. Since the tenure of a caterer's relationship with an airline is only as good as the service provided relative

B757–200, N908AW – N910AW, Equipment Requirements

ITEM DESCRIPTION	AWA PART #	SERVICE LEVEL		QTY ONBD
		F/C	M/C	
Cart, Beverage, Full Size	960589		2	2
Cart, Dead Head, Full Size	960589		1	1
Cart, Folding	960592	1		1
Cart, Liquor, Full Size	960589	1	2	3
Cart, Meal, Full Size	960589	1	5	6
Cart, Support, Full Size	960589	1		1
Cart, Waste, Full Size	960594	1	1	2
Container, Waste Cart, Grey	960612	1	1	2
Drawer, Beer #1	960591	1		1
Drawer, Beer/Wine #1	960591		4	4
Drawer, Condiment #2	960591	1	2	3
Insert, Condiment	960932	1	2	3
Drawer, First Class Cocktail Snack		1		1
Drawer, Juice #2	960591	1	8	9
Drawer, Liquor #1	960591	1	2	3
Insert, Liquor	962010	1	2	3
Drawer, Mix #2	960591	1	8	9
Drawer, Soda #1	960591	1	8	9
Drawer, Supply #2	960591	1		1
Drawer, Supply #4	960591		1	1
Drawer, Supply #5	960591	1		1
Drawer, Wine #1	960591	1		1
Drawer, Wine #2	960591	1		1
Ice Container, Grey (each with 20 lbs wet ice)	960582	3	6	9
Oven	960595	2	6	8
Oven Tray (8 per oven)	960596	16	48	64
Pallet Serving Tray (White)	960328		2	2
Pot, Coffee	961772	2	4	6
Standard Carrier (STC)	960597	3	5	8
Table, Auxiliary	960593	1		1
Waste Bin, Galley 2–11	961607	1		1
Waste Bin, Galley 4–16, 27	960585		2	2

FIGURE 12.10 Listing of equipment required for the provision of one airline's food and beverage services on the B757-200. (Courtesy of America West Airlines)

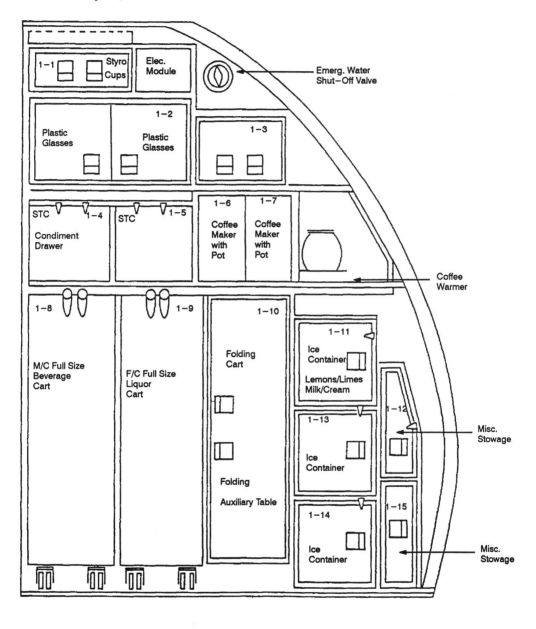

(a)

FIGURE 12.11 One airline's loading diagrams for the galleys on a B757-200 aircraft. Parts a–d illustrate each of the four galleys on the aircraft. All of the equipment listed in Figure 12.10 should have a placement location somewhere on the four galley loading diagrams. (Courtesy of America West Airlines)

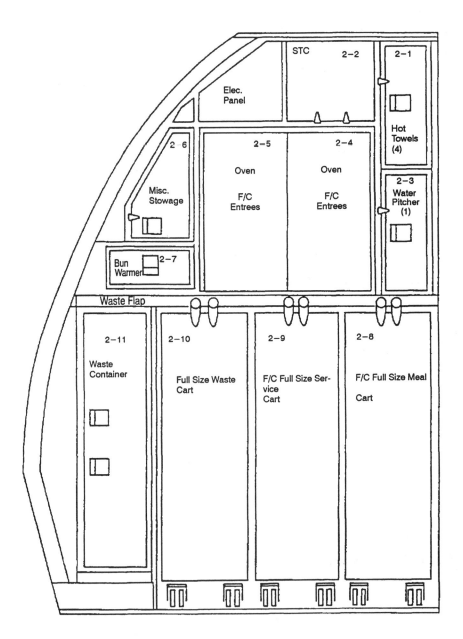

(b)

FIGURE 12.11 *(Continued)*

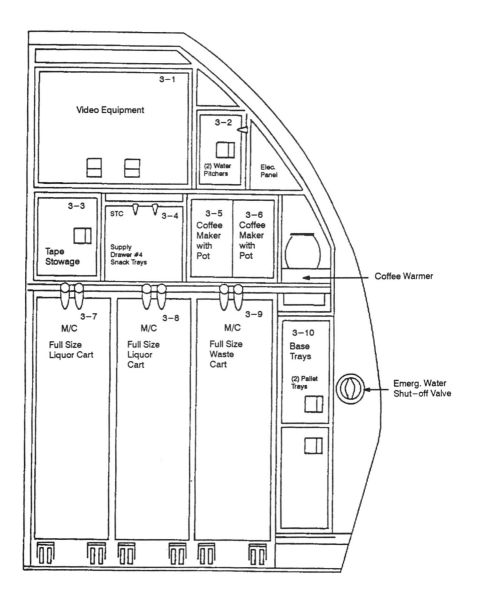

(c)

FIGURE 12.11 *(Continued)*

B757–200 Galley #4 Aircraft N908AW – N910AW

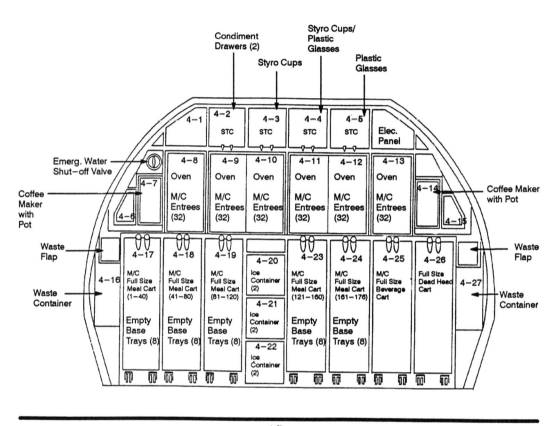

(d)

FIGURE 12.11 *(Continued)*

FIGURE 12.12 Example of a menu form which an airline requires the caterer to board onto the aircraft with the meal service supplies and equipment. The form indicates the menu, the load factor that was to be used, and provides an area for the flight attendants to make comments about the caterer's service, the food and beverage products provided, and the way the provisions were boarded onto the aircraft. (a) Form for first-class service. (b) Form for coach-class service. (Courtesy of Trans World Airlines)

MENU DESCRIPTION SHEET

CYCLE 3

FLT: 312   **CLASS: F**   **DATE**

CATERER: OGDEN AVIATION SVES STATION BOARDING: LAS

FOR SERVICE OUT OF: LAS

F/C SMC4-	**ONE ENTREE- HOT LUNCH/DINNER**	**50%**
F/C D70-	**ONE ENTREE- HOT LUNCH/DINNER**	**50%**

100% ZUCCHINI/RADISH/CARROT SALAD
      (FANCY SALAD MIX/DICED ZUCCHINI/SLICED
RADISHES/SHREDDED CARROTS)   1 EA.
BLUE CHEESE DRSG., 1 OZ.   1 EA.
WHOLE WHEAT TWIST ROLL   1 EA.
CONTINENTAL BUTTER CHIP   1 EA.
BLACK FOREST CAKE SLICE   1 EA.
SALT AND PEPPER SHAKERS   1 EA.

50% SMC4
D20 CHICKEN FLORENTINE
CHICKEN FLORENTINE (SLICED IN 4 SLICES)   1 EA.
CHERRY TOMATO, GRILL MARKED   1 EA.
YELLOW RICE W/TOASTED ALMONDS   3.00 OZ.
LEMON HERB SAUCE   1.00 OZ.

50% D70 BEEF ENTREE ROTATION
BEEF MEDALLIONS
BEEF MEDALLIONS, 2 OZ.   3 EA.
SAUCE DIABLE   1.50 OZ.
YELLOW RICE W/TOASTED ALMONDS   2.00 OZ.
BUTTERED ASPARAGUS   1.50 OZ.
SAUTEED MUSHROOM SLICES   1.00 OZ.
RED PEPPER STRIPS   .50 OZ.

REMARKS:_____

_____

_____

_____

ATTENTION: FLIGHT SERVICE MANAGERS/FLIGHT ATTENDANTS

Meal or provisioning discrepancies should be reported immediately. Prompt corrective action will be initiated with the appropriate personnel. Your help is appreciated.

FIGURE 12.12(a)

MENU DESCRIPTION SHEET

CYCLE 3

FLT: 312 CLASS: Y

CATERER: OGDEN AVIATION SVES STATION BOARDING: LAS

FOR SERVICE OUT OF: LAS

Y/C SMC2-COACH ONE ENTREE-HOT LUNCH/DINNER	D3
100% SALAD (1 OZ. SALAD GREENS/1 EA. RED PEPPER RING/ 5 EA. GARBONZO BEANS)	1 EA.
RANCH DRSG., 1/2 OZ. PKT	1 EA.
COUNTRY CROCK MARGERINE CUP	1 EA.
LA VOSH CRACKER PKT.	1 EA.
AMARETTO RASPBERRY CAKE	1 EA.
SALT & PEPPER PKTS.	1 EA.
ENTREE: RAVIOLI W/ITALIAN GLAZE	1 EA.

REMARKS: _____

_____

_____

_____

ATTENTION: FLIGHT SERVICE MANAGERS/FLIGHT ATTENDANTS

Meal or provisioning discrepancies should be reported immediately. Prompt corrective action will be initiated with the appropriate personnel. Your help is appreciated.

FIGURE 12.12(b)

to the airline's standards and expectations, the inflight caterer must focus considerable attention on quality assurance to make sure that its service is consistent and always meets the standards of the airlines as well as the standards of other inspecting agencies such as the health department or the FDA. Thus, the proactive caterer will develop a quality assurance system within its inflight kitchen and assign one or more of its senior employees responsibility for the maintenance of the desired quality and service standards.

Menu presentations (or menu reviews) are one important component of an inflight caterer's quality assurance program. Menu presentations should be routinely done whenever the menu cycle changes. Under the menu presentation process, the employees make a spare tray during their regular tray setup activities. This tray is set aside and is then *closely* checked to be sure that *all* the items on the tray are prepared exactly as they should be, (for example, weights, specs, assembly, and taste) that the brands of prepackaged products used are correct, and that everything is set on the tray exactly as it should be. After the evaluation of the tray, a menu presentation summary is prepared to document that this activity was completed as well as to let everyone concerned know what was right and what was not done correctly so that any errors found can be corrected as quickly as possible. In addition to these planned menu presentations, random checks of trays should be done periodically by the caterer's management staff to ensure menu quality, accuracy, and consistency.

Since the inflight foodservice system is a cook–chill system, an important area of concern for the maintenance of quality (and food safety) is the freshness of the products to be used for the meals. The general usage standard is that products must be served to the passengers within 48 hours of their production. Put another way, hot foods are produced and chilled one day. They may be plated or set up on trays ready for boarding onto the aircraft either that same day or the next day. Cold plates should be made the same day they are to be boarded and served.

The inflight catering industry has developed a standardized system to help track the flow of items produced in the kitchen to help assure product usage within the allowable time constraints. Under this system, all products prepared in the kitchen are color coded to indicate the day that they were produced. These codes are indicated in Table 12.1.

There should never be more than two days' production color codes in the caterer's facilities at any time. A third code indicates that product was not used within the time frame that it should have been. Any products, other than salad dressings and some sauces, that have not been used within this allowable time period must be thrown away as unusable product. From Table 12.1, it can be seen that everything prepared on Monday would have a green tag. By Wednesday, there should be no items on hand in the refrigerators with green tags. If there are some green-tagged items, they must be removed and thrown out.

TABLE 12.1
Daily Food Production Codes

Monday/Lunes	Green
Tuesday/Martes	Brown
Wednesday/Miercoles	Yellow
Thursday/Jueves	Orange
Friday/Viernes	Light green
Saturday/Sabado	Blue
Sunday/Domingo	Red

AIRLINE CONCERNS WITH QUALITY ASSURANCE

It is not just the inflight caterers that are concerned with quality assurance as a means of making sure that they meet the performance standards established by the airlines. The airlines are also concerned, and they regularly conduct inspections and evaluations of each caterer's facilities and operations to ensure that the caterer is performing in accordance with their published manuals and producing the expected product and service quality. Since the airlines usually do not have direct control over the meal production and the service provided to the aircraft, this type of caterer inspection program becomes an important part of their quality assurance program for their inflight food and beverage services.

Usually each airline has a regional representative or a dining service representative or perhaps a team of site evaluators who periodically visit each kitchen catering to that airline to conduct a visual inspection of the kitchen. The frequency of these inspections varies with the different airlines, but could be as often as monthly and should usually be at least quarterly. An inspection that indicates poor performance on the part of a caterer could be closely followed by another inspection to verify that the caterer is making the recommended quality improvement changes.

These inspections are concerned with all aspects of the kitchen and its operations, including areas such as kitchen cleanliness, handling of the airline's equipment, food quality, trucking and safety issues, administrative accuracy, and overall performance of the kitchen personnel. They are thorough and detailed. Following these inspections, reports are provided to the caterer's management staff as well as to the airline's foodservice department.

In today's atmosphere of partnering between the airline and its caterers, these inspections are meant to be positive in tone rather than punitive. While the airline wants to assure the quality of the products served on its flights, the inspection is also done to identify weaknesses in the caterer's operation which, from the airline's perspective, could be potentially detrimental to its food and beverage services. While on site, the airline's representative has an opportunity to sit down with the caterer's general manager and other staff, as appropriate, and discuss problems noted. An objective of these discussions would be to develop ways in which the problems noted can be corrected within the caterer's operating constraints. Of course, if a potential solution or correction to observed problems can be developed at this time, the airline's inspector will expect to see that solution operationalized by the next inspection. Should that not be the case and the problem be a recurring problem, ultimately some type of action will be taken by the airline to make sure that the caterer is in compliance with its standards or understands that there is a risk of losing the contract with the airline.

Figure 12.13 illustrates a caterer evaluation form that is used by one airline. As can be noted from this form, the inspection completed by the

CATERER EVALUATION

Instructions for completion of question 9 of the Caterer Evaluation Report.

Choose one recipe or menu currently scheduled from your station. Use a sample from the actual production for a Continental flight. For this example, refer to page 3.130.85 of the Continental Catering Information Manual.

(1) Enter the manual page number (recipe code).

(2) List each component of the menu/recipe chosen.

(3) List the Continental quantity/weight from the menu/recipe.

(4) List the actual contents of the sample menu/recipe chosen for the evaluation.

(5) Enter your follow-up action in this space if applicable. If additional room is needed, use the section "Follow-Up Notes" following question 17, or the reverse side of the page.

(6) Review the Preparation steps at the bottom of the recipe page. If the caterer prepared the menu according to these steps, mark "Yes". If the caterer deviated from the preparation steps, mark "No" and advise follow-up action.

RECIPE CODE: (1) 3.130.85

ITEM	CONTINENTAL SPEC.	ACTUAL
(2) Honeydew Melon	(3) 4 sl.	(4) 4 sl.
Cantaloupe	4 sl.	4 sl.
Grapefruit	5 sl.	4 sl.
Grapes	1 oz.	.5 oz.
Lemon Leaves	2 ea.	2 ea.

(5) Variance was reviewed with caterer and corrected

(6) Did the caterer follow the recipe preparation steps?

Yes_____ No_____

01–APR–93

FIGURE 12.13 Example of an evaluation form used by one airline to evaluate caterers' service quality. (Courtesy of Continental Airlines)

CATERER EVALUATION

1.514.4

Station: _____ Date: _____

Caterer: _____

Catering Gen. Mgr.: _____

Last Inspection Date: _____

Dining Service Rep.: _____

DSR Phone Contact: _____

Food Storage, Preparation and Handling

1. Are prepared food items covered and color-coded by day of production?　Yes____ No____

2. Did you find frozen foods received by caterer dated/color-coded to insure proper "first-in/first-out" rotation?　Yes____ No____

3. Cold Box/Freezer Temperature Check: (Indicate °C or °F)

   Freezer Temperature Observed ____°C ____°F
   Refrigerators/Holding Boxes ____°C ____°F

   Follow-Up Notes: _____

   _____

   _____

   _____

   _____

Menu Specifications and Quality Control

4. Are you reviewing the Weekly Dining Services Update in the DRS system?　Yes____ No____

5. Do you provide your caterer with a copy of the Weekly Dining Services update?　Yes____ No____

6. Are the correct products for the current cycle being boarded?　Yes____ No____

7. Does your caterer contact you for approval prior to making a menu item substitution on a CO flight?　Yes____ No____

8. Are unscheduled crew meals, when boarded on special request, properly documented, billed and entered into the billing system using a 2000 series code?　Yes____ No____

9. Review at least 1 complete caterer-prepared recipe or menu for compliance to CO specifications and list results in columns as follows:

   REFER TO PAGE 1.514.3 FOR INSTRUCTIONS.

   RECIPE CODE:

ITEM	CONTINENTAL SPEC.	ACTUAL

   Did the caterer follow the recipe preparation steps?　Yes____ No____

10. How are bank meals boarded onto the aircraft, check as applicable:
    Carriers _____　Loose on trays _____
    Carts _____　In bags _____
    Ovens _____　Other _____
    If other, explain _____

11. Are the meals used for banks in your station the same code and specification as the regularly scheduled meals?　Yes____ No____

Meal Packing and Assembly

12. Is a check sheet used to insure that all items specified are packed?　Yes____ No____

13. When provisioning a choice of entrees, does the caterer use the same color foil wrap on both entrees?　Yes____ No____

01-MAR-94

FIGURE 12.13 *(Continued)*

CATERER EVALUATION

Meal Packing and Assembly   (Cont'd)

14. When cleaning carts and carriers, does caterer remove tape and unsightly markings?   Yes____ No____

15. Are meal trays placed into meal carts or carriers so that 2 trays face one side and, 1 tray faces the other side on each level?   Yes____ No____

16. Are meal carriers and carts provisioned with dry ice prior to kitchen departure?   Yes____ No____

    Follow-Up Notes: _____

    _____

    _____

    _____

Beverage/Liquor Control

17. Are white wines, red wines, champagnes, and beers chilled and iced prior to dispatch; if no explain below.
    Yes____ No____

    Follow-Up Notes: _____

    _____

    _____

    _____

Equipment Handling and Management

18. What is the date on the Equipment Order sheet being used by your station?   _____

19. What is the date on the Inventory Form currently being used by your caterer?   _____

20. Is HDQHH being advised of excess equipment (Class I, II) and is the surplus being shipped out as required per monthly inventory procedures?   Yes____ No____

21. Did you find any CO equipment scattered throughout the kitchen and not in secured/locked areas?
    Yes____ No____

22. Is CO working stock segregated from other airline equipment?   Yes____ No____

23. Is equipment held in the storeroom properly inventoried, labeled, secured and segregated from other airline equipment?   Yes____ No____

24. Are CO stained linens being returned to hubs for the reclamation prog. per section 1.610? Yes____ No____

25. Does your caterer complete the par level column of your inventory?   Yes____ No____

    Follow-Up Notes: _____

    _____

    _____

    _____

Dishroom, Sanitation and Cleanliness

26. Are rotable equipment and untensils air-dried after sanitation, properly handled and stored to prevent contamination?   Yes____ No____

27. Did you find meal carts, carriers, ovens and trash bins properly sanitized, drained and stored? Yes____ No____

28. Is overall facility (including parking lot, dock, toilet areas and other locker rooms) clean and well maintained?   Yes____ No____

29. Are employees in proper uniforms, wearing approved hair restraints and practicing good personal hygiene?
    Yes____ No____

30. List dish machine temperatures observed during:
    operation: Wash   _____
                                  Rinse   _____
                                  Final Rinse _____

    Follow-Up Notes: _____

    _____

    _____

    _____

Transportation and Ramp Safety

31. Are all carriers, contents of bins and Class 1 equipment being removed from RON aircraft properly sanitized prior to recatering?   Yes____ No____

32. Are drivers and helpers neat in appearance and currently licensed and safety trained?
    Yes____ No____

01-MAR-94

FIGURE 12.13   *(Continued)*

CATERING INFORMATION MANUAL

CATERER EVALUATION

1.514.6

Transportation and Ramp Safety (Cont'd)

33. Was any airline equipment or debris found under the seats of the catering truck cabs?
    Yes_____ No_____

34. Are originating flights catered 30 minutes (45 minutes for head starts) prior to ETD and through flights met on arrival?
    Yes_____ No_____

35. Indicate number of catering delays (60/61) in the last 30 days (includes ferry and charter flights):
    _____

36. Indicate number catering related aircraft damage incidents (64) in last 30 days:
    _____

    Follow-Up Notes: _____

    _____

    _____

    _____

Administration and Miscellaneous

37. Are there any recurring pricing problems with specific billing codes?
    Yes_____ No_____
    If yes, list codes: _____

    _____

    _____

    _____

38. Who corrects/adjusts CAT sheets when there is an aircraft swap?
    Caterer: _____
    Station: _____

39. Does your station receive a separate Enroute Report covering catering problems in addition to the complete system Enroute Report?
    Yes_____ No_____

40. Is the catering Enroute Report handed over to the caterer in a timely manner and thoroughly reviewed with follow-up corrective action?
    Yes_____ No_____

41. Are CO and caterer representatives jointly attending a billing reconciliation weekly?
    Yes_____ No_____
    List the last reconciliation date: _____

42. List the last update received by the DSR / Caterer:

	DSR	Caterer
Manual Revision		
System Memo.		
Select Memo.		
System Teletype		

43. Is the local station management reviewing the caterer laundry logs?
    Yes_____ No_____

44. Have previous problems been corrected?
    Yes_____ No_____

Notes / Remarks:

_____

_____

_____

_____

_____

_____

_____

_____

_____

_____

_____

_____

_____

_____

_____

_____

_____

_____

_____

_____

_____

_____

_____

JG/cc
(Effective 3/1/94)
Original: CO Dining Services / GTWDS
    Copy: CO General Manager
          CO Dining Service Representative
          Caterer

Completed by: _____
Dining Service Representative   /   Date

Reviewed by: _____
Catering GM / Account Rep.   /   Date

01–MAR–94

FIGURE 12.13 *(Continued)*

airline representative is quite comprehensive. However, a copy of this form and the airline's expectations in regard to the caterer's performance and its evaluation process are included in the information manual provided to each caterer. Therefore, the items considered in the inspection should be no surprise to the caterer, and the kitchen should be operated in such a way that these inspections pose no problem. Indeed, some kitchens will conduct periodic self-inspections using the airlines' inspection standards, as well as the standards of other inspecting agencies, such as the FDA, as a self-evaluation of how well they are doing. By conducting such self-evaluations on a regular basis and carefully considering the findings, caterers are able to identify problems and take appropriate remedial action well before such problems are called to their attention by an outside inspection, such as a representative from an airline.

The inspection form illustrated in Figure 12.13 evaluates each item inspected on a "yes" or "no" basis. However, some airlines use an inspection form that requires the inspector to give a numerical score to each of the items inspected. Figure 12.14 illustrates one page from such a multipage form.

CHART 5 KITCHEN QUALITY ASSURANCE	STD	SCORE	COMMENTS
5.1 Menus All menu Specifications Per Current Cycle or Substitution Approved	5		
5.2 Pictures and Specifications Pictures and Specifications Posted and Accessible to Product Workers	5		
5.3 Products/Beverages Good Quality Acceptable Brands Approved Beverage Brands	10		
5.4 Finished Product Color Coded Refrigerated Promptly	10		
5.5 Orange Juice and Dairy OJ (Quarts & PC) Storage/Rotation/ Thawing Procedures	5		
5.6 Timeliness No finished product over 24 hrs old used. No more than two color codes in use.	10		
5.7 Management Supervision End Product Proper supervision of food production	5		
5.8 Scheduling - Food Preparation Food prep. timely to maximize freshness Galley timeliness for kitchen departures	10		
5.9 Kitchen Timeliness Galleys ready and cheched at posted kitchen departure time	5		
TOTALS	65		

FIGURE 12.14 Excerpt from a different version of a form that might be used to evaluate a caterer's service quality. (Courtesy of Ogden Aviation Services)

To receive a rating of "good," the caterer must score between 95 and 100 percent on the evaluation. A score of 88 to 94 percent will earn the caterer a rating of marginal, and a score of 87 or below is unsatisfactory. Thus, the scoring is strict, allowing the caterer little variance from the expected standards. Indeed the airline's objective for the quality assurance program is 100 percent performance in all areas by all caterers. While that objective may seem unrealistic, it is no different from the performance objectives which most chain operations have for the management of their restaurants.

THE DISPATCH SHEET

The dispatch sheet is another important quality assurance document. Figure 12.15 illustrates a sample dispatch sheet that one caterer used for one airline. Inflight caterers usually develop their own dispatch sheets to meet their particular needs. At some catering facilities, there may be a different dispatch form for each airline which helps to avoid confusion and possible boarding errors. This is especially true when one or two airlines make up a major portion of the total flight activity serviced by the caterer. The dispatch sheet might be considered to be the driving force for the kitchen as the focal point of all kitchen operations is to have the proper food for each flight ready to go to the aircraft at the proper time. All of the kitchen activities are conducted with that goal in mind. Therefore, the dispatch sheet and the indicated scheduled flight departure times really do drive the kitchen. From that perspective, it is an excellent quality assurance tool as careful checks are made of all products and the equipment pack prior to their loading for transport (or dispatch) to the aircraft.

The dispatch sheet summarizes a great deal of information concerning the flights in an easily readable format. Not only is basic information, such as the flight number, type of aircraft, aircraft tail number, and estimated times of arrival (ETA) and departure (ETD) indicated, but information such as the actual arrival and departure times, the time the boarding crew leaves the kitchen, and notes about the service are included. The dispatch sheet lists the preliminary passenger counts for the flights. These counts come in to the caterer's office 24 to 48 hours ahead of the scheduled flight departure, and they are the figures used by the production area to plan its meal production for the day of the flight. The final count is also indicated. This is the passenger count indicated by the airline about 1 to 1.5 hours ahead of the scheduled kitchen departure time for domestic flights. The final count is indicated about three hours ahead of time for international flights. Kitchen departure time varies by airport (that is, how long it takes to drive from the kitchen to the ramp), but generally it is 1 to 2 hours before flight departure.

The dispatch sheet is really a record of everything that is done in the flight kitchen. Because this sheet contains both estimated, or planned, data

INBOUND # & CITY	OUT # & CITY	A/C #	A/C	GAL CNT	TYPE OF SERVICE	ETA	ACTUAL ETA	ETD	FBH/ LOADER	KD	PRELIMS F/C	PRELIMS Y/C	PRELIMS CREW	FINALS F/C	FINALS Y/C	FINALS CREW	FREQUENCY & SERVICE NOTES
ORIG	448/LAX		737	2	V43/V42	ORIG		0815									X 7 BRD 3 EMPTY F/C C
ORIG	1936/LAX		737	2	V43/V42	ORIG		0710									7 ONLY BRD 3 EMPTY F/C C
ORIG	1272/SFO		737	2	C31/V42	ORIG		0845									REMOVE G INBD ONLY
1518/PIT	1125/LAX		737	2	V43/V42	1104		1150									G A
CHARTER	912/LAX		737	2	V43/V42	1120		1230									7 ONLY
1046/LAX	1131/PIT		737	2	L11/L12	1228		1320									A G H
2529/LAX	RON		737	2	STRIP	1923		RON									
299/SFO	RON		737	2	STRIP	1956		RON									X 6
2112/TPA	2112/LAX		737	2	V43/V42	2100		2140									F A #1940 6 ONLY
307/CMH	307/SFO		737	2	V43/V42	2113		2155									REMOVE G INBD #2735 6 ONLY
1483/IND	618/PHL		737	2	S11/S12	2115		2200									X-5 A H G
608/LAX	608/PHL		737	2	S11/S12	2150		2230									A H G
177/EWR	623/CLT		737	2	S11/S12	2155		2245									A H G
601/SFO	601/CMH		737	2	S11/S12	2216		2255									A G H
1575/CLT	610/PIT		737	2	S11/S12	2205		2335									A H G
1915/BWI	605/BWI		737	2	S11/S12	2245		2345									A H G
1669/PHL	633/IND		737	2	S11/S12	2256		2355									A G H

SPECIALS

CODES   F= F/C STRIP   G=GLASS CAR   A=ALLADIN STRIP   H=HEADSETS

FIGURE 12.15 Example of a dispatch sheet typical of such forms used by inflight caterers. (Courtesy of Ogden Aviation Services)

concerning flight times and meal counts as well as actual data, it can readily be used to track patterns regarding an airline's flights and its actual meal usage patterns which can help the caterer with planning for improved product production and labor usage efficiency. It is also used as the source document for billing airlines for the caterer's services, and for researching historical information to respond to airline inquiries, passenger complaints, and so on.

SUMMARY

The airlines' catering manuals govern the way most of the work in the caterer's kitchen is done. The manuals contain the menus to be served, recipes to be used, product specifications for all types of items, how the meals are to be served, provisioning standards, packing diagrams and other such operational and policy information. The information contained in the manual is very specific, and it is the caterer's responsibility to follow the directives exactly as they are specified.

Because of the volume of information and the extensive detail included in the airlines' catering manuals, it would be difficult for most employees working in a flight kitchen to accomplish their work as they should if they always had to individually reference manuals to see what should be done. Both employee productivity and accuracy of communications regarding airline expectations are improved if only one or a few persons are assigned responsibility for studying the manuals carefully and communicating needed information and any changes from the airlines to the proper kitchen staff.

Quality assurance is a critical aspect of an inflight kitchen's operations. Because of the desire for 100 percent accuracy regarding many product and service details, both the airlines and the inflight caterers develop quality assurance programs to help ensure that the airlines' requirements are met as they should be. These programs include activities such as detailed inspections of the caterer's equipment, facilities, and operational activities, and menu presentations. Developing a viable quality assurance program can be an important tool that a caterer can use to maintain long-term relationships with the airlines it services.

Dispatch sheets can also be valuable tools for a caterer's quality assurance efforts as they provide a record of the caterer's activities as well as a chronology of each airline's operational data, such as the plane (tail) number, passenger load, and schedule activity. Data gained from dispatch sheets can be utilized by the inflight caterer to evaluate the flow of the overall operations and to make projections for future service demands. They are also used as the basis for billing the airline for services rendered.

KEY TERMS

Activity Report

Color Coding

Dispatch Sheet

Dispatcher

Dock (Loading Dock)

ETA

ETD

Liquor Cart

Menu Cycle (Cycle Menu)

Menu Presentation

Meter

Partnering

Presentation Summary

Provisioning

Provisioning Change

Provisioning Chart (or Standards)

Quality Assurance

Sample Meal

Specification

Support Cart

DISCUSSION QUESTIONS

1. What type of information do the airlines put into their catering manuals? Why are these manuals the heart of the inflight caterer's operations?

2. Why is it important for caterers to simplify these manuals for their line employees through the use of worksheets, models, and other such guidance materials?

3. Discuss how a person assigned to prepare entrees for the next day's menu would use the airline's catering manual to know what to do.

4. Why do the airlines use a lot of codes in the manuals that they give to their caterers?

5. How are changes that the airlines want to make to some part of their manuals handled in the inflight kitchen? Who is responsible for seeing that the desired changes are made? What happens to the change sheets that the airlines send to the caterer?

6. What are some of the reasons that the airlines change their menu cycles?

7. How do frequent cycle changes impact on the inflight caterer's purchasing and storage of products specified by the airlines in their menus? What can the caterer do with leftover products?

8. What must the caterer do if a vendor is unable to supply a product that is needed for a particular day's menu?

9. Why do airlines set provisioning standards for all stock items, even items as small as coffee creamers? What happens when an airline decides to change these provisioning standards for one or several items? How might such changes impact a caterer's operations?

10. Who decides where the different pieces of boarding equipment will go in an aircraft's galleys? Who decides what is put in each of those pieces of equipment? How does the caterer's staff know how to pack the equipment and where to place it on board the aircraft?

11. What are menu presentations? How are they related to a caterer's quality assurance program?

12. Why are all food products prepared in an inflight kitchen color coded to indicate the day the products were prepared? What must be done if out-of-date food products are found in a kitchen's refrigerators?

13. Why are airlines interested in inspecting their caterers' kitchens? About how often do they conduct inspections?

14. What types of things are looked at when airline inspectors come to review an inflight kitchen? How detailed is the inspection?

15. What action is taken if a flight kitchen does poorly or does not pass an airline's inspection?

16. Why is the dispatch sheet so important to the caterer, both in terms of the caterer's quality assurance efforts and the caterer's billings to the airlines?

13

Food Safety and Sanitation

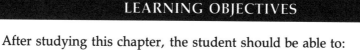

LEARNING OBJECTIVES

After studying this chapter, the student should be able to:

1. Discuss why food safety and sanitation are especially important concerns of the inflight foodservice industry.
2. Explain the HACCP system and how it can be incorporated into an inflight foodservice facility as part of the facility's quality assurance program.
3. Explain how Critical Control Points can be used to help ensure the safety of foods served on board aircraft.
4. Identify the five factors found to most frequently contribute to the incidence of food-borne illness.
5. Discuss key areas of concern for the prevention of food contamination in the receiving and storage of food products.
6. Discuss the responsibility of suppliers in regard to the prevention of food-borne illness in inflight foodservices.
7. Discuss key areas of concern for the maintenance of food safety during cold food preparation and handling.
8. Identify potential food safety problem areas and possible controls for those areas during hot food preparation and handling.
9. Discuss the food safety problems that might occur during the setup, packing, and final holding of inflight meals and actions that could be taken to control problems.
10. Explain why the transportation of food products to the aircraft poses unique food safety problems and what actions must be taken to control potential problems.

Inflight foodservice is particularly susceptible to food safety problems because of the extensive handling of the food products through the production, transport, and service processes. Indeed, one of the major objectives of the Inflight Food Service Association has always been "To develop and promote uniform standards of quality, sanitation and safety . . . (Foreword, HACCP Management Systems on Airline Foodservice). Because of this high level of susceptibility, it is imperative that inflight caterers pay very close attention to the sanitation level of their facilities, the work habits of their employees, and all other aspects of their operation that could contribute to food safety problems.

Since the deregulation of the airline industry, several trends have indicated the need for a comprehensive, industrywide quality assurance program regarding food safety. Some of these trends include:

1. Consolidation of airline companies and the evolution of megacarriers and superhubs, bringing about larger kitchens and more complex operations.
2. Self-regulation trends within the federal government.
3. A recession that led to a highly competitive atmosphere in the airline industry, thus creating a need to have more effective programs while also containing costs.
4. Increased concern for temperature control of potentially hazardous foods, particularly since the emergence of refrigeration-temperature pathogens as a cause of food-borne illnesses.
5. The generally recognized validity of Hazard Analysis and Critical Control Point (HACCP) systems of food protection by the regulatory community.

THE HACCP SYSTEM

Many inflight caterers are currently incorporating the HACCP system as their approach to the maintenance of food safety. HACCP is an acronym for Hazard Analysis of Critical Control Points. The implementation of a HACCP system in an inflight kitchen provides the manager with a systematic means of looking at all parts of the food production and service system to assess what hazards might be present in the system. It also enables the kitchen management to systematically determine what the critical control points are to prevent problems as well as to monitor those points once they have been identified.

There are seven distinct steps to an HACCP system. They are as follows: (1) Assess hazards. (2) Identify Critical Control Points (CCPs). (3) Set up control procedures and standards for CCPs. (4) Monitor CCPs. (5) Take corrective actions. (6) Establish effective record keeping. (7) Verify system is working.

Each step of the flow of product through the flight kitchen to the aircraft is reviewed for the possible risk of food-borne illness. When hazards or possible risks or sources of contamination are identified in the flight kitchen, they are assessed to identify the possibility of: (1) the food becoming contaminated with pathogenic organisms; (2) the organism multiplying if the food is contaminated; (3) the organisms surviving for a sufficient time to cause illness; and (4) eliminating or reducing the hazard. Particular attention should be paid to foods that are known to be carriers of diseases, have a high risk of becoming contaminated, or are prepared and stored in quantity.

Once the potential hazards have been identified and analyzed, the next step in the HACCP process is to identify critical control points. A critical control point is a location or a process which, if not correctly controlled, could lead to unacceptable contamination, survival, or growth of foodborne pathogens or spoilage microorganisms. The objective of identifying these points is to gain *control* over the process, which incorporates raw materials, the environment, and the people working in the area, as early in the system as possible. Critical control points must meet *all* of the following criteria: (1) The hazard can be controlled or prevented. (2) Control criteria are already established. (3) The point can be monitored. (4) Corrective action can be implemented to reduce or eliminate the hazard. (5) The risk of illness is high to moderate.

Once control actions have been initiated at the identified critical points, the final step is monitoring these controls for effectiveness. Monitoring might be done by direct observation, measurement of criteria such as food temperatures or bacterial counts, a physical check, or an application of a warning label (or statement). All activities incorporated into the monitoring process should be recorded or maintained in a log.

Should any of the critical control points be found to be out of control at any time, immediate action on the part of the caterer's management staff is critical. The prevention of microbial problems is highly dependent on proper, thorough cooking and proper storage of *cooked* product because there is inadequate pathogenic microbiological control of all raw products. Until the suppliers of raw food products are better able to control the pathogenic microbiological contamination of their products, even the entrance to the storeroom is a critical control point.

There are several microbiological principles associated with the HACCP system, listed in Table 13.1. A review of these principles underscores the importance of *control* as the means of maintaining food safety in inflight food service, given the types of foods served and the potential for contamination that exists within the production and service system.

CAUSES OF FOOD-BORNE ILLNESS

Based on data collected for the United States, England, and Canada, there are a number of factors which contribute to food-borne illness. Five of those

TABLE 13.1
Microbiological Principles Associated with HAACP

1. Most foods of concern are *potentially hazardous foods*. These foods are capable of supporting:
   a. The rapid, progressive growth of organisms that can make people sick; or
   b. The slower growth and toxin production of the bacteria *Clostridium botulinum*.
   They include foods of (1) animal origin that are raw or cooked; and (2) plant origin that are (a) cooked; or (b) raw seed sprouts (bean or alfalfa); or (c) cut melons; or (d) garlic and oil mixtures; (3) cheese manufactured with unpasteurized milk; (4) raw eggs used in desserts not requiring cooking; (5) partially cooked poultry, seafood, or pork requiring further cooking onboard the aircraft where safe internal cooking temperatures cannot be guaranteed; (6) gravies, sauces, and soups; (7) egg and dairy products and products made from them such as custard, cream desserts, or meringue; (8) meat salads; or (9) sandwiches and canapes.
   They do not include (1) foods with a water activity value of 0.85 or less; (2) foods with a pH level of 4.6 or below; (3) properly processed commercial foods in unopened hermetically sealed containers; and (4) foods for which laboratory evidence demonstrates that rapid and progressive growth of harmful organisms cannot occur.
2. All foods may contain some level of hazardous ingredients. The levels must be below that which can make the consuming population ill. Examples of some ingredients which are in many foods, but which can make people sick if consumed in excess include: salt, sugar, spices, preservatives that are naturally occurring or manmade, viruses, and bacteria that are naturally occurring, contaminating, or used in the preparation of the food itself.
3. While cooking food to the proper temperature controls bacterial growth, it does not control all bacterial toxins or spores that could have formed if the food were previously temperature abused or contaminated.
4. The rate of microbiological growth can be controlled by time, temperature, chemical additives, acidity (pH), or water activity.
5. Freezing food will not adequately control high bacteria or virus counts already present, but proper freezing can control parasites in food.
6. Those handling food may always be potential carriers of infectious organisms whether they appear sick or not. Good personal hygiene, handwashing, sanitary food-handling practices, and proper supervision are the only controls available.

factors are implicated in 25 percent or more of the reported cases. Table 13.2 lists these contributing factors and indicates how they might be controlled through monitoring at critical control points within an inflight kitchen. More than one of the factors listed in Table 13.2 are usually implicated in a food-borne illness outbreak; thus, the percentages sum to more than 100 percent. However, these factors have remained quite constant over a number of years, and have been adopted as the foundation for the HACCP approach.

TABLE 13.2
Causes of Food-Borne Illness and Injury

Hazards

1. Less than adequate employee and management knowledge.

2. Less than adequate command and control.

3. Presence of microorganisms, chemicals, and hard foreign objects.

Critical Control Points

63%	Inadequate cooling and cold holding
29%	Preparing food ahead of planned service
27%	Inadequate hot holding
26%	Poor personal hygiene/infected persons
25%	Inadequate reheating
7%	Use of leftovers
5%	Inadequate cooking or heat processing
9%	Inadequate cleaning of equipment
6%	Cross-contamination
2%	Contaminated raw ingredients
1%	Unsafe sources
4%	Containers adding toxic chemicals
2%	Intentional chemical additives
1%	Incidental chemical additives

Unknown Hard foreign objects

Courtesy of the Inflight Food Service Association.

Since the preparation, distribution, and service of food is carried out through a series of processes and events, certain key steps within those processes are critical to the safety of the final product. Table 13.2 indicates what those key steps are (i.e., cold hold, cooling, etc.) relative to each of the listed factors contributing to food safety problems. Previous systems designed to control food-borne illness relied on spot-checking for physical deviations from the established operational standards. In contrast, the HACCP system focuses on the development of controls for specific critical points as part of a total process which is incorporated into the flight kitchen's management system.

FOOD PROCUREMENT

There is increasing concern with the safety of the food supplied to the inflight caterer as suppliers have been implicated as the source of the contamination in several recent cases of food-borne illness in the restaurant industry. Suppliers of products to the inflight industry must be sure that their products meet the specifications established by the airline on whose flights they will be used and that their products will withstand the conditions to which they will be subjected during the inflight meal production, transport, and service process. They need to also make sure that the caterer understands the limitations on the handling and storage of the products if their quality and safety level is to be maintained.

While some requested products may not have specifications stated by the airlines, such products are usually covered by federal or local regulatory mandates regarding their composition and quality. For example, all pop-out meals must be purchased from either FDA or flight industry inspected and approved suppliers. Another example is that all milk and dairy products must be purchased from suppliers that are listed in the *FDA's Interstate Milk Shippers List* and that retain a rating of "approved" because the milk is being used in interstate commerce.

Suppliers Responsibilities

When responding to airlines' or caterers' bids for products, suppliers to the inflight foodservice industry must be aware that their products will be used in a federally inspected facility and will be transported in interstate commerce by the airlines. They should realize that their products are assumed to have met federal standards upon arrival at the flight kitchen and that certain federal regulations may be different from local or state requirements, particularly in regard to food additives and labeling. The supplier is responsible for knowing the applicable regulations with which their products must comply.

The suppliers of potentially hazardous foods to inflight kitchens should also be prepared to supply the kitchen management with data such as the maximum refrigerated shelf-life of each product held at 45°F (7.2°C) and the maximum allowable shelf-life of each product held at 55°F (13°C) and at 70°F (21°C). The maximum times quoted should be based on the growth rates of pathogenic organisms that are of significance to their products.

In addition, suppliers must make sure that their customers are aware of any hidden hazards that may characterize their food products. Examples of products with hidden hazards would be a pop-out meal that contains partially cooked chicken. If the onboard cooking process is not monitored to ensure that an internal temperature of 165°F (73.8°C) is attained, the chicken could represent a hidden hazard to the passengers on board the flight. Other examples would be any products containing raw shell eggs as an ingredient that must be cooked to an internal temperature of 140°F (60°C) or any gas-packed or vacuum-packed product (i.e., sous vide) that could support the anaerobic growth of *Clostridium botulinum* if proper storage temperatures were not maintained.

Suppliers are also responsible for the conditions under which their products are shipped to the caterer's kitchen. Trucking temperatures and conditions must be appropriate for the products shipped. The supplier must make sure that common carriers used for food product and packaging supply deliveries have not previously hauled chemicals, garbage, or other products that might potentially contaminate their products.

Ultimately, the general manager of each kitchen is responsible for seeing that a safe food supply is ordered and delivered for use in the flight kitchen. That responsibility means the manager makes sure that supplies are purchased from approved and/or specified sources and that the supplies received meet the specifications established for each product. It also means that all incoming supplies are checked for sanitary delivery and condition by an experienced manager or trained staff person, that records of critical control point checks on the receiving dock and in the storeroom will be maintained where necessary, and that vendors will be held accountable for the products' delivered condition. The general manager is responsible for seeing that all supplies not meeting the specified minimum sanitary conditions, temperatures, quality, weight, and grades will be rejected and immediately returned to the vendor.

Suppliers to the inflight foodservice industry are expected to immediately notify all their customers of any suspected food safety problems or possible problems that are being investigated by regulatory officials. All suspected products under investigation will immediately be recalled by the supplier. Suppliers are expected to have a recall procedure in place, and they should have adequate means by which products can be retrieved quickly. If a recall is necessary, all products should have lot numbers printed on them that identify specific time periods or processes. While this coding will usually be on all cases, the individual packages should be coded as well, where applicable. Open coding systems (i.e., those using calendar days or dates rather than a producer's internal code) are preferred since these systems can also help the caterer with proper stock rotation in the flight kitchen's storeroom.

Inspections of Suppliers' Facilities

Suppliers to inflight caterers should expect both announced and unannounced sanitation inspections that will be conducted by their customers (either the airline or the caterer or both) or their designated representatives. The sanitation guidelines used for these inspections will be either those from the appropriate regulatory agency, such as the FDA or the USDA, or the sanitation guidelines promulgated by IFSA, as a part of their service to the inflight foodservice industry. Suppliers should view these inspections as opportunities to discuss the quality aspects of their products that are most important to their inflight customers. They could also be opportunities for the suppliers to discuss how their products are being used (or misused) by their customers and to suggest to them better handling and usage procedures.

These inspections should be conducted in a manner that will minimize any disruption of the supplier's operation. Generally, an official from the supplier's plant will accompany the inflight food safety auditor. This official should willingly answer all pertinent questions concerning the products they manufacture and sell to the inflight foodservice industry. Any sanitation-related documents or records should also be made available on request. Such documents might include complaint files, recall procedures, HACCP documents, and microbiological test reports. The inflight food safety auditor should meet with plant officials, including the official who was the inspector's escort, at the close of the inspection to discuss all pertinent sanitation observations. A written report of these observations should be provided to the suppliers' plant management, as well as to the airline and/or the caterers conducting the inspection.

RECEIVING DOCK AND STOREROOM

Food safety control on the receiving dock entails controlling the suppliers' delivery schedules so that all deliveries can be properly inspected and quickly moved into proper storage areas. Large shipments will probably contain several different types of supplies that require different levels of attention for food safety concern. Some items will have food safety factors that should be periodically checked (control points), while others may require the higher level of surveillance and management control called for by Critical Control Points (CCP's). When a mix of products is received in the same shipment, the items should be handled in the order indicated in Table 13.3 for maximum food safety control.

The most recent FDA food code, released in 1993, will eventually require refrigerated foods to be maintained at 41°F (5°C) or below when received at the foodservice facility. However, the required refrigeration level of food items in transit falls under the USDA's regulatory authority, and the USDA and the FDA do not have the same requirements for cold food storage in transit. Therefore the 1993 FDA Food Code would require the foodservice facility to cool these food items to 41°F (5°C) within four hours of receipt. Since the average refrigeration unit in most flight kitchens is designed to maintain food temperatures, particularly for items stored in large quantities, rather than to cool them quickly, this regulatory conflict may place an undue burden on inflight caterers and other foodservice operations. Thus, it is suggested that caterers require their suppliers to deliver food products at the required maintenance temperature of 41°F (5°C) or below, particularly since flight kitchens are regulated and regularly inspected by the FDA.

It should be remembered that there are a number of common practices in a kitchen's operation that can excessively raise the internal temperatures of refrigerators to the extent that the units are unable to maintain the required storage temperatures for products stored in the unit. For example, when large volumes of room-temperature items are placed in a refrigerator, the interior temperature is raised for an extended time; when the door

TABLE 13.3
Order of Priority for Handling Products Delivered by Suppliers

1. *Refrigerated potentially hazardous foods.* Randomly sample for temperatures over 41°F, (CCP) (5°C). If higher temperatures are found, record temperatures, initial all cases, and reject the lot.
2. *Frozen potentially hazardous foods.*
   (a) Check for temperatures above 0°F (-17.7°C) but below 32°F (0°C). If found, notify supplier.
   (b) Check for evidence of prior thawing. If found, reject lot.
   (c) Check for evidence of current thawing on pallet extremities and top corners of cases (checkpoint). If found, but temperatures are below 41°F (5°C), the decision to keep or reject may be based on the need for the product. Notify supplier of condition. If temperature is above 41°F (5°C), reject lot.
   (d) Check for thawed condition in center of pallet. If found, initial all cases and reject lot.
3. *Refrigerated non-potentially-hazardous foods.* Check for temperatures above 41°F (5°C). If found, notify supplier.
4. *Frozen non-potentially-hazardous foods.* If not solidly frozen, notify supplier.
5. *Clams, mussels, and oysters received raw.* Check for shellfish shippers' tags. Date and keep tags on file for 90 days.
6. *Produce.* Check for quality and accept or reject as quality standards indicate for the specific items delivered.

is open excessively, the temperature is not maintained—and the rise is particularly noticeable if the outside air is high in humidity. When the evaporator is frosted over or iced up, the cooling capacity of the unit is significantly reduced, if it cools at all. An important aspect of any HACCP program is the determination of the adequacy and cool-down capacities of existing refrigeration equipment so that procedures can be developed to avoid these types of high-temperature problems.

Food-borne illness statistics indicate that when storeroom operations have been implicated as a cause, it is most likely from improper refrigerated storage, thawing or dating of potentially hazardous foods, or problems with cross-contamination during storage with foods such as raw chicken. One of the lesser-known contributing factors to storeroom-related food-borne illness is the survival and growth of some bacteria at refrigeration temperatures. Rotation of stock in refrigerators is an important means of controlling the development of these slow-growing bacteria. Table 13.4 lists the pathogenic psychrophilic (cold-loving) bacteria that can grow slowly at refrigeration temperatures along with their minimum growth temperatures. One of these Clostridium botulinum, is also anaerobic. It should be noted that this listing includes E. coli, the bacteria that has recently been found to be the cause of serious cases of food-borne illness, a few of which have resulted in death for the victims, primarily children.

Controls for these cold-loving organisms that will receive no further heat processing should be either refrigeration below 34°F (1.1°C) or limiting the available time for refrigerated growth. Also, the working time after these products are thawed or delivered must be carefully limited. Some potentially hazardous foods may become hazardous after thawing, opening, and preparing in as little as three days under refrigerated storage. Other critical control points that should be considered for frozen and refrigerated products include: (1) never returning thawed foods to the storeroom freezer; (2) redating or double-dating all frozen foods with the date they were placed in the refrigerator for thawing; (3) individually dating cases of potentially hazardous products, such as pop-outs or kosher meals, when the cases are unpacked; (4) dating or color-coding products, such as turkey loaf, that are thawed prior to slicing, refrigerated on sheet pans, made into sandwiches,

TABLE 13.4
Pathogenic Psychrophilic (Cold-Loving) Bacteria

Bacteria	Minimum Growth Temperature*
Yersinia enterocolitica	34°F (1°C)
Listeria monocytogenes	39°F (4°C)
Escherichia coli	39°F (4°C)
Clostridium botulinum	39°F (4°C)

* The minimum growth temperature is the lowest temperature at which these bacteria can grow.

and then refrigerated again (such products should be dated with new handling dates through all the subsequent steps following the initial thawing so the time between the completion of the thawing and the actual use will be known; and (5) dating all refrigerated potentially hazardous supplies in food production areas and rotating them out before three days or before the supplier-documented refrigerated shelf-life has expired.

COLD FOOD

Cold food operations are the most critical of all flight kitchen areas since these foods will receive no further cooking. Also the caterer's personnel have many labor-intensive tasks associated with the hand preparation of such items as snack plates, sandwiches, hors d'oeuvres, and special meals. Thus, the personal hygiene of staff becomes important, not only because of the possibility of contaminating potentially hazardous foods, but also because of the possibility of contaminating raw vegetables, fruits, and garnishes. A further problem is that many of these items take considerable time to prepare with personnel working on the items at room temperature, accelerating bacterial growth. All of these factors combine to make the cold food preparation area a particular HACCP challenge.

The statistics presented previously in Table 13.2 indicated that inadequate cooling and cold holding was a contributing factor to food-borne illness 63 percent of the time. Poor personal hygiene was a contributing factor an additional 15 percent of the time. Of those cases, 94 percent were caused by bacteria and 6 percent by viruses. Of the sixteen most prevalent food-borne illness organisms studied, seven can infect, or multiply, within workers and have been organisms consistently implicated through poor personal health and hygiene practices. These organisms are: (1) *Salmonella*, (2) *Staphylococcus aureus*, (3) *Shigella*, (4) *Campylobacter*, (5) *Hepatitis A*, (6) *E. coli*, and (7) *Streptococcus*. Other nonresident pathogenic organisms that are picked up on the hands or uniforms of personnel could be spread to food products through cross-contamination.

If any of the seven organisms of greatest concern contaminate raw or already cooked food, they will *not* be neutralized as they would during hot food preparation. They can only be controlled by good personal hygiene, sanitary equipment, and proper refrigeration of food products. All of these organisms except the hepatitis virus can grow in contaminated cooked foods that are not properly refrigerated if the pH and water activity levels are appropriate for growth. However, unlike most bacteria, the hepatitis virus does not need to grow to infect someone eating contaminated food.

Further, organisms such as *Hepatitis A, Shigella*, and *E. coli* need only very low numbers to cause food-borne illness. Thus, even non-potentially-hazardous foods, such as celery or lettuce, can become contaminated by poor personal hygiene and cause a food-borne illness outbreak. These and other indicated organisms can be carried in the bodies of sick or well employees. All of them can be controlled on the hands of kitchen personnel by proper handwashing.

Control of Time at Room Temperature

Both the amount of time that potentially hazardous foods are out at room temperature during preparation and the time it takes for the kitchen's refrigeration equipment to cool potentially hazardous foods to below 41°F (5°C) should be carefully monitored as this information is needed to determine CCPs in cold food operations. The total time that cold foods are exposed to higher temperatures may be minimized through the use of quick preparation techniques, proper refrigeration, and the prechilling of ingredients. Where possible, it is helpful to do cold food preparation tasks, such as the slicing of meats, under refrigeration.

It may be helpful for a facility to graph the actual amounts of time it takes for various types of foods commonly served on inflight meals to cool back down to 41°F (5°C) in various refrigeration units. By varying the amounts and placement of these foods within the refrigerator, it would be possible for the staff to determine the fastest cooling combinations for their food products. The cooling times for each cold food product can also be measured and flowcharted to be sure that they are within the allowable time. Cooling times on new menu items should be tested and shortened where necessary. The 1993 FDA Food Code requires that foods be cooled from 140°F (60°C) to 70°F (21°C) within two hours and from 70°F (21°C) to 41°F (5°C) within four hours. If a food originates at room temperature, it must be cooled to 41°F (5°C) within four hours.

Contamination by Personnel

Personnel working in the food production area, particularly in the cold food area, are among the most common sources of food product contamination. Government regulations prohibit anyone from working with food who is ill, or appears to be ill, has open cuts or lesions, or has any possible source of microbial contamination. Such personnel should be excluded from work, required to wear plastic gloves if the cuts or lesions are on the person's hands, or assigned to some other position where they will not have direct contact with the food until they are able to return to their regular position.

The personal hygiene habits of employees are also a major area of concern. Employees must maintain proper grooming standards and follow proper hygiene practices while on duty. Even though it may sometimes be embarrassing to do so, it is important for the overall sanitation level of the facility that all members of the staff are instructed on proper hygiene habits and reminded to take remedial action when hygiene problems are noted. A mistake that is commonly made is to *assume* that everyone practices good personal hygiene. Experience has shown that even persons in supervisory or managerial positions do not always follow expected hygiene practices.

HOT FOOD

Hot food operations have a very effective built-in food-borne illness control as the proper cooking process is the most reliable food safety tool available to the inflight caterer. Of the sixteen most prevalent food-poisoning microorganisms, the following twelve can be completely eliminated by proper cooking: (1) *Salmonella spp.*, (2) *Listeria spp.*, (3) *Yersinea*, (4) *Trichina*, (5) *Shigella*, (6) *Streptococcus*, (7) *Vibrio spp.*, (8) *Hepatitis A virus*, (9) *Campylobacter*, (10) *Escherichia coli*, (11) *Brucella*, (12) *Norwalk virus*.

However, some pathogenic bacteria produce spores that can survive the cooking process and grow during subsequent temperature abuse. These bacteria are: *Clostridium perfringens*, *Clostridium botulinum*, and *Bacillus cereus*. Two of the sixteen bacteria can produce heat-stable toxins. If these bacteria are temperature abused in cooked food, normal recooking procedures, without special temperature controls, will not destroy the toxin that the bacteria produced in the food. These bacteria are *Staphylococcus aureus* and *Bacillus cereus*.

After potentially hazardous food is properly cooked, only *Clostridium botulinum* can survive and multiply under extended refrigerated conditions. However, in addition to proper date coding and monitoring of food items, this bacteria can be controlled while products are refrigerated by protecting them from anaerobic (no air) conditions. Practices such as placing sauces and gravies in shallow containers and avoiding foods stored under a layer of oil will help prevent botulism growth and product contamination.

Some foods common to hot food operations have certain factors that affect how they should be cooked for optimum safety. Raw chicken, for example, is generally highly contaminated with numerous pathogenic bacteria and ground meats are generally contaminated as the surface contamination is spread throughout the meat in the grinding process. The required internal temperatures for cooked foods or the required cooking process for certain items are listed in Table 13.5.

After the products have been cooked in accord with these parameters, their handling must be minimized. If handling is necessary, clean, sanitized utensils should be used. If hands are used, employee hygiene becomes a CCP, and HACCP monitoring is called for.

Previously cooked foods for airline meals pose additional problems for the inflight caterer. When potentially hazardous foods are recooked, there can be a higher risk of contamination from the presence of toxins and spore-

TABLE 13.5
Hot-Food Cooking Critical Control Temperatures and Procedures

Item	Required Internal Temperature	Procedure
Raw poultry	165°F (73.8°C)	N/A*
Raw pork cuts	150°F (65.5°C)	Seared on surface
Raw ground pork	155°F (68.3°C)	N/A
Shellfish to be eaten raw	N/A	Approved, reliable source
Shellfish to be cooked	140°F (60°C)	N/A
Raw red steaks	N/A	Seared on surface
Raw hamburger	155°F (68.3°C)	N/A
Multiple raw foods	N/A	Cook at temperature for the most hazardous ingredient
Previously cooked foods	165°F (73.8°C); unless part of HACCP system	N/A
Other potentially hazardous commodities	N/A	Conduct a hazardous analysis; cook accordingly

* Not applicable.

forming bacteria if temperature abuse has occurred. The initial cooking process will eliminate natural bacterial competitors that would normally slow the growth of the higher-risk bacteria. The cooling and storage temperatures after cooking are always critical. If all steps following the initial cooking period have been successfully controlled, the kitchen recook temperature needs only to reach and/or be held at 140°F (60°C) except where a higher temperature is specified by the airline. It is important to note that on-board cooking temperatures cannot be adequately controlled to meet this objective; so, all previous steps must be controlled to assure safety.

Hot food supplies should enter cooking areas in ways to minimize contamination. Frozen meats and seafoods should have been previously thawed under refrigeration. Thawing in a sink under cold running water should only be done for emergencies or for small portions. Microwave thawing or thawing as part of the cooking process may also be done. The smallest mass possible should be thawed to shorten thawing times.

Cartons of foods, such as those used for raw chicken, should be handled so there is no leakage. Liquid spills from these cartons must be treated as hazardous. Contaminated areas and equipment must be washed, rinsed, and sanitized before any other operations are allowed to take place. If raw foods are stored with cooked foods in the same refrigerator, they must be separated, either vertically with raw poultry, shell eggs, and raw meats at the lowest level and cooked products on top, or horizontally on separate racks.

Cooking Specifications

All cooking specifications should be reviewed for proper cooking temperatures. If the cooking temperatures are CCPs, but are *not* noted as such on an airline specification, the airline representative should be contacted, the proper cooking temperatures determined, and these temperatures written into the specifications and adhered to in the production process. All new menu cycles received from airlines should be carefully reviewed for new specifications or critical control points.

When newly specified products arrive at the caterer's facility, they should be carefully examined and a hazard analysis conducted on them. In the analysis, they should be checked for the following: (1) Is the product raw, partially cooked, or completely cooked? (2) If it is raw, where are the bacteria likely to be—throughout the product or on the surface? (3) Will the specified cooking process kill the bacteria of concern? (4) If there are several different raw products mixed together, which is the most hazardous , and what temperature is needed for that component? (5) Can different cooking processes, such as baking, broiling, frying, steaming, or boiling, be used or combined to address known hazards? (6) If the product is partially cooked, could there be a problem with toxins or spores if it has been temperature abused? (7) Will the final product need additional microbiological barriers, such as pH adjustment or water activity adjustment? (8) If it has already been cooked, have all the subsequent critical points been controlled adequately?

Some foods, such as raw chicken, will have critical cooking steps that must be controlled by temperature measurement. Others, such as the searing of steaks or the slow boil of a soup, may be visually monitored. Accurately calibrated thermometers should be available for employees carrying out these operations. If additional microbiological barriers, such as pH adjustments, are called for, a pH meter and fresh calibrating solution must be available to kitchen personnel. For water activity adjustment, a water activity meter and calibration media are needed.

Hot Food Cooling and Coding

The proper cooling and cold holding of cooked food is the most important food safety step in a flight kitchen. HACCP procedures have shown that deep pots of hot food in a walk-in refrigerator are an unacceptable means of cooling potentially hazardous foods. Sheet pan racks of hot entrees shrouded in plastic in a walk-in refrigerator are not likely to cool within specified times, either, because the plastic limits the movement of cool air over the product. Previous concerns about covering hot foods for protection from inadvertent contamination have been outweighed by the need to encourage air movements for quick, effective cooling. As with cold food products, it may be helpful to graph the actual amounts of time it takes for various types of common hot foods to cool back down to 41°F (5°C) in various refrigeration units. By varying the sizes of containers, amounts of food, and placement of these foods within the refrigerator, it is possible to find the fastest cooling combination for these foods.

Some date coding procedures are different for hot food operations than they are for cold foods. There are two distinct categories of cooked, potentially hazardous foods to consider: (1) *Raw Foods* that will go through an initial HACCP cooking process. After the cooking is completed, the resident population of pathogenic organisms is greatly reduced or temporarily eliminated. Under these conditions, a new date coding period may begin with the cooking process. (2) *Foods to be Reheated* for which all critical points have been controlled since the initial cooking process (such as pop-out meals). These foods may be rethermalized with no critical temperature requirements for the second cooking period.

SETUP AND PACKING

Setup and packing operations include the final kitchen handling of prepared potentially hazardous food items. These operations are generally done under room-temperature conditions. An efficiently managed team can quickly assemble all the components and pack them in carts, carriers, or modules with only minimal changes in food temperature. However, time and temperature controls must be carefully monitored, or much of the food safety efforts from previous steps could be lost.

Staff setting up and packing food are responsible for the final use of date coding information. Each person working in this area should know the oldest acceptable food in use each day. Each should know what to do when older food is found.

Potentially hazardous foods that have been closely temperature controlled can withstand short temperature excursions without promoting bacterial growth. This lag in bacterial growth can be quite long if temperatures remain below 60°F (15.5°C). However, as temperatures enter the 70°F to 120°F (21.1°C to 48.8°C) range, the bacterial lag phase becomes shorter, and multiplication becomes more rapid. Setup and packing operations handle both cold snacks that have received no in-house cooking steps as well as previously cooked hot foods that are usually in a refrigerated state.

This operation is usually short in duration and entails no direct hand contact with food items. Therefore, the time needed to pack meals is the primary hazard that must be controlled. It is important to track potentially hazardous food temperatures and time through the packing operation to determine if any time-consuming steps could be combined or eliminated. Care should be taken to be sure that potentially hazardous foods are not left out at room temperature during breaks or lunch periods. Packed cold food carts or carriers should immediately be placed into the final holding refrigerator with the doors open to facilitate air circulation or be ready for transportation to an aircraft just as soon as they are packed. They should not be left sitting by the packing area until several are packed and ready for storage.

The cooling of foods prior to cold packing is very important if the final container has insulating properties. Only small amounts of cold supplies being packed should be kept at room-temperature at one time. All supplies should be stored under refrigeration until just prior to use. Closed plastic boxes, cardboard carriers, or bags will stabilize the temperatures of snack items quite well, particularly if the containers are then tightly packed into trolleys or carriers. Thus, if potentially hazardous foods are loaded at 70°F (21.1°C) in such containers, they could remain above 41°F (5°C) for over eight hours inside the final holding refrigerator.

Dry ice is commonly used for holding cold temperatures of foods for transport. In many operations, it is loaded during packing. It can be effective if properly placed and properly used. Dry ice is *not* effective for cooling down warm foods. It is also not particularly effective if placed in the bottom of carriers, next to doors that do not seal well, or on the outside top of carriers.

Electric modules for hot packing should not be used for heating meals. These units are capable of sustaining the specified hot temperatures—the temperatures at which the food should be when it is packed—but not raising those temperatures. Hot-packed potentially hazardous foods should leave packing and be delivered to the aircraft at a minimum temperature of 140°F (60°C) or at the temperature specified by the airline—whichever is higher.

Insulated hot-pack trays (e.g., the Aladdin Service) should be stacked with a good seal (snug fit) between all trays to maintain adequate heat. Temperature checks should *not* be made on hot-pack trays after they have been sealed and belted. Breaking one seal can cause all the meals in the stack to loose temperature. The loss of seal and/or temperature of an insulated hot-pack tray should mandate the destruction of those meals.

FINAL HOLDING

After meals have been packed, they are held awaiting transportation. Hot-pack foods will generally not be held very long. Cold-pack foods, though, may be held many hours as a final cooling step. With either system, all aspects of final holding must be carefully controlled as this is the last step over which the flight kitchen operations will have complete control.

Cold foods that have been packed at room temperature will normally rise above 41°F (5°C) during packing. The final refrigerated holding will lower the packing temperatures to the required level. It will also determine the transportation and boarding temperatures as well as the final service temperatures for cold foods. The culmination of the packing, transport, boarding, and service steps can represent the longest time-out-of-temperature for the whole HACCP procedure. When final holding temperatures of foods are adequately controlled, small rises during delivery and service are expected to remain within the maximum of four hours' optimal temperature equivalents for bacterial growth.

The adequacy of the heating or cooling equipment is a major factor in this operation. The capacity of the refrigeration equipment should be checked under actual conditions. The doors of carriers and carts must be left open in the final holding refrigerator to allow the airflow that will assure adequate final cooling of all potentially hazardous foods. Foods that are packed into closed containers for cold delivery either must be of a size or depth that will cool quickly to below 41°F (5°C) or already be packed at that temperature or below. If these conditions are not possible, the lids of the containers must be left open in the final holding refrigerator to facilitate cooling. The final checking of cold food counts should be done in the final holding refrigerator so that potentially hazardous foods are not again exposed to room-temperature levels. It is imperative that all potentially hazardous foods leave the final holding area at a temperature that, during normal operations, will assure their arrival at the aircraft while still out of the temperature danger zone.

TRANSPORTATION

For the inflight caterer, transportation is the final step in a long series of HACCP procedures. The adding together of all the previous time-out-of-temperature segments for a particular food will determine if this final step can deliver a safe product. In most flight kitchens, the transportation procedures and schedules are determined in-house. Transportation procedures are a CCP when they can be controlled by the caterer. However, there are some cases where the kitchen operations have no direct control over food transportation to the aircraft as that transportation is done by the airline. In this situation, there can be no CCP during transportation, and all other in-house steps must make up for any anticipated out-of-temperature conditions during transportation, boarding, and onboard service. Here, it is imperative that the caterer and the airline work together to make these operations part of the HACCP program.

Transportation departments must contend with such problems as flight delays, equipment switches, gate switches, mechanical problems, tarmacking, hot ramps, hot trucks, air traffic control backups, and canceled flights. All of these factors can adversely impact the safety of the food products being transported to an aircraft. All previous HACCP procedures become very important when several of the above problems make transportation and loading times unpredictable.

Cold foods should be left under refrigeration until just prior to departure. Counting and finaling operations should be done under refrigeration where possible. All cart and carrier doors should be closed prior to exiting the final holding refrigerator. The doors of carts and carriers should not be opened again under room temperature conditions prior to delivery. Dry-iced carts and carriers can hold temperatures only until the door is opened. Once the temperature rises, temperature recovery may not take place. Since the departure temperature can be of great importance, the use of a log of temperatures taken just before the carts leave the final holding refrigerator is called for as a monitoring tool for this CCP.

A well-run HACCP program can be designed to deal with such adverse instances. Maximum limits for time and temperature must be set. When circumstances go beyond the designed limits of temperature abuse, previous plans should have been made with the airlines to recater rather than use boarded food. This is the final critical control point in the HACCP process.

Kitchen departure times should be continually monitored to assure that flights are dispatched no sooner than necessary. Times and temperatures should be monitored carefully when more than one flight is catered per truck. Transportation personnel should be equipped with calibrated thermometers so delivery temperatures can be checked as per airline specification. Potentially hazardous foods should ideally arrive at the aircraft at 45°F (7.2°C). The temperatures should be no higher than 50°F (10°C) at the conclusion of catering, and cold foods should be no higher than 55°F (13°C) prior to onboard service.

TABLE 13.6
Useful HACCP Post-Kitchen-Life Times for Boarded Foods*

Cooled Foods Useful Life Is . . .	If Boarded at . . .	And/or Served Prior to Reaching . . .
9 hours	50°F (10°C)	60°F (15.5°C)
12 hours	45°F (7.2°C)	55°F (13°C)

Freshly Prepared Foods Useful Life Is . . .	If Boarded at . . .	And/or Served Prior to Reaching . . .
3 hours	70°F (21°C)	90°F (32°C)
6 hours	60°F (15.5°C)	70°F (21°C)

* Time and temperature projections are based on the *USDA Pathogen Modeling Program* (PMP) Version 4.0 and Controlled Inflight HACCP Systems for all foods.

Foods are assumed to slowly rise in temperature during transportation, boarding, and onboard storage. Table 13.6 shows the useful cooled post-kitchen life of potentially hazardous foods prepared under an inflight HACCP system. The times portrayed in this table are longer than those allowed by any food production and distribution system with less control. Upcounts can result in freshly prepared meals being boarded without the usual cool-down times. Table 13.6 also shows the useful post-kitchen life of these freshly prepared products. *If* all the proper *Inflight* HACCP steps have been followed during the preparation of these fresh products, these extended times may also be used as a guideline for product life. Again, it should be noted that the times listed in Table 13.6 are *only* for food prepared under the *Inflight HACCP System*, and they are longer than would be appropriate for foods not prepared under this closely monitored control system.

System Verification

As is the case with any system, it is important to verify through an independent audit that the HACCP system implemented by a flight kitchen is functioning as planned. Such verification should at least entail periodic checks of food product temperature monitoring systems during different stages of the flow of food products into and through the kitchen. It should also include auditing the times that food products are outside the same temperature range so that the actual sum of these times for different products can be determined. Since the objective of these, and all other food safety activities of the inflight caterers, is to assure the safety of foods served on board aircraft, when problems with the HACCP system, as it is being used, are found during the verification process, prompt remedial action should be taken to make the system effective, as planned.

SUMMARY

Inflight foodservices pose unique food safety problems, and trends since the deregulation of the domestic airlines have made the need for a comprehensive, industrywide quality assurance program for food safety apparent. The Inflight Food Service Association has consistently taken a leadership role in regard to airline food safety and has promoted the use of the HACCP system as a means of food safety control in inflight kitchens. The HACCP systems focuses on the identification and analysis of hazards that might impact on food safety and the development and monitoring of critical control points for those hazards to help ensure the safety of food products served on board aircraft.

Many factors are associated with the incidence of food-borne illness, but inadequate cooling and cold holding and poor personal hygiene are factors involved in a high percentage of reported cases. Other important contributing factors are preparing food ahead of planned service, inadequate hot holding, and inadequate reheating. All of these factors are very much related to a cook–chill (freeze) type of foodservice system commonly used in most inflight kitchens.

All components of the inflight foodservice kitchen, from the arrival of product on the receiving dock to the boarding of products on the aircraft, can potentially contribute to food safety problems. Using the HACCP system, key hazards can be identified and appropriate control points and procedures to implement desired controls can be developed. Careful attention to the identified control points and close monitoring of activities there can help an inflight caterer ensure that only safe food is boarded on the aircraft serviced by that flight kitchen.

REFERENCES

Food Safety Quality Assurance Manual. (1994). Louisville, KY: Inflight Food Service Association.

HACCP Management Systems for Airline Food Service. (1994). Louisville, KY: Inflight Food Service Association.

Jay, James M. (1986). *Modern Food Microbiology*, 3rd ed. New York: Van Nostrand Reinhold, pp. 437–519.

Microbial Ecology of Foods. (1980). Vol 1, ICMFS. Orlando, FL: Academic Press, pp. 23–27.

"Significant Changes Within the FDA Food Code 1993." (May 1994). Technical Bulletin. Washington, DC: National Restaurant Association.

KEY TERMS

Anaerobic Bacteria	Maximum Allowable Shelf-Life
CCP	Microbiological Barriers
Control Points	Open Coding System
Critical Control Point	Out-of-Temperature Conditions
Danger Zone	Pathogen
Final Holding	pH
Finaling Operations	Potentially Hazardous Foods
Food-Borne Illness	Psychrophilic Bacteria
HACCP	Upcount
Inflight Food Safety Auditor	Water Activity Level
Maximum Refrigerated Shelf-Life	

DISCUSSION QUESTIONS

1. What trends have contributed to the need for a comprehensive industrywide quality assurance program regarding inflight foodservice safety? Why have these trends called attention to food safety needs?

2. What is the HACCP system? Explain how it can be incorporated into a flight kitchen as a means of quality assurance for food safety.

3. What are Critical Control Points (CCPs)? How are CCPs used to establish and monitor safe food-handling procedures?

4. What are the microbiological principles associated with the HACCP system? Why do these principles provide a foundation for HACCP activities?

5. What are the five contributing factors most commonly associated with incidents of food-borne illness? How are these factors related to an inflight caterer's cook–chill foodservice system?

6. What are the suppliers' responsibilities for the prevention of food-borne illness on board aircraft?

7. Who can conduct inspections of suppliers' facilities and what is the purpose of those inspections?

8. What are the temperatures and product conditions required for refrigerated and frozen food products at the time of delivery to the inflight caterer's receiving dock? What should be done with products that do not meet the minimum temperatures and conditions?

9. What are some problems potentially compromising food safety that can arise in the caterer's refrigerators and other storage areas?

10. What special controls have to be considered to ensure that food products are not contaminated with cold-loving bacteria?

11. Why are cold food production areas particularly vulnerable to compromises in food safety and potential food-borne illness problems?

12. Why must the inflight caterer be particularly concerned with the cooling times of products and the total time that products are at temperatures in the danger zone [above 41°F (5°C) and below 140°F (60°C)]?

13. Why is personal hygiene always an important consideration for foodservice employees and a particularly important concern in cold food production and handling?

14. Why do previously cooked foods used in hot food products pose a problem for the inflight caterer?

15. Why are cooking temperatures and final internal temperatures important for some foods? What are some of the foods and the final internal temperature requirements that inflight caterers should be especially concerned with?

16. What is date coding? Open Date Coding? Why should some foods be date coded more than one time (after they arrive on the caterer's receiving dock)? When should they be recoded?

17. Why is it particularly important for the setup and packing time to be kept as

short as possible? Why should foods to be packed in bags or boxes be as chilled as possible prior to packing?

18. What is the purpose of the final holding of packed carts and carriers in refrigerated units? Should the doors of this equipment be open or closed? Why?

19. Why does the final transportation of products to the aircraft pose some unusual food safety problems for the inflight caterer? What can the caterer do to reduce the risks to food safety that might be encountered during this period? What are the temperatures that food products should be at the time they are boarded on the aircraft?

20. Why might a well-run HACCP program be critically important to the service of safe food on an aircraft, particularly if the inflight caterer does not do the transportation of the food products to the aircraft?

14

Waste Management

LEARNING OBJECTIVES

After studying this chapter, the student should be able to:
1. Identify at least four reasons for the inflight foodservice industry's concern with waste management and waste management issues.
2. Discuss waste management issues resulting from limited on-board storage space.
3. Describe the impact of airlines' servicing different political jurisdictions on solid waste management within the inflight foodservice industry.
4. Discuss the USDA's requirements for the disposal of wastes from international flights landing in the United States and the rationale for those requirements.
5. Identify the extent to which inflight foodservice operations participate in recycling programs.
6. Discuss the potential impact of source reduction activities on the management of solid waste within the inflight foodservice industry.

Along with food safety, waste management is another area of special concern to the inflight foodservice industry. Although all types of foodservice operations are now concerned with solid waste management because of the ever-increasing costs of waste handling as well as an increased sense of environmental responsibility within the industry, there are unique problems faced by inflight foodservice operations that make solid waste management a particularly critical issue for the inflight caterers. Inflight foodservice must be particularly concerned with waste management for several reasons, including: (1) limited space available on board the aircraft; (2) differing waste-handling requirements in different political jurisdictions (different states; different countries) (3) possibilities for international agricultural epidemics from foreign pests brought into this country by garbage from food products boarded by foreign caterers; and (4) airlines' sensitivity to environmental concerns and the need to recycle solid waste products.

LIMITED SPACE AVAILABILITY

Waste and trash that accumulates from food and beverage services during the flight must be put somewhere. Either new storage space must be found (which means that there must be some empty space left in the galley structure that is not used for boarding food and beverage service supplies) or the waste and trash must fit into the boarding equipment that originally held the food and beverages that were served to the passenger, or some combination of both. No matter how much waste and trash is generated, some means must be found to secure it on board the aircraft until it lands, where the waste and trash can be removed by the inflight caterer's boarding crew at the landing site.

The usual procedure for trash and garbage management on board an aircraft is to pack all trash and garbage generated on the flight back into the carts, carriers, or other boarding equipment, replacing the food trays, entrees, and other such items consumed by the passengers during the flight. Since onboard space is so limited, the less trash and waste generated, the less the storage problem that is faced by the airlines. As airlines have reduced the level of foodservice offered to coach-class passengers to gain operating cost savings, they have recognized a further benefit in the reduction of solid waste generated from a flight.

Another way to save onboard space is through the use of trash compactors. Several different compactor models, all of which are configured as a trolley which fits into one compartment in the galley, are currently available. Some of these models also facilitate the sorting of the solid waste for recycling by having separate compartments within the compactor for different types of waste (i.e., aluminum, paper, etc.). Figure 14.1 illustrates one trash compactor model that is designed with three interior bins so that the flight attendants can separate plastic, aluminum, and paper trash on board the aircraft during the flight. Other models of compactors come in both full and half sizes to better accommodate the space available on a particular aircraft model. Figure 14.2 illustrates ATLAS-size trash compactors in both full and half sizes.

The solid waste storage problem is compounded on international flights serving multiple meals to all classes of passengers. Not only must more food and beverage products be boarded onto the aircraft prior to takeoff, but more space must be found during the flight to store the solid waste generated from the food and beverage services. In this situation, too, it is

FIGURE 14.1 One model of a trash compactor that might be used on an aircraft. This model is designed to facilitate the sorting of trash on board the aircraft. (Courtesy of Aero-design Technology, Inc.)

important that all waste is properly handled to make sure that waste generated from the first meal and beverage service does not come into contact with or otherwise contaminate products being held in galley storage for later meal service. As will be noted later, this storage space problem can become an even greater concern for the airline if its destination landing site will not allow solid waste from the inbound flight to be off-loaded. In that case, the airline is, in effect, hauling its own solid waste as freight on the return flight, a costly endeavor when trash displaces paid freight in the aircraft's baggage compartments.

FIGURE 14.2 Full- and half-size versions of a different model trash compactor designed for use on an aircraft. (Courtesy of Godfrey Aerospace, Inc.)

DIFFERENCES IN WASTE-HANDLING REQUIREMENTS IN DIFFERENT POLITICAL JURISDICTIONS

Because the food and beverage service waste is generated while the aircraft is in flight, in most cases the waste from the products loaded at the departure site is automatically transferred to the landing site for handling. What sometimes makes this situation unique is that the landing site is usually in a different political jurisdiction (i.e., different state or country) than the departure site. Thus, the regulations governing solid waste management may be very different in the two locations. How the solid waste has been handled during the flight can have an important impact on the caterer's workload at the landing site. For example, some states, such as California and Florida, have mandatory recycling laws while others do not. If recycling is mandatory, and the airlines have sorted their recyclable trash on board, it is much easier for the caterer's personnel to properly handle the solid waste for recycling. If they do not, then either the caterer must do the sorting or must have an arrangement with its trash-handling company to do the sorting (a potential cost to the caterer).

Within the United States, the airlines can move solid waste from one state to another and be assured that the waste can be taken off the aircraft at the landing site. However, the picture is different, in some instances, for international flights. Some countries, such as Germany, have very strict solid waste management laws. These laws prohibit the entry of solid waste from some parts of the world. Because solid waste from the country from which the flight originated cannot enter the destination country, the airline must package the waste generated on board the aircraft during the first segment of the flight, store it in the baggage compartment, and return it to the country of origin. As was noted in the previous section, this requirement can be costly to the airline as the stored trash (producing zero revenue) may displace freight which would be generating revenue.

Because of the many differences in laws governing solid waste management throughout the world, inflight catering firms with kitchens in multiple locations (particularly international locations) must be well versed in the local solid waste management laws and policies to make sure that they are properly handling the solid waste which they take off all inbound aircraft that they service. For example, in the United States, solid waste from inbound international flights must be either incinerated, steam sterilized, or ground and placed directly into a sanitary sewer system. The airlines, too, must be well versed in these laws to be sure that they are using proper food and packaging products and are allowing appropriate amounts of space in the galleys and freight storage areas for solid waste storage. Failure to comply with appropriate local laws and regulations can result in substantial fines for the caterer, the airline, or both.

CONTAMINATION POSSIBILITIES

Because many airlines travel worldwide and board food and beverage products from many countries, they are possible carriers of food and water contaminants, bacteria, or other sources of disease, or agricultural pests from one area of the world to another. In addition to a strong concern with the environment, this concern with possible agricultural disease transfer is an important rationale for some countries' laws which preclude the disposal of trash originating in certain other countries. It is also an important rationale underlying the U.S. requirement that solid waste from international flights must be either incinerated, steam sterilized, or ground and placed directly into the sewer system.

The primary concern is the agricultural industry. This concern centers around plant and animal disease organisms entering the area through free rides on the fresh fruits, vegetables, animal products, or other products used for the meal service. When the waste from the flight is casually handled, these organisms may be provided with a temporary home until they can invade their new home site. Different political jurisdictions establish laws and regulations for solid waste management which they feel will offer them the desired level of protection from a possible invasion of contaminants, disease, and agricultural pests. In the United States, the primary concern is with possible infection of livestock with diseases such as hoof and mouth, which could severely damage the U.S. cattle industry. Thus, the United States Department of Agriculture (USDA) is the agency which regulates and monitors the handling and disposal of solid waste from international flights which land in the United States.

Generally, the USDA requires that anything that comes into the United States that has plant or animal materials or comes into contact with these plant or animal materials has to be treated a certain way. Food products and food waste obviously fall into this category of USDA-regulated materials. However, food trays, utensils, and any other items that have come into contact with the food products also fall under the jurisdiction of the USDA handling regulations and must be properly disposed of or sanitized by the inflight caterer. The special handling requirements for the waste stream from international flights will be discussed later in this chapter.

ENVIRONMENTAL CONCERNS—RECYCLING

The airline industry has become involved with environmental concerns, just as most other major industries have, and many airlines and inflight caterers have developed environmental programs. Some of the programs which impact inflight caterers entail the airlines' replacing disposable items with rotable serviceware, recycling disposables, and contributing leftover food products to food banks or other programs, such as the Second Harvest program. Some airlines are using proceeds from their recycling programs as donations to other environmental causes as well as supporting efforts of large U.S. businesses to encourage the purchase and usage of products manufactured from recycled materials.

A survey conducted by the IFSA Waste Management and Recycling Committee in 1993 (Adams, 1993) found that most of the 163 respondents (153 flight kitchens and 10 airlines) were trying to recycle some of their waste. By far, the products most commonly recycled were corrugated cardboard and aluminum cans. Figure 14.3 illustrates the number of respon-

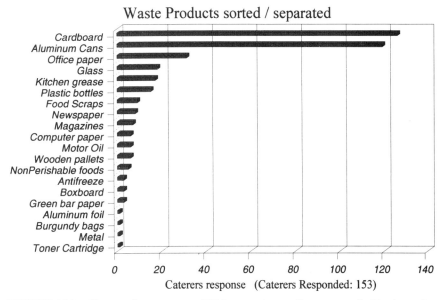

FIGURE 14.3 Caterers' response to IFSA caterer recycling survey indicating what waste products they sorted and/or separated. (From Adams, 1993; courtesy of the Inflight Food Service Association)

dents indicating that they recycled any of twenty products included in the survey.

The survey also indicated that five states plus Dulles Airport outside of Washington, D.C. in northern Virginia mandated recycling of goods from the solid waste generated on flights. These states are California, Florida, New York, Pennsylvania, and Texas. Caterers operating kitchens in these states need to be in compliance with their respective state's recycling laws, and managers have the responsibility of knowing what those laws are and what actions are expected to insure compliance.

The growth of the recycling movement has led to the involvement of the airlines, the caterers, and the airports in the recycling of materials from airline flights. All parties are now trying to claim the rights to revenues generated (if any) from the sale of recycled goods. Some companies are interested in these revenues as resources they can use to fund local charities—a community goodwill program for them. Others want the revenues to off-set their trash pickup costs, and the trash haulers themselves, who are often willing to separate the recyclable products for the caterer, want the recyclable materials to sell for additional revenues. Some cities in which the airports are located are now also interested in airline trash. Their interest is primarily focused on this trash as fuel for their waste-to-energy incinerators, which they are using for power generation.

A very positive aspect of the recycling pictures is that now almost all the aluminum cans leaving airports and catering operations are recycled.

It is now even possible to recycle aluminum cans from international flights. Cans that have not been in direct contact with any food products such as those remaining on the bar cart or those which were used primarily during beverage service periods which are separately collected by the flight attendants and kept separated from the remainder of the food and beverage service waste and the garbage can be recycled. However, if a can has been smeared with food or food waste during the meal service or the collection period, it cannot be recycled unless it is sterilized first. Indeed, any items that have been sterilized by a process acceptable to the USDA can be recycled. Because of this strong aluminum recycling effort of the airline industry, as well as by individuals and other industries throughout the United States, the price of aluminum has begun to decrease.

Discussions at the 1994 IFSA Waste Management and Recycling Committee meeting indicated that members felt that soft-type plastic recycling represented the best potential future revenue resource if these products could be used more in airline foodservices and if cost-effective recycling programs were developed. These products can be recycled and returned to use as exactly the same product, thereby saving remanufacturing costs. PET (the soft-type plastic that soda bottles are made of) and polystyrene have been recyclable for some time. In addition, the U.S. Food and Drug Administration has recently approved the recycling of certain plastic equipment and serviceware from airline and other types of foodservice back into food containers.

Although it may seem desirable, from a recycling point of view, to use PET two-liter soda bottles on board aircraft for soft drink service, there are problems for the use of PET products on airlines in the future. The size and configuration of the PET soda bottles has meant that they can only be loaded into the beverage carts on their sides. Thus, only a very low percentage of the soda served on board airline flights has been poured from PET soda bottles. To date, there have been only very limited efforts to recycle PET containers. One airline, working with one of the container manufacturers, attempted to develop a container recycling program in one airport. However, a much larger-scale effort is required to make this recycling effort efficient and cost effective for the airline and the inflight caterer.

There has been some interest in the possible recycling of plastic from international flights, but to date, little has been done in this area. The lower market level for plastic than for aluminum has limited interest in the plastic component of the international flights' waste stream in the United States.

Polystyrene, often used for hot beverages, can also be recycled. Although polystyrene holds heat very well, and passengers like it for that reason, it has posed problems because of its bulk. Polystyrene trash simply takes a lot of space to store. One international airline has completely eliminated the use of polystyrene on its flights after more than two years of work. This carrier now stocks washable coffee cups and claims that it saves about 330 tons of plastic waste per year.

However, the recent development of a solvent made from citrus products that can be used to reduce polystyrene to a liquid (even on board aircrafts) has the potential to significantly improve the feasibility of polystyrene recycling as the bulk storage problem would be eliminated. Thus it would become economically practical to ship large volumes of liquid polystyrene from users collection points to recycling plants.

DECIDING WHAT PRODUCT TO USE

As a whole, the inflight foodservice industry has substantial purchasing power. Because the airlines very closely control the specifications of the products used for their flights' food and beverage services, it would be possible for this industry to have a significant economic impact on the use of products made from recycled materials. Although a number of airlines are specifying the use of recycled products in some instances, the current economic structure of the airline industry has precluded more extensive specification of products manufactured from recycled materials.

The major stumbling block to date has been that products made from recycled materials still cost more than do comparable products made from new materials. Since many airlines are operating at an overall loss and looking for ways to reduce costs (not increase them), especially in their food and beverage services, they have not supported the use of products manufactured from recycled materials on the basis of their cost. It will be difficult to increase the usage of these products in inflight foodservices until such time that their purchase becomes cost effective for the airlines.

One of the difficulties encountered in trying to increase the use of products made from recycled materials is simply that such products cost more. This higher cost is the result of several factors. One factor is the cost of collecting and separating the materials to be recycled which have to be included in the overall manufacturing costs. Another is that there are increased processing costs for remanufactured products compared with the same products manufactured from new materials. This cost hurdle may be reduced or eliminated sometime in the future as the supply and demand for recycled and newly processed products becomes more equitable.

The other question faced by the airlines is whether to use rotable (or reusable) or disposable serviceware. The more reusable ware is used, the less solid waste is generated. However, there are still environmental questions related to the water used for ware washing, as well as concerns about the increased boarding weight (and thus increased aircraft fuel consumption) of rotable serviceware. Consideration must also be given to the additional labor time requirements that the inflight caterer has for washing the rotable serviceware. As the airlines move to more simplified food and beverage services and the use of more snack and cold meal service, replacement of rotable serviceware with disposables becomes more feasible. Thus, an important question that all airlines will have to consider as they continue to review and restructure their foodservices is whether to use disposables and help with the development of a viable recycling program for these products (many of which are made from PET plastics or polystyrene) or to use reusable serviceware (china, glassware, and some types of plasticware) and impact municipal water treatment systems and the rivers and streams into which they empty.

CHANGES IN PRODUCT PACKAGING (SOURCE REDUCTION)

The packaging for food and beverage products used for inflight foodservices can have a significant impact on the waste stream generated by the caterers' operations as well as by the service on board the aircraft. Disposal of solid waste is now a significant operational cost of all inflight caterers and is becoming more so as the availability of landfills becomes increasingly limited. Thus, actions that can be taken by the industry to reduce the use of packaging materials for the products used (reducing the *source* of the solid waste stream) would help reduce the caterers' solid waste disposal costs, reduce the need for the recycling of materials, and have an overall positive environmental impact. One caterer has noted that its kitchens generated one pound of corrugated cardboard for every seven meals produced—a sad environmental statistic for an industry producing several hundred thousand meals per day. Worse yet, that weight did not include all of the plastic, styrofoam, and other packaging materials that the products they used came packaged in.

Because the caterers follow the specifications provided by the airlines they are servicing, the airlines and the product manufacturers will have the leading role in this source-reduction effort. The airlines have control over the products that are purchased for their inflight foodservices. Because of the large purchase volumes for very specific products, they can often specify to their vendors how they want their products packaged. Airlines, and their caterers, need to consider ways in which they could discourage excess use of packaging materials, such as by purchasing products that they use a great deal in bulk quantities even though it may be more convenient to purchase them packaged individually or in smaller, more readily handled units, or by encouraging product manufacturers to package or deliver products in reusable containers. Of course, there is always a possible differential in labor costs or other environmental impact considerations that must be taken into account when addressing the question of product packaging.

Unless they take a leading role in this effort, the airlines will be paying for the cost of the vendors' use of excess packaging materials that are not always needed or wanted, as well as adding to inflight caterers' costs for disposing of the excessive solid waste stream. It may take a group effort on the part of the airlines, but there is opportunity for product cost reduction, as well as savings for the environment, through the airlines working with the vendors and caterers to reduce the amount of packaging materials and water used.

Reducing the excessive use of packaging materials also offers opportunities for the vendors, and they are in a position to respond to the concerns of the airlines and the inflight caterers. The vendors are in control of the packaging process, and know what the government regulations are for packaging, and how packaging has to be specified. They can use this expertise to work closely with the airlines to develop new approaches to product packaging. Reducing the use of packaging materials could lead to considerable production cost savings for the vendors, as well. These cost savings could enable the vendor to bid more effectively in the competitive market for the airlines' business.

However, a caveat is that the airlines have to be willing to accept their vendors as true partners in this endeavor. Such partnering will quite likely mean the development of long-term purchasing contracts with the vendors who work cooperatively with the airline in regard to environmental issues. The vendors will need the long-term assurance of a customer base that would be implied through the development of such purchasing contracts in order to justify the research and development expense that would be involved in studying this problem area jointly with the airlines and the inflight caterers.

The caterers, too, can assist with this partnership effort. Just by surveying what comes into their kitchens—how products are packaged, how much packaging material is used, what type of materials are used and so on—they can help both the airlines and the vendors identify products with excessive packaging. They can also offer suggestions for alternative packaging approaches, both for products coming into the kitchen and for products being boarded onto the airlines' flights. For example, they could request that prepackaged bakery products be delivered on reusable racks rather than in cardboard boxes, or they could request that their chemical drums be returned for reuse by the chemical company. Indeed, this need for source reduction of the solid waste stream offers an excellent opportunity for the partnering concept to work through cooperative efforts among the airlines, the vendors, and the caterers.

Buying products packaged in larger bulk quantities is another approach that can help reduce the amount of packaging used. However, care must be exercised here. Buying products in larger quantities than can be used can cause an increase in product cost resulting from loss due to spoilage, inappropriate usage, and increased storage costs. There must always be a match between the amount of the product to be used within a reasonable length of time and the amount purchased at any one time, as well as how that amount is packaged for use, to optimize product costs overall. For example, one airline at one time purchased styrofoam cups in tubes holding 75 cups. However, they found that the flight attendants were either throwing out the excess cups or holding tubes back for their own use. As a result, the airline now purchases these cups in tubes of 25. Although the cost per tube is greater, the overall tube usage is less since the boarded cup count better matches the actual cup usage on the flights.

DISPOSAL OF INTERNATIONAL WASTE

It is generally much more costly for a caterer to dispose of international solid waste than to dispose of domestic waste. Caterers who are able to effectively separate their two streams of waste (international and domestic) are able to dispose of them in two different ways—using the more costly incineration or steam sterilization process only for international waste. However, if they cannot separate their waste products in a way acceptable to the USDA, then *all* their solid waste must be treated as international waste and disposed of in accord with USDA procedures for international solid waste disposal. Having to combine their waste disposal, of course, increases the cost of waste handling for the caterer. In many areas, the USDA seems to be pressing the caterers to combine their waste streams and either incinerate or steam sterilize *all* their waste, regardless of the airline from which it came. Generally, the USDA has this preference, especially for incineration, as it is usually a more simple process to regulate than separation (although it is more costly to the inflight caterer).

Solid waste separation procedures that are acceptable to the USDA vary from one location to another. Thus, inflight caterers wanting to separate their domestic and international trash streams need to consult with their local USDA officials to determine what will be acceptable. In general, the following would be acceptable procedures:

1. Corner off the area where the carts from the international flight(s) will be coming into the flight kitchen sanitation area.
2. Do not leave any of the international carts outside on the loading dock where they may possibly come into contact with domestic carts or where birds and other pests may scavenge food scraps.
3. Mark the areas where the trash and waste from the international carts is being stored and account for its whereabouts at all times until it is incinerated or sterilized.
4. Run all of the carts and equipment from the international flight(s) through the dish machines separately from carts and equipment from domestic flights.
5. When the washing of the international carts and equipment is completed, strip and clean the dish machine before any domestic carts and equipment are washed.

Increasing use of extruders and high-compression compactors by inflight caterers as a means of reducing the solid waste volume so that a lower volume of materials goes to sanitary landfills must also be considered when disposing of international waste materials. Extruders and high-compression compactors reduce the volume of waste by extracting or squeezing out the water from the waste materials. When this process is applied to international waste, a stream of liquid waste is produced which would be just as contaminated as the solid residue remaining, if the products were contaminated in any way when they came from the aircraft. The USDA has agreed that as long as this liquid waste is contained and it goes down a sanitary sewer, this approach to the disposal of international waste is acceptable.

There is still a problem, though, with the extruder itself. It is not always possible to economically and efficiently clean the extruder between processing international and domestic waste, as is possible with the dish machine (although also cumbersome). Therefore, if an extruder is used for international waste, either the caterer must treat all waste going through the extruder as international waste or must have two extruders and two processing areas—one for domestic waste and one for international waste. This latter alternative, though, would be feasible only for large kitchens with a high volume of international flights because of the capital investment that would be required to create two waste processing areas.

It is also acceptable for a caterer to grind international waste and put it down a sanitary sewer. While there is equipment available on the market today that will grind some nonfood items for disposal, the grinding of waste is most applicable to food product waste, as opposed to trash (paper, glass, etc.), which is more readily handled through incineration or sterilization.

Another solution to the separation problem which is used by some of the larger caterers with a large number of both domestic and international flights at a particular airport is to have completely separate kitchens for each type of flight. Then, all of the waste at the international kitchen is handled as international waste and all the waste at the domestic kitchen is clearly from domestic flights only.

SUMMARY

Waste management is an important area of concern for the inflight foodservice industry. Space limitation on board the aircraft, wide variances in legal regulations from one political jurisdiction to another, and the industry's concern with environmental issues while also being faced with the need to reduce operating losses are some factors contributing to this concern. Because some landing sites restrict the disposal of waste products from some sources, airlines are sometimes required to back-haul the trash generated during a flight to the flight's point of origin, or at least to a destination within the country of origin. Space that must be used for hauling trash cannot be used for producing revenue.

There is wide variance in the laws and regulations governing waste management and disposal at different landing sites around the world. Most of the legal restrictions are the result of concerns about the spread of plant and animal disease through contaminated food products. However, in some areas of the world, such as in Western Europe, there are also concerns about inadequate landfill space to accommodate the large volume of trash generated by the airlines. In the United States, the USDA is the regulatory agency with oversight of waste management from international flights. The selection of the USDA, and not the FDA or the FAA, is a result of the primary concern with the possible spread of disease among livestock.

The airline industry is aware of and involved with environmental concerns. Thus, inflight foodservice operations are also involved, environmentally, and recognize the need to reduce the volume of the solid waste stream to best use limited available landfill space. While such reduction can be done through equipment such as compactors, pulpers, or shredders, more viable approaches are increased recycling of all types of products and source reduction of packaging materials. Most inflight caterers are involved in some type of recycling program. However, much more could be done through cooperative efforts between the airlines, airport authorities, inflight caterers, local waste management companies, and the regulatory community.

Source reduction, too, will require a cooperative effort between the airline, the caterer, and the vendors supplying the needed product. The airlines have much control regarding product packaging because they specify the specific products that will be used on their flights and, in that specification, can address the packaging that will be used. The vendors could potentially benefit from source reduction through product manufacturing cost savings as well as through increased favorable partnering with the airlines and the inflight caterers. In addition to their recycling efforts, the caterers also have responsibility for observing packaging problems and excesses and discussing what might be done with the airlines and the vendors.

REFERENCES

Adams, Bill. (Summer 1993). *Inflight Food Service Association Recycling Survey*. Louisville, KY: Inflight Food Service Association, 63 pps.

"Recycling: Opportunities and Disappointments." (July/August 1994). *Onboard Services*, 26(6):17.

Sims, Susanne. (May 1993). "Cleaner Skies." *Successful Meetings*, 42(6):29.

"Transcription of IFSA's Waste Management and Recycling Committee Meetings Held Since its Inception in 1990." (Spring 1993). Louisville, KY: Inflight Food Service Association.

KEY TERMS

Back-haul
PET
Remanufacturing
Sanitize

Solid Waste
Source Reduction
Sterilize

DISCUSSION QUESTIONS

1. Why is the inflight foodservice industry particularly interested in waste management issues?
2. What do the flight attendants do with the trash generated on board an aircraft?
3. What must the airline do with its waste if the local laws and regulations prohibit the waste from being off-loaded at that destination?
4. Are there differences in the waste management considerations of U.S. domestic flights and international flights? If so, what are they?
5. What is the primary concern of the USDA in regard to waste coming into the United States from international flights?
6. What methods can an inflight caterer use to dispose of waste from an international flight?
7. What are the two materials most commonly recycled by the inflight foodservice industry?
8. Is recycling mandatory anywhere within the United States? If so, where?
9. Why does the inflight industry not use more products manufactured from recycled materials? What would need to happen to encourage increased usage of these materials (and subsequent increased demand for recycles)?
10. What is meant by the term *source reduction?* How is source reduction related to waste management within the inflight foodservice industry?
11. What actions might the airlines take to increase source reduction of waste materials? The vendor? The caterers?
12. Is purchasing products in bulk the best approach to source reduction? Why or why not?
13. What is a suggested procedure for ensuring that international solid waste is separated from domestic solid waste?
14. What can the inflight caterer do with liquid waste from international flights?
15. Why would the airline, the caterer, the trash hauler, and the airport all be interested in having the recyclable materials from an airline's flights available to them?
16. What are two problems currently inhibiting the recycling of PET programs by the airlines? What has been the major problem with polystyrene recycling?
17. What are some of the factors that the airlines should consider when trying to decide whether to use rotable or disposable serviceware on their flights? Why are these factors important? What potential impact do some or all of these factors have on the environment?

15

Meeting Airline Needs through Product Manufacture and Distribution

LEARNING OBJECTIVES

After studying this chapter, the student should be able to:

1. Discuss the challenge associated with product development and distribution in the inflight foodservice industry.
2. Describe the role of the product manufacturer in support of inflight foodservices.
3. Describe the need for the specialized distributor in support of inflight foodservices.
4. Identify at least three products representative of manufacturers' research and development efforts and use of technology to meet the needs of the airlines.
5. Discuss the importance of branding to inflight foodservices and how branding is being incorporated into inflight foodservice operations.
6. Identify at least three products which were either especially developed for airline use or for which special packaging has enhanced the usability of the products for the airlines.

CHALLENGES IN PRODUCT DISTRIBUTION

There is a need for a wide diversity of products in any inflight foodservice operation. Items used include those such as both frozen and shelf-stable

357

foods, carbonated beverages, noncarbonated juices, mineral waters, alcoholic beverages, reusable meal tray components, disposable paper and plastic products, and packaging materials (foils, film, tapes, and labels). When an airline is operating out of several hundred cities, often both domestic and international, it has to deploy these products to inflight caterers at most of these cities if the airline wishes to provide food and beverage services to its passengers. The quantities of any of these items that are used can range from thousands of cases at major hub cities to minimal quantities at the smaller airport locations.

The logistical process that is involved in providing products to the airlines' caterers is further complicated as many items are directly sourced and specified by the airlines. Yet the supplies are needed at the widely dispersed catering company locations so that they can perform their service function for the airlines. As has been noted earlier in this text, airlines prefer to use their own purchasing departments to deal directly with product manufacturers to obtain the lowest possible prices for the items purchased for their inflight food and beverage services.

Some manufacturers, though, will ship products only by the truck load—in quantities usually too large for inflight caterers to receive and store at their airport kitchens. Thus, it is necessary to have some intermediate stage between the manufacturer and the caterer to provide product storage and distribution services. Manufacturers, such as the entree manufacturers, however, will work directly with the airlines and their caterers in regard to product shipment. These manufacturers will ship their products directly to the caterer; thus, the distributor fees, or middle-man costs, are saved.

Originally, airlines used their own *stores*, or warehouse facilities, as storage centers for the truck loads of products shipped directly to them from the manufacturers. Then, they used their own aircraft fleet's cargo capability to distribute these materials (referred to as COMAT, or company owned materials) to their caterers. However, as air traffic increased over time, the volume of product flow became too great for the airlines to handle internally. Also, air freight revenues have increased dramatically for the airlines in recent years. Thus, their cargo space became too valuable as a source of freight revenue, and it was no longer cost effective for them to ship company materials themselves. Therefore, most major airlines stopped using their stores' facilities for such goods and began to use the services of specialized distribution companies to warehouse the products to be used and to ship these products to the caterers as needed.

This entire process of product distribution in support of inflight food and beverage services is very expensive. Having products positioned at many locations, as well as in transit to caterers, is very complex and difficult to control. There is a need for airlines and caterers to work very closely with product manufacturers and distributors to better incorporate modern, efficient distribution techniques into the process of product acquisition and distribution to help contain the costs associated with this part of inflight foodservice operations (see discussion of EDI, Chapter 7).

THE ROLE OF MANUFACTURERS

Both the product manufacturers and the specialized distributors that service the airline industry are key members of the inflight foodservice partnership. Product manufacturers work closely with the airlines to develop products which will meet the needs of the airlines. The most notable example of this development process which is widely used today are the frozen pop-out meals discussed earlier.

Another example are the frozen *mealtime components* which have been developed by frozen entree manufacturers. Here, meal components such as meat, vegetables, starch, sauces, and gravies are prepared and frozen separately into individual portions. The airline can then mix and match these portions as they develop menus to achieve menu variety for their passengers without creating a heavy, frequently changing workload for the caterers. One of these manufacturers has used technology to develop a new microwave cooking process for the manufacture of its entree products to help maintain product freshness.

Manufacturers commit research and development resources to be able to respond to the requests of the airlines. They do so because the volume of products purchased by the airlines (especially if the product can be used by several airlines) is high. Also, since the airlines prefer to purchase directly from manufacturers, if manufacturers can contract directly with one or more airlines to be the supplier of a particular product, or line of products, they are assured that a particular volume of that product will be purchased over the time period of the contract. Thus, they are able to tailor their manufacturing level to that known sales quantity, eliminating some risk from their product inventory management.

Another approach that airlines often use for product procurement is to deal directly with an airline broker. An airline broker serves as an intermediary between the airline and manufacturers that could potentially supply a product to meet an airline's need. Essentially the broker becomes the problem solver for the airline, the distributor, and the product user (the caterer). Generally about 50 to 60% of airline-contracted items are "worked" (or procured) through such a broker.

Because the product research and development is the product of the supplier (even if the supplier was directed by the airline), if the airline later chooses to change suppliers for their meal products they do not have the right to access and transfer a recipe and product information to another company. Since the manufacturers bear most of the meal development costs, the recipes and production processes used are the proprietary property of the manufacturers, not the airlines. However, in contrast, when a caterer develops the recipe for the airline, it may be asked to give it to all entree manufacturers interested in bidding on the product. This recipe would then be a proprietary item of the airline and not the caterer.

In many instances, research done to develop a product for the airlines has led or could lead to the development of a product with applications to other parts of the foodservice industry or to the retail market. Classic examples of this situation would be the development of the convection oven for the airlines and the flight-type dish machine for the caterers, both incorporating technology which was later applied throughout the foodservice industry. Thus, when this situation occurs, much of the research and development investment costs can be recovered through the airline contracts enabling the manufacturer to gain a desirable profit level from sales to other areas.

Manufacturers also listen to the comments of the caterers using their products, and conduct research to try to make product improvements based on the comments they receive. If the product is not functional for the caterer's operations or if it cannot be used efficiently by the caterer's personnel, the life of the product within the inflight industry may be quite limited. Manufacturers must keep abreast of the latest developments in food technology, food manufacturing, and product packaging to be able to produce a product that will be usable within the inflight foodservice system, will be of high quality, and will be economically feasible for airline usage. Figure 15.1 illustrates products developed by manufacturers which utilize product recipe research and packaging technology to provide new menu options to the airlines while enabling the inflight caterer to prepare a highly consistent product of known quality with a minimum investment of labor.

Many product manufacturers are conducting research to find ways to reduce the labor requirements of inflight caterers. One such effort which incorporates the use of cryovac packaging technology is the pre-preparation of fresh produce, as shown in Figure 15.2. As also shown in this figure, fresh meats can also be precut and trimmed ready to be cooked and similarly packaged. Figure 15.3 illustrates another such application of the cryovac packaging process to make ready-to-use high-quality foods available to the airlines. Here the manufacturer has developed a line of gourmet hors d'oeuvres which the inflight caterer or the flight attendants responsible for first-class meal service need only slice and place on a tray for service.

Product manufacturers are both leaders and followers within the inflight foodservice partnership. They are followers in the sense that they must be responsive to the airlines' needs and wants, as well as to the product handling problems and concerns of the caterers, when developing and refining their products for use in this industry. At the same time, they are leaders as they have the technological knowledge needed to make innovative recommendations to the airlines about products that would be applicable to this type of service as well as being capable of withstanding the product handling required for inflight foodservices.

FIGURE 15.1 Examples of products developed by manufacturers which simplify the inflight caterers' production processes while also enabling them to produce products with more consistent product quality.

SPECIALIZED PRODUCT DISTRIBUTORS

Specialized product distributors are equally important members of the team. They must work closely with the manufacturers to know about the products that they will be handling for distribution—how they are packed, what kind of storage space will be needed, and so on. They must also work closely with the airlines to know how much of any one product the airline anticipates using over a specific time period to determine what amount of storage space will be required and what the flow of the product will be through their distribution channels. Airline distributors put items into their inventory with the assurance that their stocks of these items will be depleted by the contracting airline.

Finally, they must also be in close contact with the caterers to know what the storage and handling capabilities of each of the caterers is as well as to know what the anticipated purchase volume (distribution flow) for each product will be for each of the caterers they service. They must be sure that they have the product in stock when a caterer needs a delivery; yet they do not want to have an excessive level of product inventory on hand. They can also help the caterers they service monitor their usage of specific products to help the caterers' purchasing representatives make sure that orders are placed when they should be and stock outages do not occur at the caterers' facilities.

FIGURE 15.2 Precut, trimmed, ready-to-use products packaged through cryovac processing. (Courtesy of Gourmet Foods, Inc.)

The distributors that handle the products commonly used in the inflight foodservice industry generally specialize in product distribution to this industry. Such specialization enables these distributors to focus on providing service of specialized products, prepared to precise specifications, to caterers located over a wide geographic area. Because manufacturers are often developing and manufacturing products specifically to meet airline specifications, their market for those products may be more limited than would be the case for other products that they might develop for retail or for the general foodservice industry. The more limited market, and the production of fewer units of the product, means that fewer distributors are needed for efficient product distribution—another factor contributing to distributor specialization in the inflight foodservice market.

Caterers, though, also try to buy products from local distributors servicing the foodservice industry in their area. While many products specified by the airlines may not be available through these distributors, other products, such as produce or many bakery and dairy products, are available. It is also important that caterers have a good knowledge of all types of products on the local market because the usage volume for some products used on more upscale services (such as charter flights by an airline like MGM Grand Air) may not be enough to warrant using a distributor. It is not unusual for caterers to make special trips to the local produce market, or even the nearby supermarket, for specialty goods needed in limited amounts. Another reason for maintaining local contacts is that, should something happen to interfere with the specialized distributor's delivery schedule, it is important for the caterer to have on-going contacts and working relationships with local distributors so that a reasonable substitute for the specified product can be obtained quickly, as needed, from the local market.

BRANDING IN THE INFLIGHT FOODSERVICE INDUSTRY

Branding (the use of brand name products familiar to the customer) has become an integral part of inflight foodservices, just as it has throughout the noncommercial sector of the foodservice industry. Passengers associate

FIGURE 15.3 Ready-to-serve hors d'oeuvres packaged in cryovac packaging for freshness. (Courtesy of Hannelore Gourmet Foods, Inc.)

a particular level of quality with a particular brand. By using recognized brands with a high-quality image, the airlines are able to raise the passengers' perspective of the quality of the food and beverage services offered on their flights.

Branded products are used at all levels of service, including beverage, snack, and meal services in first, business, and coach classes on both domestic and international flights. Many branded items are purchased prepackaged, and these products are ready to use without any further preparation in the caterer's kitchen. Such items not only enhance the passengers' perception of the service provided, but they may also reduce the caterers' labor costs.

Even though prepackaged items often cost more per unit than would comparable units of the same product purchased in bulk packaging, the labor-cost savings potential may be greater than the product purchase cost increase; thus, the caterer (and ultimately the airline) may save money overall. However, if the airline was already using a prepackaged product without a known brand name or one that carried a brand name with a lesser-quality image (a good brand of yellow mustard versus Grey Poupon), then the labor-cost savings potential is lost, and the airline must weigh the increased product cost of the high-quality brand-name product against the marketing advantage of passengers perceiving an improved service quality. Although branded products do often cost more than generic products, there may also be instances when such products are priced very favorably to the airlines as some manufacturers view airline usage as a marketing tool for them—or as a means of gaining wide exposure of their products to a clientele that they want to reach.

One airline provides cold snack trays that are composed entirely of branded products, including sandwiches from a franchise fast-food company. The sandwiches are made in the inflight caterers' kitchens in accord with the sandwich company's specifications using the products they specify. These products are delivered to the caterers' kitchens by the distributors that service all company franchises in the area. All the other items on the trays are purchased prepackaged and ready to use. They are handled by the caterers' personnel only during the tray assembly process. Figure 15.4 illustrates such branded snack trays. These branded snacks have been very well received by airline passengers as they feel they are eating familiar food products which are quality products—not just traditional airline food. The use of McDonald's Happy Meals for children's meals on one airline's flights from the upper Midwest to central Florida's family resort area is another example of this type of branding which is designed to encourage children's enjoyment of their inflight experience, as well as motivate their parents to select that airline for their family flights.

Figure 15.5(a and b) illustrates a variety of branded items that might be used on different types of meals. A number of manufacturers make condiments, jellies, bagels, muffins, candies, and other such items similar to those illustrated here from which the airlines might choose.

FIGURE 15.4 Example of cold meal and snack trays made entirely from branded items. (Courtesy of Continental Airlines and Subway)

(a)

FIGURE 15.5(a) Illustrations of branded, ready-to-use items that might be used for inflight services. (a) Courtesy of Harvey Alpert & Co.: (b) courtesy of Love and Quiches®, Ltd and Susan's Sweet Talk®

FIGURE 15.5(b)

The increasing use of shelf-stable branded items is one of the most important trends within inflight foodservices. As the airlines move toward the service of more cold snacks and fewer hot meals, these shelf-stable items offer them menu versatility without increasing their caterer's labor costs. At the same time, the use of recognized brands creates value in the minds of the passengers served in regard to the foodservice of the airline. Examples of such self-stable items might be Kraft's cheese-and-cracker snack packs (enabling the airline to serve a formerly refrigerated item at room temperature in shelf-stable packaging) or Mrs. Field's cookie packets. The variety of such shelf-stable items now on the market enables an airline to purchase large quantities of a number of items (thus realizing the best possible cost price) and then to mix and match these items in varied snacks which helps to prevent boredom with the "same old meal." This consideration is particularly important with frequent flyers. As suppliers become more and more innovative in the range of food items that are packaged to be shelf-stable, the use of such products by the airline can only continue to grow.

Branding is equally important in liquor service. Figures 15.6 to 15.8 illustrate displays of spirits and wines that might be used on board aircraft, particularly for first-class and business-class service. As can be seen from these displays, airlines use a variety of alcoholic beverages for their passenger beverage services. While the bottle size shown in these displays, designed to promote the particular beverages handled by the several distributors who prepared the displays, may sometimes be used in first-class service on long-distance international flights, the small 50 ml (1.69 ounce) bottles of spirits is the size commonly used for inflight beverage service. The liquor industry first used small 1.5 ounce bottles as samples of their products. Later, these small bottles were introduced to the airline industry as an answer to their need for individualized portions on board aircraft. When the liquor industry converted to metric sizing, the 1.5 ounce bottles became 50 ml in size as they are now.

FIGURE 15.6 Airlines serve an extensive variety of alcoholic beverages as a part of their inflight food and beverage service. (Courtesy of Brown-Forman Beverages Worldwide)

FIGURE 15.7 Brand names are important in passengers' perception of quality beverage service.

Branding and brand recognition is a major factor in airlines' decisions regarding the soft drinks boarded on their flights. An airline will generally have an exclusive contract with one of the major cola beverage companies, usually either with Coca-Cola or Pepsico. Changes in consumer preferences for soft drinks and reduced demand for alcoholic beverages and more demand for water and juices has had an impact on the airlines' usage of different types—and brands—of soft drinks, waters, and juices. While cola products are still the product with the greatest demand, there is substantial demand for other types of soft drinks by today's passengers.

FIGURE 15.8 Wine is gaining an ever increasing importance in inflight beverage service.

PACKAGING AND SERVICEWARE PRODUCTS

Packaging and serviceware products are also often especially developed for the inflight foodservice industry. However, on some flights, first-class meals are served on traditional serviceware that might be found in any fine dining establishment. Figure 15.9 illustrates one such first-class setting using traditional serviceware.

Sometimes special equipment may be needed to handle the glassware that might be used for an airlines' first-class, fine dining service. This equipment is needed to help reduce the breakage of the glass, particularly the stemware, that might otherwise be associated with the ware washing and boarding process. Figure 15.10 illustrates special racks that are designed

FIGURE 15.9   First-class service setting using traditional fine dining dinnerware.

FIGURE 15.10   Racks especially configured to accommodate crystal that might be boarded on airlines for first class passenger service. (Courtesy of Air Representatives, Inc.)

FIGURE 15.11 Examples of china serviceware that might be used for inflight foodservices. (Courtesy of the Pfaltzgraff Co.–Contract Development)

to handle crystal stemware during these processes. They are sized to fit into the trolleys for transport to and storage on board the aircraft.

Figure 15.11 illustrates a number of different pieces of china that could be used for inflight meal service, and Figure 15.12 illustrates different pieces of rotable plasticware that might be similarly used. As was mentioned in the waste management discussion in Chapter 14, many airlines are using more rotable serviceware, such as that illustrated here, (versus the use of disposables) to help reduce their serviceware costs as well as to reduce the solid waste stream generated on their flights. Note that the one snack plate in Figure 15.12 has a disposable cover, although the plate itself is made from plastic that can be washed and reused.

In comparison, Figures 15.13 and 15.14 illustrate meals and snacks packaged in disposable plastic boxes. The major manufacturers of disposable serviceware for the inflight foodservice industry are in constant contact with the airlines to better determine what their needs are, and they are always working on new product development that would make their products more widely used throughout the industry.

GOURMET PRODUCTS

Because of their emphasis on foodservice as a marketing tool for first-class and business-class service, airlines purchase a number of gourmet items.

FIGURE 15.12 Examples of rotable plastic serviceware that might be used in inflight foodservices. (Courtesy of DeSter Corporation-Atlanta, Georgia, USA)

One such item, ready-to-serve hors d'oeuvres, has previously been noted. Other items that are often purchased are gourmet chocolates, and caviar or other specialty fish and seafood products. While the airlines can use these products in the commercial packaging used for other components of the foodservice industry, sometimes they are interested in special packaging of a particular size or type. The manufacturers of these products, too, work with the airlines to develop both products and packaging for specific needs. Once developed, these products are generally distributed to the caterer through the distributors specializing in the inflight foodservice industry. Figures 15.15 to 15.18 illustrate some of the many gourmet products that might be used by the airlines for their first-class and business-class meal service.

FIGURE 15.13 Examples of meal and snack service using disposable plastic ware for packaging products. (Courtesy of Bonfaire, by Placon Corporation)

FIGURE 15.14 Full meal tray using disposable plastic ware for packaging the food products included on the menu. (Courtesy of Bonfaire, by Placon Corporation)

FIGURE 15.15 There are many options for gourmet products using fish and seafood. (Courtesy of LaMaree and Caviar Importers, Inc.)

FIGURE 15.16 Caviar is an item often used for first class fine dining, particularly on international flights. (Courtesy of LaMaree and Caviar Importers, Inc.)

FIGURE 15.17 Chocolates are always a popular item. Here gourmet chocolate offerings available to the airlines are shown.

SUMMARY

Airlines use a wide array of products to accomplish their inflight food and beverage services. They are concerned with product quality for all classes of service, but often seek a gourmet-level product quality for their first-class service and sometimes for business class. Their product needs are always in flux, particularly today as airlines are restructuring their food and beverage services to better meet the changing preferences of their passengers.

Developing products which will meet the specific needs of the airlines, including the need to fit into the space available for on-board storage and handling, is a challenge to manufacturers. Once appropriate products are developed, another challenge is their distribution to multiple-usage sites dispersed over wide geographic locations although they are often purchased centrally by the airlines. The development of strong partnerships between the airlines, the product manufacturers, their distributors, and the caterers who actually use the products to service the airlines' aircraft is essential. Modern technology is making new products, new product packaging, and new efficient distribution systems possible. However, cooperative interrelationships between the partners in this production-distribution-usage system will be critical if all parties are to realize the potential for improved product quality and long-term cost savings.

FIGURE 15.18 Another example of the many types of gourmet chocolates that are available for airline service. (Courtesy of Classic Confections, Inc., Atlanta, GA)

KEY TERMS

Branding   Sourced
Mealtime Components

DISCUSSION QUESTIONS

1. Why is the process of providing needed products to the inflight caterer complicated?
2. Why are specialized distributors needed for inflight foodservice industry products?
3. What roles do product manufacturers play in the provision of inflight foodservices?

4. Why would product manufacturers want to invest research and development resources into the development of products specifically requested by the airlines?

5. Why would product manufacturers be concerned with the inflight caterers' labor requirements for product usage?

6. What are two products that manufacturers have developed which reduce the inflight caterers' labor requirements while also improving the quality consistency of the food products served on airline flights?

7. What is the role of the specialized distributor in the provision of inflight foodservices?

8. Why don't inflight caterers purchase all needed items from distributors specializing in support of the inflight foodservice industry?

9. Why do the specialized distributors have to closely manage their inventory levels of products specified by an airline for use in a particular menu cycle?

10. Why has branding become an integral part of inflight foodservices?

11. How are branded products being used in inflight foodservices? Would you expect the usage of branded products to continue? To expand? Why or why not?

12. Why are brands becoming important in the airlines' soft drink stockage decisions?

13. What are the pros and cons of using rotable serviceware? For using disposable serviceware?

14. Why are specialized packaging and serviceware products needed for inflight foodservices? Give some examples of such specialized products.

15. Where are gourmet food products used in inflight foodservices? Give some examples of gourmet products that might be used.

16

Career Potential in the Inflight Foodservice Industry

LEARNING OBJECTIVES

After studying this chapter, the student should be able to:

1. Discuss the career opportunities available with inflight catering firms.
2. Discuss the foodservice career opportunities available with airlines.
3. Describe the diverse career opportunities available with product manufacturers and distributors servicing the inflight foodservice industry.
4. Describe the future potential of the inflight foodservice industry.
5. Discuss the impact that future technological developments may have on the inflight foodservice industry.
6. Discuss the need for diversification within the inflight foodservice industry and possible directions that such diversification might take in the future.

The inflight foodservice industry can offer a number of exciting career opportunities for those interested in this field of work. It is an exciting field that is ever changing—one where there is "never a dull moment"! There are a variety of paths that one might take to pursue a career in this field, each of which might require different skills and interests, but any of which could offer desirable long-term career development opportunities.

CAREERS WITH INFLIGHT CATERERS

One career path in this industry is employment with an inflight catering firm. The general organizational structure of an inflight catering kitchen was discussed in Chapter 6. Someone wanting a career with a caterer might start as an hourly employee and gradually work up into the management structure of the kitchen (Chapter 6). However, someone with a degree in foodservice management or a related field might start at an assistant manager level. Such an entry-level position might be as a shift supervisor, an equipment supervisor, a truck maintenance supervisor, or a building maintenance supervisor. It would also be possible to obtain an internship position with an inflight caterer to learn the basics of the kitchen's operations and then work into an entry-level management position.

Generally, any supervisory position under the operations manager position would be considered to be a junior-level management position. The inflight foodservice industry is no different than any other aspect of the foodservice industry. Companies here, too, believe that people interested in management careers in this field need to gain ground-floor experience to really understand the operation. Because of the unique logistical considerations involved in inflight foodservices, most catering firms believe that hands-on experience is particularly important. Junior management positions are training grounds through which employees can gain that necessary hands-on experience.

Since these entry-level, or junior management, positions are considered to be learning positions, the salary scales paid here are reflective of that learning or training perspective. However, in some organizations, the company's bonus program may extend down to the junior management level, providing some additional performance incentive. In others, though, the bonus program may not extend below the operations manager level.

The operations manager position and other managerial positions at that level within the organization are considered to be senior management positions. Thus these positions have considerably higher salary structures, have some company perks associated with them, and are incorporated into the firm's bonus program. Good performance in these positions can result in very positive bonus rewards for these managers.

A typical progression for someone with a foodservice management degree seeking a career with an inflight catering firm would be entry into the firm through a junior management position. To learn as much about kitchen operations as possible, it would be desirable to work in several different junior-level positions, as opportunities become available. The scope of responsibilities associated with these positions, though, will vary depending on the size of the kitchen in which they are located. From the junior-level positions, promotions would be to operations manager, or quality control manager, or to other such senior management positions. Generally, it would be desirable to work in several senior management positions within the firm in order to gain the breadth of experience required for promotion to general manager of a kitchen.

Most large inflight catering companies also have a regional structure. An employee could stay in the direct operations line and be promoted from a kitchen general manager to a regional operations management position. However, another alternative would be to move into a specialized regional position, such as that of controller, training or human resources management, or sanitation management. Those interested in the specialized positions may or may not progress to that level through the general manager's position within a kitchen. They may stay within the specialty field they are interested in and not have to assume the overall operations management responsibilities to move into regional, or even corporate office positions in their specialty field.

Above the regional positions are the corporate positions. Here, too, there are positions concerned with the direct management of the corporation's inflight kitchen operations and positions in specialty areas, such as finance, human resources, marketing, and so on that would be available. The type of position sought and the level to which a person rose within the total corporate structure would all be a function of each individual's interests, their willingness to work the required hours, and their success in the performance of their assigned job responsibilities.

IS THERE A FUTURE WITH INFLIGHT CATERING FIRMS?

With the recent changes in the food and beverage services being offered by the airline, people interested in this field may ask if there is a future in this industry. The answer to this question has to be yes. While the promotion opportunities may be more limited in the short run than they have been in the past when the airlines were a growth industry, they will still be there for those who perform well in their positions. Also, it seems highly likely that airline transportation is the transportation system of the future; therefore, there should be long-term growth in the industry in spite of the difficulties being encountered today. The industry has a long history of business cycles, and there is nothing to suggest that this cyclical nature will not continue. People entering this career field now will be able to gain the basic experience which would position them well for advancement opportunities later on as the airline industry resumes its growth.

Inflight catering firms' current interest in diversifying their operations also means that there will be continued opportunities in this field that may become even more varied than they are at present. Inflight catering firms have the skills, the production, packaging, and distribution equipment, and the product handling and management capabilities that make them able to provide foodservices to a number of different customers in addition to the airlines. Rather than watch their sales decline as the airlines curtail meal services, a number of inflight catering firms are taking innovative actions to secure other types of foodservices contracts that will enable them to gain improved usage of their production capacity. As these initial ventures into the production and distribution of meals and food products for nonairline customers prove to be successful, caterers will look to continued expansion into these other types of services. As they expand, an increasing array of career opportunities will be available with these firms.

CAREERS WITH THE AIRLINES

As was indicated in Chapter 5, all airlines have a staff component that is responsible for the food and beverage services on their flights. Just how large or how small that component is and exactly how it is structured varies markedly from airline to airline. The extent to which the airlines see their food and beverage services as a key operational and marketing area for them will often be a factor underlying the structure of this component of their organization. Positions available within an airline's structure might range from that of executive chef responsible for menu development to purchasing agent responsible for food product purchases within the airline's purchasing department, to account manager responsible for interfacing with caterers at the airline's landing sites, to the overall manager of the airline's inflight foodservice operations. Other positions available within an airline's structure might include responsibility for beverage selection, galley equipment selection, the development of galley packing plans, and the scheduling of food services on flights. Depending on an airline's structure, there also may be field positions available that are responsible for the airline's commissary activity at airports.

People aspiring for careers within an airline's organization should also consider the possibility of having to move up within the airlines' overall structure, outside of the foodservice field, if they are to achieve maximum advancement. Some may not want to do this and may be satisfied with the more limited career progression options available if one stays only within the airline's foodservice organizational structure.

Entry into operational positions will entail either having a degree in the area with which the position is concerned (finance, food technology, chef training, etc.) or having experience in airline or inflight kitchen operations. For example, chef training or training in food technology might be required for product recipe development positions; chef training or foodservice operational training and experience might be required for menu development positions; a financial background might be required for budget development positions; or some knowledge of and experience with products used in inflight foodservices might be required for purchasing positions.

Airlines, generally, have a strong policy of promoting from within as positions become available within their structure. Therefore, someone wanting to pursue foodservice-related careers within an airline may need to consider taking any available entry-level position to get into the airline's structure. Such a position might be as a flight attendant or a customer service representative. The entry-level salary structure for these positions may not be what graduates of four-year professional education programs might want to receive as their starting salary. However, employment in any position with an airline offers the opportunity for free or discounted flights for employees and their immediate families on a space-available basis, a great benefit for someone who is interested in travel.

Over the long term, foodservice career opportunities with the airlines seem limited. As the airlines work to streamline their operations and cut costs, it seems likely that they will rely more on their inflight foodservice partners—the caterers, the manufacturers, and the distributors—for the staff support that may have, at one time, been done in-house by the airline. It seems likely that the airlines will continue to make the operational decisions regarding the menus to be served, the products to be used, and the suppliers for most of those products in order to maintain consistency in their on-board services. However, the trend toward more use of branded, prepackaged products and the research and development that manufacturers are doing to develop new products usable on board aircraft would seem to indicate that there would be less need for development support personnel within the airlines' organizational structure. Therefore, there will simply be fewer foodservice-related positions available within any one airline.

Those interested in an inflight foodservice career should not eliminate airlines from their consideration list, though. Since the inflight foodservice industry exists to service the needs of the airlines, the more one knows about airline operations and the more experience one can gain with the airlines, the better that person's experience background is relative to this career field. Several airlines offer internships in their operations areas (generally as customer service representatives) or in corporate staff areas (such as foodservice), which can provide insights into airline operations and the role of inflight foodservices to the airline. Also, training and experience as a flight attendant or in other customer-contact positions can help one understand the needs and concerns of the passengers served by the inflight foodservice industry. Gaining this kind of experience can be helpful, whether one continues to work for the airline within its foodservice organization or whether the individual moves to other career opportunities within the inflight foodservice industry.

CAREERS WITH PRODUCT MANUFACTURERS AND DISTRIBUTORS

Perhaps the greatest number, and surely the most diverse, of career opportunities within the inflight foodservice industry are with the product manufacturers and the distributors that service the industry. Those interested in working in this industry, particularly those completing two- or four-year degrees in food service management, should seriously consider these often-overlooked career opportunities.

When seeking opportunities with these firms, some experience with the inflight foodservice industry is helpful, even for entry-level positions. This experience might be gained while in school through internships or part-time hourly positions either with an inflight caterer or an airline. Or, an individual might choose to take an entry-level position with a caterer or an airline and then transition to a product manufacturer or a distributor as a second or third step along the career path.

Manufacturers and distributors can offer career opportunities for people with a variety of backgrounds and interests. For example, manufacturers may have positions available in research and development, sales and marketing, finance and accounting, and human resources as well as in production operations, product inventory management, purchasing, and product shipment. Distributors will have positions available as sales representatives to caterers and manufacturers as well as positions in marketing, finance and accounting, and product logistics (inventory management, purchasing, and distribution). Both manufacturers and distributors will have positions that are concerned with interfacing with the airlines to be sure that they are communicating with them regarding their needs.

Some advantages of careers with these types of firms might include opportunities to work with other segments of the foodservice industry, depending on how specialized the firm is that one might be employed with. A firm manufacturing and distributing dish washing, cleaning, and sanitizing chemicals, for example, might work with every facet of the foodservice industry. In contrast, another firm manufacturing frozen pop-out meals might work almost exclusively with the airline industry and a limited number of other foodservices that would utilize pre-prepared frozen entrees (such as some school lunch programs or some health care facilities). Other advantages could include: (1) opportunities for creativity in product development; (2) working with the airlines and their caterers in solving logistical or product problems; and (3) opportunities for advancement within the firm while still working with the foodservice industry.

Positions with these types of firms also generally offer excellent salary structures and perks as advancement occurs. While salaries for entry-level positions will generally be comparable to those paid by other manufacturing and distribution firms, many positions offer opportunities to earn bonus and commission payments. If the fit is good between an individual and a particular sales/distribution position, the potential for commission earnings and other reward perks can be quite substantial. With hard work and commitment to the job, fairly rapid advancement is also possible in these firms, particularly in the sales and product representative areas.

Product manufacturing and distribution firms are also expected to continue to grow in the future, making new opportunities for career advancement available. Even if the airlines' product usage stabilizes or declines, these firms have the potential to diversify into other foodservice areas. Indeed, many already service other components of the foodservice industry in addition to inflight foodservices. This expansion will be enhanced as inflight caterers diversify their operations to service other segments of the foodservice industry (primarily in the noncommercial foodservice sector). For example, the health care industry is generally considered to be an expanding industry for the future. Many of the products, equipment, and distribution procedures applicable to the inflight industry are also applicable to the health care industry. Thus expansion into this area is often a natural fit for the inflight caterer and the manufacturing and distribution firms servicing the inflight foodservice industry. Other expansion areas with close fits to inflight mass production and distribution systems are the school foodservice systems and the rapidly growing prison foodservice systems.

THE FUTURE OF THE AIRLINE INDUSTRY AND INFLIGHT FOODSERVICES

Globalization

As indicated previously, it seems likely that airlines will be a key means of transportation in the twenty-first century. Thus, overall, airline operations will probably continue to expand, worldwide. An important factor in this expansion will be the increased globalization of the industry. While domestic services will continue to be an important aspect of U.S. airline operations, most U.S. airlines will also develop strong international operations or linkages with international airlines. It also seems likely that international airlines will seek to offer services within the U.S. market. Inflight foodservice managers must anticipate this globalization and be prepared to work in the international market in terms of food products served, preparation methods used, and interacting with multicultural personnel—whether as employees in their kitchens, airline representatives, or representatives of the international markets they service.

Many airlines are already taking steps to increase their cultural sensitivity on their international flights as they see such sensitivity as a key factor in proactively meeting the needs of their multicultural passengers. One example of actions the airlines are taking is the development of menus that are country specific with the development process occurring outside the United States, in the countries serviced by the airlines. Be developing menus on site in different countries, the airlines are able to have a greater awareness of food product availability there as well as food preferences and cultural practices regarding foods and meal service than would be possible if all menu development was done in the United States. Another example is the airlines' development and implementation of cultural awareness programs for their flight attendants. In addition to making their flight attendants aware of and sensitive to their passengers' needs (which may be quite different from those of U.S. passengers), one purpose of these programs is to help ensure that no cultural taboos are broken on flights heavily populated with international passengers.

The Emergence of Low-Cost, No-Frills Carriers

The low-cost, no-frills airlines, such as Southwest, have changed the face of commercial aviation. They have brought down the level of airfares to the point where they are competitive with rail and bus fares, as well as with the cost of driving personal autos. Not only are the fares of these airlines competitive with alternative transportation options, but they are able to get their passengers to their destinations faster than trains, busses, or cars can. Thus, they have introduced many people to flying who otherwise might not have considered flight as an alternative. Because of the success of these no-frills airlines in attracting market share, other airlines have been forced to compete with them and offer low-cost flight options, as well.

The Impact of Technology

Technological developments will also impact inflight foodservice operations. As aircraft technology improves and aircraft style and efficiency increase, more people will be flying. Increasing use of flight as the preferred mode of transportation will be aided by the new generation of commercial aircraft that will be utilizing secondary (or smaller) airports.

Technology may reduce the need for food services as entertainment for passengers during flights as the new hi-tech entertainment and work units become commonplace on aircraft. Passengers will have options to play video games, listen to their favorite music, conduct business on their video phones, use on-board computers for work projects, or engage in other activities made possible through advances in computer technology. Food may be relegated to a "nice to have," as opposed to a "necessary for entertainment" position on these new high-speed, technologically sophisticated aircraft of the twenty-first century.

Technological advances are also likely to continue to impact the types of products used for inflight foodservices, as well as the packaging available and the way that they are served. Branding is the most important trend to impact the noncommercial foodservice industry in recent times. There is little doubt that the importance of branding and the use of prepackaged products will continue to increase in all classes of service. Some of the most frequently used branded items will probably be the increasing number of high-quality, shelf-stable items as these items have an extended life and do not require higher-cost refrigerated storage.

Even though fresh food preparation has been the hallmark of fine service in first class, improvements in technology may well mean that it will be possible to have better-quality products prepared by a food manufacturer using ingredients delivered directly from the growers, cooked and frozen using equipment incorporating the latest technological developments, and delivered directly to the caterer on a just-in-time basis. Rethermalized on board the aircraft using new technologically advanced rethermalization equipment, the products that the first-class passengers (as well as the business and coach passengers) receive are perceived to have been freshly prepared that day by the caterer's chefs. This new technically advanced production and distribution system would eliminate variances in product quality from station to station, reduce caterers' labor requirements, and enhance products' nutritional quality because of the rapid transition of the products from the grower to the consumer.

Technology also seems certain to impact the flow of information between the airlines and their inflight foodservice partners—the caterers, the manufacturers, and the distributors. Technically sophisticated interactive computer systems are already available that could eliminate the extensive paperwork required for communications today. As airlines develop menus, specifications, and so on, this information could be downloaded to their caterers' computer systems and transmitted to their product manufacturers and distributors for their planning, as well. At the caterers', this information could be automatically reviewed for applicability to flights serviced by each individual caterer. Applicable information, then, could be automatically transferred to a report form or file for review or printout by the caterer. On-line terminals could be strategically placed throughout the caterers' kitchens so that employees responsible for a particular flight or a particular type of production could review their production requirements, the menu to be used, the latest passenger count, or other such information.

It also seems likely that in the twenty-first century inflight caterers will be on-line with all of the airlines they service so that they can receive information necessary for their dispatch operations in real time directly from the computer. There would likely be linkages between the airline systems and the caterers' systems that would allow data to be automatically transferred to the caterers' system so that each caterer could print dispatch forms in the format they desired. It is also likely that there would be a terminal at the loading dock which the caterer's transportation personnel could use to verify flight times, as well as passenger counts, as they were preparing to load the necessary equipment for a particular flight.

One of the greatest impacts of technology on inflight catering operations may well be in inventory management and control. Developments in automated distribution systems have the potential to simplify the very complex procedures now required to keep track of product needs for the different menus used for the different airlines and to have product on hand at the right time to meet those needs without having excessive amounts on hand at the time the menu changes. Increasingly sophisticated inventory management systems which would be interactive with the product distributors' systems would make it possible for inflight caterers to move toward just-in-time inventory management. Doing so could reduce both product losses and storage space requirements.

Much of this technology is already available, but it has seen limited application within the inflight foodservice industry. IFSA has an Electronic Data Interchange committee studying these questions and trying to determine the best course of action to get increased application of these systems to the management of inflight caterers' inventories in the future.

Diversification

As has been noted in the discussion regarding career opportunities, as the airlines reduce their requirements for food and beverage services, there may be an increasing trend toward diversification in the servicing of other demands for the production and distribution of prepared meals and snacks. In the future, inflight kitchens may be viewed as production and distribution sites which specialize in (1) the production of fresh products (i.e., salads or desserts made of fresh produce or other ingredients which manufacturers have not yet been able to process off-site), (2) the assembly of meals or snacks packaged to the customer's specification, and (3) the delivery of the proper quantity of assembled products to the site and at the time specified by the customer. Such diversification enables the inflight caterer to build a new customer (and revenue) base to augment the revenue from inflight foodservices provided to the airline using the unique strengths of the inflight foodservice systems as they presently exist.

Another opportunity for diversification for the inflight caterers would be into airport concession operations. There are a limited number of inflight caterers, such as CA One Services, Inc., that currently both operate inflight kitchens and contract for the management of airport foodservices; most of the large inflight caterers are no longer involved with airport foodservice operations. Because of their close proximity to airport terminals and their current interaction with airport authority personnel, diversification in this field may be a possible survival strategy for inflight caterers in the future.

However, airport foodservice is really a new line of business for the inflight caterer, and different expertise is required than that for servicing a flight's food and beverage needs. The growing importance of branding and the use of branded outlets in airport terminals would require the inflight caterer to develop new relationships with well-known branded foodservice operations. Branding would also require the development of new management skills which would enable the caterer either to qualify as a franchisee of the branded operation or to be able to function as a management coordinator of a number of concessionaires operating foodservice outlets within the terminal. Even though they are geographically co-located with the airport terminals, managing terminal foodservice operations would be a completely new line of business for many inflight caterers. Because expansion to terminals does not draw upon the existing strengths of the catering operation, this diversification option may be less attractive for the future than diversifying into providing catered prepared meal services to entities other than the airlines.

SUMMARY

The inflight catering industry offers many diverse career opportunities, which may be pursued through employment with inflight caterers or with the airlines themselves, or through the product manufacturers and distributors servicing the inflight foodservice industry. Even in the face of declining demand for inflight foodservices at the present time, career opportunities are expected to expand as a result of both overall long-term growth in the airline industry and diversification in the range of services and the clientele served by the inflight caters. As the caterers' operations expand, so too will those of the manufacturers and distributors servicing them.

No matter what path they choose to follow, people interested in careers in this field would be well advised to gain at least some basic experience with either the airlines, directly, or an inflight caterer. Such experience might be gained through internships, part-time hourly positions, or entry-level positions after graduation with a two- or four-year degree. This experience is necessary to gain an understanding of the industry and the unique aspects of inflight foodservice that must be addressed when providing food and beverage services to the airlines.

Airlines are expected to be an important mode of transportation in the future; thus, there will be a continuing need for inflight food and beverage services although the structure of these services may change over time. New developments in technology are expected to have a significant impact on what services are desired by the airlines, the products that are used for these services, the flow of these products within the industry, and the communication systems used to coordinate and accomplish the desired services. People interested in this career field are well advised to develop sophisticated computer skills which will enable them to understand technological developments as they occur and be on the leading edge as interactive, real-time, multimedia systems are incorporated into the inflight foodservice industry.

The field of inflight foodservice is undergoing great change, and such change is expected to continue well into the twenty-first century. No two days are the same, and opportunities for creativity are plentiful. Indeed, it is an exciting and diverse field for anyone looking for interesting, personally challenging, long-term career opportunities.

DISCUSSION QUESTIONS

1. Discuss what actions one would take to begin a career with an inflight catering firm.
2. What paths for advancement might be available for someone pursuing a career with an inflight catering firm?
3. How does the salary structure of an inflight catering firm compare with comparable positions in other sectors of the foodservice industry? Are there bonus opportunities available?
4. Are inflight catering firms expected to offer career opportunities over the long term? How does diversification impact on the career paths that may be available within these firms?
5. What types of foodservice career opportunities are available with the airlines?
6. What actions might one take to enter into a career with the airlines which would include working in their foodservice division? Are entry-level positions necessarily in the foodservice area?
7. Why is it important for someone interested in the inflight foodservice industry to gain basic experience, either with an airline or with an inflight caterer?
8. What kind of career opportunities are available with product manufacturers and distributors? Are these related to the inflight foodservice industry?
9. Why are the inflight foodservice career opportunities available with product manufacturers and distributors probably the most numerous and the most diverse of all?
10. How will the increasing globalization of the airline industry impact on the management of inflight foodservices and the skills needed by managers working in this area?
11. Where might advances in technology significantly impact the provision of inflight foodservices? What changes might occur?
12. How will changes in information/communication technology further the partnership between airlines, inflight caterers, product manufacturers, and distributors?
13. What are the strengths of inflight kitchen operations that would enable them to diversify into other market areas?
14. Why would diversification of inflight catering firms into airport concession operations possibly be desirable? Or possibly be problematic and not an appropriate area for diversification?

Glossary of Terms

ACTIVITY REPORT: For the inflight caterer, a report prepared by the caterer's boarding crew regarding their actions while transporting and boarding the food and beverage service items onto an aircraft. Any unusual events are to be included in this report, which is usually written on the dispatch form for the shift.

AIRCRAFT NUMBER: See *Tail Number.*

AMBIENT AIR: The air surrounding something or the environment around an object.

ANAEROBIC BACTERIA: Bacteria that can grow without oxygen.

AVAILABLE SEAT MILES (ASM): The number of seats on an aircraft multiplied by the number of miles in a flight segment that aircraft is scheduled to fly. ASM is a factor used by the airlines to consider the profitability of a particular flight segment. It might also be used in airline budgeting for flight expenses.

BACK-HAUL: Carrying goods from their final destination back to their point of origin.

BALANCE: For aircraft, refers to the distribution of weight throughout the aircraft. Generally, having the tail of the aircraft slightly heavier than the nose is preferred for best performance.

BANK MEALS (also called *top-off meals, supplementary meals,* or *standby meals*): Extra meals that are made for additional passengers, stored at the gate area either in one of the caterer's trucks or in a permanent location used by the caterer, and boarded as needed at the last minute prior to the aircraft's departure.

BELT: See *Tray Line.*

BEVERAGE FLIGHT: A flight on which only beverages are served (as opposed to a snack flight on which a plated or packaged snack is served or a meal flight on which a full meal is served). The beverages may be accompanied by a packet of peanuts, pretzels, or other such snack. (See *Meal Flight* and *Snack Flight*.)

BIN: See *Drawer*.

BLAST FREEZER (CHILLER): A cooling unit used in cook–chill or cook–freeze systems. The food products are rapidly chilled by passing high-velocity flows of superchilled air over the food products. This type of chiller is used with individual meal components, with preplated products, or with products stored on racks in steam table pans.[1]

BOARDING: The act of going onto a ship or an aircraft. In inflight catering, the term refers to the act of loading food and beverage provisions and service equipment onto the aircraft to prepare it for the food and beverage service activities that are scheduled to occur during a flight.

BOARDING EQUIPMENT: The equipment into which the meal components, serviceware, beverages, and all other necessary supplies and products are packed for transport to and boarding onto the aircraft. The boarding equipment fits into designated spaces in the aircraft's galley structure. May also be called *food service equipment*.

BOARDING MODULES: A large piece of specially designed equipment that contains meals, serviceware, beverages, and all other needed supplies for the food and beverage service planned for a particular flight on a particular type of aircraft. The items are packed into the boarding module and loaded onto the aircraft as a unitized module rather than as individual items, as would be the case on some other types of aircraft. Boarding modules are most frequently used with the very large, wide-body aircraft where the food and beverage service items are often loaded into the lower level of the aircraft and transferred to the passenger deck for service via specially designed elevators within the aircraft.

BONDED STORAGE: A specially constructed storage area, which meets U.S. Customs requirements, designed to secure items on which U.S. taxes have not been paid. The caterer usually carries a fidelity bond as well as comprehensive theft insurance to secure the value of the products stored in bonded storage. Inflight caterers serving international flights are required to have a bonded storage area to store liquor and other products on which U.S. taxes have not been paid. Such items are brought to the United States on a duty-free status for exclusive use on their outbound international flights.

BRANDING: Refers to the incorporation of brand-name products or concepts into inflight foodservices.

BULK LOADING: A situation in which the food products are boarded onto the aircraft in bulk (or in one large quantity rather than in individual portions). This approach to loading food supplies, beverage, condiments, or supplies is used in lieu of these items being individually preplated in the inflight caterer's kitchen or placed onto a tray that has been individually preset in the caterer's kitchen.

BURN OFF SUPPLIES: Refers to the practice of using up excess stock that was on hand in inventory for a previous cycle menu that needs to be used up (and not become waste) when a new cycle menu is introduced or a decision is made to discontinue or change a product.

BUSINESS CLASS: An intermediate class of service found on some domestic flights and most international flights. The food and beverages served to this class of passengers are more typical of those served to the first-class passengers. However, the foods are generally packaged in coach-class format, especially in the use of tray service for presentation of the meal service.

CARRIER: A container, usually made of aluminum, in which meal entrees, snacks, utensils, or supplies might be packed for boarding onto an aircraft.

CART: Also termed a *trolley*. A modular piece of boarding equipment into which passenger trays, beverages, utensils, supplies, can be loaded for boarding onto an aircraft.

CART SERVICE: A type of service sometimes used for first-class passengers when the service emphasis is on providing a fine dining experience tailored to the individual desires of each passenger. The food products are bulk-loaded onto the aircraft. When they have been prepared for service, they are placed on a cart which the flight attendants wheel to each passenger's seat. Once there, they prepare the passenger's plate, serving only the items desired by the passenger. Cart service is generally not used for business-class service and would never be used for coach class, even on international flights. Cart service in the sense noted here should not be confused with cart distribution of meals where meals are served from trolleys (or tray carts) in the aisle versus being run individually or in groups of two or three from the galley by the flight attendants.

CCP: See *Critical Control Point*.

CHARTER FLIGHT: A flight that is not regularly scheduled, but is planned for a particular purpose. (See also *Scheduled Charter Flight*.)

CHECKER (FLIGHT CHECKER): An individual who works in the flight assembly (staging) area checking the prepared meals for a flight. Depending on the location, checkers may work either inside the kitchen or on the ramp.

CHLOROFLUOROCARBONS (CFCs): Ozone-threatening compounds, such as freon, which have been commonly used as refrigerants for commercial refrigerators and freezers in the past. The U.S. Clean Air Act now restricts the use of CFCs and will gradually phase out their use altogether.

CIRCLE OF SAFETY: An imaginary ring that extends ten feet out from the wing tips, nose, and tail section of the plane.

COACH (ECONOMY) CLASS: The least costly, or most economical class of service available on most airlines' flights. Some airlines offer one class service which generally means that all their seats are sold as coach-class seats. The majority of the passengers on almost all scheduled airline flights are coach-class passengers who are seated in the main cabin of the aircraft.

On domestic flights, these passengers must pay for ammenities such as alcoholic beverages or headsets if they want them. Alcoholic beverages are generally complimentary for coach-class passengers on international flights. Food, snacks, and nonalcoholic beverages are complimentary for coach-class passengers on all types of flight. Although varying from airline to airline, the types of foods served and the level of service is considerably more restricted then that offered to first-class or business-class passengers. (See *Main Cabin*.)

COLOR CODING: Refers to the practice of affixing colored stickers coded to the day of the week a product is produced or otherwise handled on all freshly prepared or purchased items. When a product is handled several times during the production and service process (i.e., is received, stored, thawed, cooked, etc.) it is given a new code each time it is handled. Color coding is done in accord with industrywide color codes for the seven days of the week.

COMAT: An acronym for *Co*mpany owned *Mat*erials. Used to refer to the company-owned goods and equipment that an airline ships to and from its caterers when freight space is available on the airline's aircraft.

COMMERCIAL FOODSERVICES: Foodservice operations which have the primary objective of providing food and beverages to their customers for the purpose of making a profit from their operations.

COMMISSARY: A large, centralized food production and handling facility that purchases products and prepares and packages foods for distribution to numerous sites where the products are assembled and served to clientele, such as airline passengers. (See *Flight Kitchen*.)

CONTRACT: A legal document indicating an agreement between the airline (the client) and the caterer (the contractor). An inflight caterer may contract with an airline to provide specified services for the airline; the airline contracts to receive and pay for the services provided in accord with agreed-upon pricing as defined in the contract terms.[1]

CONTROL POINTS: Food safety factors characteristic of some types of food products which should be checked carefully prior to product acceptance when shipments are received on the caterer's loading dock.

CONVECTION OVEN: An oven that heats (or rethermalizes) products by means of rapid circulation of heated air.

COOK–CHILL (COOK–FREEZE) FOODSERVICE SYSTEMS: Assembly-line food production systems that prepare food on a cook-to-inventory basis. Food products are batch-produced in large quantities whenever it is necessary to restock existing inventories of products to the par stock level required. After the food products are prepared, they are rapidly chilled or frozen, either in bulk or as preplated meals. They are then stored in constant-temperature chilled or frozen storage areas until they are needed for service to the foodservice's clientele. The storage shelf-life of these products varies depending on the type of storage used (chilled or frozen), how they are stored (bulk or preplated), and the type of chilling equipment used. Once removed from storage, the products are either rethermalized at the production site and portioned hot for service or transported in the chilled or frozen state to the point of service (such as onboard an aircraft) and rethermalized there before service.[1]

COUNT: Often referred to as *pre-lim*, the count is the number of passengers by class of service for that flight as designated by the airline. Also referred to as *first count*, *second count*, and *final count*, depending on how far in advance of the flight's scheduled departure time the count is received.

CRITICAL CONTROL POINT (CCP): A location or process, which if not correctly controlled, could lead to unacceptable contamination, survival, or growth of food-borne pathogens or spoilage microorganisms. Under the HACCP system, CCPs are monitored to prevent new product contamination or to ensure that conditions do not promote microbial growth.

CUBE: For aircraft, refers to the total volume of items to be boarded onto the aircraft. Because there is limited space available on an aircraft to board the many needed items, the dimensions and total volume of all items are very important. For inflight foodservices, the boarding equipment used to board all food, beverages, utensils, and supplies must fit into equipment for which the cube corresponds to the designated storage areas in the aircraft's galleys.

CURED ICE: Ice that has been taken from the ice machine, bagged, and placed in a freezer to become hard-frozen prior to boarding onto an aircraft.

CYCLE (also known as *cycle rotation*): A set of menus rotating periodically; the exact rotation schedule depends on the individual airline's policy.

DANGER ZONE: The temperature range between 41°F and 140°F (5°C to 60°C). Bacteria and other microorganisms are able to grow and reproduce when food products are held within this range.

DEADHEAD: A system required by each airline whereby equipment balance is maintained by the caterer depending on the passenger volume of that flight. For example, if an aircraft's maximum passenger capacity is 250 and the final meal count is 150, an additional 100 pieces of equipment would be *deadheaded* on that flight. (See *Dummies*.)

DECK STRESS LIMITS: The weight-bearing capacity of the flooring in the aircraft.

DELAY: The failure of a scheduled passenger flight to depart at the scheduled time. A delay may be due to problems with the aircraft, poor weather conditions, air traffic control, inflight catering service, or a number of other factors or service areas. A delay that is caused by an inflight caterer could result in the caterer being assessed a substantial monetary penalty by the airline.

DEREGULATION: Originally all operational activities of the U.S. domestic airlines were controlled, or regulated, by the federal government. Deregulation refers to the lifting of most of those regulations in the late 1970s. Following deregulation, the airlines were free to compete in the market place, making their own decisions about matters such as flight routes, destinations served, and fares charged.

DISPATCH SHEET: A form prepared by a caterer which summarizes a lot of information regarding an airline's flights. This sheet would contain data such as the times of flight arrival and departure, the passenger counts, and the aircraft tail number. Dispatch sheets are used by the caterer's transport and boarding crews as guidelines for their boarding activities.

DISPATCHER: The individual in a kitchen who communicates the latest arrival, departure, passenger counts, special meal requests, and aircraft changes. The dispatcher usually works very closely with the transportation manager.

DISPOSABLE (SINGLE-SERVICE) ITEMS: Items designed to be used once and then thrown away. Some inflight foodservices use disposable items for product packaging as well as for utensils and some serviceware. Airlines must determine whether their policy will be to use disposable or rotable items or some combination of both for their food and beverage services.

DIVERSIFICATION: Refers to the practice of manufacturing a variety of products or servicing a variety of customers in a variety of ways so that a failure or economic slump in one area will not be disastrous to the inflight catering firm.[2]

DOCK (LOADING DOCK): The outside area of the kitchen where trucks load and unload airline equipment and meals.

DOMESTIC (FLIGHT OR AIRLINE): Of or pertaining to the United States. A domestic flight is one that both originates and terminates within the United States; a domestic airline is one that is owned by a U.S. company.

DOUBLE PROVISIONING: Refers to the practice of boarding enough food and beverage supplies at a previous landing (upline) location so that no additional supplies are needed from a caterer at the next site (downline) where the aircraft lands. In addition to saving expense for an airline, this practice may be done when an aircraft's destination is an airport where a caterer that the airline does not want to work with has exclusive catering rights, where the aircraft's destination does not have catering services or the foods or standards of service are unacceptable to the airline, where there is space on the aircraft for the additional provisions and ground time can be saved at the aircraft's destination, or other such reasons.

DOUBLE-STACKING (PIGGY-BACKING) TRAYS: When the tray requirement for a flight exceeds the carrying capacity of the carts and carriers that can be boarded onto an aircraft, a full tray with two sets of meal components may be placed over an empty tray before it is placed into the cart or carrier. During the meal service, the flight attendant will separate the trays, divide the components between them, and have two fully set trays for passenger meal service.

DOWNLINE: The next flight segment(s) city(ies) of a departing flight.

DRAWER: A compartment in carts or trolleys that can be pulled out for access and removed and replaced. Drawers are interchangeable from one cart to another, as long as the carts are of the same type. Caterers maintain a stock of spare drawers so that their employees can prestock them ahead of time and simply exchange a filled drawer for a used one when equipment is returned for restocking. Each airline provides detailed specifications on what should go into their cart drawers and how the products will be arranged in the drawers. May also be called a bin.

DRIVER: The individual responsible for driving the truck to transport the prepared meals and supplies from the kitchen to the aircraft.

DRY ICE: Carbon dioxide (CO_2) solidified either under great pressure or as a result of rapid evaporation of liquified CO_2. It is used as a refrigerant as it passes directly from a solid to a gas at $-78°F$, absorbing a great amount of heat in the process.[2]

DUMMIES: Empty tray setups of equipment that are boarded on aircraft in addition to the actual number of meals boarded onto the aircraft. The purpose of boarding dummies is to balance the equipment supply among the caterers. The system of boarding dummies (individual trays) or dead-heading (bulk-boarding of extra equipment in designated locations) serves the same purpose.

DUTY FREE: Products sold free of customs duty or import taxes.

ELECTRONIC DATA INTERCHANGE: The electronically automated flow of business transactions in a standard format between two companies. These business transactions are created, received, and acted on by the companies' internal computer-based business management system.

EQUIPMENT BALANCE: The appropriate distribution of equipment to caterers within an airline's system so that the caterers always have the proper equipment in the amounts needed to properly board the required food and beverage service products, equipment, and supplies on the airline's flights.

ERGONOMICS: The study of the relationship between human beings and machines, especially in terms of physiological needs.[2]

ETA: Estimated time of arrival of a flight.

ETD: Estimated time of departure for a flight.

FINAL HOLDING: The last storage period for food products that have been prepared and packaged or packed into boarding equipment for later transport to an aircraft. Generally, the final holding area for food products is a holding refrigerator where products are thoroughly chilled prior to transport to the aircraft.

FINALING OPERATIONS: The activities associated with the final assembly of the exact number of meals and related products and supplies needed for a particular flight prior to loading them all onto the transport truck.

FINGER BELT: The conveyor belt in a flight-type dish machine. The protrusions on the belt which hold the dishes and glassware in place resemble fingers.

FIRST CLASS: The most expensive class of service available on scheduled airline flights. All foods and beverages and other cabin amenities (e.g., movies, audio, etc.) are complimentary, and the types of foods and beverages available as well as the range of selections rival those offered in fine dining establishments. Service is often accomplished using napery, china, silverplate, and glass or crystal, and either cart or tray service may be used. First-class dining is particularly elegant on international flights. Food and beverage service has become more restricted on domestic flights, where there are often few first-class passengers aboard the aircraft and flight segments are shorter.

FLIGHT ATTENDANT: Aircraft personnel who are responsible for passenger safety and emergency procedures, and who provide inflight passenger service, such as food and beverage service, passenger boarding, etc. (This term has replaced *steward* and *stewardess*.)

FLIGHT CHECKER: See *Checker*.

FLIGHT DECK: The aircraft compartment containing the instruments and controls for flying the aircraft, which is occupied by the pilot, copilot, and flight engineer (if part of the crew).

FLIGHT KITCHEN: A production kitchen facility operated by an inflight caterer for the purpose of preparing food products for boarding onto passenger aircraft. (See *Commissary*.)

FLIGHT SEGMENT: A flight from a point of origin (or aircraft takeoff) to the point at which the plane next lands. A passenger's flight may consist of only one flight segment or it may consist of several segments if the passenger is traveling an extended distance.

FLIGHT-TYPE DISHWASHER: A finger-type conveyor dishwasher where dishes, glassware, etc. can be placed directly onto the fingers and passed through the machine and the wash/dry cycle without having to be placed into racks. This type of machine is desirable for very-high-volume ware washing requirements.

FOLDING CART (SERVICE CART): A collapsible cart that remains on board the aircraft as part of the aircraft galley equipment. It is generally used to provide cart service to first-class passengers.

FOOD-BORNE ILLNESS: Any illness, the cause of which—whether bacteria, viruses, toxins, or other contaminants—is passed to victims through the food they eat.

FOOD FACTORY: A food production facility that prepares food products on a large-quantity, *cook-to-inventory* assembly-line basis rather than on the *cook-to-order* basis common in commercial foodservices. Food products are prepared in large batch lots when inventory stocks of items indicate a need for new production. Prepared foods are portioned, packaged, usually chilled or frozen, and placed into inventory for use as needed.[1]

FOOD SERVICE EQUIPMENT: See *Boarding Equipment*.

FOREIGN: See *International (Foreign)*.

FORWARD CABIN: The first-class seating compartment on a passenger aircraft.

FULL-SERVICE FIRM: An inflight catering (or inflight services) firm that provides not only foodservices, but an array of other services to airlines, including fueling, baggage handling, or aircraft cleaning.

GALLEY: The kitchen or food preparation area used for meal storage and preparation on board a ship or an airplane.[1]

GALLEY STRUCTURE: The structural configuration of the galley on board an aircraft. The galley structure has places built into it for insertion of the boarding equipment used to board the foods, beverages, and other supplies. It is usually modular in design so that different types of items can be inserted into some of the spaces. Also referred to as the *fixed galley*.

GUIDE: See *Loader*.

HACCP (HAZARD ANALYSIS OF CRITICAL CONTROL POINTS): A systematic means of looking at all parts of the food production and service system to assess what hazards might be present in the system. Once these hazards are identified, HACCP enables kitchen management to systematically determine what the critical control points are to prevent problems, as well as to monitor those points once they have been identified.

HELPER: See *Loader*.

HIGH-LIFT TRUCK (SCISSORS TRUCK): A type of truck specially designed for boarding food and beverage service items onto aircraft. The whole bed of the truck can be raised (or high-lifted) to the level of the aircraft door by means of a hydraulically operated scissorslike lift mechanism which expands to raise the level of the bed and folds down to lower the bed.

HIGH-TECH CARTS: Specially designed ambient air or refrigerated carts that heat the entree by conduction of heat only to the entree unit while allowing all other components of the tray to remain chilled in the refrigerated cart. The conduction occurs when the bottom of the plate or the special tray on which the entree plate sits makes contact with the heating pad specially constructed into each runner or shelf of the cart.

HOLDING OVEN: An oven designed to maintain a near-constant temperature level which will hold preheated meals at temperatures at least equal to 140°F from the time they are loaded into the oven until they are served to the passengers on board an aircraft.

HYDROCHLOROFLUOROCARBONS (HCFCs): A class of refrigerants that can legally be used on an intermediary basis as *transition* refrigerants between the use of CFCs and the development and use of refrigerants which have no impact on the ozone layer.

INBOUND EQUIPMENT: Equipment that is off-loaded from an arriving aircraft that is taken to the caterer's kitchen to be washed, inventoried, and used for boarding outbound flights.

INFLIGHT CATERER: A firm in the business of providing foodservices to airlines for the flights flown by that airline.

INFLIGHT FOOD SAFETY AUDITOR: A representative of an airline or an inflight catering firm that goes to a product supplier's facility for the purpose of conducting a food safety inspection on the products used by the airline or the caterer.

INFLIGHT FOODSERVICES: That part of the foodservice industry that is concerned with the provision of meals and beverages served to passengers on board aircraft.

INTERNATIONAL (FOREIGN): Of or pertaining to countries other than the United States. An international (or foreign) flight is one that either originates in the United States and terminates in another country, originates in another country and terminates in the United States, or both originates and terminates in another country (domestic to that country, but foreign to the United States). A foreign airline (or foreign flag carrier) is operated by a company or government other than a U.S. firm.

LETTER OF AGREEMENT: A letter written to a caterer by the airline which indicates to the caterer that it has been selected to service that airline's flights at a particular airport. It also indicates the terms of that agreement. Generally, the caterer would sign and return a copy of the letter to the airline to indicate accord with the terms of the agreement. This document might be used in lieu of a contract in the inflight foodservice industry.

LIFT: On wide-body aircraft, refers to the elevator(s) inside the aircraft used to move the food and beverage carts from the lower level where they are boarded to the upper level (passenger level) for meal and beverage service. Some lifts will accommodate only carts; others will also accommodate personnel. For aircraft, lift also refers to the forces which direct the plane upward.

LIQUOR CART: A boarding cart packed with the liquors, mixes, and other supplies that are necessary to provide bar service on an aircraft.

LOAD FACTOR: The proportion of the passenger count to be used as the count for boarding the several items listed on the menu or on the provisioning list.

LOADING DIAGRAM: A schematic drawing or written guidance that indicates specifically where different items are to go when a vehicle, such as an aircraft, is loaded with supplies, equipment, freight, etc. Airlines have specific load plans for their aircraft galleys which indicate which specific pieces of boarding equipment go into specific galley areas. These load plans help ensure that all necessary foods, beverages, supplies, and equipment are on board the aircraft, and they help reduce flight attendant uncertainty about where particular items are located during a flight.

LOADING DOCK: See *Dock*.

LOADER: The individual who assists the driver in transporting the prepared meals to the aircraft. The loader usually acts as a guide when the truck is near aircraft.

LOGISTICS: That aspect of military science dealing with the procurement, storage, maintenance, and transportation of supplies, facilities, and personnel.[1] Applied to inflight foodservices, it refers to the management of the details of procurement, storage, maintenance, transportation, and distribution of the large amounts of foods, beverages, supplies, and equipment needed to service the world's fleets of passenger aircraft.

MAIN CABIN: The largest passenger compartment within a passenger aircraft. Generally, the main cabin is used to seat coach-class passengers since this class usually represents the majority of passengers on board the aircraft. (See *Coach Class*.)

MAN MINUTE: A measure of the work output of one person for one minute. Labor requirements for specific tasks can be evaluated in terms of the number of man minutes required to accomplish the task. May also be referred to as a *work value point*.

MAN MINUTE RATE: The average (or adjusted) wage rate paid by a caterer for one man minute of work.

MAXIMUM ALLOWABLE SHELF-LIFE: The maximum time that a product can be held at 55°F (13°C) and still be safe to consume as an edible food product.

MAXIMUM CERTIFIED WEIGHT: The maximum total weight (including fuel weight) that a particular aircraft can be and still safely take off, given certain runway lengths and other parameters. This maximum weight is certified by the FAA for each particular aircraft model.

MAXIMUM REFRIGERATED SHELF-LIFE: The maximum time period that a product can be held at 45°F (7.2°C) and still be safe to consume as an edible food product.

MEAL FLIGHT: A flight on which a meal is served. The meal could be breakfast, lunch, dinner, or snack.

MEALTIME COMPONENTS: Entree components, such as the meat, vegetables, starches, sauces, or gravies that are prepared and frozen separately into individual portions. These portions can then be assembled into a variety of entrees to meet different menus.

MENU CYCLE (CYCLE MENU): A period of time for which a particular set of menus is planned (or the menu set planned for that period). At the end of the predetermined time period, or cycle, the menu set is repeated. This cycling of menus continues until a new menu set is prepared; then it starts anew.

MENU PRESENTATION: The preparation of a sample meal or a spare tray for a particular menu on an airline's menu cycle. This spare tray is then presented to the other employees and management for study and evaluation.

Errors in the tray setup noted during the presentation period are noted for correction through employee training. Also refers to major presentations of menu concepts made by caterers to airline personnel. Such presentations could be for a system menu project or at a particular kitchen, usually for international service, where an airline may rely on locally developed and prepared menus.

METER: An electronically printed message or memo similar to a teletype message. A flight kitchen might receive such a message from an airline indicating a change that is to be made in the food and beverage services. Generally, when transmitted this way, the change is to be made instantaneously.

MICROBIOLOGICAL BARRIERS: Actions or conditions, such as lowering the pH or the water activity level of products, regulating the cooking or storage temperatures used, and so on that will prevent further microbial development in the particular food product.

MODULAR EQUIPMENT: Equipment that is interchangeable with other equipment in an installation space because all the equipment possibly used in that space is built to standards for external dimensions as well as for other factors, such as power and plumbing requirements.

NARROW BODY: Any of a number of aircraft with a single-passenger ingress/egress aisle and, generally, five- or six-abreast seating.

NONCOMMERCIAL FOODSERVICES: Foodservice operations located in host organizations that do *not* have foodservice as their primary business or purpose.[1]

OFF-LOADING (also referred to as *stripping* or *strip*): The complete removal of catering equipment, including trash and garbage stored in this equipment, from the galleys in an aircraft.

OPEN-CODING SYSTEM: A coding system used by a manufacturer to indicate the expiration date of food and beverage products which uses readily understandable calendar time or dates rather than an internally developed code which persons outside of the product's manufacturing firm do not understand.

OPEN SKIES POLICY: Early in the history of airline flight, political agencies (such as state or country governments) claimed control of the airspace above their land area. However, it soon became evident that airline operations were not possible unless the operations were coordinated by a central authority and unified policies were established. Thus, the federal government determined that the local political agencies did *not* have control of the airspace above their lands; that that airspace was open to anyone for flight; and that the federal government was the appropriate agency to determine policies regarding flight operations and the use of airspace.

ORIGINATING FLIGHT (also termed *originator*): The first leg of an aircraft's flight itinerary; usually the first departure of a new flight number.

OUTBOUND EQUIPMENT: Equipment that has been packed with the products and equipment for a particular flight and is to be boarded on an aircraft prior to its departure.

OUT-OF-TEMPERATURE CONDITIONS: Environmental conditions in which food products might be placed during the acquisition, preparation, transport, and service activities where the ambient temperature is between 41°F and 140°F (5°C to 60°C). Time during which food products are exposed to out-of-temperature conditions is cumulative in regard to the growth potential of pathogenic microorganisms.

OUTSOURCING: Going outside of the firm to procure a good or service.

OVEN RACK: Carrier designed to hold entrees which is placed into an oven built into the galley structure when boarded onto the aircraft.

OZONE DEPLETION POTENTIAL: A factor used to indicate the extent to which a chemical compound might have a detrimental effect on the earth's ozone layer if released into the atmosphere.

PARTNERING: Refers to the efforts of the airlines to work in a mutually cooperative manner with their caterers and suppliers so that the inflight catering process becomes a win–win situation for all parties.

PATHOGEN: Any disease-producing organism.[2]

PET: An acronym for the complex chemical name of the soft plastic that is used to make items such as 2-liter soda bottles or 1-gallon milk containers.

pH: A measure of the acidity level of substances such as foods or beverages. The lower the pH level, the higher the acidity level of the food product and the more difficult it is for pathogenic microorganisms to grow. Pathogenic organisms grow best at a pH around 7, which is a neutral environment that is neither acidic or basic.

PIGGY-BACKING TRAYS: See *Double-Stacking Trays*.

PLACARDED WEIGHT LIMIT: In order to maintain the planned balance of an aircraft, as well as to not exceed the deck stress limit within an area, each storage area in an aircraft galley has a specific weight limit which is posted on a placard near the space to which it refers. Carts and carriers should not be loaded to a weight that exceeds the posted limit for the storage space designated for that cart or carrier.

PLUG-IN TRAY TABLE: A type of tray which had collapsible arms which would fit into (plug into) the arms of the passenger seats on many types of early passenger aircraft. The tray then served as a table for the passenger's meals. Prior to the development of this table, the passengers had to eat their meals on trays that were set either on pillows in their laps or on the lid of the tray, inverted on their laps. Other than for the bulkhead seats on some types of aircraft, the plug-in tray table has been replaced by the fold-down tray table that fits into the back of the seat in front of each passenger. Also called *bayonette tables*.

POP-OUT MEALS (POP-OUTS): Frozen individual entrees pre-prepared to airline specifications by commercial food product manufacturers that are packaged in plastic formed to the shape of the entree dish. When the entree is plated for use, it is pushed out, or popped out of the plastic form onto the serving plate or casserole.

PORT: The left-hand side of or direction from a vessel or an aircraft facing forward.[2]

PORTION PACKS: Small items, such as condiments, crackers, nuts, etc., that are packaged into individual portions. They are generally served to the diner in unopened packages. Also called *PCs*.

POTENTIALLY HAZARDOUS FOODS: Foods which would provide an excellent growth environment for bacteria if they were not properly handled throughout the food procurement, production, and service process.

PRE-LIM: See *Count*.

PRESENTATION SUMMARY: A report prepared to document the activities completed at a menu presentation. Such documentation is necessary to make sure that everyone concerned is aware of the outcomes of the presentation.

PRESSURIZED CABIN: The interior of modern aircraft is pressurized to maintain an air pressure similar to that found at ground level. However, the usual practice of most airlines is to pressurize a cabin to a pressure approximately equal to 8,000 feet in altitude, or about the pressure that would be found on the ski slopes of the Rocky Mountains. If the cabins were not pressurized, passengers could not survive without oxygen masks and forced breathing of oxygen. The air temperature, too, would be too cold for normal passenger survival.

PROVISIONING: The process of supplying an aircraft with meals, beverages, and supplies in the amount estimated as the requirement to serve the number of passengers on board the flight.

PROVISIONING CHANGE: A change made by an airline in the amount of a provision that should be boarded onto an aircraft. Because of the tightly structured food and beverage service on board an aircraft, making a provisioning change may be a very complex, and sometimes costly, task for an airline.

PROVISIONING CHART (OR STANDARDS): A chart prepared by an airline for its caterers which indicates the proportionate amount of all items, such as condiments, flatware, supplies, and entrees, that should be boarded for a particular flight. Generally, the amounts are indicated on an allocation per passenger, and the caterer must multiply that allocation by the passenger count to determine the exact count to board.

QUALITY ASSURANCE: Activities undertaken by a firm or organization to control the quality level of a product or service provided or received. Quality assurance activities are designed to see that performance is in accord with product or service quality standards established at the beginning of the relationship.

RAMP: Also called *Tarmac*. The area at the airport where the catering truck delivers the prepared meals to the aircraft.

REDUNDANT AIRCRAFT SYSTEMS: The duplication of all systems on board an aircraft to help ensure that, should a system fail, there would be a backup system that was still functional to keep the aircraft aloft and enable it to achieve a safe landing.

REGISTERED DIETITIAN: A person who has completed a Bachelor's or Master's degree in dietetics, has completed an approved dietetic internship program or a preplanned dietetic work experience program, and has passed the dietitians' registration examination, which is administered by the Registration Commission of The American Dietetic Association.[1]

REGULATED AIR FARES: Air fares that are set by a regulatory agency, such as the Civil Aeronautics Board in the United States (prior to deregulation in the 1970s) or IATA for international flights.

REMANUFACTURING: The process of reducing recycled products to their original materials and manufacturing them again into usable products (which may or may not be the same product the materials were manufactured into originally).

RETHERMALIZE: To heat a food product that has been previously cooked, portioned, and chilled or frozen for storage back to the proper temperature for service to the foodservice's clientele. Common rethermalization procedures include the use of microwave ovens, convection ovens, or specialized equipment (sometimes referred to as high-tech transport equipment in the inflight foodservice industry) that reheats products by conduction. Also referred to as *reconstitution* or *recon*.[1]

RETROFIT: To modify equipment that is already in service using parts developed, or made available, after the time of original manufacture.[2]

REVENUE PER PASSENGER MILE (RPM): The amount of revenue generated by a flight for every passenger mile flown, calculated by dividing the total revenue from all paying passengers on a flight by the number of miles on the flight segment multiplied by the number of paying passengers on the flight. This factor is used to evaluate the profitability of a flight segment as well as for airline budgeting activities.

ROTABLE EQUIPMENT: Equipment, such as china, glassware, or reuseable plasticware, that can be washed and reused as serviceware for inflight food and beverage service.

SAMPLE MEAL: A meal or portion of a meal prepared according to written airline specifications and made under the supervision of a departmental manager, supervisor, or lead employee. The sample meal is then used by employees as a gauge for the remaining meals.

SANITIZE: The process of freeing a surface or object from dirt and germs.

SCHEDULED CHARTER FLIGHT: A charter flight, i.e., a flight that is arranged for a specific purpose outside of a regular commercial airline schedule, but one which operates on a regular schedule (weekly, monthly, etc.).

SERVICE CART: See *Folding Cart*.

SERVICEWARE: Utensils and other pieces of equipment such as pitchers, bowls, or trays used in the service of meals and beverages.

SETUP AREA: Also referred to as *setup* or *bulk*. The area where first-class, business-class, and coach equipment are assembled.

SHELF-STABLE: Able to be stored at room temperature without spoiling. Shelf-stable products do not require refrigeration or freezing, they are typically canned products or products packaged in a way that microorganisms cannot grow in the product—either too dry (rice, flour, noodles, etc.) or with no air available (packaged in a vacuum).

SHIP NUMBER: See *Tail Number*. Also same as *aircraft number*.

SNACK FLIGHT: A flight on which only a snack service (less than a full meal service) is planned. Beverage flights (i.e., those on which only beverages are served) would not be considered a snack flight.

SOLID WASTE: For the inflight caterer, solid waste generally refers to non-hazardous materials such as paper, paperboard, corrugated cardboard, glass, plastics, metals, textiles, or wood. It is essentially the trash that results from the caterer's operations. Municipalities look at solid waste as sewer waste. Inflight caterers also contribute to solid waste from that perspective as well. For example, garbage disposed of through garbage disposals or the liquid waste stream produced by extruders or high-compression compactors all enter the municipal sewer system. There is also hazardous solid waste, which is composed of items such as light fixtures, chemicals, and medical or biological waste. The inflight caterer would normally generate only a low level of hazardous waste and most of that would be chemicals, such as paint or some cleaning compounds.

SOURCE REDUCTION: Refers to the reduction in the use of packaging materials at the product manufacturer's facility where the product is originally packaged for distribution and use (the *source* of the packaging used). Generally, if less packaging can be used originally (or at the source), then there is less packaging throughout the total waste stream as there is less packaging entering the distribution flow that has to be disposed of later.

SOURCED: The process of identifying a source of supply for items needed by the airlines or their caterers for the provision of inflight foodservices.

SPECIAL MEALS: Meals prepared especially for a passenger's diet, taste, or religious preference and prepared under the airline's specifications. International special meal codes and guidelines have been agreed upon by the airline industry in an effort to improve the consistency of special meals for passengers.

SPECIFICATION: A detailed description of requirements, products, layout, and other such parameters of an airline's inflight food and beverage services that is prepared by each airline. Its specifications are presented to its caterers in manuals which the caterers are expected to become familiar with and follow precisely.

STAGING (STAGED): The process of assembling all of the necessary trolleys, carriers, and other boarding equipment and supplies that are required for a particular flight in the caterer's staging area. When all such equipment and supplies are assembled, they are *staged*—ready for inspection.

STAGING AREA: An area near the loading dock where the trolleys, carriers, and all other necessary equipment and supplies for a flight are assembled for final inspection prior to being loaded into the caterer's truck for transport to an aircraft.

STANDARD TYPE CERTIFICATE (STC'D): A certificate awarded by the FAA to pieces of equipment which can be used in aircraft construction or as part of the interiors of aircraft. This certificate is awarded only after extensive testing by the FAA to ensure the structural durability of the equipment.

STANDARDIZED PRODUCT: A product prepared by a food product manufacturer which is prepared in accord with precise specifications, portioned into specified portions, and packaged in portions—either in individual portion packs or as a bulk pack of portioned product. These products may be ready to cook or ready to serve when they are received in the inflight kitchen.

STAND-BY MEALS: See *Bank Meals*.

STARBOARD: The right-hand side of or direction from a vessel or an aircraft facing forward.[2]

STEAM AUTOCLAVE: A piece of equipment in which steam, under pressure, reaches high enough temperatures to sterilize the material placed inside the equipment.

STERILIZE: The process of destroying microorganisms.

STEWARD: An attendant on a ship or an aircraft who is there to serve the passenger. Generally stewards handle foodservice responsibilities, as well as emergency safety, passenger boarding, etc. The term refers to a male attendant, and is no longer used on aircraft (though it is on cruise ships) as it has been replaced by the term *flight attendant*, used to refer to both male and female attendants. (See *Flight Attendant*.)

STEWARDESS: An attendant on an aircraft who is there for passenger safety and to provide inflight passenger service. Generally, stewardesses handle foodservice responsibilities, as well as emergency safety, passenger boarding, etc. Originally, a stewardess had to be a registered nurse because the primary focus of her responsibility was passenger safety. Today, this term is not used on aircraft as it has been replaced by the term *flight attendant*, used to refer to both male and female attendants. (See *Flight Attendant*.)

STRIPPING THE AIRCRAFT: See *Off-loading*.

SUPPLEMENTAL MEALS: Also called supps. See *Bank Meals*.

SUPPORT CART: A cart packed with supplies and equipment, such as cups or serving utensils, that support the service of meals and beverages on board an aircraft.

TAIL NUMBER: A serial number usually located on the tail, fuselage, or nose landing gear door of an aircraft that is used to identify the specific aircraft by ramp personnel and catering personnel.

TARMAC: See *Ramp*.

TEMPERED: Refers to a product that has been gradually thawed to refrigerator temperature. The purpose of tempering a product is to reduce the time required to rethermalize it when it is to be used for meal service. Generally, products are tempered in refrigerator units. In the inflight industry, most portioned frozen items are tempered for approximately 24 hours prior to boarding on the aircraft for meal service. Also called *slack* or *slacking*.

TERMINAL FOODSERVICES: The food and beverage services found inside the airport terminal which are open to the general public, including airline passengers waiting for flights. The term could also be used to refer to the foodservices found inside a bus, ship, or railway terminal.

TERMINATING FLIGHT (TERMINATOR): A flight that has arrived at its destination following the final leg of an aircraft's flight itinerary. The flight number will not continue with this aircraft.

THROUGH FLIGHT: An intermediate stop on an aircraft's flight itinerary. After its origin, a through flight may land at one or more airports to deplane and board passengers, and take on fuel, food supplies, baggage, etc., and then continue on toward the terminal point of the flight itinerary with the same flight number.

TOP-OFF MEALS: See *Bank Meals*.

TRANSOCEANIC FLIGHTS: Flights that are made over oceans; usually intercontinental flights which have long flight times.

TRAY CARRIER: A piece of transport equipment into which preset passenger meal trays can be loaded for transport to and boarding onto an aircraft. The tray carrier is lifted or carried and designed to fit into a designated space in the aircraft's galley. After the meal service, the dirty trays are loaded back into the tray carrier for removal from the aircraft and transport back to a caterer's facilities when the aircraft lands at its destination.

TRAY LINE (also called a *belt*): A mechanical device, often supported by carts, lowerators, or other mobile supply storage equipment, used by the caterer's employees to assemble individual meal entrees or to set individual trays before placing them into an airline cart. Depending on the number of items to be placed on an entree or onto a cart, there may be two to four employees working on the tray line, or belt, at any one time.

TRAY RUNNER (SHELF): The slides on which the meal trays fit when they are loaded into the cart or carrier.

TRAY SERVICE: The service of meals to passengers on board aircraft through the use of preset trays. The trays are generally preset by the inflight caterer with all cold food items, condiments, and utensils. If a hot entree is part of the meal service, it is added to the tray just prior to service by the flight attendants on board the aircraft. The tray is then offered to the passenger as the meal service.

TROLLEY: See *Cart.*

TURBULENCE: Meteorologically, irregular motion of the atmosphere, as that indicated by gusts and lulls in the wind.[2] Inflight turbulence can cause an aircraft to make sudden, unplanned drops or rises in altitude or may buffet the plane from side to side. During periods of heavy turbulence, meal and beverage service must usually be discontinued to avoid spillage and other possible accidents which could harm either the passengers or the flight attendants.

TURN: A quick exchange of catering equipment and meals. Also known as a *quick turn.* If full meal service is involved, a turn will usually take about 1.5 hours.

TURN FLIGHT: Essentially an aircraft on a round-trip flight. The aircraft's itinerary is to fly to a destination, deplane and board passengers, load baggage, fuel, food and beverage supplies, etc., and then return to its point of origin which would also probably be its point of termination. A caterer treats a turn flight similarly to a through flight in that it may remove and board food, beverages, and equipment in the same service sequence. The outbound departure of a turn will have a different flight number than the inbound segment.

TURN TIME: The time required to complete a turn for an aircraft. An airline will usually have turn time standards which caterers must adhere to for their flights.

TURNAROUND TIME: For an inflight caterer, the time between when the caterer's boarding crew starts to load a truck for a flight and when it comes back, is off-loaded, cleaned, and ready for reloading for another flight.

UPCOUNT: An increase in the number of passengers estimated for a particular flight (airline's estimate or exact count at the gate).

WATER ACTIVITY LEVEL: A factor which represents a ratio of the vapor pressure of food to that of pure water. It indicates how much available water is in a product that microorganisms can use for growth. Products that have very low water activity levels, or are very dry, will not support the growth of bacteria and other such microorganisms.

WEIGHT: For aircraft, can refer either to the full weight of the aircraft and all persons and items loaded onto it or to some particular portion of the full load.

WET ICE: Frozen water. It is called *wet ice* because it turns to a liquid (water) as it melts, as opposed to dry ice, which passes directly from a solid to a gas.

WIDE BODY: Refers to any one of several types of large passenger aircraft in which seats, particularly in the main cabin, are set in three columns with one along each side of the aircraft separated from a center column by two aisles. There may be as many as nine or ten seats in a row on a wide-body aircraft. The term originated from the wide (cross-section) fuselage shape of these aircraft. There are two ingress/egress passenger aisles.

WORK VALUE POINT: See *Man Minute.*

WORK VALUE POINT RATE: See *Man Minute Rate.*

ZERO FUEL WEIGHT: The weight of the aircraft, passengers, baggage, freight, and all other items to be loaded onto the aircraft *without* the weight of any fuel.

NOTES

1. McCool, A. C., F. A. Smith, and D. L. Tucker. (1994). *Dimensions of Noncommercial Foodservice.* New York: Van Nostrand Reinhold, Glossary.

2. *Webster's New Universal Unabridged Dictionary.* (1992). Avenel, NJ: Outlet Book Company (Barnes & Noble).

Index

Page numbers in *italics* refer to figures.